AF663925

EARLY INDIAN RELIGIOUS THOUGHT

EARLY INDIAN RELIGIOUS THOUGHT

P.D. MEHTA

BHARATIYA KALA PRAKASHAN
DELHI (INDIA)

Edition : 2007

ISBN : 978-81-8090-118-8

Published by : **C.P. Gautam**
for **BHARATIYA KALA PRAKASHAN**
3421-A, IInd Floor, Narang Colony, Tri Nagar,
Delhi-110035. Ph. : (O) 27393083, 32967505
E-mail : bkp3421@yahoo.co.in

Laser Typesetting by : Twinkle Graphics, Delhi-110088.

Printed by : BDH Printers at D K. Fine Art Press, Delhi

PREFACE

Whilst the main bulk of the book deals with early Indian Religious Thought, I have occasionally drawn upon other religious teachings, especially upon those in the Old and New Testaments.

In the presentation of the subject matter of the first part of this book, I have availed myself of the work done by a number of distinguished scholars, both non-Indian and Indian, in the field of Indian Religious Thought. Those points on which I am not in sympathy with the evaluations or judgments of some scholars, are included among the questions treated in the second part of the book. The reader will understand, therefore, why certain statements in this second part, or the implications of these statements, are either inconsistent with or directly contradict those in the first part.

Through long years spent in the West, I have had the good fortune to come to know the heart of Christian civilization. To know means to love and to respect. Only he who loves may enjoy the privilege of being outspoken. I have exercised this privilege in a few pages of this book.

My grateful thanks are due to Dr. William Stede for help in the translation of the Bhagavad-Gītā, VIII. 1–4; to Dr. and Mrs. R. W. Haines for critically reading the script of part two of the book, and for corrections and suggestions; and to Mr. M. C. Pitts for remarks and suggestions in connection with pages 451 to 468.

I am most deeply indebted to Miss I. B. Horner. She read the entire script, and made valuable suggestions and corrections. She carefully revised all the translations of the Pāli Texts quoted. She has given most generously of her time and her ripe scholarship. Her encouragement and help have been invaluable. It would have been my sorrowful loss not to owe, and always to owe, so great a debt of gratitude to Miss Horner, one of the very true and quiet friends and servers of India and of the Buddhist world.

My thanks are also due to those who have taught me deep lessons in life. For eight and a half years I studied the piano under Solomon, whose kindness and generosity it is impossible to forget. From him I learned, as from no other, the meaning of self-dedication to an ideal of perfection. Our friendship since we first met in 1924 has been one of unclouded sunshine—a unique experience for me.

Dr. H. J. Fleure, F.R.S., is one of those rare personalities possessed of deep, critical and appreciative insight into the culture of other lands. I am happily in his debt. For twenty years I searched for my vocation in life. Then Dr. Fleure introduced me to it as easily as giving me a cup of tea.

I am deeply and thankfully indebted to all who brought me joy and sorrow and all that the round of life can hold for a man, without which it is not possible to realize and to fulfill.

P.D.M.

CONTENTS

PART ONE

PAGES

PART TWO

Part One

INTRODUCTION

CHAPTER I.

PRE-VEDIC RELIGIOUS THOUGHT

IN THE absence of conclusive evidence, the religious thought and practice of the earliest humans can only be a matter of conjecture. It is not unlikely that among the influences shaping the rise of such thought were dreams. In these, living man sometimes met the dead. On waking up he must have felt confused. What was the reality? That the other man was really dead, impotent to harm or help, or that he still existed in some mysterious condition, with power to affect the living?

Life was full of other mysteries. Reflections in water were a mystery. Shadows were another mystery. They took the forms of known objects, yet changed in a strange manner throughout the day, sometimes disappearing altogether. And where did they betake themselves at night? Most things could be seen and handled. But what was the wind which could be felt, yet could not be seen or held? What was the terrible mystery of thunder and lightning? Of cloud and sky? Of the stars? Of the moon, waxing and waning? And above all, what was the wonderful mystery of birth, and the awful mystery of death? Perplexity and confusion, fear and superstition characterized early man's mental life. Yet side by side with these were hope, initiative and effort, born of the instinctive clinging to life and the urge for survival. There was probably little or no power of discrimination. Life, both physical and mental, was under the dominion of impulse and desire, imperfectly controlled by experience, by remembered pain or pleasure. There was probably a sense of kinship with nature, of a "participation mystique" with her.

Unable to distinguish the real from the unreal, dreams and persisting memories of the dead perhaps gave rise to a belief in spirits. If early man recognized death as an absolute cessation of physical existence, then the belief in survival may also have originated from his dreams of the dead. Everyday experience showed him the necessity for placating those whom he feared on acccount of their superior strength. But in dreams, it may often have happened that his weak foes whom he had killed in actual life now enjoyed a mysterious immunity from being hurt or killed by him. Further, if these spirits were in possession of what to him was magic, they were perhaps able to see him all the time whereas his vision of them was restricted to dreams, or to hallucinations. Perhaps, just as he could make things like rude flint implements, could shout, procreate, destroy, even so the spirits must surely be the controllers of natural phenomena. Also, just as there were strong men who ruled the weak, just as women could attract men sexually and give them joy, produce infants and mother them, so too there must be strong spirits who ruled in the spirit world, and spirits who attended to the life processes of organic nature. Naturally, then, the spirits must be superior beings.

Everything was shrouded in mystery. The unknown or inexplicable is the parent of fear, of fantasy and superstition. Such fear may have induced early man to find out ways of placating these spirits endowed with mysterious powers. Placation is effected by renouncing possession of what one values in favour of the power to be placated. Such renunciation of cherished possession sanctifies the one who renounces, and binds the superior power to himself with cords of favour, protection, grace and love. The whole ritual is a sacrifice—a making sacred.

Other elements too were present such as the comforting warmth of the sun, spring coolness, tree-shade, colour and magic and form in nature, and love-delight, all of which filled man with happiness, and fostered the growth of his sense of wonder and of beauty, and of his feelings of gratitude and reverence. Conceivably, therefore, happiness and gratitude, besides fear and the desire to placate, contributed elements to the rituals he devised.

One other factor : although very early man lived much like an animal, a member of a herd, it is unlikely that his gregariousness could have entirely suppressed a dawning sense of individuality.

The ego, the consciousness of separate selfhood, was slowly emerging out of the dark recesses of elemental existence. Man, the thrall of his ego-bound vision, cannot bring himself to deny personal continuance. Somehow, the "I" *ought* to survive the death of the body.

Thus, the emergence of religious thought and practice out of the experiences of life can be imagined. Though rooted in the concrete reality of life, man in his mental infancy inevitably misinterpreted this reality. He was misled by his fantasies. In course of time, civilization and community life provided the indispensable opportunity and leisure to extract truth out of knowledge and experience. After a million years or so of extremely primitive existence, civilization came on the scene a bare six thousand years ago. The domestication of animals, agriculture, weaving, pottery and the use of metals were the foundations of civilized existence. There emerged tribe, clan and family, an increasingly marked division of labour, increasing organization for the protection of the group and of the individual, property, marriage, tribal customs, and rights and duties. Sanctions, especially religious sanctions, played a paramount part in the life of the group. Spirits, or gods, had to be placated. As man's activities multiplied, so did his gods; and the rites to be performed became more elaborate.

Since subsistence agriculture was the basis of all civilization from Egypt to China, fertility rites were of prime importance. Since life's mysteries were but the magic of unseen, powerful spirits or gods, placatory rites had also to be performed. Magico-religious fertility cults had more to them, nevertheless, than mere superstition. Their symbolism was near the facts of organic existence, and it embodied psychological insight. To feel and acknowledge our vital kinship with nature to the extent of treating her with reverent worship is not necessarily barbarous or obscene. The worship of the fig tree as the symbol of fertility may have been, and still may be, a fitting expression of a true religious sense for certain people placed in a certain environment. Phallic worship is in essence an expression of reverence for creativeness.

Undoubtedly, fear and ignorance, evidenced by the anxiety to placate wrathful powers by propitiatory rites, played a dominant part in the religious life of early man. But knowledge grew in the soil of civilized life, dispelling ignorance and lessening fear. The significance of ritualistic symbolism became profounder psychologically, but tended to greater esotericism in relation to the toiling masses deprived of adequate opportunities for intellectual and spiritual growth. Power went to the priests, the repositories of knowledge. And power corrupts! Making due allowance for sincerity and real ability, the priestly class sometimes exercised tyrannous authority over the people. Magic was the priest's prerogative; and the wielder of magic was above any temporal power.

Prior to the third millennium before Christ, the totemistic Proto-australoid and Austro-asiatic inhabitants of India, Indonesia and farther India believed in soul-matter or life itself as a transferable and indestructible substance possessed of magical powers. They believed that it was situated in the head, and that on death it passed into the earth and fertilized crops and again produced life. The origin of various tabus concerning occupation, commensality and intermarriage, and of the principle underlying head-hunting, human sacrifice and cannibalism may be sought in the belief in soul-matter. Possibly, the erection of megalithic monuments and wooden images of the dead was associated with it.

In the tribal religions of India, the soul is pictured as a little man located in the head. This conception, inconsistent with the belief in soul-matter as a fertilizing substance, is probably due to man's tendency to anthropomorphize, so much in evidence in the god-conceptions of most religions. The manikin idea of the soul, together with the idea of the indestructibility of this fertilizing soul-matter, paved the way for the doctrine of reincarnation. This doctrine is logically irreconcilable with the original premises; but primitive man could hold the two simultaneously, unconscious of their inconsistency.

The religious beliefs and rites of these ancient times not only affected the religious practices brought into India by later more developed cultures but have survived in their pristine character to this day in various tribes scattered throughout the country, as in Eastern Bengal and Assam, Chotā Nāgpur and Central

India, Travancore and Cochin, and in the Andamans and Nicobars. In addition to animistic beliefs, ancestor worship, and propitiation of ghosts or gods, some tribes hold a belief in a supreme god, or at least in a chief god. Nāga Rāja, the snake god is the chief god of the Kolis and Khasiyas of Tehri-Garhwal. The Birhors of Central India seem to have forgotten the gods or spirits of their ancestors and worship Mahādeo. The Majhwars of Udaipur State worship only Mahādeo. The Kar Nicobarese appear to have some conception, however vague and undefined, of a Supreme Being as distinct from spirits of the dead or evil spirits.

A Supreme Goddess, Palichi-Ammal is worshipped by the Paliyans of Madura district. They know no other god or goddess, although they imagine Palichi-Ammal must have had a husband on the principle that no woman can live without a husband. In Travancore, the Mala-Arayans consider the sun as the natural son of a mother-Goddess, and the moon as the adopted son ; the Kānikār regard the sun as a female and as creator, while the moon is male ; the Ūrālis, the sun as the creator of the universe and the father of all souls, and the moon as the mother. Offerings to the moon and prayers to the sun are made.

Creation stories involving the belief in a creator-god who makes human beings out of mud are found in Assam and Burma, among the Santals of Chotā Nāgpur, the Kar Nicobarese, and also in Indonesia and Oceania. The Santals consider thunder and lightning and other natural phenomena as acts of the Supreme Being. Legends of destruction by fire, and /or flood are common to the hill tribes of Assam, the Mundas, the Santals, the Andamanese and Nicobarese.

The Negrito and Proto-australoid peoples of India founded the village system. A social order was in existence over fifty centuries ago. An order based on subsistence agriculture needs industry, frugality and co-operation in its members, and dutiful submission to authority. The need for security, continued existence, and the happiness of the moment were probably the main driving forces. Individual freedom, initiative, enterprise, expansion and cultural development had still to be born. Fixed custom, a " democratic " village government, and a conservative, communal life seem to have been the features of Proto-australoid

India. This phase is likely to have lasted many centuries, and it is thought that Proto-australoid culture may be even seventy centuries old. The fact that the people representing this culture, coming originally from the direction of western Asia, were enterprising enough to spread all over the million and a half square miles of India, to push through the daunting jungles of Burma down to the south-easternmost corner of Asia and into the Indonesian islands, is evidence of progressiveness, of fine human qualities. But mentally, they were backward, measured by the standard of later cultures. So their religious thought and practice consisted largely of fantastic beliefs, fears and superstitions built out of their concrete real life. The fantastic play of imagination, not disciplined philosophical enquiry or speculation, was predominant.

This may have proved a powerful influence in fixing the mode of life of the people. " The Unchanging East " is true to a degree. An established routine whose objective is merely continued existence, lacking the urge for experimentation, may well tend to resist change. But it stands for stability and security.

During the late fourth or early third millennium before Christ, the next great immigration into India took place : the entry of the Mediterraneans. The early groups, people with dark brown skins, may have come from the north African shores and the Levant, followed later on by others from the cities of the Persian Gulf and Mesopotamia, and by the broadheaded people from Armenia. They founded the Indus Valley Civilization whose culture was on a level with the cultures of Egypt and Sumeria of the same period, and later on penetrated eastwards into the Gangetic region and southwards down the western coast. Their well-planned cities and well-built houses, their crafts and industries in textiles, pottery and metals, their tools and weapons and their trade and commerce, extending westwards to Kish and Elam, their pictographic script, their personal cleanliness and adornments, all prove the great advance in civilized life made over Proto-australoid totemistic culture with its little villages, rude huts, primitive agriculture and tools.

In consequence of their control over the material world, the Mediterraneans introduced systematization in life. The people of the Indus Valley cities had a definite political economy and social organization, and an artistic and an intellectual life. Engineering skill was not inconsiderable and at least the elements of music, mathematics and astronomy were known. Conceivably, systematic education was prevalent in some sections of society, and it is likely that at least there was an educated, priestly class which wielded influence over the people.

Our knowledge of the religion of the Mediterraneans is gleaned from the figurines, amulets, ring and baetylic stones, and seals unearthed at Mohenjodāro and at Harappā. Chief among these are the figurines depicting the Mother Goddess, regarded, at least in later times, as the guardian of the village, as presiding over child-birth, and as taking a human interest in the needs of her votaries. The small size of her breasts, compared with those of the more matronly figures which are thought to have been used for votive purposes, may indicate that she was regarded as a virgin by the Indus Valley people. But it is uncertain whether this was so, or whether she was one of a trinity involving a husband and son, as in many villages today. If she was the wife of Śiva she was the prototype of Umā, Pārvatī, Durgā and Kālī. It might be hazarded that she was both virgin and wife, even as Śiva is both ascetic and lord of reproductive nature, and as such, is related to the concept of the Virgin Mother in later systems. The association of the Mother Goddess with other deities was a common feature of her cult in other countries.

It is not known why the figures of male deities in pottery are distinctly rare. These, in contrast to the skimpily skirted female deities, are entirely nude, apart from being decorated with necklaces and bangles sometimes, or with a cincture round the waist. They have horns ; and sometimes a sprig of flowers or leaves rises from the head between the horns suggesting the idea of a fertility or vegetation god.

The most important of the finds is a seal amulet portraying a nude deity with three faces and horns, seated on a stool, with heels pressed closely together, in what is evidently a religious attitude, a precursor of Yogic Āsanas. He is surrounded by two deer (or antelopes ?), a rhinoceros, an elephant, a tiger, and a buffalo. His horns resemble those of a bull or a buffalo, and a fan shaped erection, like the headdress worn by many of the female figurines, rises from his head between them. Like the female goddesses on the amulets he wears a large number of bangles on either arm. Of three such seals unearthed, two represent him seated on a stool and one on the ground.

This is the deity which Sir John Marshall identified with Śiva in his aspect of Paśupati, Lord of Beasts, on account of his many faces. Paśupati has been represented with as many as five faces. The beginnings of Hinduism thus go back five thousand years. The fertility god who was the lord of the reproductive powers of nature was destined to undergo several transformations before becoming the third person of the Hindu trinity. The personal, anthropomophic concept of the Indus Valley people was to grow into the impersonal embodiment of the destructive-regenerative activity of the universe.

At least three kinds of trees were worshipped, the nim, a tree resembling an acacia, and the pipal, *Ficus religiosa*. In modern times too, the pipal is believed by some to be the abode of Lakshmī, the goddess of wealth, Viṣṇu's consort. Women make offerings to it in order to have a male child. A vessel of water is fastened to its branches for the refreshment of the souls of the dead. Prayers are said round it. This tree was connected by the Indus Valley dwellers with the urus-ox. Since this type of animism dates from very primitive times, the worship of trees may have been confined to the uneducated.

Small cones made of lapis-lazuli, jasper, chalcedony and other stones, beautifully cut and finished, are thought to be liṅgas, whilst certain large stone rings thought to be yonis, may have been employed to build up columns. The question cannot be decided until liṅga and yoni are found in close association. Phallic worship, a legacy from the past, may have been associated with Śiva by the Indus Valley people.

In evidence of animal worship, designs of the elephant, tiger, buffalo, two kinds of cows, one a short horned animal and the other a humped bull, rhinoceros, crocodile, hare, antelope, urus bull, an unusual creature with a head at either end not unlike certain Sumerian animal designs, and a queer, composite beast with a human face, an elephant's trunk, the horns and fore-quarters of a bull, and the hindquarters and tail of a tiger, probably representing several deities fused into one form, have been found on seal amulets. The gharial, or fish eating crocodile, was an emblem of a river god. Only one figure of a snake was unearthed at Harappā.

As in Crete and Mesopotamia, the dove, sacred to the Mother Goddess, is portrayed with outstretched wings and tail.

Bearing striking likeness to a certain Sumerian demigod or hero, a horned human figure with the feet and tail of a bull is depicted struggling with a horned tiger (? demon). But the amulet in human shape is a small steatite figure, just over half an inch in height, of a deity wearing the curling horns of a ram. The bronze figure of a dancing girl may represent the predecessor of the Devadāsis.

An unusual amulet of shell has a knot carved upon it. Knots have always had a magical significance in the East as well as in the West. On one seal a six-rayed skirl has one ray in the form of a urus-bull's head. Skirl devices are uncommon, and are generally considered to be solar symbols. The six animal heads on them may represent the premier deities of the Indus Valley pantheon. The Svastika and Greek Cross are often found on the seal amulets.

A cemetery has been discovered at Harappā. The Indus Valley people also cremated their dead and scattered the ashes into the river.

The worship of horned deities, which disappeared with the Indus Valley people, and of the man-bull, occur in contemporary Sumerian mythology.

There was a cult of snakes in Crete, where some terracotta figurines of the Mother Goddess that have been excavated are not dissimilar to those from Mohenjodāro and Bihār. The cult of the bull is also common to early Crete, Egypt, the Near East, the Indus Valley and Hindu India. The sanctity of the cow in India is older than Vedic religion, and is foreign to the Ṛig Veda. Reverence for cattle characterizes the pre-equine civilizations of the eastern Mediterranean regions. In India, it is suggestive of the religions of Asia Minor, Egypt, and Crete rather than of the Ṛig-vedic Indians.

The deification and worship of kings, typical of the Hindu attitude to kingship, is characteristic of Sumerian religion in contrast to Semitic.

Associated with Mesopotamia or Asia Minor is astronomy and the worship of the heavenly bodies, which form an important part of Hindu culture. The moon is male and the sun is female until the influence of the Ṛig-vedic invaders changed the sex of the sun into male, although as late as in the Tenth Book of the Ṛig Veda, the male Soma (moon) is represented as marrying Sūryā, the daughter of the sun.

What precisely was the religious system of the Mediterraneans is yet to be discovered, if it can be discovered. It may be permissible to infer that the religious thought of these people who achieved an admirable material civilization was more refined and better developed than the cruder animism and phallicism of their Negrito and Proto-australoid precursors. Belief in magic was probably universal, as also faith in the priest, the divinely appointed wielder of magic through the medium of rites and ceremonies. The conception of various deities is definite. Possibly there was a belief in an abode appropriate to these deities. In a civilization which knew the meaning of law and order, which had sufficient intellectual development to have skilled arts and crafts, it is quite likely that the other world too, was invested with law and order which the gods obeyed, even if their treatment of mortals was capricious.

Regarding the soul, its sojourn on earth and its fate after death, the Mediterraneans probably had ideas far in advance of the Proto-australoids. They had the germs at least of the belief in reincarnation, and possibly they developed the theory to some extent. Their stable background of material prosperity gave them the leisure, and their mental development the ability to speculate on the deeper things of life, and work out some sort of religious system. Their worship of the heavenly bodies may imply a belief that these bodies were the vehicles of gods and goddesses, or at any rate of beings possessed of supernatural power. The Sumerians and Indus Valley people possibly connected these planetary deities with human lives and human destiny, and so believed in astrology. They must have had some sort of psychological system. Man is, of course, a psychologist since Adam's days, in so far as he could not help understanding elementary facts about human nature. But the reactions of fundamental human nature to different circumstances and environments furnish the material for a systematic study; and it is not inconceivable that the rudiments of such study existed in Sumeria and in the Indus Valley. Unable to explain the whole of life in terms of human behaviour and circumstance, the *deus ex machina* of planetary deities had to be brought in. Fatalism and obedience, not initiative and over-riding joyous hope, must have been keynotes.

It is probable that the developing anthropomorphism of these people, as evidenced by Śiva and the Mother Goddess, was one in which the gods were regarded as being apart from and above mortals. The universe consisted of separate elements, unrelated, except by winning the favour of supernatural powers through sacrificial propitiation. The wrath of gods, the evil wrought by malignant forces, had to be feared. All civilizations were based on slave labour in those days. Man was of little account. He could not enjoy the dignity of his own individuality or his unchallengeable right as an individual to existence. He did not think of looking within himself; he bowed in fear before unknown and incomprehensible might. He never dared to imagine freedom for himself; he was the slave of mysterious powers. Man and god were apart.

Nevertheless, because of material control and mental development, the god-conceptions of the Mediterraneans were a great advance upon the Proto-australoid ideas. Not so very many centuries were to elapse before man realized that these conceptions were but projections of himself. The lower rungs of the ladder to freedom necessarily rest upon the dark soil of ignorance, fear and superstition.

There is one very significant fact to notice: the figure of Śiva is portrayed in a religious attitude. Despite the influence of fear and superstition, man's aspiration towards something wonderful, satisfying, protective and inclusive, something ideal, plays a powerful, perhaps the most powerful part in his religious growth. Perhaps the significance of Śiva's attitude is that his votaries recognized the worth of religion as religion, in its profounder sense. So the gods themselves must be religious beings. Abstract values are beginning to emerge out of concrete experience. The worship of the gods is not mere barter or insurance, and the temple of god is no mere bargaining counter.

Further, if the artist who made the figure, and the priests who accepted and used the symbol were aware of its significance, it may be inferred that the practice of meditation, of inner spiritual communion of some sort, was not unknown to them. There must have been mystics amongst the Indus Valley people. The use of a special physical attitude in order to produce a receptive or exalted state of mind could not have been unknown to them. The very fact that art goes very far back into man's early history, as proved by the cave drawings which have been discovered, means that an inner "soul life" was active at the same time. Art, sex, religion, and mysticism all go together, and through one or more forms, singly or simultaneously, the inherent creative imagination of man finds expression. The religion of the Indus Valley may well have been the product of deep psychological understanding. The discipline at the psychical level was the prelude to the later growth of philosophy and science.

CHAPTER II

THE VEDAS

" May we attain that excellent glory
of Savitar the god :
So may he stimulate our prayers "
Ṛig Veda III.62.10.

PRIOR TO THE spread of the Āryan-speaking peoples over the civilized world, the cultural development of man takes place in the lands bounded by the equator and the fortieth parallel of north latitude. Egypt, Sumeria and the Indus Valley knew not the use of the horse, nor of the iron sword or plough. Then about twenty-seven centuries before Christ, somewhere in the snowy slopes between Mongolia and Siberia, man first learned to tame the horse.[1] The mobility, amenability and adaptability of the horse gave his master advantages great enough to alter history. Later on, about fifteen centuries before Christ, the Hittites of Anatolia[2] developed the art of smelting iron to such a pitch, that iron replaced copper and bronze in the making of tools and weapons. The iron sword became an instrument of decision.

Climatic changes were partly responsible for the movement of the Āryan speaking peoples southwards from the central Asian steppe lands towards Afghanistān and westwards into Irān and Mesopotamia under the shadow of the Elburz mountains, and, probably a little later in time eastwards over the passes of the Hindu Kush into what is today, the Panjāb. Armed with horse and sword, these pastoral nomads from beyond the fortieth parallel of north latitude, fair-skinned, haughty, vigorous and virile, rudely intruded as conquering barbarians and overran the

[1] See "*The Steppe and the Sown*" (Vol. V of *The Corridors of Time*) by Peake and Fleure pp. 8, 19, 146.

[2] See "*The Horse and the Sword*" (Vol. VIII of *The Corridors of Time*) by Peake and Fleure pp. 53 - 55.

prosperous, fertile lands of the Indus and its great tributaries, where flourished Dravidian civilization. Their intrusion may have begun during the eighteenth or seventeenth century before Christ. Certainly not closer to our times than the fifteenth century before Christ, the Āryan speaking peoples were lords of Pañcanada and Kurukshetra, confined between the basins of the Indus and the Sutlej. Before a thousand years had rolled away their domination had spread to the Ganges-Brahmaputra delta, over Pañcāla, Kosala, Bhoja, Videha, Kāśī, and Magadha.

Great and powerful states were these, some kingdoms, others republics. The third stage in political development in India was now reached, the village system of the Proto-australoids being the first, and the city-states of the Indus Valley people the second. Whereas, formerly, inclusion in the community depended upon kinship and personal allegiance to the head of the tribe, now, nationality was determined by the territory on which one was born and by military allegiance to the sovereign power over the kingdom. The personal basis of the small group changed into the impersonal basis of the modern state, the organized kingdom. In course of time, religion and philosophy underwent changes in the new order. Man learned to seek reality objectively, to discover himself and learn the truth impersonally.

It is hard to say what was Dravidian religion. When the Āryan conquerors came, Mohenjodāro was under the sands—literally the city of the dead. Mediterraneans and Proto-australoids had mixed in blood to some extent, though on the whole the aborigines were segregated in less accessible and less fertile parts. The elements of caste distinction were already present, even from Proto-australoid times, based on colour, personal strength and degree of civilization. The principle of avoidance was already in operation. Dravidian civilization had reached a pitch of luxury, and consequent decadence. There were castles ; and women bathed in milk fifteen centuries before Poppea Sabina.

A privileged and learned priestly class existed. Its members enjoyed the advantage that they knew how to propitiate the gods of the soil. They succeeded finally in establishing their ascendancy over the intrusive culture of the Āryan invaders. There is evidence to show that the true brāhman families were of pre-Vedic origin. The Āryan kings of Madhyadeśa were their own priests and had no brāhmans, until the influence of the Dravidian priesthood over the new conquerors brought a separate brāhman caste into being. The Āryans themselves probably consisted of the Rājanya (the ruling class, the Kshatriyas or warriors), the Vaiśyas (the merchants and traders) and the inspired poets of the Vedic hymns. Magical spells and incantations appear in the Atharva, the latest of the Vedas. The first, the Ṛig Veda, which came with the Āryans into a new land, is marked, in the opinion of most scholars, by a naïve realism, by joyous optimism, characteristic of a happy, successful, hedonistic people. Only later, through interaction with the decadent culture of the conquered, fear and superstition crept in, till in fact the Dravidian gods triumphed, counterbalancing the physical victory of Āryan arms. It may be, then, that Vedic bards and Dravidian priests interacting with the Āryan rulers gave rise to a brāhman caste.

Often, it is hard to draw a line between tribal religions and Hinduism. The word *brahma* may have meant, originally, supernatural power or influence, like the Proto-australoid, *mana* ; and *brahman*, according to Oldenberg, meant a magic spell, the meaning being derived from the magical spells of Dravidian times. The name Viṣṇu, has a Dravidian origin according to Przyluski, who also shows that *liṅga* is definitely of non-Āryan origin. The śakti cult, bound up with Śiva worship is probably derived from the Great Mother goddess of Asia Minor. The great gods of Hinduism, Viṣṇu, Śiva, and Kālī are not Ṛig-vedic gods.

Dravidian religion thus contributed major elements to Hinduism, especially in its ritualistic aspect, though possibly less in its philosophical aspect. The Upanishads are the distillate of that thought and enquiry foreshadowed in the monotheistic and monistic tendencies of the Ṛig Veda, although the influence of Dravidian ceremonial doubtless moulded that thought to some extent. And these special tendencies of the Ṛig Veda, are the distinctive contribution of a race of different calibre from those earlier immigrant races from western Asia.

As far as can be gathered, man and god in Dravidian religion were still apart from each other. Propitiation was necessary. A man was not yet generally regarded as an integrated whole, as a personality. Reality was still the unknown, and perhaps unknowable. Man had still to acknowledge his serfdom to the gods, and to live in fear of malign powers.

The Āryan speaking peoples of the Northern Steppe had outstanding qualities. They were adventurous and explorative; tolerant and practical minded; good organizers and experimenters; and they were a race of poets, their greatest gift to mankind being their language which was more highly developed than any other. Their westward migrations spread to Greece and other parts of Europe; in Asia they spread over Irān and Mesopotamia and India. Such has been their prowess that they produced great civilizations in the past, and are masters of the world today. In India, they established stable and prosperous kingdoms and republics in course of time, and through their tolerance, a heterogenous mixture of peoples was welded into a single, social order. True, the caste system emphasized and perpetuated caste distinctions; but the Āryan rulers did insist upon the organic unity of the different castes as a social whole. If each member of each separate caste performed his duty, all society would flourish. And the ideal was backed by religious sanction. It was related to the individual's spiritual salvation. Thus Hinduism, unique by virtue of not possessing any single founder, grew out of the seed of a social experiment based on a religious motive as well as a practical objective, a way of life which was found to be good and workable, and to which, in time, were added philosophy, mysticism and yoga. A phenomenon, isolated in world history.

What is the Ṛig Veda? A collection of hymns, the earliest document of the human mind, representing, according to most scholars, the religion of an unsophisticated age, the creation of inspired poets and seers. Many of the hymns, it is said, are simple and naïve, in praise of nature gods and goddesses; some deal with formal ritual; and others, especially in the last book, the tenth, present the results of conscious reflections on the origin of the world, and on the Supreme Being. These last show deep insight. They embody penetrating intuitions. But no system of philosophy is presented at this stage, for mythology and poetry precede philosophy and science.

Three other Vedas came into being; the Sāma Veda which is purely liturgical; the Yajur Veda (from Yaj—to sacrifice) which is like the Sāma Veda, only more elaborately ceremonial; and the Atharva Veda, the last to be compiled and accepted as a Veda, and which is largely a book of spells. The word Veda means knowledge. Associated with, and derived from the hymns, or Saṁhitā (i.e. a collection), called Mantras, arose the treatises called the Brāhmaṇas, the Āraṇyakas and the Upanishads. The Brāhmaṇas consist of precepts and religious duties, symbols and sacrificial rituals. The explanations of the symbols and rituals, found by contemplation by forest hermits, constitute the Āraṇyakas. They are the transition link to the Upanishads, the intuitive perceptions of those who won spiritual vision by moral and intellectual discipline. The Upanishads laid the foundations for all the subsequent thought of India.

Each Veda thus consists in the main of the Mantras, the spontaneous expression of poets, embodying the religion of nature; the Brāhmaṇas, the elaborate system built by priests, embodying the religion of Law; and the Upanishads, the mature creation of philosophers, embodying the religion of the spirit.

Nowhere in the world is the process of god-making so clear as in the Ṛig Veda. In this unique scripture are to be found animism, naturalistic polytheism, pantheism, monotheism, and, in the final stages, monistic suggestions.

The Āryan overlords of India believed in gods, gracious and kindly powers, and in demons, grim and hostile powers. In the Vedic universe of heaven, mid-air and earth, the demons were confined to mid-air and earth, while the gods ranged freely through the three domains. The demons are variously named: Dasyus, Paṇis (niggards), Rākṣasas (injurious ones, or, to be guarded against), Yatus (demons), Yātudhānas (sorcerers), Druhas (deceivers), Arātis (illiberal ones), and Asuras, which became their standing designation in later Vedic literature. But little attention is given to the demons by the Ṛig Veda, devoted as it is to the worship of the gods, of whom Indra and Agni are the great demon-slayers. The demons loom larger in the later Atharva Veda.

The evil spirits are endowed with the evil qualities characterizing evil men. They are fools, tricksters, evildoers, haters of prayer, slanderers and false accusers, robbers and thieves, malicious, and above all liars. Their ultimate fate is hell :

1. Indra and Soma, burn, destroy the demon foe, send
   downward, O ye Bulls, those who add gloom to gloom.
   Annihilate the fools, slay them and burn them up :
   chase them away from us, pierce the voracious ones.
2. Indra and Soma, plunge the wicked in the depth,
   yea, cast them into darkness that hath no support,
   So that not one of them may ever thence return : so
   may your wrathful might prevail and conquer them.

Ṛig Veda VII. 104
(identical with Atharva Veda VIII.4.1,3.)

The celestial family appears to be conceived anthropomorphically after the pattern of the human family. Father Sky and Mother Earth are the parents of all the gods, the devas, and also of men. The divine race is composed of various groups, such as the Ādityas, Vasus and Rudras, the semi-divine Aṅgirases, and lower deities such as the Ṛibhus, Apsarases and Gandharvas. Collectively, they are called Viśvedevāh, or " all-gods ". The gods have, like men, their specific functions. Agni and Bṛihaspati are priests, Indra and the Maruts warriors, Tvaṣṭar and the Ṛibhus artizans, while Kshetrapati, lord of the field, Urvarā, she of the ploughland, and Sitā, she of the furrow, are agricultural deities. But they are not exclusive functionaries. Parjanya, Varuṇa, Indra, Dyaus, Rudra and the Maruts are all rain-makers ; Indra and Trita Āptya make lightning ; Rudra and the Maruts, Varuṇa, Soma, the Aśvins, Vāta and the Waters are all physicians ; Agni, Indra and the gods of light are demon-slayers ; and Bṛihaspati, the Maruts and the Aṅgirases are divine minstrels.

The gods work in perfect accord, mutually helping and serving each other. Indra alone appears to introduce a discordant note, but only occasionally. Agni serves all the gods as a messenger ; the Maruts serve Indra as soldiers (Ṛig Veda III.35.9.) ; Agni serves Indra since Indra drinks soma, the nectar of the gods, with the tongue of Agni (Ṛig Veda III.35.9 and 10) ; Indra serves all the gods by his victory over the demon Vṛitra so giving them their freedom (Ṛig Veda III.34.7) ; Varuṇa prepares a path for Sūrya (Ṛig Veda I.24.8.) and Sūrya reports to Varuṇa and Mitra the sinfulness of men (Ṛig Veda VII.62.2.). All the gods are characterized as shining, as Asuras or mysterious—their mystery emphasized by māyā or their occult power, as immortal, in contrast with mortal humans, as endowed with power, beauty and benevolence and as upholders of Ṛta or the Eternal Order, cosmic and ethical. Varuṇa and Mitra are most intimately connected with Ṛta. All the gods function as a unity, a unity not of an individual will but of a collective clan, reflecting the unity of nature, of the cosmos as an ordered whole, or Ṛta. Thus the tendency of the Ṛig Veda was towards a pantheistic unity.

Until man achieves self-realization, he feels insecure, incomplete, unloved, insignificant. He remedies this by endowing his anthropomorphic gods with infinite power, stability, majesty and any other qualities which appeal to him. He defines stability and security as that which never alters, is permanent and infinite. The Ṛig-vedic Indian observed birth, growth and decay. Storms come and go ; the tides and seasons and years roll on ; the very sun and moon and stars change. Only the firmament abides. Dyaus Pitar, Father Heaven, was the boundless infinite, the supporter and mainstay of all. The Zeus of the Greeks, Jupiter of the Romans, deus of the Latin tongue, are related to Dyaus Pitar. As heaven above, so earth below was deified, made the wife of heaven, addressed in the Homeric poems as " Mother of Gods, the wife of the starry Heaven ". Heaven and Earth, the universal parents, are regarded in the Ṛig Veda as the parents[1] of men and gods, and are endowed with righteousness, beneficence and omniscience.

Varuṇa is the lord of the firmament. He is Ouranos with the Greeks, Ahuramazda with the Irānians, the one who encompasses or enfolds the universe. Devoid of caprice, he is one of fixed resolve, a dhṛtavrata, whose orders are obeyed by other gods. " Varuṇa's character ", said Macdonell (*Vedic Mythology*, p.3) " resembles that of the divine ruler in a monotheistic belief of an

[1] Ṛig Veda I.185.4; I.159.1,2; I.160.3; III.3.11; IV.56.2; VI.17.7; VII.53.1, 2 IX.85.12; X.1.7; X.35.3; X.64.14; X.65.8; X.11.9.

exalted type". He is the embodiment of law and order[1], and is the most moral of the Vedic gods. All seeing,[2] omnipresent,[3] majestic,[4] with the sun as his eye,[5] the sky for his garment and the wind as his breath,[6] he is the punisher of the guilty but gracious and forgiving to the penitent sinner. Confession of guilt, repentance and prayers for forgiveness[7] abound in the hymns to Varuṇa. Though God of gods, Varuṇa obeys the universal moral law[8] which he himself has established. By sin, man breaks his fellowship with Varuṇa who inflicts disease as a punishment. Varuṇa is lord of life and death, and his grace can be won and his mercy gained by trying to discover one's hidden faults and confessing them, by longing to be justified in Varuṇa's sight, by prayer for the remission of the penalty due, by renewed obedience, by oblation and sacrifices, and by hymns of praise.

1. Who now is he, what god among the immortals,
   of whose auspicious name we may bethink us?
   Who shall to mighty Aditi restore us,
   that I may see my father and my mother?

2. Agni the god the first among the immortals,
   of his auspicious name let us bethink us.
   He shall to mighty Aditi restore us,
   that I may see my father and my mother.

3. To thee, O Savitar, the lord
   of precious things, who helpest us
   Continually, for our share we come—

4. Wealth, highly lauded ere reproach
   hath fallen on it, which is laid,
   Free from all hatred, in thy hands.

5. Through thy protection may we come
   to even the height of affluence
   Which Bhaga hath dealt out to us.

6. Ne'er have those birds that fly through air attained
   to thy high dominion or thy might or spirit;

[1] Ṛig Veda V.66.1 and 68.1.
[2] Ṛig Veda I.24; I.25; VII.34.
[3] Atharva Veda IV.16.4.
[4] Ṛig Veda V.85.
[5] Ṛig Veda VI.51.1.
[6] Ṛig Veda VII.87 and 88; VIII.41.
[7] Ṛig Veda I.24; VII. 86.87.88.89.
[8] Ṛig Veda V.67.4.

Nor these the waters that flow on for ever,
nor hills, abaters of the wind's wild fury.

7. Varuṇa, king, of hallowed might, sustaineth
erect the tree's stem in the baseless region.
Its rays, whose root is high above, stream downward.
Deep may they sink within us, and be hidden.

8. King Varuṇa hath made a spacious pathway,
a pathway for the Sun wherein to travel.
Where no way was he made him set his footstep,
and warned afar whate'er afflicts the spirit.

9. A hundred balms are thine, O king, a thousand ;
deep and wide-reaching also be thy favours.
Far from us, far away drive thou Destruction.
Put from us e'en the sin we have committed.

10. Whither by day depart the constellations
that shine at night, set high in heaven above us ?
Varuṇa's holy laws remain unweakened,
and through the night, the moon moves on in splendour.

11. I ask this of thee with my prayer adoring ;
thy worshipper craves this with his oblation.
Varuṇa, stay thou here and be not angry ;
steal not our life from us, O thou wide-ruler.

12. Nightly and daily this one thing they tell me,
this too the thought of mine own heart repeateth.
May he to whom prayed fettered Sunaḥsepa,
may he the sovran Varuṇa release us.

13. Bound to three pillars captured Sunaḥsepa
thus to the Āditya made his supplication.
Him may the sovran Varuṇa deliver,
wise, ne'er deceived, loosen the bonds that bind him.

14. With bending down, oblations, sacrifices,
O Varuṇa, we deprecate thine anger :
Wise Asura, thou king of wide dominion,
loosen the bonds of sins by us committed.

15. Loosen the bonds, O Varuṇa, that hold me,
loosen the bonds above, between, and under.
So in thy holy law may we made sinless
belong to Aditi, O thou Āditya.

Ṛig Veda I.24.

1. Whatever law of thine, O god, O Varuṇa, as we are men,
Day after day we violate,

2. Give us not as a prey to death, to be destroyed by thee in wrath,
To thy fierce anger when displeased.

3. To gain thy mercy, Varuṇa, with hymns we bind thy heart, as binds
The charioteer his tethered horse.

4. They flee from me dispirited, bent only on obtaining wealth,
As to their nests the birds of air

5. When shall we bring to be appeased, the hero, lord of warrior might,
Him, the far-seeing Varuṇa?

6. This, this with joy they both accept in common: never do they fail
The ever-faithful worshipper.

7. He knows the path of birds that fly through heaven, and, sovran of the sea,
He knows the ships that are thereon.

8. True to his holy law, he knows the twelve moons with their progeny:
He knows the moon of later birth.

9. He knows the pathway of the wind, the spreading, high, and mighty wind:
He knows the gods who dwell above.

10. Varuṇa, true to holy law, sits down among his people; he
Most wise, sits there to govern all.

11. From thence perceiving he beholds all wondrous things, both that hath been,
And what hereafter will be done.

12. May that Āditya very wise, make fair paths for us all our days:
May he prolong our lives for us.

13. Varuṇa, wearing golden mail, hath clad him in a shining robe:
His spies are seated round about.

14. The god whom enemies threaten not, nor those who tyrannize o'er men,
Nor those whose minds are bent on wrong.

15. He who gives glory to mankind, not glory that is incomplete,
To our own bodies giving it.

16. Yearning for the wide-seeing one, my thoughts move onward unto him.
As kine unto their pastures move.

17. Once more together let us speak, because my meath is brought : priest-like
Thou eatest what is dear to thee.

18. Now saw I him whom all may see, I saw his car above the earth :
He hath accepted these my songs.

19. Varuṇa, hear this call of mine : be gracious unto us this day :
Longing for help I cried to thee.

20. Thou, O wise god, art lord of all, thou art the king of earth and heaven :
Hear, as thou goest on thy way.

21. Release us from the upper bond, untie the bond between, and loose
The bonds below, that I may live.

Ṛig Veda I.25.

1. The tribes of men have wisdom through his greatness
who stayed even spacious heaven and earth asunder ;
Who urged the high and mighty sky to motion,
and stars of old, and spread the earth before him.

2. With mine own heart I commune on the question
how Varuṇa and I may be united.
What gift of mine will he accept unangered ?
When may I calmly look and find him gracious ?

3. Fain to know this my sin I question others :
I seek the wise, O Varuṇa, and ask them.
This one same answer even the sages gave me,
Surely this Varuṇa is angry with thee.

4. What, Varuṇa, hath been my chief transgression,
that thou wouldst slay the friend who sings thy praises ?
Tell me, Unconquerable Lord, and quickly
sinless will I approach thee with mine homage.

5. Loose us from sins committed by our fathers,
from those wherein we have ourselves offended.

O king, loose, like a thief who feeds the cattle,
as from the cord a calf, set free Vasishṭha.

6. Not our own will betrayed us, but seduction,
thoughtlessness, Varuṇa! wine, dice, or anger.
The old is near to lead astray the younger:
even slumber leadeth men to evil-doing.

7. Slavelike may I do service to the bounteous,
serve, free from sin, the god inclined to anger.
This gentle lord gives wisdom to the simple:
the wiser god leads on the wise to riches.

8. O lord, O Varuṇa, may this laudation
come close to thee and lie within thy spirit.
May it be well with us in rest and labour.
Preserve us evermore, ye gods, with blessings.

Ṛig Veda VII. 86.

1. The mighty Ruler of these worlds beholds as though
from close at hand
The man who thinks he acts by stealth: all this the
Gods perceive and know.

2. If a man stands or walks or moves in secret, goes to
his lying-down or his uprising,
What two men whisper as they sit together, King
Varuṇa knows: He as the third is present.

3. This earth, too, is King Varuṇa's possession, and
the high heaven whose ends are far asunder.
The loins of Varuṇa are both the oceans, and this
small drop of water, too, contains him.

4. If one should flee afar beyond the heaven, King Varuṇa
would still be round about him.
Proceeding hither from the sky his envoys look,
thousand-eyed, over the earth beneath them.

5. All this the royal Varuṇa beholdeth, all between
heaven and earth and all beyond them.
The twinkling of men's eyelids hath he counted. As one
who plays throws dice he settles all things.

6. Those fatal snares of thine which stand extended,
threefold, O Varuṇa, seven by seven,
May they all catch the man who tells a falsehood, and
pass unharmed the man whose words are truthful.

7. Varuṇa, snare him with a hundred nooses! Man's watcher!
   let not him who lies escape thee.
   There let the villain sit with hanging belly and
   bandaged like a cask whose hoops are broken.

8. Varuṇa sends, and drives away, diseases: Varuṇa is
   both native and a stranger,
   Varuṇa is celestial and is human.

9. I bind and hold thee fast with all these nooses, thou
   son of such a man and such a mother.
   All these do I assign thee as thy portion.

Atharva Veda IV.16.

In the prayers for pardon[1] the removal of the penalty for sin is emphasized. Sin consists in the transgression of the laws or ordinances, the Vrata, of Varuṇa,[2] the ordinances being themselves founded upon Varuṇa.[3] What are these sins? To kill, curse, deceive, gamble and cheat, indulge immoderately in wine, anger, dice. A tribal ethic. But there is also the conception of sinning against a stranger, and a distinction between intentional and unintentional sinning.[4] The Vedic Indians did believe that to err is human,[5] and pleaded thoughtlessness, weakness of will, wine, anger, dice, bad example and evil dreams as causes of sin. In Ṛig Veda VII.86.5, the poet says, "Loose us from sins committed by our fathers". Varuṇa can combine mercy with justice, provided there is a true repentance on the part of the sinner. To his true worshippers, who are his beloved ones, he grants protection and happiness.

Varuṇa as Lord of the Ethical Order is a holy God; as lord of the Cosmic Order he is a Creator and Sovereign. The Vedic poets, observant worshippers of nature, were believers in the established order of things. The stars in heaven, day and night, the seasons, all followed an all-compelling law, Ṛta, "the course of things", of which Varuṇa is the custodian[6] and ruler:

[1] Ṛig Ved II.28.5 & 9; V.85. 7 & 8; IX.14; 1.24.
[2] Ṛig Veda I.25.1 & 2; VII.89. 5.
[3] Ṛig Veda II. 28.8.
[4] Ṛig Veda V.85.7 & 8.
[5] Ṛig Veda I.25.1; VII.89.5.
[6] Ṛig Veda I.141.9.

1. I am the royal ruler, mine is empire, as mine who
   sway all life are all the immortals.
   Varuṇa's will the gods obey and follow. I am
   the king o'er folk of sphere sublimest.
2. I am King Varuṇa. To me were given these first
   existing high celestial powers.
   Varuṇa's will the gods obey and follow. I am
   king o'er folk of sphere sublimest.
3. I Varuṇa am Indra : in their greatness, these the
   two wide deep fairly fashioned regions,
   These the two world-halves have I, even as Tvashṭar,
   knowing all beings joined and held together.
4. I made to flow the moisture-shedding waters, and set the
   heaven firm in the seat of Order.
   By law, the son of Aditi (i.e. Varuṇa), Law-observer,
   hath spread abroad the world in threefold measure.

(The hymn is to Varuṇa and Indra.)

Ṛig Veda IV.42.

Ṛta is a universal principle, the unchanging law, physical and moral, the real and eternal, on which the whole universe is founded. All objects, all creatures, all gods are subject to Ṛta.

(Agni)	Ruler of sacrifices, guard of Law Eternal	Ṛig Veda I.1.8.
	Who, deathless, true to Law, 'mid men a herald bringeth the gods as best sacrificers	,, ,, I.77.1.
	Such as thou art, born after Law	,, ,, I.189.6.
	Whose foresight keeps the Law from violation	,, ,, II.9.1.
	True knower of the Law	,, ,, IV.3.4.
	Thou art the eye and guard of mighty order	,, ,, X.8.5.
(Viṣṇu)	Primeval germ of Order	,, ,, I.156.3.
(Indra)	The holy Law's commandments make me mighty	,, ,, VIII.89.4.
(Savitar)	God, Law's fulfiller	,, ,, II.30.1.
(Bṛihaspati)	Son of Law	,, ,, II.23.15
	Guilt-scourger, guilt-avenger . . . who slays the spoiler and upholds the mighty Law	,, ,, II.23.16.

(Varuṇa and Mitra)	. through Law, lovers and cherishers of law, Have ye obtained your mighty power	Ṛig Veda I.2.8.
	By thee, O Agni, Varuṇa who guards the Law, Mitra and Aryaman, the bounteous are made strong	,, ,, I.141.8.
	For Varuṇa, whose form is law, place offerings for his great delight	,, ,, V.66.1.
	For they are true, they cleave to Law, held holy among every race	,, ,, V.67.4.
	They, mighty lords, are lofty Law	,, ,, V.68.1.
(The Ādityas)	Mighty through Law, . . . is your greatness	,, ,, II.27.8.
	Upholders of the Law	,, ,, II.29.1.
(The gods generally)	Strengtheners of the Law	,, ,, I.14.7.
	The gods approached the ways of holy Law, there was a gathering vast as heaven itself	,, ,, I.65.2.
	The waters fed with praise the growing babe, born nobly in the womb, the seat of Order	
(In Nature and cosmos)	The flowing of the floods is Law, Law is the Sun's extended Light	,, ,, I.105.12.
	The holy Law hath quelled even mighty men of war	,, ,, VIII.76.5.
	Ye raised the Sun to heaven by everlasting Law	,, ,, X.62.3.
	Ye (Heaven and Earth) sanctify each other's form, by your own proper might ye rule, And from of old observe the Law	,, ,, IV.56.6.
	By Law, the Aṅgirases cleft the rock asunder	,, ,, IV.3.11.
	By Law, he (Indra) lighted up the host of Mornings.	,, ,, VI.39.4.
	He moves with steeds yoked by eternal Order	
	With mighty strength, most liberal	,, ,, VI.68.2.

	of the princes (Indra and Varuṇa), chiefs of the host, by Law made Vṛitra's slayers	
(In relation to man)	None, Varuṇa and Mitra, harms the mortal man who honours and obeys your laws	Rig Veda VIII.22.15.
	He makes his house endure, he gathers plenteous food who pays obedience to your Will	,, ,, VIII.22.16.
	Born in his sons anew he spreads as Law commands, and prospers everyway unharmed	
	Seeing that Mitra, Aryaman and Varuṇa are guarding us, the paths of Law are fair to tread	,, ,, VIII.31.13
	This holy hymn, sublime and seven-headed, sprung from eternal Law	,, ,, X.67.1.
(The Maruts)	As best of all foreknowers, excellent to guide, like Somas, good to guard the man who follows the Law	,, ,, X.78.2.
	O Indra, Lead us beyond all pain and grief along the path of holy Law	,, ,, X.133.6.

The above quotations indicate the deep conviction of the Ṛig-vedic Indians of the existence of the Law, its power and its importance, and its undeviating operation. And yet, throughout the Ṛig Veda there is not a single hymn exclusively devoted to Ṛta! Moreover, the term—the Law, or eternal Law, or Order, or the seat of Order—is introduced without explanation of itself. There is no analysis of the nature of the Law itself, or its mode of operation. Three consecutive verses deal with Ṛta:

Eternal Law hath varied food that strengthens;
Thought of eternal law removes transgressions.
The praise-hymn of eternal law, arousing, glowing,
hath oped the deaf ears of the living.

Firm-seated are eternal law's foundations; in its fair
form are many splendid beauties.
By holy law long-lasting food they bring us; by holy
law have cows come to our worship.

Fixing eternal law he, too, upholds it : swift
 moves the might of law and wins the booty.
To law belong the vast deep earth and heaven :
 milch-kine supreme, to law their milk they render

Ṛig Veda IV.23.8–10

The verses are illuminating. Yet even here there is no analysis of the nature of universal law. India had to wait centuries before the Buddha announced the law of causation as being universally operative in all the realms of our experience—material, moral and spiritual. The inspired seers of the Ṛig Veda lived in unquestioning obedience to their vision of the fact of Law and Order. Not for them to enquire into its nature, still less to challenge it. Life in an ordered cosmos was good. There was no stimulus to a deeper or wounded curiosity in a world which, by and large, offered a happy and successful life.

What is most significant, however, is that the concept of the supremacy of the law prevailed in Vedic times if not earlier. Man lived in a just world, even if justice as humanly understood was not clearly discernible in concrete events. Such a belief was an instrument for destroying fear and winning freedom. What was a simple religious faith in the Vedic age, grew into a philosophic truth with the Buddha, into a scientific fact in modern times. In the field of government, ancient Hindu political philosophy, based upon the king as the sovereign authority and power in the land, acknowledged the supremacy of the law as even higher than the king's. The chief priest of the land, the sage and the saint, as expounders of divine law, were sacrosanct, and even a king had to accept their rebuke with humility, and listen to their advice with respect. Though the wielder of sanctions, the king himself was liable to penalty and punishment, more severe in some cases than that meted out to the humble and ignorant, if he did wrong. The Manu Saṁhitā, the Rāmāyaṇa and Mahābhārata and many other writings extol the king who upholds the highest moral principles and spiritual ideals as the best king. The moral imperative for living the good life, for social justice and political integrity have their roots in Varuṇa of the Vedic Pantheon.

Joint keeper of Ṛta and forgiver of sin with Varuṇa is Mitra, sun, and god of the morning light. He watches over truth-speaking and sincerity between man and man in all man's promises, contracts and treaties. Three thousand years ago in India, treaties were not " mere scraps of paper ". Mitra helps men to keep faith in all covenants between man and man, and tribe and tribe. He punishes where necessary :

> For thee, even Aryman, Varuṇa and Mitra, are
> the chastisers of all guile and falsehood.
>
> Ṛig Veda VII.60.5.

He is the dearest friend of mortals :

> Let us not anger Varuṇa, nor Vāyu, nor him,
> the dearest friend of mortals, Mitra.
>
> Ṛig Veda VII.62.4.

and he is invoked as a protector from distress caused by friends :

> From trouble caused by man the Lord preserve us ;
> from woe sent by his friend let Mitra save us.
>
> Ṛig Veda IV.55.5.

All the qualities ascribed to Mitra, also characterize Varuṇa.

It is difficult to believe that the spiritual vision of the inspired bards who sang of Varuṇa was clouded with anthropomorphism. He who was regarded as omniscient and omnipresent, as lord of law, as justiciar not without ruth, was not altogether an external anthropomorph, but rather an enlightened concept born of emancipated intelligence. To unburden the soul's sense of guilt through confession, to pray for forgiveness, trusting in a supreme power characterized by both dispassionate justice and kindly mercy, evidences psychological insight. The race of man is outgrowing its intellectual and spiritual childhood and adolescence—such is the significance of Varuṇa.

The sun as the source of life, light and warmth has always attracted worship. Sun worship was at the core of Greek religion and Zarathustrianism. Sūrya is the sun by day ; Savitar too, is the sun by day and also the invisible sun at night. Both are addressed as Creators. Prayers are addressed to Savitar for granting blessings and for the forgiveness of sin. (Ṛig Veda IV.54.3.) Sometimes Sūrya and Savitar are indentified with each other (Ṛig Veda VII.63.)

Viṣṇu appears in the Ṛig Veda as a form of Sūrya (Ṛig Veda I.21 and 154). He typifies greatness, for in three strides he covers heaven, earth and the rest of the universe. Though he holds a subordinate position in the Vedic Pantheon, he is destined for one of the highest positions in later Hinduism as Lord of Wisdom. Pūṣan, a pastoral, solar god, the guardian of cattle and friend of man, is the god of wayfarers and husbandmen. The praise of Uṣas, goddess of the dawn, the Greek Eos, is sung in several hymns of lyric beauty (Ṛig Veda I.113, 123 and 124; IV.51; V.80). The fleet and strong Aśvins, twin brothers of Uṣas, are the lords of brilliance, of dawn and dusk, who later on become the protectors of conjugal love and life, deliverers of the oppressed and suffering, the physicians of gods and men.

Indra is the most frequently sung of the Vedic gods. Born of water and cloud, he is the wielder of the thunderbolt, god of the blue sky, lord of rain, the bringer of light and life, before whom heaven bows and at whose approach the earth trembles. He is also lord of victory in battle, the champion of the Āryan hosts. In course of time he displaces Varuṇa (though by identification with him), becomes ruler of sky, earth and all its creatures, waters and mountains.

(Indra's Sovereignty)

Indra is king of all that moves and moves not,
of creatures tame and horned, the thunder wielder.
Over all living men he rules as sovran, containing
all as spokes within the felly.

Ṛig Veda I. 32.15.

(His power and might)

1. He who just born chief god of lofty spirit
by power and might became the gods' protector,
Before whose strength in majesty of valour
the two worlds trembled, He, O men, is Indra.

2. He who fixed fast and firm the earth that staggered,
and set at rest the agitated mountains,
Who measured out the air's wide middle region
and gave the heaven support, He, men, is Indra.

7. He under whose supreme control are horses,
all chariots, and the villages, and cattle:

He who gave being to the sun and morning,
who leads the waters, He, O men, is Indra.
9. Without whose help our people never conquer;
whom, battling, they invoke to give them succour;
He of whom all this world is but the copy,
who shakes things moveless, He, O men, is Indra.
10. He who hath smitten, ere they knew their danger,
with his hurled weapon many grievous sinners;
Who pardons not his boldness who provokes him,
who slays the Dasyu, He, O men, is Indra.
13. Even the Heaven and Earth bow down before him,
before his strength the very mountains tremble.
Known as the Soma-drinker, armed with thunder,
who wields the bolt, He, O ye men, is Indra.

Ṛig Veda II.12.

Indra's two most characteristic epithets are Vṛitrahan, the slayer of the dragon Vṛitra, and Maghavān, the bountiful. Victorious warrior, he wins from the aborigines (the Dasyus) gold, horses, cows and ploughland (Ṛig Veda II.21.1; IV.17.11.) which he gives as booty to his followers. Bestower of wives, treasure-lord of treasures (Ṛig Veda III.36.9), he is generous to his true worshippers. Men pray to him:

Indra, bestow on us the best of treasures,
the spirit of ability and fortune;
Increase of riches, safety of our bodies,
charm of sweet speech, and days of pleasant weather.

Ṛig Veda II.21.6.

In contrast to the righteous and merciful Varuṇa, majestic in his reposeful, meditative calm, guiding the universe by merely watching it, Indra is the apotheosis of heroic action, the embodiment of the strenuous doer. Cosmically, Indra generated the lightnings of the sky, found the hidden heaven and earth, made the earth visible to heaven and the sun visible to earth, slew the dragon Vṛitra and released the waters, and separated and supported heaven and earth. On behalf of his votaries, the divine warrior delivered many Āryan chieftains, demolished the ninety-nine forts of Śaṁbara for Divodāsa's sake, broke down the forts of Pipru and helped Ṛijiśvān at the slaughter of the Dasyus, helped Sudās in the battle of the ten kings and drowned his foes in the Paruṣṇi, and arrested the floods so that Turvīti and Vayya could cross over.

The incomparable Indra is described as unique in his exploits, matchless, for even the two boundless worlds are a handful to him, and his greatness extends beyond his filling of heaven and earth. Heaven trembles at the birth of his blinding splendour, and he makes the world out of nothing. In many respects he reminds one of Yahweh, the Semitic "lord of hosts and god of battles"

4. For, overthrowing what hath ne'er been shaken,
   thou goest forth alone destroying Vṛitras.
   For him who followeth thy law the mountains
   and heaven and earth stand as if firmly stablished.

5. Yea, much invoked! in safety through thy glories
   alone thou speakest truth as Vṛitra's slayer.
   E'en these two boundless worlds to thee O Indra,
   what time thou graspest them, are but a handful.

Ṛig Veda III.30.

Indra, impetuous one hath waxed immensely:
he with his vastness hath filled earth and heaven.
E'en beyond this his majesty extendeth
who hath exceeded all the worlds in greatness.

Ṛig Veda IV.16.5.

Heaven trembled at the birth of thine effulgence;
Earth trembled at the fear of thy displeasure.
The steadfast mountains shook in agitation;
the waters flowed, and desert spots were flooded.

Ṛig Veda IV.17.2.

Like Varuṇa, Indra is lord of Ṛta. Whereas Varuṇa's lordship is mainly ethical, Indra's is cosmic, for he controls, through Law, plants, rivers, and the dawns. Perhaps Indra may be regarded as the executive arm of Varuṇa. Varuṇa is Law-maker, Law-giver; Indra is Law-enforcer. Like Varuṇa, Indra punishes the guilty. Himself the guiltless one, he is a saviour even from great sin. But the relationship of penitent sinner and graciously forgiving god, so characteristic of man and Varuṇa, is absent in the case of Indra. This is natural and proper. Varuṇa, psychologically considered, represents the beneficient un-conscious, the *sweetly*-compelling law that moves all things to righteousness. Varuṇa exerts no choice. Goodness only is possible to angels, the choiceless ones incapable of doing evil, as evil alone is possible to devils, the choiceless ones incapable of doing good. Individuality means choice—both free and unfree choice !—and personal responsibility. Man eats of the fruit of the dual tree of knowledge of good and evil. Man chooses rightly at times, wrongly at other times. Indra, lord of individuality, guiltless god, is the apotheosis of right choice. Indra leads man to conscious right action, to a knowing perfection, whereas Varuṇa, the everlasting arms underneath, implants the unconscious urge to goodness. Indra represents that power in man which by personal action lifts him to godhead, Varuṇa, the power which man calls up, the beneficent grace he invokes, from his inner depths.

As the Āryan tribes expanded eastward with conquest, established kingdoms, and settled down to an ordered civilized life, the note of individuality sounded more insistently. It is not surprising that Indra receives some two hundred and fifty hymns, nearly a quarter of the whole Ṛig Veda, in his praise. But in no sense must the quantity of hymns be regarded as the final criterion of Indra's worth in the Vedic Pantheon, apart from it being a possible indication of the trend of Āryan development. It is not unlikely that all the gods, or at least all the main gods, stood equal in all respects, in the sight of holy Law and Order.

Agni, first born of holy Order,[1] is the god of Fire. Mātariśvan brought fire from heaven[2] and entrusted it to the safe keeping of the Bhṛgus. As with Indra there is a naturalistic origin of Agni —the scorching sun, lightning, flintstone, fire sticks. With sharp jaws and burning teeth[3] with wood and ghee (clarified butter) for his food, and possessing a tawny beard, Agni shines like the darkness-dispelling sun. With a voice like heaven's thunder,[4] he cleaves a black path through forests, smoke for his banner[5], for

[1] Ṛig Veda X.5.7.
[2] Ṛig Veda III.9.5; VI.8.4; I.60.1.
[3] Ṛig Veda IV.7.9-11.
[4] Ṛig Veda IV.10.4.
[5] Ṛig Veda X.12.2.

he is dhūmaketu. On hearth and altar, in sun and lightning he dwells, a supreme god. As the conception of Agni deepens he becomes the mediator between gods and men (Ṛig Veda IV.2.4. X.70.11.), the friend of all (Ṛig Veda IV.1.3 and 5; X.7.3; Atharva Veda IV.23).

Agni as the sun in heaven, the lightning in the firmament, and the altar-fire on earth represents the earliest Indian triad. His threefold nature is well expressed in Ṛig Veda III.20.2. :—

> Three are thy powers, O Agni, three thy stations,
> three are thy tongues, yea, many, child of Order !
> Three bodies hast thou which the gods delight in :
> with these protect our hymns with care unceasing.

In one of his primitive aspects, Agni is a houselord, and he is regarded as kinsman and friend.

> 2. Who for the fivefold people's sake hath seated him
> in every home, wise, youthful, master of the house.
>
> 7. Lord of the house, whom men must seek, we set thee
> down, O worshipped one.
>
> Ṛig Veda VII.15.

> Thou, Agni, art the homestead's lord, our herald
> at the sacrifice.
> Lord of all boons, thou art the cleanser and a sage.
> Pay worship and enjoy the good.
>
> Ṛig Veda VII.16.5.

> Agni, men seek thee as a father with their prayers,
> win thee, bright formed, to brotherhood with holy act.
> Thou art a son to him who duly worships thee, and as
> a trusty friend thou guardest from attack.
>
> Ṛig Veda II. 1.9.

Agni's function as a dispeller of evil spirits, hostile magic and darkness is his other primitive aspect :

> With fervent heat exterminate the Yātudhānas (demons) ;
> destroy the Rākṣasas (fiends) with burning flame, O Agni.
> Destroy with fire the Mūradevas' (foolish gods') adorers ;
> blaze and destroy the insatiable monsters.
>
> Ṛig Veda X.87.14.

O Agni, radiant one, to whom the holy oil is poured, burn up
Our enemies whom fiends protect.

Ṛig Veda I.12.5.

Smite with thy weapons those of evil speech and
thought, devouring demons, whether near or far away.

Ṛig Veda I.95.9.

So thou, O Agni, rich in light, beaming like
Sūrya with thy rays
Boldly demolishest the gloom.

Ṛig Veda VIII.43.32.

The world was swallowed and concealed in darkness:
Agni was born, and light became apparent.

Ṛig Veda X.88.2.

To thee, dispeller of the night, O Agni.

Ṛig Veda I.1.7.

The priestly god, Agni, as the sacrificial fire, is the mediator and messenger between gods and men:

1. Thee, Agni, have the gods, ever of one accord, sent hither down, a god, appointed messenger, yea, with their wisdom sent thee down.
   The immortal, O thou holy one, mid mortal men, the god-devoted god, the wise, have they brought forth, brought forth the omnipresent god-devoted sage.
2. As such, O Agni, bring with favour to the gods, thy brother Varuṇa who loveth sacrifice, the chief who loveth sacrifice.
   True to the Law, the Āditya who supporteth men, the king, supporter of mankind.
3. Do thou, O friend, turn hither him who is our friend, swift as a wheel, like two car-steeds in rapid course wondrous! to us in rapid course.
   O Agni, find thou grace for us with Varuṇa, with Maruts who illumine all.
   Bless us, thou radiant one, for seed and progeny,
   yea, bless us, O thou wondrous god.
4. Do thou who knowest Varuṇa, O Agni, put far away from us the god's displeasure.
   Best sacrificer, best of priests, refulgent, remove thou far from us all those who hate us.

5. Be thou, O Agni, nearest us with succour, our closest friend
while now this Morn is breaking.
Reconcile to us Varuṇa, be bounteous : enjoy the
gracious juice ; be swift to hear us.

Ṛig Veda IV.1.

Aryaman, Mitra, Varuṇa, and Indra with Viṣṇu,
of the gods, Maruts and Aśvins—
These, Agni, with good car and steeds, bring hither,
most bountiful, to folk with fair oblations.

Ṛig Veda IV.2.4.

Agni performs the functions of every type of priest : the Hotar or Herald who invokes the gods ; the Potar, Purifier or Cleanser who is the assistant of the brahman or praying priest who remedies any defect in the ritual ; the Neshṭar or leader who leads forward the wife of the sacrificer ; the Agnidh or Kindler who lights the sacrificial fire ; the Praśāstar or Director who is the assistant of the Hotar ; and the Adhvaryu or ministering priest who is the deacon who measures the ground, builds the altar, and makes all the preparations necessary for the sacrifice. Agni's essential and archetypal priesthood is his outstanding feature. He is ruler of sacrifices, guard of Law eternal, radiant one (Ṛig Veda I.1.8.), and he is the most bountiful rewarder, both directly and indirectly, of the pious whose oblations he carries to the gods.

Even as Varuṇa and Indra are lords of Ṛta, moral and cosmic, so Agni is lord mainly of ritualistic Order. He is called the eye and guardian of mighty Ṛta. He, the " imperial lord of sacred rites " (Ṛig Veda I.27.1.), is often described as " sprung from Law "," faithful to Law ", " true to Law ". He of the thousand eyes (Ṛig Veda X.79.5.) makes known man's sin to Varuṇa and all the other gods. He punishes sin. He also intercedes with Varuṇa, appealing to his mercy on man's behalf. Prayers are offered to him for the remission of sins.

The problem of the One and the Many first emerged in Indian thought with the question of the relationship between Fire, Agni, and the infinite fires, agnis, which were a material fact of everyday life. The trend of thought was towards unity :

Thou art the same in many a place.

Rig Veda VIII.11.8.

Kindled in many a spot, still one is Agni.

Vālakhilya Hymn 10.2.

Sharing in the activities of both Indra and Agni is Bṛihaspati, lord of prayer. He is an abstract god, with no physical basis except sound. He is the personification of the creative power of the " brahman ", the magical word ; and he is the principal god who helps priests in making effective prayers. He is, like the other gods, born of Law. He punishes and avenges, and remits guilt, especially the guilt of hating prayers.

The special interest of Bṛihaspati consists in his being a link between the primitive ideas of brahman or the creative word as " mana ", or some magical life-essence (as with the Proto-australoids ?), and the later Upanishadic concept of Brahman as the essence of the universe, the ultimate reality.

The three ritualistic gods of the Vedas are Agni, Bṛihaspati and Soma. The last gives his name to the Soma sacrifice, which is regarded as the soul of the Ṛig Vedic ritual :

Winner of kine, Indra (another name for Soma), art
thou, winner of heroes, steeds and strength :
Primeval soul of sacrifice.

Ṛig Veda IX.2.10.

Soul of the sacrifice, the juice effused flows
quickly on . . .

Ṛig Veda IX.6.8.

His celestial origin is thus expressed :

High is thy juice's birth ; though set in heaven,
on earth it hath obtained
Strong sheltering power and great renown.

Ṛig Veda IX.61.10.

He is borne to earth by a falcon, as related in hymn 26 and hymn 27 in Book IV of the Ṛig Veda. Physically, Soma is the juice extracted out of the Soma plant, called mountain dwelling in several passages,[1] also mountain grown,[2] and is closely connected with rock.[3] After the Āryans entered India, they had to

[1] Ṛig Veda III.48.2; V.43.4; IX.18.1; IX.62.4.
[2] Ṛig Veda IX.46.1;
[3] *Journal of the Royal Asiatic Society*, July 1920, pp. 349-351.

find a substitute for the " madhu " or honey-mead of their original homeland. Besides the Sarcostemmas (Viminale, Intermedium, Brevistigma and Brunonianum[1]) there was the grape from Afghanistān, a preparation from sugar-cane or a hop preparation as suggested by Max Müller. E. B. Havell[2] suggested that the drink might be made from rāgi, the common millet (Eleusine coracana, " cultivated " says Havell, " along the Himālayas up to a height of 8,000 feet "). The Soma plant of the Veda, and the Irānian Haoma of the Zarathustrian Avestā, are identically described as having hanging branches and yellow colour, and as growing on mountains. Whatever it was, Soma, both god and drink, held the highest ritualistic place. That the whole of the ninth book of the Ṛig Veda should be exclusively devoted to Soma indicates the importance of Soma. The preparation of the juice, and the sacramental ritual, are elaborately described. The ceremony was hieratic in character, only gods and priests partaking of the Soma ; and the Soma offering, a free will and not an obligatory offering, gave the rich and the noble an unusual opportunity for liberality to gods and priests.

Soma produced exhilaration in the warrior ; it particularly induced a feeling of strength and greatness, dispelling anxiety or fear for personal safety. It inspired the seer and it healed the sick ; it bestowed wealth and prolonged life ; it scared away malign powers, gave joy and comfort, and it preserved one from the wrath of enemies.

1. Thou, Soma, art preeminent for wisdom ;
   along the straightest path thou art our leader.
   Our wise forefathers by thy guidance, Indu,
   gained for themselves among the gods great riches.
2. Thou by thine insight art most wise, O Soma,
   strong by thine energies and all-possessing ;
   Mighty art thou by all thy powers and greatness,
   by glories art thou glorious, guide of mortals.
3. Thine are king Varuṇa's eternal statutes ;
   lofty and deep, O Soma is thy glory.
   All-pure art thou like Mitra the beloved ;
   adorable, like Aryaman, O Soma.

[1] See Hillebrandt, *Vedische Mythologie* 1.4ff.
[2] *Journal of the Royal Asiatic Society*, July 1920, pp. 349-351.

4. With all glories on the earth, in heaven,
 on mountains, in the plants, and in the waters—
With all of these, well-pleased and not in anger,
 accept O royal Soma, our oblations.
5. Thou, Soma, art the lord of heroes, king, yea,
 Vṛitra-slayer thou ;
Thou art auspicious energy.
6. And, Soma, let it be thy wish that we may live and
 may not die ;
Praise-loving lord of plants art thou.
7. To him who keeps the law, both old and young, thou
 givest happiness,
And energy that he may live.
8. Guard us, king Soma, on all sides from him who threatens
 us ; never let
The friend of one like thee be harmed.
9. With those delightful aids which thou hast, Soma, for
 the worshipper—
Even with those protect thou us.
10. Accepting this our sacrifice and this our praise,
 O Soma, come,
And be thou nigh to prosper us.
11. Well skilled in speech we magnify thee, Soma, with our
 sacred songs :
Come thou to us, most gracious one.
12. Enricher, healer of disease, wealth-finder, prospering
 our store,
Be, Soma, a good friend to us.
13. Soma, be happy in our heart, as milch-kine in the
 grassy meads,
As a young man in his own house.
14. O Soma, god, the mortal man who in thy friendship
 hath delight—
Him doth the mighty sage befriend.
15. Save us from slanderous reproach, keep us, O Soma,
 from distress :
Be unto us a gracious friend.
16. Soma, wax great, from every side may vigorous powers
 unite in thee :
Be in the gathering-place of strength.
17. Wax, O most gladdening Soma, great through all the
 filaments and be
A friend of most illustrious fame to prosper us.

18. In thee be juicy nutriments united,
  and powers and mighty foe-subduing vigour,
 Waxing to immortality, O Soma:
  win highest glories for thyself in heaven.
19. Such of thy glories as with poured oblations
  men honour, may they all invest our worship.
 Wealth-giver, furtherer with troops of heroes,
  sparing the brave, come, Soma, to our houses.
20. To him who worships Soma gives the milch-cow,
  a fleet steed and a man of active knowledge,
 Skilled in home duties, meet for holy synod,
  for council meet, a glory to his father.
21. Invincible in fight, saver in battles,
  guard of our camp, winner of light and water,
 Born amid hymns, well-housed, exceeding famous,
  victor—in thee will we rejoice, O Soma.
22. These herbs, these milch-kine, and these running waters—
  all these, O Soma, thou hast generated.
 The spacious firmament hast thou expanded,
  and with the light thou hast dispelled the darkness.
23. Do thou, god Soma, with thy godlike spirit,
  victorious, win for us a share of riches.
 Let none prevent thee: thou art lord of valour.
  Provide for both sides in the fray for booty.

Ṛig Veda 1.91.

1. This here is Soma, ne'er restrained, active,
  all-conquering, bursting forth,
 Ṛishi and sage by sapience.
2. All that is here he covers o'er, all that is
  sick he medicines:
 The blind man sees, the cripple walks.
3. Thou, Soma, givest wide defence against the hate
  of alien men,
 Hatreds that waste and weaken us.
4. Thou by thine insight and thy skill, impetuous
  one, from heaven and earth
 Drivest the sinner's enmity.
5. When to their task they come with zeal, may they
  obtain the Giver's grace,
 And satisfy his wish who thirsts.
6. So may he find what erst was lost, so may he speed
  the pious man,
 And lengthen his remaining life

7. Gracious, displaying tender love, unconquered, gentle
   in thy thoughts,
   Be sweet, O Soma, to our heart.
8. O Soma, terrify us not; strike us not with alarm,
   O king:
   Wound not our heart with dazzling flame.
9. When in my dwelling-place I see the wicked enemies
   of gods,
   King, chase their hatred far away, thou bounteous
   one, dispel our foes.

Ṛig Veda VIII.68.

A distinction is drawn between the earthly Soma juice and the heavenly Soma, about which the brāhman priests alone have knowledge.

1. Truth is the base that bears the earth; by Sūrya are
   the heavens sustained.
   By Law the Ādityas stand secure, and Soma holds his
   place in heaven.
2. By Soma are the Ādityas strong, by Soma mighty is
   the earth.
   Thus Soma in the midst of all these constellations
   hath his place.
3. One thinks, when they have brayed the plant, that
   he hath drunk the Soma's juice; of whom
   brāhmans truly know as Soma no one ever tasted.
4. Soma, concealed by covering rules, guarded by
   hymns in Bṛihatī,
   Thou standest listening to the stones: none tastes
   of thee who dwells on earth.

Ṛig Veda X.85.

Let heavenly Soma gladden thee, O Indra, let
that effused among mankind delight thee.

Ṛig Veda X.116.3.

Indra waxes in might and accomplishes his wonderful exploits only through the inspiration and exhilaration of the heavenly Soma. Indeed, the immortality of the gods is the creative work of Soma, the ambrosia and nectar of the gods. The blessed dead, the Fathers, became immortal when Soma, father of the gods, unites with them.

For, verily, Pavamāna (Soma), thou hast, splendidest,
called all the generations of
The gods to immortality.

Ṛig Veda IX.108.3.

2. Let Indra drink, O Soma, of thy juice for wisdom,
and all deities for strength.
4. Flow onward, Soma, as a mighty sea, as father of the
gods, to every form.

Ṛig Veda IX.109

Let Vṛitra-slaying Indra drink Soma by Śaryaṇāvān's
side,
Storing up vigour in his heart, prepared to do heroic
deeds.

Ṛig Veda IX.113.1.

Soma helps the truthful and righteous man, and punishes the evil doer. He is, as indicated above in I.91.3, one with Varuṇa and the Ādityas.

9. Those who destroy, as is their wont, the simple,
and with their evil natures harm the righteous,
May Soma give them over to the serpent,
or to the lap of Nirṛiti (Death or Destruction) consign them.
12. The prudent finds it easy to distinguish
the true and false : their words oppose each other.
Of these two that which is true and honest,
Soma protects, and brings the false to nothing.
13. Never does Soma aid and guide the wicked or him
who falsely claims the warrior's title.
He slays the fiend and him who speaks untruly :
both lie entangled in the noose of Indra.

Ṛig Veda VII.104.

Splendid by Law ! declaring Law, truth-speaking,
truthful in thy works,
Enouncing faith, king Soma ! thou, O Soma, whom
thy maker decks. Flow, Indu, flow for Indra's sake.

Ṛig Veda IX.113.4.

Finally there are these verses in the Ṛig Veda IX.113.

7. O Pavamāna, place me in that deathless, undecaying world
Wherein the light of heaven is set, and everlasting lustre
shines. Flow, Indu, flow, for Indra's sake.

8. Make me immortal in that realm where dwells the king, Vivasvān's son,
Where is that secret shrine of heaven, where are those waters young and fresh. Flow, Indu, flow for Indra's sake.
9. Make me immortal in that realm where they move even as they list,
In the third sphere of inmost heaven where lucid worlds are full of light. Flow, Indu, flow for Indra's sake.
10. Make me immortal in that realm of eager wish and strong desire,
The region of the golden Sun, where food and full delight are found. Flow, Indu, flow for Indra's sake.
11. Make me immortal in that realm where happiness and transports, where
Joys and felicities combine, and longing wishes are fulfilled. Flow, Indu, flow for Indra's sake.

Ṛig Veda IX.113.

Max Müller was of opinion that the Lithuanian god of thunder Perkunas, corresponds to the early Āryan sky god, Parjanya who is the god of cloud and rain (Ṛig Veda V.83), who rules over the world and who is the life of all that moves and rests (VII.101.6.). After the Āryan entry into India he seems to have become Indra.

Only in the last book of the Ṛig Veda abstract deities appear, such as Manyu or Ardour (Ṛig Veda X.83.4), and Śraddhā or Faith (Ṛig Veda X.151).

1. By Faith is Agni kindled, through Faith is oblation offered up.
We celebrate with praises Faith upon the height of happiness.
2. Bless thou the man who gives, O Faith ; Faith, bless the man who fain would give.
Bless thou the liberal worshippers : bless thou the word that I have said.
3. Even as the deities showed their Faith against the potent Asuras,
So make this uttered wish of mine true for the liberal worshippers.
4. Guarded by Vāyu, gods and men who sacrifice draw near to Faith.
Man winneth Faith by yearnings of the heart, and opulence by Faith.

5. Faith in the early morning, Faith at noonday will
   we invocate,
Faith at the setting of the sun. O Faith, endow
   us with belief.

Ṛig Veda X.151.

There are several goddesses in the Ṛig Veda : Uṣas, goddess of Dawn ; Sarasvatī, a river invoked as a goddess ; Vāc, goddess of speech, Araṇyānī of the forest. Most interesting is Aditi (literally, unbound or unlimited), who stands for the infinite substratum of all. In the Ṛig Veda I.89.10, she is referred to thus : " Aditi is the sky ; Aditi is the intermediate region, Aditi is father, mother and son, and all the gods and five tribes. Aditi is whatever has been born and shall be born ". She is the precursor of an all embracing and all producing Nature, of the Prakṛiti of the Sāṁkhya philosophy, of Anaximander's Infinite.

Both Greeks and Ṛig-vedic Indians were Āryans in origin. The Greeks developed clarity and a crystallized sense of form. Physical perfection, logical thought, and poetry were their keynotes. Prosperity, the free play of bodily desires, and happiness tempered by social virtues were their objectives in life. Spiritual development, mysticism, morality and asceticism played a lesser part in their lives. They were humanist and practical, not otherworldly. A sensible people. But for that very reason their civilization was the end of that particular road of human development. When aspiration and endeavour finally crystallize in physical form, the end is at hand. The form must perish when it outlasts its usefulness. The emergence of a new form and of renewed activity out of the life of the people depends upon the creative spiritual power of the people. The spirit is the fount of renewal in terms of distinction, greatness and individual expression. The vital power of the living body will only produce more bodies, to be inhabited by slave minds if the spiritual forces have ebbed away. The altar of devotion for the Greeks was the state. But patriotism is a minor creative force, if creative at all, beside aspiration to the Transcendent. So the Greek flower perished though it left the memory of a fragrance so exquisite that later civilizations in Europe knew a rare blossoming.

It was different with the Vedic people. They were not so clear cut. There was not only light but also shadow. Beautifully chiselled form had an amorphous background, and there was always a rich store of virgin material to draw upon. The unseen and the formless are the hidden, mysterious source of continuous creation and growth. With the old Indians, the peak points of their creative thought are seen in their answers to three profound questions—ultimate reality ; the phenomenal universe ; and man —in the Upanishads and in the teachings of the Buddha.

So at first, the Vedic gods are somewhat mixed, as where, instead of a single Sūrya as sun god, Indra, Agni, Savitar, are all part sharers of solar divinity. Inter-acting with Dravidian religion, many new gods and godlings crept into the Āryan fold. Whilst this showed the considerate tolerance which characterized the Āryan conquerors, it proved an intellectual burden, and set in motion the tendency towards monotheism. Each of the Vedic bards emphasized his own special deity as the supreme god. But the worship of each divinity in turn, as if it were the supreme or only one, was a logical contradiction. Such henotheism (a word coined by Max Müller) was only a dim groping towards monotheism, and the road became clearer for the later ascent from polytheistic anthropomorphism to a spiritual monotheism. Little did India dream that before she reached the full height of monotheism she was to scale the loftier summit of monism ! In addition to henotheism, the conception of Ṛta and the idealized god-conception of Varuṇa powerfully led the mind to monotheism.

It was only natural to enquire who was the true supreme Being. Since there was no single Revealer, the several inspired seers postulated different supreme Beings : Viśvakarman (Ṛig Veda X.81.82), Bṛihaspati (Ṛig Veda II.23 and 24 ; X.72), Prajāpati, lord of creatures, and Hiraṇyagarbha (Ṛig Veda X.121). But a supreme Being garbed in many names can be as unsatisfying as a plurality of gods. Questioning arose : " To which god shall we offer our oblations ? " (Ṛig Veda I.121). Doubt and scepticism appeared. Indra's very existence was challenged (Ṛig Veda X.86.1 ; VIII.89.3 ; II.12.5.) and the spirit of denial was rife. The whole host of gods might be a pure figment of imagination. Who had seen them come into being ? Who had any irrefutable firsthand evidence of their exiṣtence or power? The twilight of the gods was at hand; and when the Upanishadic thinkers arose two centuries later, the twilight turned into night, in a certain sense.

No one can question the sincerity and humility with which the Vedic seers sought the Supreme Being:

> Ṛig Veda I.164—Who hath beheld at birth the
> Primal Being? —Verse 4
> Unripe in mind, in spirit
> undiscerning, I ask — „ 5
> I ask, unknowing, those who know, the sages, as
> one all ignorant, for sake of knowledge,
> What was that One who in the Unborn's image
> hath stablished and fixed firm these worlds' six
> regions? —Verse 6.

and the answers were:

> They call him Indra, Mitra, Varuṇa, Agni, and
> he is heavenly nobly-winged Garutmān (the Sun).
> To what is one, sages give many a title: they
> call it Agni, Yama, Mātariśvan.
>
> Ṛig Veda I.164.46.

> Kindled in many a spot, still One is Agni; Sūrya
> is One though high o'er all he shineth.
> Illumining this All, still One is Ushas.
> That which is One hath into All developed.
>
> Vālakhilya Hymn X.2.

> 2. Mighty in mind and power is Viśvakarman,
> Maker, Disposer, and most lofty Presence.
> Their offerings joy in rich juice where they speak
> of One, only One, beyond the Seven Ṛishis.
> 3. Father who made us, he who, as Disposer,
> knoweth all races and all things existing,
> Even he alone, the deities' name-giver—
> him other beings seek for information.
> 5. That which is earlier than this earth and heaven,
> before the Asuras and the gods had being—
> What was the germ primeval which the waters
> received where all the gods were seen together?
> 6. The waters, they received the germ primeval
> wherein the gods were gathered all together,

It rested set upon the Unborn's navel,
that One wherein abide all things existing.
7. Ye will not find him who produced these creatures:
another thing hath arisen up among you.
Enwrapt in misty cloud, with lips that stammer,
hymn-chanters wander and are discontented.

Ṛig Veda X.82.

In all the worlds That was the best and highest
whence sprang the mighty god (Indra), of
splendid valour.

Ṛig Veda X.120.1.

1. In the beginning rose Hiraṇyagarbha,
born only lord of all created beings.
He fixed and holdeth up this earth and heaven.
What god shall we adore with our oblation?
2. Giver of vital breath, of power and vigour,
he whose commandments all the gods acknowledge!
Whose shade is death, whose lustre makes immortal.
What god shall we adore with our oblation?
3. Who by his grandeur hath become sole ruler
of all the moving world that breathes and slumbers;
He who is lord of men and lord of cattle.
What god shall we adore with our oblation?
5. By him the heavens are strong and earth is steadfast,
by him light's realm and sky vault are supported:
By him the regions in mid-air were measured.
What god shall we adore with our oblation?
8. He in his might surveyed the floods containing
productive force and generating Worship,
He is the god of gods, and none beside him.
What god shall we adore with our oblation?

Ṛig Veda X.121.

Clearly enough, the Vedic seers affirmed their conviction that the Ultimate is One, and is unknowable by man (Ṛig Veda X.82.7. above). This One is regarded as the Supreme Being, differently named by different seers though similarly conceived, and is also described as " it " (" To what is one, sages give many a title; they call it Agni, Yama, Mātariśvan") or "That" ("That which is One hath into All developed " ; and, " In all the worlds That was the best and highest whence sprang the mighty god, of splendid valour "). As Supreme Being, Viśvakarman is conceived of as Maker, Disposer, most lofty Presence and Father. Considering how frequently the love of a father for his son is mentioned in the Ṛig Veda, it is probably not illegitimate to credit the Vedic seers with the concept of the loving fatherhood as embodied in Dyaus the father of gods and men, or in Varuṇa (Ṛig Veda X.124.3 and 4) or Agni (Ṛig Veda V.4.2.). What is striking, however, is that whereas the earlier gods like Varuṇa, Indra, Agni, Bṛihaspati or Soma were all intimately bound up with Holy Law and Order, there is no mention whatever of Ṛta in connection with Hiraṇyagarbha or Viśvakarman. Moreover, while the earlier Ādityas, though invested with divine majesty, authority and sanction, were regarded and addressed as kinsmen of mortals, Hiraṇyagarbha or Viśvakarman are more aloof, unapproachable.

This is not unnatural. In seeking the Ultimate, the Vedic Ṛishis grew to a greater awareness of the Transcendent. The Supreme Being was not so near home as were the great, but familiar, Ādityas. God—very God of very God—was beyond mortal comprehension they felt. The confidence associated with youthful curiosity was giving place to the wistful uncertainty and greater humility characterizing maturer enquiry. There is even complete uncertainty, an agnostic attitude, and a feeling for suspended judgment in the famous Creation Hymn (Ṛig Veda X.129). Possibly the Vedic Ṛishis were experiencing a sense of what is beyond good and evil. If that were so, the ethical quality of Varuṇa and Agni, the righteousness of the Āditya host, so taken for granted, may well find no mention in the later god-conceptions.

Again, with the deepening feeling of the unity of the Universe, the sense of impersonality was growing. Varuṇa the Holy and Righteous, the Just but Merciful to repentant sinners, the friendly, fatherly protector and guide of mortals, omniscient and omnipresent, knowing all about a man's personal life, was a Personal God par excellence, a Personal Being in his own right, having a clear-cut, non-mystifying, direct relationship with personal beings like men and women. How safe, well ordered and crystal clear was such a universe! The other gods of the Āditya clan were like Varuṇa in their relationship to man. But intellectual curiosity undermined this solid palace of Personal Gods. Instead, the embodiment of God-like-ness was emerging. Hence Vedic religion did not produce a monotheistic concept of the type developed in later Hinduism.

Finally, a new element had entered: looking within. In Ṛig Veda X.81.4, the poet says "Ye thoughtful men inquire within your spirit" and in Ṛig Veda X.129.4. "Sages who searched with their heart's thought . . .". With deeper introspection, associated with the physical, moral and intellectual discipline which led to spiritual vision it appears as if two streams of realization were emerging: the one, personal, subjective, concerned with the problems of individual life and conduct, and developing the idea of a personal, holy, loving, just and merciful God, whom to love, worship and obey was the highest duty and deepest felicity; the other, impersonal, objective, fundamental, absolute, transcending human qualities and beyond good and evil, the Ultimate Reality, indefinable, inexpressible, unknowable by intellect, but yet the incontrovertible ground of faith through spiritual insight or through pure, mystic intuition, and to realize which meant complete liberation, the end of human development and the final fulfilment of existence. Varuṇa is the embodiment of the first; Viśvakarman and Hiraṇyagarbha partly belong to the first and partly lead to the second; and the few Creation hymns, especially Ṛig Veda X.129, approach even closer to the second. The emergence of the second stream of realization is charged with profounder intellectual and spiritual significance, and, as will be seen later, with more powerful practical consequence to man, than the first. The first, however, is the sufficient and central factor in a vital, developed religion.

Vedic religion has, then, a highly developed god concept, henotheistic in fact, monotheistic in tendency; a developed priestly ritual of worship involving sacrifices, chanted hymns, prayers and invocations, assembly or congregation, and celebration of rites; a sense of living relationship between god and man; and a code of ethics. Besides the belief in God and the worship of God, the bond between man and God and its fulfilment in ethical conduct, two other elements, the belief in immortality, and freedom, constitute the essentials of religion. To begin with, infinity or eternity is represented by Aditi, the eternal element, the celestial light which is the essence of Aditi's sons, the twelve Ādityas, the imperishable immortal gods. It was said that first Agni alone was immortal and he conferred immortality on the other gods :

> Gods through thy glory, god who art so lovely !
> granting abundant gifts gained life immortal.
> Ṛig Veda V.3.4.

> To thee, immortal ! when to life thou springest,
> all the gods sing for joy as to their infant.
> They by thy mental powers were made immortal,
> Vaiśvānara (Agni), when thou shonest from thy parents.
> Ṛig Veda VI.7.4.

Savitar and Soma are also said to confer immortality on the gods :

> For thou at first producest for the holy gods,
> the noblest of all portions, immortality :
> Thereafter, as a gift to men, O Savitar,
> thou openest existence, life succeeding life.
> Ṛig Veda IV.54.2.

> Thy drops that swim in water have exalted Indra to delight :
> The gods have drunk thee (Soma) up for immortality.
> Ṛig Veda IX.106.8.

> We have drunk Soma and become immortal ;
> we have attained the light, the gods discovered.
> Ṛig Veda VIII.48.3.

The Vedic seers thus postulated infinity or eternity, Aditi, as the unborn and undying essence. The gods obtain or are granted immortality, in the sense of a personal continuance as conscious Beings, endowed with distinctive qualities, fulfilling distinctive functions. Mortal man prays for immortality :

> " In immortality Vivasvān set us !
> Go from us Death, come to us life eternal "
> Atharva Veda XVIII.3.62.

> " Agni . . .
> Vouchsafe us length of life and give us hope of immortality."
> Atharva Veda XIX.64.4.

(See also Ṛig Veda IX.113.7–11, quoted above.)

He aspires towards a celestial paradise. The Fathers, the blessed, sainted dead, are there, enjoying fellowship with the gods and with Yama, the king of the dead, in the realms of eternal light and bliss. Heaven is the reward of merit—pious offerings and gifts ; liberal sacrificial fees ; risking life in battle ; austerity ; following Holy Law (Ṛig Veda X.154). And hell is the place of punishment for the wicked (see Ṛig Veda VII. 104.2. above).

Although there is no special mention of a ruler of hell, there is a belief in a sort of Diabolus or Evil One :

> If by some grievous sin we have provoked the
> gods, O deities, with the tongue or thoughtlessness of heart,
> That guilt, O Vasus, lay upon the Evil One,
> on him who ever leads us into deep distress.
>
> Ṛig Veda X.37.12.

There are stray lines in the Ṛig Veda which may incline some to say that the Vedic Indians believed in transmigration or reincarnation :

> May Earth restore to us our vital spirit,
> may Heaven the goddess and mid-air restore it.
> May Soma give us once again our body,
> and Pūṣan show the path of peace and comfort.
>
> Ṛig Veda X.59.7.

> Wearing a new life let him increase his
> offspring : let him rejoin a body, Jātavedas.
>
> Ṛig Veda X.16.5.

> Thereafter as a gift to men, O Savitar,
> thou openest existence, life succeeding life.
>
> Ṛig Veda IV.54.2.

If the full context of these passages is examined it is difficult to concede that they stand for a definite belief in reincarnation. It is true that from the earliest times the peoples of India believed in life-essence or soul-matter as an indestructible material substance (see Chapter I) which passed, on death, into the soil and plants, and reappeared in a human being when the mother ate the particular food into which this life-essence had entered ! It is true, also, that the phenomenon of recurrence was ever present in their minds. Dawn succeeded dawn, season followed season, and so on, apparently unto all eternity. And yet, if these passages implied a belief in reincarnation, there would doubtless have been more unequivocal statements on the belief, and, more important, some speculations about the rationale, and the purpose or value of such rebirths.

In the world-process, there is recurrence with reference to the type of event and not with reference to objects or persons participating in the event. The phenomenon is typical and recurrent: its constituent elements are new and different. The Vedic seers sang lovely lyrics about succeeding dawns. They invested dawn with a divine spirit, the Goddess Dawn. Certainly, the one Goddess Dawn drove her resplendent car with unerring precision, through an endless succession of dawns. She was, if one likes, re-incarnated in endless bodies, the real dawns. But she was merely a lovely creation of fancy, one and permanent, whereas each single dawn was a concrete and unique fact of experience, never to be reborn, but to be followed by entirely new dawns.

No, the Ṛig Veda has no unequivocal affirmation of reincarnation. What it does present is the idea of continual existence after death either with the Fathers and Gods in Heaven, or with the other folk down below—a grim prospect! The idea of unending suffering in hell did not unbalance the sturdy spirit of a people who were by no means insensitive. To aspire to immortality in sunny, joyous heaven was positive enough for their souls' needs. And they believed in another form of immortality:

> As I, remembering thee with grateful spirit,
> a mortal, call with might on thee immortal,
> Vouchsafe us high renown, O Jātavedas,
> and may I be immortal by my children.
>
> Ṛig Veda V.4.10.

Life in heaven is enjoyed by the soul clothed in a heavenly body of light, free of the imperfections of the gross body which lived on earth.

> Meet Yama, meet the Fathers, meet the merit
> of free or ordered acts, in highest heaven.
> Leave sin and evil, seek anew thy dwelling,
> and bright with glory wear another body.
>
> Ṛig Veda X.14.8.

The personality in heaven consists of " manas " the soul, " asu " the spirit (=breath, not spirit in the modern sense of the word) and the luminous, heavenly " śarīra " or body. It is welcomed, on arrival, by the Fathers and Gods. Soma is drunk and immortality attained. Family reunion with the departed, sainted parents, friends, wife and children takes place, and blessedness and perpetual felicity reign supreme (Atharva Veda VI.120.3; XII.3.17.)

Such a belief may have been one of the powerful hidden forces responsible for the vigorous survival of the Indian peoples and their way of life.

Although there are doubts expressed regarding the existence of the gods, and there are a few speculations tending to lead the mind towards the concept of an impersonal That or It as the ultimate reality, Vedic religion, in its literal aspect, is on the whole a clear-cut system with simple doctrines and well defined ritual. It is remarkable, and significant, that though the hymns were composed over a period of several centuries by seers and poets belonging to different families, perhaps widely separated from each other in habitation, there is unanimity in the descriptions of the gods and their functions. Of course, there is henotheism, which indicates the particular slant of individual Ṛishis. But there is no usurpation of function or dereliction of duty. Agni is Agni and Soma is Soma, every inch faithful, dutiful and majestic gods. The conduct of the celestial host is ethical, and the ethic laid down for man is undoubtedly high.

It is not surprising, then, that there is no dogmatic assertion of individual freedom: of the dignity, worth and rights of the individual as an individual. There seems to be no obvious struggle to win and to express the freedom of the mind and spirit of man, or of the right to make mistakes, to challenge established beliefs, to explore new avenues. There is no rebel angel, no Promethean conquest, tragedy and emancipation. The lordly Ādityas rule; the priests celebrate the holy rites; man obediently fulfils duty. All is well.

There is only one hymn (Ṛig Veda X. 100.) in which the first eleven of its twelve verses end with the refrain, " We ask for freedom and complete felicity " [Griffith translates it as " We long for the universal Aditi," (the infinite, the un-fettered)]. An examination of the context shows that the purport of the hymn is to obtain freedom from illness, loss, sin's consequence and unhappiness.

In practice, Vedic man remained dependent, therefore, upon the gods. His constant endeavour was to win their favour by prayer and sacrifice, and store up merit in heaven by the good life here.

And yet, there is an assertion of inward personal freedom, the magnitude of which is proportional to the profundity of the question asked and the daring limit to which the agnostic thinker rose. This is the famous Creation Hymn in the Ṛig Veda, X.129. Though not concerned directly with religious thought, the philosophical speculation in this hymn is of the utmost importance. It was the greatest forerunner of the monistic trend which culminated some centuries later in the Upanishads, in that greatest of all concepts, the concept of Brahman. In this hymn, the speculative search for the first origin of creation did not, however, crystallize into a concept, but remained as a question, as a tentative suggestion. The monism of the Ṛig Veda is a tendency not an accomplishment. Yet it is undoubtedly the true seed whence grew the tree and fruit of the Upanishadic concepts of Brahman and Ātman. The Nāsadīya hymn expresses what is probably the crowning glory of the Ṛig Vedic speculative thought:

1. Then was not non-existent nor existent:
 there was no realm of air, no sky beyond it.
 What covered in, and where? and what gave shelter?
 Was water there, unfathomed depth of water?

2. Death was not then, nor was there aught immortal:
 no sign was there, the day's and night's divider.
 That One Thing, breathless, breathed by its own
 nature: apart from it was nothing whatsoever.

3. Darkness there was: at first concealed in darkness
 this All was indiscriminated chaos.
 All that existed then was void and formless:
 by the great power of Warmth was born that Unit.

4. Thereafter rose Desire in the beginning,
 Desire, the primal seed and germ of Spirit.

Sages who searched with their heart's thought discovered
the existent's kinship in the non-existent.

5. Transversely was their severing line extended:
what was above it then, and what below it?
There were begetters, there were mighty forces,
free action here and energy up yonder.

6. Who verily knows and who can here declare it,
whence it was born and whence comes this
creation?
The gods are later than this world's production.

7. He, the first origin of this creation,
whether he formed it all or did not form it,
Whose eye controls this world in highest heaven,
he verily knows it, or perhaps he knows not.

This poem bears the influences of several lines of thought—naturalistic, psychological, philosophical, speculative and agnostic. The poet begins in the mood of enquiry. What is the ultimate underlying both existent and non-existent? Dyaus Pitar himself is abolished. Life, death, night, day, and hence process, action, growth and consciousness are all non-existent. Then, comes the assertion, "That One Thing, breathless, breathed by its own nature: apart from it was nothing whatsoever." Anthropomorphism and monotheism are transcended. Reality is felt objectively. The terms are "it" and "itself" for the one-ness. Even further, other than "it" there was nothing. All manifestation is but the one, the ultimate "it", undergoing continuous transformation. Since there is no other than it, then surely the manifestation of it is indeed a universe. "Breathed without breath". The poet cannot put into mere words the light that gave him vision. He could have said "It was". But he belongs to a naturalistic, vitalistic tradition, to a day which regarded all the universe as "living", with no sharp cleavage between dead matter and living creations. So he uses the term "breathed", perhaps indicating the potentiality within the ultimate for action, growth and being.

"Darkness there was". Symbolic of non-differentiation—symbolic too of matter and of un-consciousness. "All that existed then was void and formless"! Again, portraying non-differentiation, absence of organization, control or direction or of law in operation. The poet next uses naturalistic language. He draws upon his own life-experience when he says " Thereafter rose Desire in the beginning, Desire the primal seed and germ of Spirit ". And immediately afterwards he plunges into profundity when he says " Sages who searched with their heart's thought discovered the existent's kinship in the non-existent ". Herein lies a suggestion of looking inwards to find reality. Intellectual examination is an out-turned activity, touching the periphery of experience. So much escapes sense and brain, but is nevertheless there, part and parcel of active being. Searching the heart means searching the hidden depths. The later poets of the Ṛig Veda had insight and intuitive perception as proved by the poets' words: " discovered the existent's kinship in the non-existent ". For indeed the roots of the seen lie in the unseen ; knowledge slumbers in the womb of ignorance ; and the substantial emerges out of the seemingly non-substantial. This is not to deny the dictum " ex nihilo, nihil fit ", but rather to indicate the relationship between the factual and conceptual, the complex organism and its seed, between the concrete result of process and the original forces giving rise to the process.

Magnificent is the agnostic frame of mind in which the poet asks: " Who verily knows and who can here declare it whence it was born and whence comes this creation ? The gods are later than this world's production. Who knows then whence it first came into being ? " With great daring he asserts that the gods came later than the world, and so could not be makers of heaven and earth. Perhaps he wants to suggest they were born out of men's minds, that primitive animism was the parent of a more sophisticated anthropomorphism, and that even the exalted conception of Varuṇa or Viśvakarman was only a shadow of the substance of underlying reality. But the poet does not yet personally seek reality. He still looks for some other, man or god, who may know. Although he has abolished the gods de jure he has not dethroned them de facto. Although he seeks inward reality, essential truth, he is still looking outwards, himself remaining a separate entity from the all-inclusive one-ness, despite his own previous assertion: " That One

Thing, breathless, breathed by its own nature; apart from it was nothing whatsoever." The climax comes in the last verse: " He the first origin of this creation, whether he formed it all or did not form it, whose eye controls this world in highest heaven, he verily knows it, or perhaps he knows not ". " It " is replaced by " he " and the vitalist triumphs over the objective transcendentalist of the earlier verse. The question whether the ultimate is a first cause, a being, fashioning already present matter into a universe, or is the impersonal, unknowable absolute out of which emerges the universe, remains unanswered. The earlier search for the absolute ends up with the poet wondering whether even the highest seer in the highest heaven knows. And even he may not know. The greatest of the gods is fearlessly challenged! Gone is the day of blind faith, of baseless trust in the unverified or unverifiable. The individual right to question without fear or favour, is asserted. The spirit of selfless, objective search for truth is born, the new flame to light man's path on his quest, to lead him to spiritual freedom. That the path lay through his own inner being was the discovery which fell to the lot of a later generation.

Prajāpati Parameṣṭhin, poet of the Nāsadīya hymn, was an ancestor of the scientific spirit and method. To him belongs the honour of being the first liberator of the mind and spirit of man from the shackles of fear and superstitious propitiation of unknown gods, of being the first champion of free individuality. The mind and spirit of man had come of age.

* * *

Generations later, the poets of the Atharva Veda take up the theme. In a dialogue between Varuṇa and Atharvan, the primeval priest after whom the Atharva Veda is named,

Atharvan says:

O self-dependent Varuṇa, wise director,
thou knowest verily all generations.
What is, unerring one! beyond this region?
What more remote than that which is most distant?

Atharva Veda V.11.5.

Varuṇa answers:

> One thing there is beyond this air, and something
> beyond that one, most hard to reach, remotest.
> I Varuṇa, who know, to thee declare it.

But Atharvan does not proceed to reveal the secret, except that further on, in verse 10, he says: "One origin, Varuṇa! one bond unites us: I know the nature of that common kinship." This may be a hint that the ultimate origin, IT, is un-knowable and indescribable. Yet IT is the ground of the indissoluble link of the kinship between man and god. And so, only the nature of that kinship can be known.

The first hymn of Book II of the Atharva Veda begins thus:

> 1. Vena (the rising sun) beholds that Highest (the
> Supreme First Cause) which lies hidden, wherein
> this All resumes one form and fashion.
> Thence Pṛiśni (the creative power of Nature)
> milked all life that had existence; the hosts
> that know the light with songs extolled her.
>
> 2. Knowing Eternity, may the Gandharva (Vena, or,
> according to Weber, the sage) declare to us
> that highest secret station.

In the second hymn of Book X, the poet asks many questions about Purusha or Primeval Man: Who made his heels, ankles, feet, legs, hips, thighs, stomach, breast, arms, head—in short every part of his body—and how? Who gave him form, shape, motion, consciousness? How is he made up of the pleasant and unpleasant, want, evil, suffering, success, opulence, prosperity, truth and falsehood, death and immortality?

Further, by whom was this earth disposed and heaven placed above, the expanse of air lifted on high and stretched across?

The answer is Purusha himself identified with Brahman the phenomenal Creator. Man's body is called Brahman's castle, or "fort girt about with immortality" (Verse 29). And a little further on:

> 32. Men deep in lore of Brahman know that Animated
> Being which
> Dwells in the golden treasure-chest that hath
> three spokes and three supports.

33. Brahman hath passed within the fort, the golden castle ne'er subdued.
Bright with excessive brilliancy, composed with glory round about.

The eighth hymn of Book XI is concerned with the origin of the gods and of man. Questions are asked: who brought together hair, sinews, bones, marrow, flesh and joints? The answer is such and such a god or gods, who thereafter entered man. Who constructed head, hands, face, tongue, neck and intercostal parts? Another god, who thereafter entered man. And so the hymn goes on, and at verse 18 says:

"Gods made the mortal their abode and entered and possessed the man."

Then sleep, sloth, sin, baldness, old age, prosperity, hunger, knowledge, ignorance, in short everything constituting man's body, life and character entered into the body. Again from verse 29:

". . . then the Gods entered into man."

30. All Waters, all the Deities, Virāj with Brahmā at her side:
Brahmā into the body passed: Prajāpati is Lord thereof.

31. The Sun and Wind formed separate, the eye and the vital breath of man.
His other person have the Gods bestowed on Agni as a gift.

32. Therefore whoever knoweth man regardeth him as Brahman's self.
For all the deities abide in him as cattle in their pen.

Beyond question, there is psychological insight into the nature of man shown here, and a mystical conviction of the oneness of all existence, man and God being included in one whole reality. What is so significant is that the mind of man arrives finally at the sense of the unity of the universe, whatever be its approach—religion, philosophy, mysticism, science, art, mythology, psychology—to truth. Whether the approach is sound or partly sound, verifiable or partly verifiable, whether it is made to-day or was made yesterday, last year, or in the pre-christian millennium, no difference is made to the result—the ultimate fact, the end of revelation, the fruit of all vision, is the One Reality, myriad though its manifestations be.

Unlike Parameṣṭhin, the seer of Ṛig Veda X.129, the poets of the Atharva Veda commit themselves to a positive answer. Brahmā is the Supreme Being.

> 1. Worship to loftiest Brahmā, Lord of what hath been
>   and what shall be,
> To him who rules the universe, and heavenly light
>   is all his own—
>
> Atharva Veda X.8.

In the last two verses of the same hymn, the poet indicates who are the seers who can know these things :

> 43. Men versed in sacred knowledge know that living
>   Being that abides
> In the nine-petalled Lotus flower (the body),
>   enclosed with triple bands and bonds.
> 44. Desireless, firm and immortal, self-existent,
>   contented with the essence, lacking nothing,
> Free from the fear of Death is he who knoweth
>   that Soul courageous, youthful, undecaying.

Skambha, the embodiment of the Divine Power, and considered as the Pillar or Support of all existence, is celebrated in Atharva Veda X.7 :

> 12. Who out of many, tell me, is that Skambha
> On whom as their foundation earth and firmament
>   and sky are set ;
> In whom as their appointed place rest Fire and
>   Moon and Sun and Wind ?
> 15. Who out of many, tell me, is that Skambha
> Who comprehendeth, for mankind, both
>   immortality and death,
> He who containeth for mankind the gathered
>   waters as his veins ?
> 17. They who in Purusha understand Brahman know
>   Him who is Supreme.

He who knows Him who is Supreme, and he who
knows the Lord of Life,
These know the loftiest Power Divine, and
thence know Skambha thoroughly.

Here it is declared that man can know the Supreme, a view different from that expressed in the Ṛig Veda. Both views are reconciled, later, by the Upanishadic thinkers. It is significant that the adage " Man, know thyself " finds expression in the Atharva Veda, for, as declared in XI.8.32, he who knows man knows Brahman.

Hymns like the above are very few in the Atharva Veda. Some of the mystical hymns are beyond comprehension at times. The fault may be laid at the door of their composers ; or, more likely, the key to their interpretation has not yet been found. The ancients were prone to convey their wisdom in symbolical and poetical rather than explicit and scientific language.

But, having paid due homage to the profounder elements of this fourth Veda, the fact remains that the main bulk of its hymns are prayers and benedictions, charms and imprecations. There are prayers for pardon, protection, prosperity, peace, health, and for all the desirable ends and objects mortal man longs to enjoy. There are benedictions on a newly elected king, a new-born child, a sick man, a warrior, a bridegroom. There are charms for winning love, overcoming enemies, against evil dreams, fiends and goblins, to reconcile estranged friends, cure various diseases, ensure conception, banish jealousy, to strengthen hair and promote its growth (see Atharva Veda VI.21.) and a host of other things. Conceivably, the suggestive power of those charms was not much less efficacious than modern advertisements, and the use, of pills and powders which are guaranteed panaceas ! And of course there are various imprecations and incantations against rivals and enemies. There are also hymns on the consecration of a newly built house, on the glorification of the hospitable reception of guests, and of Kāma, god of Desire or Love. Tedious, absurd, even offensive to good taste as some of the hymns are, they nevertheless give a remarkable, almost vivid picture of Āryan life of that period. Two short hymns of the more acceptable type may be quoted here. First a charm to be pronounced by a bride and bridegroom:

> Sweet are the glances of our eyes, our faces are
>   as smooth as balm.
> Within thy bosom harbour me; one spirit dwell
>   in both of us!
>
> Atharva Veda VII.36.

And next, a nuptial charm spoken by the bride:

> With this my robe, inherited from Manu, I
>   envelop thee.
> So that thou mayest be all mine own and give
>   no thought to other dames.
>
> Atharva Veda VII.37.

Charming!

There are two other hymns in the Atharva Veda which are of interest. One is a prayer for wisdom:

> 1. Intelligence, come first to us with store of
>   horses and of kine!
>   Thou with the rays of Sūrya art our worshipful
>   and holy one.
> 2. The first, devout intelligence, lauded by sages,
>   sped by prayer
>   Trusted by Brahmacārīs, for the favour of the
>   Gods I call.
> 3. That excellent Intelligence which Ṛibhus know,
>   and Asuras,
>   Intelligence which sages know, we cause to
>   enter into me.
> 4. Do thou, O Agni, make me wise this day with
>   that Intelligence
>   Which the creative Ṛishis, which the men
>   endowed with wisdom knew.
> 5. Intelligence at eve, at morn, Intelligence at
>   noon of day,
>   With the Sun's beams, and by our speech we
>   plant in us Intelligence.
>
> Atharva Veda VI.108.

The other is of special interest as it contains one of the earliest statements of the great teaching "Love one another":

1. Freedom from hate I bring to you, concord and
   unanimity.
   Love one another as the cow loveth the calf
   that she hath borne.
2. One-minded with his mother let the son
   be loyal to the sire.
   Let the wife, calm and gentle, speak
   words sweet as honey to her lord.
3. No brother hate his brother, no sister
   to sister, be unkind.
   Unanimous, with one intent, speak ye
   your speech in friendliness.
4. That spell through which Gods sever not,
   nor ever bear each other hate,
   That spell we lay upon our home, a bond
   of union for the men.
5. Intelligent, submissive, rest united, friendly
   and kind, bearing the yoke together.
   Come, speaking sweetly each one to the other. I
   make you one-intentioned and one-minded.
6. Let what you drink, your share of food be common :
   together, with one common bond I bind you.
   Serve Agni, gathered round him like the spokes
   about the chariot nave.
7. With binding charm I make you all united, obeying
   one sole leader and one-minded.
   Even as the Gods who watch and guard the Amṛit,
   at morn and eve may ye be kindly-hearted.

Atharva Veda III.30.

* * *

In Vedic religion, the daily sacrifices were performed with meticulous precision, no ritualistic detail, however minute, being neglected. If it were neglected, or if the slightest error in procedure were made, the whole effect of the sacrifice was supposed to be lost. The sacrificial offerings were made not so much as an expression of devotion to the gods as a magical technique to produce certain desired results: and unhappily, these desired results betrayed a worldliness that needed more than imagination to be characterized as religious. The sacrifice, regarded as man's prime duty, was called kriyā (action) or karma; and the belief was held that it was an unalterable law that this karma, or mystical sacrifice, must inevitably give rise to effects. Here lies the germ of the doctrine of Karma which plays so prominent a part in Indian religious thought.

It fell to the lot of the Brāhmaṇas, the prose treatises which exhaustively describe the ceremonies and explain the significance of the rituals, to develop the idea of Karma in association with the introduction of the theory of transmigration, and to make significant the concept of Brahman as the supreme principle.

The most important Brāhmaṇas are the Aitareya and the Śatapatha. The latter taught that the consequence of the incorrect performance of rites was to be reborn and again suffer death. It taught (I.9.3.) that the dead pass between two fires which let the good man go by safely but burn the evil-doer; that everyone is weighed in the balance, born again after death, and receives reward and punishment according to past good works and misdeeds. In the early period, misdeeds or good works meant little else, if anything at all, than the neglect or wrong performance, or correct performance, of the rites. Centuries later, this limited idea of karma developed into the moral concept that good or evil conduct produced a better or worse character and opportunities.

The Buddha specifically defined karma as the law of moral causation, a part, only, of his all-inclusive law of action and consequence in all spheres, namely the law of Causality.

The emergence of the idea of rebirth was inevitable. The Ṛig-vedic immortal happiness in heaven or horror in hell was unendurable. Both justice and commonsense were flouted here, to say nothing of the mockery made of mercy and loving-kindness. How could mortal man capable of finite acts merit an immortal condition of infinite consequence? So the idea of rebirth emerged. Life after life, consequences of the past were worked out, faculties developed, greater and greater good was achieved till ultimate liberation reunited the soul with Brahman. Such was the doctrine after it was fully developed, affording hope, encouragement, opportunity and satisfaction for man, and upholding righteousness, justice, omniscience and mercy in God.

Associated with this was the doctrine that the purpose of man's existence was ultimate union with the source of his being,[1] and man's concrete objective, therefore, was so to live that he escaped from the round of births and deaths. The Brāhmaṇas contained all the seeds from which these doctrines of karma and transmigration developed.

Now the Śatapatha Brāhmaṇa says:

" Verily, in the beginning this universe was Brahman."
—(*Sacred Books of the East*, Vol. 44, pp. 27, 28).

This is practically the earliest introduction of the impersonal, objective concept of an IT as the origin of the universe. Brahman creates Agni, Vāyu and Sūrya, and makes them lords of earth, air and sky, and Itself goes beyond. Then Brahman returns again by means of Name and Form, and as far as Name and Form extend, so far does the universe extend. Again, Brahman, as the ultimate thing in the universe is identified with Prajāpati, Prāṇa (Vitality or Vital Breath) and Purusha (*Sacred Books of the East*, Vol. 43, pp. 59, 60, 400 ; and Vol. 44, p. 409), and is also described as self-born.

In the sphere of ethics, the conception of man's duties first arises in the Brāhmaṇas. The five-fold system of duty consists of duties to (1) the gods (2) the seers (3) the departed shades (4) men, and (5) the lower creation. Austerity, truthfulness, praise and good works, and the sacrifice of all things as essential for spiritual freedom, are all upheld. Adultery is condemned, whilst confession of sin is encouraged. Despite the emphasis on formal ceremonial worship, there was a strong religious urge also, together with an ethic set out in greater detail than in the Ṛig Veda. The caste system, and the idea of the four stages in man's life, the Āśrama Dharma, consisting of the stages of the student, the householder, the hermit with a fixed forest abode, and the wandering mendicant with not even a home for himself, crystallized in the Brāhmaṇa period. Brāhmaṇism established itself firmly as the religion of the people from this period.

But simultaneously there was an influence which kept alive

[1] Forth from the sea the sleepless waters flow . . . their goal the sea.
Ṛig Veda. VII.49.1. Coomaraswamy's translation)

philosophical search, and which continuously fed religion itself with new life. This was the work of the forest hermits. The ritualistic life was left behind by these advanced and mature men who spent the evening of their lives in meditation, who lived austerely, and who devoted all their energy to the search for Truth. They conveyed the fruits of their labours to a select group of students who were accepted after they had proved their worthiness to receive the sacred instruction. Theirs was a protestant activity as a reaction against orthodox ritualism. Their wisdom, embodied in the Āraṇyakas, was the parent of that finest flower of ancient Hindu wisdom, the Upanishads.

THE UPANISHADS

" Behold the Universe in the glory of
  God : and all that lives and moves
  on earth.
Leaving the transient, find joy in
  the Eternal : set not your heart on
  another's possession."

" The face of truth remains hidden
  behind a circle of gold.
Unveil it, O god of light, that I
  who love the true may see ! "

Īśā Upanishad, Verses 1 and 15,
translated by J. Mascaró.

" From the Unreal lead me to the Real,
From Darkness lead me to Light,
From Death lead me to Immortality."

Bṛihadāraṇyaka Upanishad, I.3.28.

Chapter III

THE UPANISHADS

Aśvapati Kaikeya declared :
In my kingdom there is no thief,
No churl, no drunkard,
None who neglects the sacrifice
or the sacred lore,
No adulterer or courtesan.

Chāndogya Upanishad V.11.5.
(Deussen's translation).

THAT WAS probably a reasonably just statement of fact. And in the eighth century before Christ it is likely that there were other states, like Aśvapati's, of which a similar account could have been given, without straining credulity too far. The pre-Buddhistic Āryan kingdoms, republics and chieftaincies enjoyed a measure of political stability and economic prosperity, with attendant cultural and moral advances. Although the goodness of the people of a whole state may have derived from fear of punishment, secular and spiritual, yet good the people were. It must also be remembered, that since the Āryans looked down upon the conquered Dasyus, as the Ṛig Veda proves, an Āryan ruler may have kept only the Āryan population in mind when talking of his people's goodness, the conquered being left out of consideration.

It is refreshing, however, to be assured that at least some kings like Aśvapati, Janaka, Ajātaśatru and Pravāhaṇa Jaibali were not merely interested but proficient in sacred knowledge ; so much so that at times the usual convention was reversed and these royal kshatriyas imparted the supreme wisdom to brāhman pupils. Philosopher kings they were, anticipating that lone star, Aśoka Maurya, emperor of a sub-continent in the third century before Christ, to whom history accords the honour of being a true and great philosopher king. If the phenomenon of the philosopher king was not unknown in India, then the conditions producing such kings could not have been altogether missing.

In those kingdoms which were stable, strong and prosperous, orthodox religion flourished. Carpenters, tailors, farmers, goldsmiths, potters, weavers, toymakers, business men, doctors, soldiers and officials all said their prayers after their ablutions, paid the priests as lavishly as possible for all ceremonies connected with birth, death, marriage, and a host of other events, and dutifully performed the piety expected of the Brāhmaṇical faith, such as sacrifices to the departed fathers and the gods, and almsgiving. Their faith was unquestioning, their relationship with their gods was whole and bright.

Not so everywhere. A divine discontent drove others—intellectuals, devotees, seekers of the Ultimate Truth. These were not only members of the priestly caste. They were also warriors and administrators (the kshatriyas), great householders (a caste still lower), like the five gentlemen who sat at the feet of good king Aśvapati, and whose names are immortalized in the Chāndogya Upanishad (V.ii.i. et seq.); they were even Śūdras like Raikva and illegitimates born of servant girls like Satyakāma Jābāla. In Aśvapati's pleasant land there must doubtless have been opportunity for a liberal education. Perhaps the five householders sought the wisdom of the Eternal because of a natural inner urge and a cultural upbringing, or perhaps the sorrows of life, such as the denial of success in business, or being ill-mated, drove them to seek sanctuary in God. But apart from those whose efforts were inclined towards spiritual realization by pleasant or unpleasant external stimuli, there was a not inconsiderable and not inconsequential group, the sages, poet-seers, and forest-dwelling hermits who, impelled by inner necessity and inherited traditions, and who, fitted by nature and training, sought, found and expounded the Truth as they saw it.

Their exposition is not philosophy or religion by any conventional or modern standards, nor a presentation of truth as expected by a mind trained in logical processes of thought or in scientific method, but a string of statements, at times with no seeming relationship one to another, at times apparently meaningless, at times contradicting other statements. And yet, who, expounding the Absolute, can stand much higher than Yājñavalkya? Who can transcend Uddālaka Āruṇi's "That art thou" as the final answer to the question "what is man?"?

Nārada said, "Teach me, sir!" and his chosen master Sanatkumāra said, "Tell me first what you know". Came the answer: "The four Vedas, Legend and Ancient Lore, Grammar, Propitiation of the Manes, Mathematics, Augury, Chronology, Logic, Polity, the Science of the Gods, the Science of Sacred Knowlege, Demonology, the Science of Rulership, Astrology, The Science of Snake-charming, and the Fine Arts." A learned man.

But Sanatkumāra tells him, "All that is mere Name"! (Chāndogya VII.1.1–3).

The Taittirīya Upanishad says (I.11.) that, having taught the Veda, a teacher further instructs the pupil to be truthful, virtuous and studious; not to neglect welfare and prosperity, nor fail to beget children; not to neglect duties to the gods and fathers; to regard mother, father, teacher and guest as god; to revere and perform good deeds, and to respect and serve superiors; to give with faith, generosity, modesty, fear and sympathy; and when in doubt oneself, to behave as one's superiors behave.

The seekers of Truth, therefore, were not unqualified men. The discipline and training available in their age was theirs. Their facts were not exactly the facts of modern science. But they had trained minds and disciplined characters.

The authority of the Philosophy of the Upanishads rests on such characters. How profound their influence was, is well attested by the fact that the fundamental ideas of the Upanishads are the fundamentals of Indian Religion and Philosophy up to modern times. And since the days of du Perron, Schopenhauer, Schlegel, Max Müller, Deussen and others, the brilliance of that spiritual flame has inspired many minds in the modern world, and brought them enlightenment and peace.

Picture the Upanishads coming into being. Man's thirst for

the answers to the Great Questions can never be wholly slaked. The findings of the forest hermits came to the ears of kings and commoners who also had pondered deeply. Free disputation was a birthright of India's thinkers. The professional sage or priest had no monopoly of genius. So king and commoner partook of the intellectual feasts which were a feature of old India. Nor were women debarred. Indeed, Gārgī drew upon her head a solemn rebuke from Yājñavalkya for asking the unanswerable question[1]—a distinction which no male questioner achieved! Maybe after dinner, at sacrifices, in the cool of the evening and through the infinite calm of glittering nights—India's starry nights!—perhaps under the shadow of the mighty Himālayas or perhaps surrounded by the indescribable beauty of snow-clad giants towering up to heaven, dramatically splendid by sunset and twilight, or glimmering under a bright moon—such was the setting in which sage and citizen, priest and pupil held discourse, with courtesy, with occasional wit, and always with deep earnestness. Sitting at the feet of the master, these pilgrims of the Great Quest drank in the secret wisdom, withheld from those who had not proved their worthiness to receive it. The teachings were committed to memory and handed down. They are embodied in condensed form, somewhat like notes of the important points in lectures, in the existing Upanishads. Had they been recorded in full, the texts would have been far bulkier.

Out of over a hundred existing Upanishads some fourteen are regarded as the principal ones. The oldest, in archaic prose, are the Bṛihad-Āraṇyaka, the Chāndogya, the Taittirīya, the Aitareya, the Kaushītaki and the Kena. The last named is on the border line of the transition to the later metrical Upanishads, the Kaṭha, the Īśā, the Śvetāśvatara, the Muṇḍaka, and the Mahānārāyaṇa. Later still are the Praśna, the Maitrāyaṇīya, and the Māṇḍūkya, in the complex, involved, repetitive style of later Sanskrit prose.

Of the minor Upanishads, some develop older themes; others, in verse, deal with Yoga; others, mostly in prose, with a few

[1] Bṛih. III.6. But see Subāla Up., Khaṇḍa X, where this very question does receive an answer.

inserted verses, are concerned with the Saṁnyāsa. Another group exalts Śiva, and another Viṣṇu. All these set down detailed instructions and dogmatic teachings.

Repeatedly given is an injunction against imparting[1] "the Brahman-wisdom to one not tranquil, Nor again to one who is not a son or a pupil" (Śvet. VI.22 ; Maitri, VI.29 ; Bṛih. VI. 3.12.). The Muktikopanishad says : "Never shall the Upanishads be imparted to an atheist, an ungrateful person, one intent on vicious actions, one having no devotion to Me, or one who loses his way in the cave of books." This wisdom, it adds, may be imparted "only after a thorough examination, to a disciple serving his Guru (teacher), to a well-disposed son, or to one devoted to Me, following good observances, belonging to a good family, and being of good intelligence," a view endorsed in most of the Upanishads.

The letter of the Upanishads is a statement of the findings of saint-seers. In the principal Upanishads much is asserted of the end of the quest. But there is no description, succinct or detailed, of the road, apart from a floodlighting of important landmarks, as in the Bṛihad-Āraṇyaka :

> When are liberated all the desires that lodge in one's heart,
> Therein a mortal becomes immortal !
> Therein he reaches Brahman !
>
> IV.4.7.

The Upanishads consist of emotive statements, the expressions of intuitive insights, and of inspiring, personal realizations. The principal Upanishads are not charted seas. Rather, they are the footprints in snow, mysterious, indelible, of those who scaled the spiritual Everest.

The tendency to seek the Truth by looking within had already begun with the late poems of the Ṛig Veda. The unity underlying all things was sensed, and it was declared that the Ultimate Power was One Thing. Later on, in the Atharva Veda, Brahman was called the Lord Supreme, the Real Power, and was reverenced and invoked as such in several hymns. The essential unity of God and man was acknowledged :

[1] Cf. Matthew, VII.6.

> Therefore whoever knoweth man regardeth him as
> Brahman's self.
> For all the deities abide in him as cattle in
> their pen.
>
> Atharva Veda, XI.8.32

But the Supreme was also other than, and over and above man, transcending everything. Brahman, this Lord Supreme, this Real Power, this Ultimate Reality, became the topic of absorbing interest to the Upanishadic sages.

What is Ultimate Reality? What is man and what is his relationship with Ultimate Reality? These questions are the central theme of the Upanishads.

The Bṛihad-Āraṇyaka says:

> In the beginning this world was Soul (Ātman) alone in the form of a Person. Looking around he saw nothing else than himself. He said first "I am". Thence arose the name "I".
>
> I.4.1.
>
> He knew: "I, indeed, am this creation, for I emitted it all from myself." Thence arose creation.
>
> I.4.5.
>
> Verily . . . the world . . . became differentiated just by name and form . . . He entered in here even to the fingernail-tips, as a razor would be hidden in a razor case . . . Him they see not, for (as seen) He is incomplete with one or other of these. One should worship with the thought that He is just one's self (Ātman), for therein all these become one. That same thing, namely, this Self, is the trace of this All, for by it one knows this all.
>
> I.4.7.
>
> Verily, in the beginning this world was Brahman. It knew only itself "I am Brahman!" Therefore it became the All. Whoever of the gods became awakened to this, he indeed became it; likewise in the case of seers, likewise in the case of men. Seeing this, indeed, the seer Vāmadeva began:
> I was Manu and the Sun:[1]
>
> This is so now also. Whoever thus knows "I am Brahman" becomes this All; even the gods have not power to prevent his becoming thus, for he becomes their self.

[1] Ṛig Veda IV.26.1.

> So whoever worships another divinity (than his Self), thinking " He is one and I another " he knows not.
>
> I.4.10.
>
> In the beginning this world was just the Self (Ātman), one only.
>
> I.4.17.

Other passages correlate the cosmic and personal :

> This earth is honey for all creatures, and all creatures are honey for this earth. This shining immortal Person who is in this earth, and, with reference to oneself, this shining immortal Person who is in the body—he, indeed, is just this Soul (Ātman) this Immortal, this Brahman, this All.
>
> II.5.

Here earth is the cosmic, correlated with the body, the personal. In the same strain, the waters and semen, fire and speech, wind and breath, sun and eye, . . . , Law and virtuousness, Truth and truthfulness, mankind and a man, the Soul (World) and the Soul (Individual) are all correlated. Then follows :

> Verily, this Soul is the overlord of all things, the king of all things. As all the spokes are held together in the hub and felly of a wheel, just so is this Soul all things, all gods, all worlds, all breathing things, all these selves held together.
>
> II.5.15.
>
> This Brahman is without an earlier and without a later, without an inside and without an outside. This Soul (Ātman) is Brahman the All-perceiving—Such is the Instruction.
>
> II.5.19.

The world-ground, realized subjectively, is termed Ātman, or Self ; designated objectively, Brahman or IT.

The unity which is Brahman is known through the conviction of one's own unitary self which is Ātman. Now the relatedness of the elements composing a person is not a merely mechanical joining. The unity of the person is due to Ātman, the all-creative " I ", without which that integrated whole called a person could not come into being, and would not be here. Ātman becomes the whole person, and is the whole person. And also, Ātman becomes the world of all created things.

As primordial Universal Person, Ātman, looking around and

seeing nothing apart from himself, says "I am".[1] Divinely self-asserted is Ātman the Self-existent. As that which becomes all men and all things, Ātman is also Ultimate Essence and Ultimate Substance, unitarily realized in self-existence.

Brahman, too, becomes "this All"—gods, men, dharma, speech, mind, breath, the worlds, the Vedas, space, light, in short, everything. Brahman, too, is the essence and origin of the universe which man observes and regards as a cosmos, and also of man. Whosoever knows "I am Brahman" knows truly, for he realizes his one-ness with this-All.

Brahman is supra-personal and also impersonal. For the Upanishadic sages, Brahman is Ultimate Reality not devoid of consciousness, and is in fact regarded as absolute consciousness —but "consciousness" meaning an infinitely and inconceivably other than consciousness in the human sense, the latter having a definite link, nevertheless, with the former. Thus Brahman, the become-this-All which is different from human personality, is impersonal; as including and simultaneously being immeasurably over and above human personality, Brahman is supra-personal.

Although the ancients distinguished the animate from the inanimate, they tended to apprehend the entire universe as a living whole. And so, Brahman too is presented, like Ātman, as the Universal Person, and is also called self-existent[2] (Svayambhū).

The macrocosm is infinite, and so is the microcosm. Seeking the Infinite macrocosmically, led to Brahman; microcosmically, revealed Ātman. The macrocosm and microcosm observed by man is the empirical real. Contained within the Infinite—lying between the extremes, so to say, of the dually conceived Infinite, the point and the boundless sphere—is the Medium, the empirical real, the observable Manifest. The Infinite is Brahman; contained within It is the Manifest, this-All. But Brahman

[1] Cf. Exodus, III. 13 & 14:—And Moses said unto God, Behold, when I come unto the children of Israel, and shall say unto them, The God of your fathers hath sent me unto you, and they shall say to me, What is his name? what shall I say unto them?
And God said unto Moses, I AM THAT I AM: and he said, Thus shalt thou say unto the children of Israel, I AM hath sent me unto you.

[2] Bṛihad-Āraṇyaka, II.6.3, IV.6.3 & VI.5.4; Kaṭha, IV.1; Īśā, 8.

becomes this-All, becomes the manifested universe, and still remains Itself.[1] The becoming has no earlier or later (Bṛih. II.5.19); it is not temporal but is of eternity; it is the Eternal Event or the Active Eternal.[2] Brahman's self-realization of Its own Svabhāva (Self-being) through Nature as Universal Process, is revealed *to man* as Ātman, the all-creative, all-becoming, all-powerful, all-present, all-knowing "I-agent".[3]

In the Bṛihadāraṇyaka Upanishad, the main elements of this-All are correlated to the elements composing man, and in the most unequivocal terms the identity of Brahman and Ātman is then categorically asserted: "He is indeed just this Ātman, this Immortal, this Brahman, this All", and again: "This Ātman is Brahman the all-perceiving".

This identity of Brahman and Ātman, the fundamental teaching of the Upanishads, is the supreme realization of the ancient saint-seers, a realization whose creative impulse has vitalised over twenty-five centuries of Indian thought.

Brahman became this-All. But in which sense is Brahman the eternal, also this-All the transient universe? How is Ātman the immortal, also empirical man the mortal? The objective universe though transient, and empirical man though mortal, are real enough in everyday experience. What theory of creation could be propounded which would concede the reality of the universe and also reconcile it with that supreme concept of the sole reality of Brahman or Ātman?

The Taittirīya Upanishad says:

> From this Ātman, verily, ākāśa arose; from ākāśa, vāyu (wind); from wind, fire; from fire, water; from water, the earth; from the earth, herbs; from herbs, food; from food, semen; from semen, the person.
>
> II.1.

> He desired: "Would that I were many! Let me procreate myself!" He performed austerity. Having performed

[1] The yon is fulness; fulness, this.
From fulness, fulness doth proceed.
Withdrawing fulness's fulness off,
E'en fulness then itself remains. —Bṛih. V.1.

[2] Cf. "As it was in the beginning is now and ever shall be, world without end."

[3] See also Tejobindu-Upanishad.

austerity he created this whole world, whatever there is here. Having created it, into it, indeed, he entered.

II.6.

II.1 states that the elements of the universe, herbs, food, semen, and men successively emerged out of Ātman; and II.6 states that Ātman having created the universe entered it. The Aitareya Upanishad (I.3.12) says: "So, cleaving asunder this very hair-part (i.e. the crown of the head) by that door (the sagittal suture) he entered."

The Bṛihad-Āraṇyaka Upanishad says:

Citadels with two feet he did make.
Citadels with four feet he did make.
Into the citadels he, having become a bird—
Into the citadels the Person entered.

II.5.18.

Hence, Brahman having created the universe and all therein, enters it and all therein, as soul.

Once reality was conceded to the empirical universe, what sort of reality was to be ascribed to Brahman? The answer was that Brahman was to be regarded as "The Real of the real", as in Bṛihad-Āraṇyaka, II.1.20 and II.3.6, and in Maitri VI.32.

Now one day King Janaka of Videha, an ancient kingdom apparently bounded by the Gandak on the west, the Ganges on the south, the Kosi on the east, and the southern Nepalese border on the north, instituted a great sacrifice. Brāhmans from the Kurupañcālas, powerful neighbours, were there, and many presents were distributed. Curious to discover who was the most learned brāhman, Janaka had a thousand cows enclosed, ten 'pādas' of gold being bound to the horns of each, and said, "Venerable brāhmans, let the best among you drive away those cows." All the brāhmans were diffident, except Yājñavalkya, who, rising to the occasion, said to his pupil: "Sāmaśravas, my dear, drive them away". Frowns spread over the brāhman faces. One by one they stepped forth and asked questions. Yājñavalkya answered each in turn. One by one they held their peace. When Uddālaka Āruṇi stepped forth he first related this tale: he, (Uddālaka Āruṇi) and others were once guests of Patañcala Kāpya, studying the sacrifice. Kāpya's wife was possessed by a gandharva (one of the higher spirits) who declared his name was Kabandha Ātharvaṇa, and asked Kāpya and his fellow students: " Do you know that thread by which this world and the other world and all things are tied together? Do you know that Inner Controller who from within controls this world and the other world and all things? " On being answered in the negative, Kabandha went on to say: " He who knows that thread and the so-called Inner Controller knows Brahman, he knows the worlds, the gods, the Vedas and created things, he knows the Soul, he knows everything." Kabandha then revealed the Truth to Kāpya and his fellow students.

So Uddālaka said to Yājñavalkya:

> " Thus the spirit explained it. And I know it.
> If you, O Yājñavalkya, drive away the Brahma-cows
> without knowing that thread and the Inner Controller,
> your head will fall off."
>
> " Verily I know that thread and the Inner Controller ".
>
> " Anyone might say ' I know, I know '. Do you tell what you know ".
>
> " Vāyu,[1] verily, is that thread. By Vāyu, verily as by a thread, this world and the other world and all things are tied together . . ."
>
> " Quite so, O Yājñavalkya. Declare the Inner Controller."
>
> " He who, dwelling in the earth, yet is other than the earth, whom the earth does not know, whose body the earth is, who controls the earth from within—He is your soul, the Inner Controller, the Immortal."

Yājñavalkya repeats the above sentence again and again, earth being substituted successively by the waters, fire, the atmosphere, wind, sky, sun, the quarters of heaven, the moon and stars, ākāśa, darkness, and light (III.7.1–14); and then adds:

[1] Vāyu, the god of wind, represents the vital breath of the Universal Being. Vāyu is best understood as an energizing principle which keeps going the universal process, which was felt by the ancients to be organic, living, not mechanical. The word wind inadequately represents Vāyu.

" Thus far with reference to the divinities,
Now with reference to material existence—

" He who, dwelling in all things, yet is other than all things etc.—He is your Soul, the Inner Controller, Immortal.

" Thus far with reference to material existence.
Now with reference to the self—

" He who, dwelling in breath, yet is other than breath, etc.—He is your Soul, the Inner Controller, Immortal."

The sentence is then repeated, breath being substituted successively, by speech, eye, ear, mind, skin, understanding, and semen. Yājñavalkya completes his exposition thus:

> " He is the unseen Seer, the unheard Hearer, the unthought Thinker, the un-understood Understander. Other than He there is no seer. Other than He there is no hearer. Other than He there is no thinker. Other than He there is no understander He is your Soul, the Inner Controller, Immortal."
>
> III.7.15-23

Thereupon Uddālaka Āruṇi held his peace. Into his place stepped Gārgī Vācaknavī, perhaps the greatest of the " Doctors of Philosophy " amongst the women of that age, and flung her challenge (III.8.)

1. " Venerable brāhmans, lo, I will ask him two questions. If he will answer me these, not one of you will surpass him in discussions about Brahman ".
" Ask, Gārgī " said the brāhmans.
2. " As a noble youth of the Kāśīs or of the Videhas might rise up against you, having strung his unstrung bow and taken two foe-piercing arrows in his hand, even so, O Yājñavalkya, have I risen against you with two questions. Answer me these ".
" Ask, Gārgī " said Yājñavalkya.
3. " That, O Yājñavalkya, which is above the sky, that which is beneath the earth, that which is between these two, sky and earth, that which people call the past and the present and the future—across what is that woven, warp and woof ? "
4. " Across ākāśa,[1] O Gārgī."

See Page 100

5. " Adoration to you, Yājñavalkya, in that you have solved this question for me . . . .

7. " Across what then, pray is ākāśa woven, warp and woof ? "

And Yājñavalkya answers :

8. " That, O Gārgī, brāhmans call The Imperishable. It is not coarse, not fine, not short, not long, not glowing, not adhesive, without shadow and without darkness, without air and without space, without stickiness, intangible, odourless, tasteless, without eye, without ear, without voice, without wind, without energy, without breath, without mouth, without personal or family name, unaging, undying, without fear, immortal, stainless, not uncovered, not covered, without measure, without inside, without outside.

It consumes nothing soever.
No one soever consumes it.

9. Verily, O Gārgī, at the command of that Imperishable the sun and the moon stand apart, the earth and the sky stand apart, the moments, the hours, the days and nights, the months, the seasons and the years stand apart. Verily, O Gārgī, at the command of that Imperishable, some rivers flow from the snowy mountains to the east, others to the west, in whatever direction each flows. Verily, O Gārgī, at the command of that Imperishable men praise those who give, the gods are desirous of a sacrificer, and the fathers (are desirous) of the sacrifice to the shades of the departed.

10. Verily, O Gārgī, if one performs sacrifices and worship and undergoes austerity in this world for many thousands of years, but without knowing that Imperishable, limited indeed is that work of his. Verily, O Gārgī, he who departs from this world without knowing that Imperishable is pitiable. But, O Gārgī, he who departs from this world knowing that Imperishable is a brāhman.

11. Verily, O Gārgī, that Imperishable is the Unseen Seer, the unheard Hearer, the unthought Thinker, the un-understood Understander. Other than It there is naught that sees. Other than It there is naught that hears. Other than It there is naught that thinks. Other than It there is naught that understands. Across this Imperishable, O Gārgī, is ākāśa woven, warp and woof."

And Gārgī Vācaknavī offered her homage to Yājñavalkya in no uncertain terms :

> " Venerable brāhmans, you may think it a great thing if you escape from this man with merely making a bow. Not one of you will surpass him in discussing about Brahman."

Thereupon the daughter of Vacaknu held her peace.

Yājñavalkya's oft repeated formula in answer to Uddālaka —" He who dwelling in *X*, yet is other than *X*, whom *X* does not know, whose body *X* is, who controls *X* from within—He is your Ātman, the Inner Controller, the Immortal "—expresses at once the transcendent and immanent nature of Ātman. The immortal spirit is in empirical man and the phenomenal universe, and is also over and above, and other than and controlling empirical man and the phenomenal universe.

Very significant is the statement that " He is the unseen Seer, the unheard Hearer, the unthought Thinker, the un-understood Understander. Other than He there is no Seer . . . Hearer . . . Thinker . . . Understander. He is . . . Immortal ". In very truth, the one Immortal Ātman alone is the Seer, Hearer, Thinker and Understander in, and through, innumerable, mortal persons severally. No human can possessively say " My Ātman ", as separate from " Your Ātman ". When mortal man says " I ", that " I " has no reality as permanent, unchanging selfhood apart from Ātman. Whenever " I " is used in the sense of separate, distinct personality, as it is indeed used in common parlance, it can only denote the transient phenomenon called a man. The " I ", as an existential[1] ego, conceded as real, is not the Immortal, the Ātman.

Plunging deeper and deeper into the ocean of inquiry,[2] the

[1] The ordinary meaning of *existential* is given in the dictionary as *pertaining to existence.*

That which exists as the observable manifest, is marked by transience, by change, and by development or retrogression. The word *existential* has been used throughout this book to denote the combination of these characteristics. It has been used in no other sense.

The existential person or thing or world is clearly distinguishable from the Immortal, the Eternal, Brahman or Ātman, or Godhead.

Brahman becomes this-All, and back into Brahman this-All is resolved. This-All, including the many gods, is the existential universe.

The Upanishads and the Buddha teach that after death there is neither survival of the person nor annihilation. All that we observe, using our senses and mind, and call a person, is the existential person. It is Ātman which becomes this existential person.

The existential is subsumed in the eternal that-which-is, Brahman or Ātman.

[2] "Bondage is through non-inquiry, emancipation through inquiry. Therefore there should always be inquiry into Ātman . . . and the universe."—Paiṅgala Upanishad, Adhyāya II.

Upanishadic sages found several pearls, instead of a one-and-only pearl of ultimate truth, but were unable to make the perfect string with the help of the needle of penetrating intellect and the thread of logical system. The insights were too deep, and the conscious realizations were too overwhelming, in relation to the extent of exploration of their contexts. The essence of wisdom was extracted, but the stuff of knowledge was in short supply. Hence in the Upanishads, not wholly compatible concepts stand side by side: The sole reality of Brahman or Ātman; Brahman as the Real of the real (satyasya satyam); a "not"-Brahman or "not"-Ātman in relation to, and included in, Brahman or Ātman. Intellectually this could spell confusion. In the lesser known Upanishads contradictory statements are to befound:

> The Universe of ākāśa . . . including Jīva (the "spark of God") is not-Ātman.
>
> Sarvasara Upanishad.

> Rest assured that not-Ātman is a misnomer . . . There is no world as not-Ātman . . . I am Cinmātra (the partless non-dual essence which is Brahman, which is Ātman, which is I) simply, and there is no not-Ātman.
>
> —Tejobindu Upanishad, Chap. 5.

and as examples from the principal Upanishads:

> In the beginning, verily, this (world) was non-existent. Therefrom, verily, Being was produced.
>
> Taittirīya, II.7.

> In the beginning, my dear, this world was just Being, one only, without a second. To be sure, some people say: "In the beginning this world was just Non-being, one only, without a second; from that Non-being Being was produced.
>
> But verily, my dear, whence could this be? said he. How from Non-being could Being be produced? On the contrary, my dear, in the beginning this world was just Being, one only, without a second.
>
> Chāndogya, VI.2. 1 and 2.

Whereas Uddālaka couched his question in personalistic terms, evoking in response Yājñavalkya's exposition of God transcendent and immanent, Gārgī (who doubtless would have read science in a modern university had she lived to-day), with charming aggressiveness makes an objective enquiry. That which is above the heavens, below the earth, between heaven and earth, and heaven and earth themselves, on what are they woven ? What is the primordial stuff ? " Ākāśa ", says Yājña-valkya. In the Sāṁkhya philosophy, of which the origin and development are not far distant from the day of Yājñavalkya, Ākāśa is distinguished as kāranākāśa, non-" atomic " and all-pervasive, and kāryākāśa, or " atomic " ākāśa. In Taittirīya, II.1, the manifested world " emerges " or " evolves " out of ākāśa through its successive transformations, while ākāśa itself derives from Ātman. In the Sāṁkhya, ākāśa derives from Prakṛiti, of which one aspect is effective and discrete, the other is causal and homogeneous and known as Pradhāna or Mūlaprakṛiti, the " rootless root " (amūlaṁ mūlaṁ) of all manifestation, itself without antecedents, the " noumenon " of the entire phenomenal (not only material) universe. The later Sarvasāra Upanishad which called the universe of ākāśa etc. not-ātman, proceeds to say that Māyā, the root of not-ātman, appears as Mūlprakṛiti. But the Sāṁkhya says that Mūlaprakṛiti is indestructible, pervasive, inactive, unique, unsupported, indissoluble, indivisible, uncontrollable. Is this not all too close to the spirit in which the Upanishadic sages talked of Brahman ?

When, therefore, Yājñavalkya answers Gārgī's second question with his exposition of the Imperishable, the Indestructible —one of the sublime passages in all Upanishadic literature—he is possibly talking of Mūlaprakṛiti which for the Vedantists, unlike for the Sāṁkhyists, is but Brahman in finality. By identifying this Imperishable with the unseen Seer, the unheard Hearer, the unthought Thinker, the un-understood Understander, Yājñavalkya identifies the Imperishable with Brahman. In the very next breath he uses the objective IT, as distinct from the subjective He in the answer to Uddālaka. Hence it may be permissible to suppose that the Imperishable may refer to Mūlaprakṛiti in the first instance, but is identified immediately afterwards with Brahman.

The contrasting methods of approach by Uddālaka and Gārgī to the one subject of inquiry, and the appropriate contrasting modes of response by Yājñavalkya, neatly illustrate that the single vision of the Ultimate can be regarded and expressed in more than one appropriate form. But all the different forms of expression are equivalent forms. The Truth is just the Truth.

The Upanishadic sages were by no means unaware that attempting to describe the indescribable, to bring within the clear but strictly limited sphere of distinctly structured comprehension, the vast, amorphous, all-permeating apprehension of whole experience, of Brahman, naturally led to " temptation ",[1] and to difficulties:

> Wherefrom words turn back,
> Together with the mind, not having attained.
>
> Tait. II.4.9.
>
> There the eye goes not ;
> Speech goes not, nor the mind.
> We know not, we understand not
> How one would teach it.
>
> Kena 3.
>
> Not by speech, not by mind,
> Not by sight can He be apprehended.
> How can He be comprehended
> Otherwise than by one's saying " He is ! " ?
>
> Kaṭha, VI.12.

The difficulty encountered in obtaining clear comprehension may be better understood thus :—

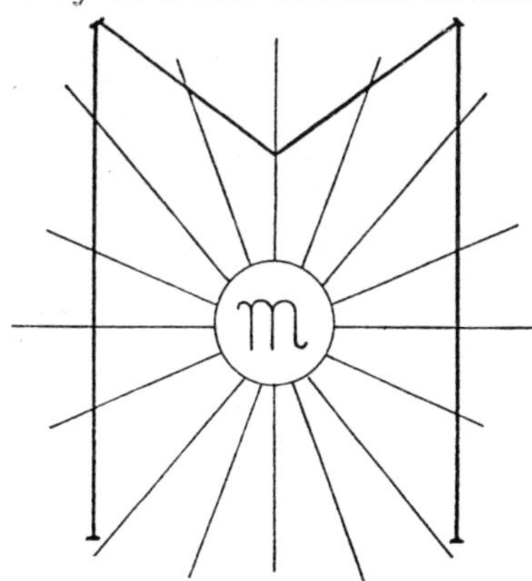

Universal process characterizes M, the macrocosm, which completely includes in itself every microcosm. One man m, a microcosm, naturally regards the universe and himself as quite separate entities at first. By virtue of being what he is and of possessing the special abilities he does possess, m gradually inter-relates himself with M, through his growing awareness and closer observation

[1] See Chāndogya Upanishad, Prapāṭhaka VIII, Khaṇḍas 7-12. In this connection consider the Christian prayer "And lead us not into temptation" —the temptation to attempt to describe God, to clothe God in the rags of our ignorance—"but deliver us from evil"—the evil of continuing to exist in the world in a state of mind unawakened to God, or in Avidyā.

of the interplay between m and M.[1] Similarly, m interrelates m_1 m_2 . . . , with M. Observation shows m how the universal process animates him, affects him adversely or favourably, controls him, and is itself affected and controlled by him. Process, the whole-happening, working in, through and upon m, is m's whole experience. Being wholly contained in M, m is wholly apprehending (by virtue of the fact of ceaseless interaction in universal process), whole experience. But whole apprehension can never be wholly comprehended, for it is too vast, all-pervasive and amorphous. Through the limiting of apprehension—only those stimuli for which man has organs of reception, his senses, reach the brain,—through a process of sorting and of relating the main elements extracted to each other, a clear structure emerges in the mind. This clear structure is comprehension, characteristic of the activity of waking consciousness. Clear comprehension[2] is a definite mental structure, (that is, a thought, or a logical sequence of thoughts), limited and precise, extracted out of whole apprehension of whole experience. Further, m m_1 m_2 . . . are each unique individuals. The "pattern" of each one of them is different from that of another. Whilst apprehension by virtue of its totality, its universality, may be the same for all, the individual comprehension emerging out of that apprehension is stamped with uniqueness. Specific becoming alone has distinctive uniqueness, whereas all-Being, or Universal process, or sole reality, has only characterless[3] one-ness. What m recognises and consciously calls his experience is a particularized form abstracted, or built out of, the whole-apprehension of his whole-experience, by means of his inter-relating, interpreting activity.

Thus, quite naturally, each sage gave out the teaching of Brahman and Ātman according to his own comprehension.

Here, pertinently, two questions must be examined. How did these sages come to know Brahman? What is the meaning of the word "know", in this context?

[1] To be meticulous, between m and M-m; after realizing that M wholly includes m, M-m is discarded for M.

[2] Comprehension is to apprehension somewhat like a word or gesture expressing love is to the whole emotion felt.

[3] Not in a derogatory sense!

Discipline is the answer to the former question, and realization to the latter. It is said in

The Kaivalya Upanishad :

> Āśvalāyana went to the Lord Parameshti, and addressed Him thus : " Please initiate me into Brahma-Vidyā (Divine Wisdom), which is the most excellent . . . mystic, by which the learned after having quickly freed themselves from all sins, reach Purusha, the Supreme of the supreme."
>
> To him the Grandfather replied : " Know IT through Śraddhā (faith), Bhakti (devotion), Dhyāna (meditation) and Yoga. Persons attain salvation not through karma (works), progeny or wealth, but by Saṁnyāsa (self-surrender) alone. Ascetics of pure mind, through realizing the meaning well ascertained by Vedānta-wisdom, and through Saṁnyāsa-Yoga, enter into THAT which is above Svarga (heaven) and is in the cave of the heart. They all attain Paramātman in the Brahma-world, and are emancipated."

The Amṛitabindu :

> Having studied the books (the scriptures) well, the learned man should persevere studiously in the acquisition of Jñāna, or Self-knowledge, and Vijñāna, or Self-realization according to such knowledge. Then he should discard the whole of the books, as a person in quest of grain gives up the straw. Though there are cows of different colours, yet their milk is of the same colour. Like milk is Jñāna, and like cows are seen the various forms (sources of information ; experiences). As ghee[1] is latent in milk, so is Vijñāna latent in every being.

The Śubāla, Khaṇḍa III.

> Some one out of many attains to Ātman by the six means of Truth, Charity, Religious austerities, non-injury to any creature, celibacy, and complete indifference to wordly objects.

The Kaṭha :

> He, however, who has understanding,
> Who is mindful and ever pure
> Reaches the goal
> From which he is born no more.[2]
>
> III.8

[1] Ghee is clarified butter.
[2] See also, below, pp. 189, 195, 225.

An intelligent man should suppress[1] his speech and his mind.
The latter he should suppress in his Understanding-Self (jñāna-ātman).
The understanding he should suppress in the Buddhi.[2]
That he should suppress in the Tranquil self (Śānta ātman).
III.13.

(and most significantly):

The self-existent pierced the openings (of the senses) outward;
Therefore one looks outward, not within himself (antarātman).
A certain wise man, while seeking immortality,
Introspectively beheld the soul (Ātman) face to face.
IV.1.

The Muṇḍaka:

This Ātman is obtainable by truth, by austerity,
By proper knowledge (jñāna), by the student's life of chastity (brahmacarya) constantly (practised).
III.1.5.

The substance of the teaching can be summed up as a physical, moral and intellectual discipline, culminating with that practice of Samādhi (meditation) through which Brahman is realized. In this discipline, silence is practised. This means abstention from talking aloud, with the voice, and also from talking silently, in one's mind. The former is not too difficult. But only those who have made a lifelong attempt to master the flow of discursive thought, the silent chatter that goes on unceasingly in one's mind, can appreciate the achievement of the ancient Yogis. In that state, the "sense impressions-mind" disturbance is at last stilled. Consciousness, as commonly understood, is transcended. The sage, far from becoming unconscious, or vacuous as scholars have sometimes said, is in a far more vivid, awakened condition—a condition faintly reflected in that of the genius so rapt in his creative inspiration that he is "lost" to the external world. It is the condition in which he gains para-Vidyā, all knowledge in the ordinary sense being a string of words,[3] and

[1] Suppress means to bring under control and make still and then enter into a profounder state of consciousness. Cf. "Be still and know that I am God" —Psalms, 46.10.

[2] Buddhi: see below, pp. 330, et seq.

[3] Indispensable and proper in its own sphere.

in which, individual consciousness, concentrated, poised, free, sparks across the gap between the conditioned self and the Unconditioned, and, fully illuminated, realizes—makes real—Brahman, the Absolute.

Returning to corporeal existence, into the world of the existential ego, the sage declares "Aham Brahma asmi", I am Brahman. The realization of Brahman, a whole apprehension in *full-consciousness* (or super-consciousness) through whole experience, is what is meant by knowing Brahman. Is it any wonder that these enthusiastic (God-intoxicated) sages sang: "There the sun shines not, nor the moon nor the stars; lightnings shine not there and much less earthly fire. From His light all these give light, and His radiance illumines all creation"—Kaṭha. V.15 (Mascaró's translation)—and again: "Brahman indeed is this immortal. Brahman before, Brahman behind, to right and to left, stretched forth below and above, Brahman, indeed, is this whole world, this widest extent"—Muṇḍaka, II.2.11.

So overwhelming, so "other-than-this" is this stupendous realization of Brahman that it is difficult to formulate it in positive terms. If a hole (which, remember, is a void, a no-thing) of a certain size were made in a room which has no other aperture, light from outside will "light up" the room, and the inside walls of the room and the objects contained in the room will become visible. It is not light which will be seen but the substantial objects which will be rendered visible by the invisible light. Analogies often mislead; but with the exercise of due caution, they are occasionally helpful. Experience of the realization of the Absolute illumines one. The 'light' of the Absolute 'makes clear' the experiences (the 'objects') of space-time existence. This, at least, is what is said by those who claim some sort of realization of the Absolute. Also, just as light cannot be made known to one who has never experienced light, the Absolute is a sealed book, or worse still, any statement about the Absolute is sense-less jargon, to one who has never had any experience embodying a touch of "absoluteness", such as "an unforgettable" joy or "the one and only beloved".

Now comprehension is rooted in the framework of dualism

together with all the grades lying between the duals (opposites). Thought cannot be conveyed to one who does not understand or has no grasp of dualism and gradation. All ordinary knowing and speaking is in terms of the subject-object, positive-negative relation. No one thing or idea has meaning, concrete, precise and logical, without its appropriate something-else (a different or an opposite) to make relation with it. The senses, mind and speech, are inexorably bound within a world of the pairs of opposites, of gradation.

How, then, in the everyday world, is one to convey the realization of Brahman to another? The greatest Upanishadic sages chose the method of negating both factors in each and every pair of opposites. In a sense, what a poor, ineffectual conveyance! And yet, no less effective than saying, at the right time, in the right place, and just exactly on the occasion of the divine stress, "I love you"!

So Yājñavalkya's presentation of the Absolute, though in negative terms, could nevertheless help to remove the obstruction offered by the ordinary interpretation of sense-experience to the realization of the nature of reality—like making a hole to let in the light. The Imperishable is "not coarse, not fine, not long, not short", not, indeed, anything that can be caught in the net of description. Nevertheless, the Absolute IS, or IT IS. Yājñavalkya had to bear witness to his Vision, if only to discharge his responsibility to answer Gārgī.

And this is complemented by a similar presentation of the Ātman in what is known as the "neti neti" (not this, not that) doctrine:

> The Soul (Ātman) is not this, it is not that. It is unseizable, for it is not seized. It is indestructible, for it is not destroyed. It is unattached, for it does not attach itself. It is unbound. It does not tremble. It is not injured.
>
> III.9.26; IV.4.22.; IV.5.15.

The Chāndogya Upanishad expresses it in a different way:

> Verily, what is called Brahman—that is the same as the ākāśa outside of a person is. Verily, what the outside of a person is—that is the same as what the ākāśa within a person is. Verily

what the ākāśa within a person is—that is the same as what the ākāśa here within the heart is. That is the Full, the Non-Active. III.12. 7-9.

Now, the light which shines higher than this heaven, on the backs of all, on the backs of everything, in the highest worlds, than which there are no higher—verily, that is the same as this light which is here within a person.

III.13.7.

1. Verily, this whole world is Brahman. Tranquil, let one worship IT as that from which he came forth, as that into which he will be dissolved, as that in which he breathes . . . .
2. He who consists of mind, whose body is life, whose form is light, whose conception is truth, whose soul (Ātman) is ākāśa, containing all works, containing all desires, containing all odours, containing all tastes, encompassing this whole world, the unspeaking, the unconcerned—
3. This Soul of mine within the heart is smaller than a grain of rice, or a barley-corn, or a mustard-seed, or a grain of millet, or the kernel of a grain of millet ; this Soul of mine within the heart is greater than the earth, greater than the atmosphere, greater than the sky, greater than these worlds.
4. Containing all works . . . desires . . . odours . . . tastes, encompassing this whole world, the unspeaking, the unconcerned—this is the Soul of mine within the heart, this is Brahman. Into him I shall enter on departing hence.
   If one would believe this, he would have no more doubt.
   Thus used Sāṇḍilya to say—yea, Sāṇḍilya !

III.14.

Earlier in this chapter was introduced the beginning of the conversation between Nārada and Sanatkumāra. The teacher tells his pupil that all he had learned so far was mere Name. Nevertheless, Name should be reverenced as Brahman, for "He who reverences Name as Brahman—as far as Name goes, so far he has freedom." Was there anything more than Name ? Yes, Speech, was Sanatkumāra's reply. Speech should be reverenced as Brahman—and the pupil could attain freedom as far as speech went—for by Speech were made known right and wrong, true and false, good and bad. Was there anything more than Speech ? Why surely, Mind—and a few points showing the importance of Mind are mentioned. And thus Sanatkumāra leads Nārada on from Mind through Conception, Thought, Meditation, Understanding, Strength, Sustenance (or Food), Water, Heat, ākāśa, Memory and Hope to Life, adding an idea or two on each topic. At this point Nārada questions no more, and Sanatkumāra continues the thread thus:

> "But he, verily, speaks superiorly, who speaks superiorly with Truth."
>
> "Then I, Sir" says Nārada, "would speak superiorly with Truth."
>
> "But one must desire to understand Truth".
>
> "Sir, I desire to understand Truth".

In this strain, Sanatkumāra leads Nārada from Truth through Understanding, Thought, Faith, Growth and Creation (or Activity) to Joy. Each one of these is the necessary condition for its immediate predecessor, up to Truth. When Nārada says, "Sir, I desire to understand Joy", Sanatkumāra leads him to the final truth:

> Where there is the Infinite there is joy. There is no joy in the finite. Only in the Infinite is joy: Know the nature of the Infinite.
>
> Where nothing else is seen or heard or known there is the Infinite. Where something else is seen or heard or known there is the finite. The Infinite is immortal; but the finite is mortal.
>
> "Where does the Infinite rest?" On its own greatness—unless, indeed, not on greatness at all.
>
> In this world they call greatness the possession of cattle and horses, elephants and gold, servants and wives, lands and houses. But I do not call this greatness, for here one thing depends upon another.
>
> But the Infinite is above and below, North and South and East and West. The Infinite is the whole universe.
>
> I am above and below, North and South and East and West. I am the whole universe.
>
> Ātman is above and below, North and South and East and West. Ātman is the whole Universe.
>
> He who sees, knows and understands this, who finds in Ātman, his delight and his pleasure and his union and his bliss, becomes a Master of himself. His freedom then is infinite.

But those who see not this become the servants of other masters and in the worlds that pass away attain not their liberation.
(VII.23 to 25—Mascaró's translation, with slight change.)

Sanatkumāra adds a few words to the effect that Life, Hope, Memory, and so on up to Speech and Name all arise from the Ātman, and finally:

" Indeed, this whole world arises from the Ātman "
VII.26.1.

It happens that Ātman or Brahman is in later times imprisoned in the cage of description ; it is catechistically docketed and becomes a subject for argument. So there arises ajñāna (un-wisdom), defined, in the Nirālamba Upanishad, as " the illusory attribution of many Ātmans through diverse vehicles such as men, beasts, angels, etc. to Brahman that is secondless (without a second), all-permeating and of the nature of all." On the other hand it was impossible to avoid catechistic docketing. Man—or at least a certain type of man—is an analyser, a pigeon-holer. He likes precision, order, method, and the concrete—something he can " bite into ". This is, doubtless, virtue in its own proper sphere, such as practical everyday life, or science. But when it intrudes into, or is forced upon, the apprehension of the all-inclusive Sole Reality, it leads to misunderstanding rather than to clear comprehension.

So the original, undifferenced unity, Brahman, identical with Ātman, gives birth in the course of centuries to Īśvara, Jīva, Brahmā, Viṣṇu, Śiva, Parameśvara, Paramātman, Jivātman, Pratyagātman, Caitanya, Kūṭastha, Antaryāmin, etc., etc.—an intellectual enrichment, but at the price, partly, of some confusion in thought, and partly, of entering the cockpit of mere argumentation at the expense of living the good life.

As an example of a catechistic definition, here is one from the Nirālamba Upanishad:

" What is Brahman ? "

" It is the Caitanya that appears, through the aspects of Karma and Jñāna, as this vast mundane egg composed of Mahat, Ahaṁkāra and the five elements, earth, water, fire, Vāyu and Ākāśa—that is secondless—that is devoid of all Upādhis (vehicles), that is full of all Śaktis (potencies), that is without beginning and end, that is described as pure, beneficial, peaceful and guṇaless and that is indescribable."

How contrasting are the presentations of Brahman in the early Great Upanishads and this late Minor Upanishad! It is necessary for a philosopher-saint to have something of the creative artist in him!

Nevertheless, the Minor Upanishads cannot be discarded without peril.

Now in the Chāndogya Upanishad, there is a charming dialogue between a father and his son, touching the question, what is man?

Uddālaka Āruṇi had a dearly loved son called Śvetaketu. When the lad was twelve years old, his father exhorted him to become a student, and receive a brāhman's education. So for twelve years the boy studied the Vedas. He returned home, thinking himself learned. Observing his son's conceit and pride, Uddālaka, with frankness not unsoftened by paternal affection, said to him:

> " Śvetaketu, my dear, since now you are conceited, think yourself learned, and are proud, did you also ask for that teaching whereby what has not been heard of becomes heard of, what has not been thought of becomes thought of, what has not been understood becomes understood? "
>
> " How, pray, sir, is that teaching? "

Uddālaka explains how by one piece of clay, or one ornament of copper, or one pair of nail-scissors of iron, the reality which is clay or copper or iron may be known, the particular object made of any of these being just a modification of the fundamental substance.

> " Verily ", said Śvetaketu, " those honoured men did not know this; for, if they had known it, why would they not have told me? But do you, sir, tell me it ".

Uddālaka then proceeds to instruct his son. Śvetaketu drinks in his father's wisdom, asking him to make him understand more. Skilfully, Uddālaka leads his son to the realization that all creatures here have Being as their root (VI.8. 4 and 6), and then says:

> "When a person here is dying, my dear, his voice goes into his mind; his mind into his breath; his breath into heat; the heat into the highest divinity.
>
> "That which is the finest essence—this whole world has that as its soul. That is Reality. That is Ātman. That art thou, O Śvetaketu."
>
> VI.8. 6 and 7.

"Do you, sir, cause me to understand even more" says the enraptured son.

"So be it, my dear" answers the father, and proceeds to express this supreme conception—That art thou—in many different ways. Two will be sufficient for quotation.

> "Bring hither a fig from there."
> "Here it is, sir."
> "Divide it."
> "It is divided, sir."
> "What do you see there?"
> "These rather fine seeds, sir."
> "Of these, please divide one."
> "It is divided, sir."
> "What do you see there?"
> "Nothing at all, sir."
>
> Then he said to him: "Verily, my dear, that finest essence which you do not perceive—verily, my dear, from that finest essence this great Nyagrodha (sacred fig) tree thus arises.
>
> "Believe me, my dear," said he, "that which is the finest essence—this whole world has that as its soul. That is Reality. That is Ātman. That art thou, O Śvetaketu."
>
> "Do you, sir, cause me to understand even more."
>
> "So be it, my dear," said he.
>
> VI. 12. 1–3.
>
> "Place this salt in the water. In the morning come unto me."
> Thus he did so.
> Then he said to him: "That salt you placed in the water last evening—please bring it hither."
> Then he tried to grasp it, but did not find it, as it was completely dissolved.

" Please take a sip of it from this end," said he. " How is it ? "
" Salt."
" Take a sip from the middle," said he. " How is it ? "
" Salt."
" Take a sip from that end." said he. " How is it ? "
" Salt."
" Set it aside. Then come unto me."
He did so, saying, " It is always the same."
Then he said to him : " Verily, indeed, my dear, you do not perceive Being here. Verily, indeed, it is here."
" That which is the finest essence—this whole world has that as its Soul. That is Reality.
That is Ātman. That art thou, O Śvetaketu ".
" Do you, sir, cause me to understand even more ".
" So be it, my dear," said he.

VI.13.1–3.

And so the patient father continues, till at last his son is fully enlightened. Śvetaketu understands, and is at peace.

For thousands of years men had wondered and speculated upon the nature of man, his origin and future. And now came an answer in the three simple words, Tat tvam asi, That art thou!

From the Imperishable, from the primordial source of the universe, emerges each person, the visible fruition of the creative forces (of whatever nature they be) which brought him into being. He lives his life. Back to the Imperishable he goes. This is the ultimate fact. Each man's emergence and final reabsorption is the Ātman's " personal " way of demonstrating that " The Absolute IS ". In that absoluteness, individual self-consciousness—I am I—is a temporary manifestation of universal activity. So Yājñavalkya says to his wife Maitreyī : After death there is no consciousness (Bṛihad-Āraṇyaka Upanishad, II.4.12, and IV.5.13.).

There is no immortality for individual self-consciousness. So there is no heaven or hell, reward or punishment, or betterment or deterioration to follow, of which I, now living, will be self-consciously aware after death. All that is thought, felt and done, affects and transforms me and my environment during my lifetime, and will continue to affect my environment (including other human beings) after I am dead, until the original impulses are " lost " in subsequent transformations. The " I am I " is mortal, like the body. But I, the Ātman, the Inner Controller, is the Immortal, being identical with the Imperishable, Brahman.

Ātman or Brahman has no " I am I "-consciousness in the everyday existential sense, nor is the Imperishable saddled with a " cosmic consciousness " as pictured by mortals, because consciousness of distinctive selfhood is impossible without " otherness ", without a duality. To attach such consciousness to the Absolute is meaningless, therefore.

But the stark, simple statement, " That art thou ", releases one from the necessity of any straining to know. From the Unknown Eternal one comes, to the Unknown Eternal one returns. This much is certain : " That " being without human limitations and sorrows, stresses and strains, there is no need for man ever to have any fear or anxiety. The Imperishable IS—That art thou.

In the Paiṅgala Upanishad, Adhyāya III, Paiṅgala asks Yājñavalkya to offer an exposition of the mahāvākyas, or sacred sentences, of which Tat tvam asi is one. Yājñavalkya answers :

> " The word Tat denotes the Cause of the universe that is variegated beyond perception, has the characteristics of omniscience, has Māyā as His vehicle, and has the attributes of Sac-cid-ānanda (existence-knowledge-bliss).
>
> " It is He that is the basis of the notion ' I ' which has the differentiated knowledge produced by antaḥkaraṇa ; and it is He that is denoted by the word Tvam."

In the Sarvasāra Upanishad :

> Who is Pratyagātman ?
>
> He is of the nature of truth, wisdom, eternity and bliss. He has no bodily vehicles. He is abstract wisdom itself like a mass of pure gold that is devoid of the changing forms of bracelet, crown, etc. He is of the nature of just consciousness.
>
> He is that which shines as Caitanya and Brahman. When He is subject to the vehicle of Avidyā, and is the meaning of the word Tvam (Thou), in Tat tvam asi, then he is Pratyagātman.
>
> Who is Paramātman ?
>
> It is He who is associated with truth, wisdom, eternity, bliss,

omniscience, etc. who is subject to the vehicle of Māyā, and is the meaning of the word Tat (That) in Tat tvam asi.

What is Brahman ?

> Brahman is that which is free from all vehicles, which is Absolute Consciousness devoid of particularities, which is Sat (Be-ness), which is without a second, which is bliss and which is māyāless. It is different from the characteristics of what is expressed by the word Tvam, subject to the vehicle (of Avidyā), and also of what is expressed by the word Tat, subject to the vehicle of Māyā. It is itself differenceless (undifferentiated) and is seen as the Seat (Source) of everything. It is the pure, the true, the noumenal, the Indestructible.

Paramātman, the Holy Creative Spirit, embodied through Māyā as the vehicle, is Parameśvar, the Supreme Being, the Father in Heaven in Christian terms. Parameśvar is the Supreme Existent, Brahman as Svayambhū or the Self-Existent, and derives from Brahman as the Ultimate.

Pratyagātman is what is commonly called " my " Spirit, God Immanent in " me ", the real I if we may so call it. Embodied through Avidyā as the vehicle, it is the Individual Self, the Jīva, the " I " as a self-existent. Pratyagātman may be said to derive from Paramātman in the first instance, and then from Brahman as the Ultimate.

The self-existent is the re-creation of the Supreme Self-Existent.

When Jesus declares " I and my Father are one ", he affirms the identity of Pratyagātman and Paramātman. He declares in his own way what the Upanishadic seer declared : I am Brahman.

The presentation in the Paiṅgala and Sarvasāra Upanishads accommodates itself to what the senses report, namely that macrocosm and microcosm appear to be separate and distinct, and also to what the inward reverence of the devotee affirms, namely that God is God and man is man. It also indicates how those ancient seers sought to relate Tat and Tvam to the Ultimate, Brahman, and to embody their intuitive insights in a metaphysical teaching. The task was, and still is, not an easy one. There are defects in the letter of the Upanishads, for the more-than-intelligible Infinite teasingly denies compression into the thought-word mould of the intelligible finite. And yet, although the ocean cannot be bottled, a sip out of a bottle of sea water is not unlike a sip of the ocean.

The monistic suggestions of the Ṛig Veda thus culminated in the Upanishads in the realization of Brahman the Absolute, as the Ultimate of which the empirical universe is but the body so to say, for Brahman is this All; and of the identity of Brahman and Ātman.

Probably it is not untrue to say that man climbed the last highest peak of thought here. Thought is not the best word. Spiritual insight or intuitive realization is a better term. Thought marches in ordered array, and where it gives rise to a logical system, a philosophy comes into being. In that sense, the Upanishads are not philosophy. But even the strictest philosophy is not merely a mechanical wonder of logical reasoning. It must have a germ, an origin. This origin is inspiration—the more-than-logical, more-than-rational, creative "feeling" or "idea" whose life and growth spell the emergence of a philosophy.

Now the Upanishads are a well of creative ideas. Their authors believed that for the finest type of development, man must *live* with a root-idea and extract all the wisdom he can out of it by his own efforts, rather than have the idea worked out into a system, the subject, thereafter, of routine intellectual exercise. Also, in those days, in the absence of paper and writing, what more natural than to enjoy a discussion on a key-idea, like free improvisation on a known theme, or to meditate in silence over it and grow in wisdom? Yet, despite the absence of close reasoning from given premises, the tendency to systematization is present in the Upanishads. The ideas cohere, even if loosely. Instead of giving logical proofs, various observations bearing on the point are made. Since the underlying purpose is that the seeker after Truth may find Truth—in finality, an individual, creative and not merely interpretative achievement—it is left to the earnest student to make what use he can of these observations.

Having said this, it must also be said that one of the world's greatest philosophies is implicit in the authoritative declarations of the Upanishads; in fact more than one, for the Vedānta, and Sāṁkhya and Yoga systems, and the philosophies of Śaṁkara and Rāmānuja have deep roots in the Upanishads.

To acknowledge that the transcendental vision of the Upanishadic sages is not clothed in the conventional garb of formal philosophy is not to impeach its value, still less to lessen its significance. The teachings, philosophical and mystical, religious and ethical, are themselves the witness of their own greatness and beauty for all time. What is of unique significance in the creation of this vision is that man has at last completely emancipated his mind and spirit. The ultimate core of his inner freedom has been reached. The anguish of his separation from the Eternal, the Tad-vana or Goal of Love-Longing, is transformed into the bliss of unending union. Here and now is the Peace that passes understanding whilst still limited by human understanding. Into the very heart of the dragon, fear, penetrated the spear of the knowledge of the true, Brahmavidyā, and the terror of the unknown and anxiety for the future ceased to torment man. In a special sense the twilight of the gods turned in two centuries into night. But for man had risen the bright day star of Truth, bringing beauty and peace and unbroken holiness. Nor in truth were the gods, or God, swept away into darkness. The tears and toil and sweat, the matchless courage and sacrificial genius of promethean man had redeemed them all, and gods and God found everlasting being in their true home, the non-duality of Brahman and Ātman.

For all time the Upanishadic seers had transformed Religion, by transforming mere conceptions of God into the realization of God. For all time they made clear the true relationship between man and God as Divine Person. Never again could God be a fearsome, vengeful, capricious or tyrannical power, to be propitiated by ignorant, grovelling, impotent man. For ever and ever henceforth, God could only be holy, ethical, righteous and wise. Destroyed was the crude superstition of God's distant separate Being, and his terrible autocracy holding man in abject slavery with the sanctions of disease, sorrow, pain, decrepitude and death. God and man, and Man and god, were one spirit, one intelligence, one vision, one desire, one life, one flesh ; of one family, familiar with each other, Loving Father and Beloved Son. All this, and more, was implicit in the new heritage of Religion, and it found fulfilment in the development of Indian religious thought in the course of some twenty centuries and more.

The Brahman-Ātman concept, and "That art thou", are expressed in varying forms throughout the principal Upanishads.

Kaṭha Upanishad (Mascaró's translation) :

> The Ātman, the Self, is never born and never dies. It is without a cause and is eternally changeless. It is beyond time, unborn, permanent and everlasting.
>
> II.18.

> Concealed in the heart of beings lies the Ātman, The Spirit, the Self, smaller than the smallest atom, greater than the greatest spaces.
>
> II.20.

> The Ātman is beyond sound and form, without touch and taste and perfume. It is eternal, unchangeable and without beginning and end : indeed above reasoning.
>
> III.15.

> There is one Ruler, the Spirit that is in all things, who transforms His one form into many . . .
>
> V.12.

> He is the Eternal among things that pass away . . .
>
> V.13

> There the sun shines not, nor the moon nor the stars, lightnings shine not there and much less earthly fire. From His light all these give light, and His radiance illumines all creation.
>
> V.15.

Īśā Upanishad (Mascaró's translation) :

> He moves, and he moves not. He is far, and He is near. He is within all, and He is outside all.
>
> 5.

The Spirit filled all with His radiance.
He is incorporeal and invulnerable, pure
and untouched by evil. He is the supreme
seer and thinker, immanent and transcendent.
He placed all things in the path of Eternity.
8.

Muṇḍaka Upanishad (Hume's translation):

That which is invisible, ungraspable, without
family, without caste—without sight or
hearing is IT, without hand or foot,
Eternal, all-pervading, omnipresent, exceedingly
subtile; That is the Imperishable, which the
wise perceive as the source of beings.
I.1.6.

As from a well-blazing fire, sparks
By the thousand issue forth of like form,
So from the Imperishable, my friend, beings
manifold
Are produced, and thither also go.
II.1.1.

That which is flaming, which is subtler
than the subtle,
On which the worlds are set, and their
inhabitants—

That is the Imperishable Brahman.
IT is life, and IT is speech and mind.
That is the real. It is immortal.
IT is (a mark) to be penetrated.
Penetrate IT, my friend.
II.2.2.

He on whom the sky, the earth, and the
atmosphere
Are woven, and the mind, together with
all the life-breaths,
Him alone know as the one Soul (Ātman).
Other
Words dismiss. He is the bridge to
immortality.
II.2.5.

Brahman, indeed, is this immortal, Brahman before,
Brahman behind, to right and to left.
Stretched forth below and above,
Brahman, indeed, is this whole world,
this widest extent.

II.2.11.

Who can deny that the Upanishads were shot through and through with deep religious feeling?

Although the sages declared that the Ultimate was hardly describable in positive terms, they nevertheless affirmed that man can "know" and become united with Brahman. Two paths open: First the objective search or looking outwards. Says the Śvetāśvatara Upanishad (IV.20):

His form is not to be beheld.
No one soever sees Him with the eye.

The Taittirīya (II.4 and 9):

Wherefrom words turn back
Together with the mind, not having attained.

The Kena (3):

There the eye goes not;
Speech goes not, nor the mind.
We know not, we understand not
How one would teach it.

Strangely baffling is this Brahman! As said in The Kena (3)

Other indeed is IT than the known,
And moreover above the unknown.

The Īśā (10):

Other indeed, they say, than knowledge!
Other, they say, than non-knowledge!

Indeed the search seems hopeless, for The Bṛihadāraṇyaka (IV.4.10—identical with Īśā 9) says:

Into blind darkness enter they
That worship ignorance;
Into greater darkness than that, as it were,
That delight in knowledge.

The Kaṭha (VI.12) says that Brahman can only be arbitrarily postulated:

> Not by speech, not by mind,
> Not by sight can He be apprehended.
> How can He be comprehended
> Otherwise than by one's saying "He is!"?

But a clue is offered by the paradoxical statement in the Kena (11):

> IT is conceived of by him by whom IT is not conceived of.
> He by whom it is conceived of, knows it not.
> IT is not understood by those who (say they) understand IT.
> IT is understood by those who (say they) understand IT not.

In short the Supreme Brahman is not to be found by objective perception; intellect is everlastingly limited by dualism.

The second path is that of the subjective search or looking within. Within the self Brahman is "known" and the unity achieved, for "Therein all these (things) become one" (Bṛihadāraṇyaka I.4.7.). The very act of looking outwards perpetuates the duality of seeing subject and observed object. But Brahman is the All. The IT includes the individual. Brahman could not be an object of consciousness, Brahman being "the unseen Seer, the unheard Hearer, the unthought Thinker, the un-understood Understander" (Bṛihadāraṇyaka III.7.23.) "Wherewith", asks Yājñavalkya, "would one understand him with whom one understands this All? Lo, wherewith would one understand the Understander?" (Bṛihadāraṇyaka II.4.14.). But Brahman and Ātman are a non-duality. The Ātman "my Soul", is "my whole Self", "is this All". In the unity which is the individual self is embodied the unity which is the Universal Self. The seer is aware of the indivisible wholeness of his own unitary being, since this unit-self, one Person, does not call for conscious objective observation to discover if he is one or two or twenty.

So, in Yājñavalka's words:

> He who has found and has awakened to the Soul
> That has entered this conglomerate abode—

He is the maker of everything, for he is the
creator of all;
The world is his: indeed he is the world itself.

Bṛihadāraṇyaka IV.4.13.

And the consequence of this realization is that the Brahman-knower becomes Brahman, becomes this All, as in Bṛihadāraṇyaka I.4.10. Elsewhere:

"Brahman-knowers become merged in Brahman"

Śvetāśvatara I.7.

"He, verily, that knows that supreme Brahman,
becomes very Brahman"

Muṇḍaka. III.2.9.

The "event" of the realization "I am Brahman" is itself simple and quiet, and at the same time extraordinary and electrifying. The separative "I-am-I" consciousness is such that whilst on the one hand it fulfils the necessary function of preserving the distinct identity of the person to whom it belongs, on the other hand it makes him behave as if he were unrelated to his environment and to other people, as if the I and the not-I were not complementaries contained within one whole. The consciousness of such separate selfhood is part of THE avidyā (ignorance) which the great thinkers of India declared was the source of suffering and evil. This ignorance is not dispelled merely by being told in words, or merely by holding the thought, that "I am Brahman." But it can be dispelled by discipline (tapas), or by study and teaching, or by the "Grace (prasāda) of the Creator" as expressed in the Kaṭha Upanishad: "One who is without the active will beholds Him, and becomes freed from sorrow—When through the grace of the Creator he beholds the greatness of the Soul (Ātman)", or by love and devotion, or by service. Then the cold, formal thought, "I am Brahman", is quickened with warm feeling. There comes a moment when the sense of separateness disappears, the imprisoning wall of ego-ism falls down, and suddenly, without losing consciousness of one's own identity, there is a flooding awareness of the environment as inseparable part and parcel of oneself, and oneself as part and parcel of the environment. The strain between oneself and the environment is changed into a state of ease never experienced before; and there is peace, and freedom, and quiet joy.

Earlier it was stated that to "know" Brahman means to "realize" Brahman. This knowing may also be considered as effecting union, or as a commingling, not mechanical as when one stream commingles with another and the united streams flow on as a single river, but as a creative harmonizing leading to new conception. ("And Adam knew Eve his wife and she conceived").[1] The Yogic discipline leads to an inner state of consciousness—conception,[2] an event inside the mother, takes place in the "dark", the "deeps"—which, coming to fruition brings forth the "knowledge of Brahman", the become-Brahman or I-am-Brahman—even as in due season there is born the child into the light.

The power which draws the Soul to God is Love. From Love alone comes, and should always come on any plane, union which is creative harmony. Hence man's Love for God, Devotion to the Lord, is indispensable. Hence the injunction that "never should the Upanishads be imparted to . . . one who is not devoted to Me . . ."[3]

The stages of knowing can be summarized thus. First, books and verbal instruction are the source of knowledge. Second, the student learns the art of applying his knowledge correctly. He is able to prove his knowledge if necessary, through what he does. To really know a truth means to be able to live it. The knowledge is part of the person's constitution so to say.[4]

The deeper reaches of knowledge are entered in meditation. Through contemplation, the knowing deepens, becomes enriched, and intensifies.[5] It grows as a creative force giving rise to profounder knowing. In the final stage, samādhi, the subject-object separation is transcended, the mind is stilled, the secret of Brahman is experienced. This experiencing, this "being Brahman" as the culmination of the successive becomings in

[1] Genesis, IV.1.
[2] See also Chāndogya Upanishad VII, especially VII.4.
[3] See also p. 89, above.
[4] "Verily, other than and within that one that consists of breath is a self that consists of mind (mano-maya)—Tait., II.3.
[5] Those who successfully practise meditation will best understand this intensification.

the manifested world, is the final "knowledge" which, not merely leads to or brings about, but itself is fulfilment, bliss, liberation, Nirvāṇa. The existential self, though enclosed within its finite bounds, realizes the Infinite, the Eternal.

Such was the knowledge of Brahman which "liberates man from all sorrow and sin", and which was possessed by and characterized the Yājñavalkyas, Uddālakas and the other Upanishadic saint-sages. Such knowledge was the Authority for their teachings.

After knowing Brahman, the "I-am-I" consciousness which hitherto was an ego-centred, exclusive, self-consciousness, becomes transformed into non-limiting (but not unlimited), inclusive SELF-awareness. The I is still I; you are still you. But the I KNOWS that Brahman is you, and also that Brahman is the I. Rightly set in the framework of the whole, the you and the I are integrated into a unity within, and with, the whole. The SELF-aware person behaves as if he and his neighbour and his environment were one whole situation. The nature of his spontaneous, uninhibited, immediate reactions proves that he "knows Brahman". He feels towards all people as if they were but different versions of himself. The barriers are down as between true lovers.

The universal and eternal fact is that Brahman dwells in the body and is the body, dwells in the mind and is the mind. Individual self-consciousness, because of ignorance, blinds vision and clouds understanding. And so a veil is thrown between man and the truth. But when this unhappy trick played by self-consciousness is done away with, when ignorance is dispelled by Brahman-knowledge, then, the vivid awareness of the truth is present and man is liberated. And the Upanishads say that man then knows immortality and bliss, whereas the absence of this saving knowledge spells misery.

The Bṛihadāraṇyaka:

> Verily, while we are here we may know this.
> If you have known it not, great is the
> destruction.
> Those who know this become immortal,
> But others go only to sorrow.
>
> IV.4.14.

Brahman is knowledge, is bliss,
The final goal of the giver of offerings,
Of him, too, who stands still and knows It.[1]

III.9.28.

"An ocean, a seer alone without duality,
becomes he whose world is Brahman, O King!"

Thus Yājñavalkya instructed him.

"This is a man's highest path. This is his highest achievement. This is his highest world. This is his highest bliss. On a part of just this bliss other creatures have their living."

IV.3.32.

The Chāndogya:

He who stands firm in Brahman attains immortality.

II.23..1.

The Taittirīya:

Both he who is here in a person and he who is yonder in the sun—he is one.
He who knows this, on departing from this world . . . proceeds on to that self which consists of bliss.

II.8.

The Aitareya:

So he, knowing this, having ascended aloft . . . became immortal, yea, became immortal.

IV.6.

The Kaushītaki:

Having reached that, he becomes immortal as the gods are immortal—he who knows this.

II.14.

The Kena:

When known by an awakening, IT is conceived of,
Truly it is immortality one finds.

[1] Cf. Psalms, XLVI.10—"Be still and know that I am God."

With the Soul one finds power ;
With knowledge one finds the immortal.
12.

If one have known (IT) here, then there is truth.
If one have known (IT) not here, great is the destruction.
Discerning (IT) in every single being, the wise,
On departing from this world, become immortal.
13.

The Kaṭha :

Higher than the Unmanifest, however, is the Person,
All-pervading and without any mark whatever.
Knowing which, a man is liberated
And goes to immortality.
VI.8.

His form is not to be beheld.
No one soever sees Him with the eye.
He is framed by the heart, by the thought, by the mind.
They who know That become immortal.
VI.9.

The Muṇḍaka :

He, verily, who knows that supreme Brahman, becomes very Brahman. In his family no one ignorant of Brahman arises. He crosses over sorrow. He crosses over sin. Liberated from the knots of the heart he becomes immortal.
III.2.9.

The Śvetāśvatara :

Higher than this is Brahman. The Supreme, the Great,
Hidden in all things, body by body,
The One embracer of the universe—
By knowing Him as Lord men become immortal.
III.7.

THAT which is beyond this world
Is without form and without ill.

They who know THAT, become immortal;
But others go only to sorrow.

III.10.

The one controller of the inactive many,
Who makes the one seed manifold—
The wise who perceive Him standing in
one's self—
They, and no others, have eternal happiness.

VI.12.

The Bṛihadāraṇyaka Upanishad has illuminating passages on the nature of immortality. King Janaka is being instructed by Yājñavalkya, who says, in the course of his discourse, that a man becomes virtuous by virtuous action, bad by bad action. Some people would say: "A person is made of desires only", to which Yājñavalkya's reply is that desire leads to resolve and resolve leads to action, and he quotes a verse:

Where one's mind is attached—the inner self
Goes thereto with action, being attached to it
alone.
Obtaining the end of his action,
Whatever he does in this world
He comes again from that world
To this world of action.

IV.12.

So much for the man who desires. But the man who is without desire, who is freed from desire, whose desire is satisfied, whose desire is the Soul, he, being very Brahman goes to Brahman. Yājñavalkya then quotes this verse:

When are liberated all
The desires that lodge in one's heart,
Then a mortal becomes immortal!
Therein he reaches Brahman.

IV.4.7.

The Upanishadic sage understood the paramount part played by desire in human life. Realizing that desire cannot be killed out but that it can be disciplined and directed to the right object, he says simply that the Soul is the right object of desire. Reaching Brahman, winning immortality, is the fruit. Yājñavalkya says immediately afterwards: "As the slough of a snake lies on an ant-hill, dead, cast off, even so lies this body. But this incorporeal, immortal Life is Brahman indeed, is light indeed."

Does incorporeal, immortal Life, which is Brahman indeed, mean the continuance of the " I-am-I " consciousness of earth life, the consciousness of individuality? Let Yājñavalkya explain. The scene is simple and touching, for Yājñavalkya, deciding that the time has come to leave the householder's life and take the next step forward, the life of the forest anchorite, is about to leave. Before leaving, he wants to make a final settlement of his worldly goods for his two wives—Maitreyī, who was advanced in sacred knowledge, and Kātyāyanī who had " just a woman's knowledge " in that matter—the Mary and Martha of that age. Maitreyī speaks:

> " If now, sir, this whole earth filled with wealth
> were mine, would I now thereby be immortal ?
>
> " No, no ! " answers Yājñavalkya. " As the life of
> the rich, even so would your life be. Of
> immortality, however, there is no hope through wealth."[1]
>
> " What should I do with that through which I
> may not be immortal ?
> What you know, sir,—that indeed explain to me."

There was no need for this heroic soul to give further proof of her spiritual quality. As always, Yājñavalkya rises to the occasion, and the tone of his discourse on Love and the Soul, on death and immortality, is on a plane with his other great discourses. But first, an expression of a great husband's love and appreciation for such a wife :

> " Though verily, you, my lady, were dear to us,
> you have increased your dearness. Behold, then,
> lady, I will explain it to you. But, while I
> am expounding, do you seek to ponder thereon ".

Then he expounds :

> " Lo, verily, not for love of the husband is a
> husband dear, but for love of the Soul (Ātman)
> is a husband dear.

[1] Cf. Mark X.25 & James II. 1-9.

> " Lo verily, not for love of the wife is a wife
> dear, but for love of the Soul is a wife dear ".

And in this strain he goes on, mentioning sons, wealth, cattle, Brāhmanhood, Kshatrahood, worlds, gods, the Vedas, beings, the All.

> " Lo verily, it is the Soul that should be seen,
> that should be hearkened to, that should be
> thought on, that should be pondered on, O Maitreyī
> Lo verily, in the Soul's being seen, hearkened to,
> thought on, understood, this world-all is known ".

Thus Yājñavalkya teaches that only by loving the Soul can one truly love husband, wife, son or anything at all; whereas in attempting to love a person or an object as something in itself instead of as a manifestation of the Soul, love is misplaced. He adds, most significantly, that everything and everyone " deserts him who knows the thing or person in aught else than the Soul ". Deathless and immortal love is possible only by the unreserved pouring of one's love on the deathless and immortal in the object of love. For if the beloved turns faithless to the lover, there is only heartbreak, ugliness and hate between the two, unless love was bestowed, not on the faithless mortal in the beloved, but on the immortal Soul in the beloved.

Yājñavalkya then proceeds to say that " everything here is what the Soul is ". He enumerates various elements out of which one arises, and then hurls this thunderbolt :

> " Arising out of these elements, into them also one
> vanishes away. After death there is no consciousness.
> Thus, lo, say I."

Maitreyī is distressed :

> " Herein, indeed you have caused me, sir, to arrive
> at the extreme of bewilderment. Verily, I
> understand not the Soul."

Then follows the exposition on immortality :

> " Lo, verily, I speak not bewilderment. Imperishable,
> lo, verily, is the Soul, and of indestructible
> quality.

"For where there is duality, as it were, there one sees another; there one smells another; there one tastes another; there one speaks to another; there one hears another; there one thinks of another; there one touches another; there one understands another. But where everything has just become one's own self, then whereby and whom would one see? Then whereby and whom would one smell? then whereby and whom would one taste? then whereby and to whom would one speak? then whereby and and whom would one hear? then whereby and of whom would one think? then whereby and whom would one touch? then whereby and whom would one understand?

"Whereby would one understand Him by means of whom one understands this All?

"That Soul is not this, is not that. It is unseizable for it cannot be seized, indestructible for it cannot be destroyed; unattachable, for it does not attach itself; is unbound, does not tremble, is not injured.

"Lo, whereby would one understand the understander?

"Thus you have the instruction told to you, Maitreyī. Such lo, indeed, is immortality".

After speaking thus, Yājñavalkya departed.

IV.5.3–15.

It is a common idea that immortality means the ceaseless continuance in time of a conscious "I", after the death of the body. This is sometimes described as living in eternity. But eternity is not just time which goes on and on into an endless future. The future has no meaning for empirical consciousness without the past; the end of time without the beginning of time. The conception, as well as the awareness of such time is directional. If attention were so concentrated that there was only awareness of a continuously transforming, but non-directional present, beginning and end, past and future, drop out of the picture. Such experience is known by the lover, the artist, the devotee, the scientist and mathematician, and by a man or woman sacrificing self for the sake of the Imperishable. Then time gives place to eternity, the ever-active, ever-present now. Process, the manifestation of Brahman, apprehended in one way produces the consciousness of time, directional and measurable; apprehended in another way, gives rise to the awareness of eternity, infinitely concentrated in the finite, and non-measurable. Time and eternity are not different from each other, being only different terms expressing man's different types of experience of reality. Time and eternity are a non-duality.

Now ordinary consciousness is a function of a mortal, finite being existing in space-time; "otherness", duality, is the essential condition for its operation. Immortality is of the Soul (Ātman), of Brahman, associable with infinitude and eternity. Immortality is not subject to formative process. In a state of finite being, that is, while a man is alive, there is consciousness but mortality. After death there is cessation of separate finite being, a cessation of "otherness", and there is immortality. Only whilst living, is it possible for some so to grow, that despite the limitations of consciousness, an awareness of Brahman is possible, and thus an awareness of the nature of immortality is possible. Here-now, one can "know" immortality by "knowing" Brahman. Consciousness is still functioning. But after death, the state of immortality supervenes, and there can be no knowing (knowing used here in its ordinary, empirical sense) of Brahman or immortality. Consciousness has disappeared.

He who, whilst living, knows That, wins immortality and experiences bliss, teach the Upanishads—"the highest bliss" says Yājñavalkya (Bṛihadāraṇyaka IV.3.32.). Man wins the experience of immortality, or an awareness of its true nature through different disciplines (suitable to different types of people) which have one factor in common: the person is brought to a state of intensely receptive and responsive consciousness, an intensely active tranquillity; a state of inward integration free of illusions, free of the turbulence of argumentative thought-processes, free of absurd and baseless fantasy, free of the tyranny of undisciplined feelings; and a state in which the desire for any particular thing or experience is absent. Then, one is ready for the holy nuptials. One "knows" the Beloved, Brahman, and the bliss of immortality is his. This bliss is a real, conscious experience, an immeasurably intense, non-sensational beatitude.

Yājñavalkya, who knew such things through experience, said, "After death, there is no consciousness", as his prelude to immortality.

It is clear, then, that the separatist "I-am-I" consciousness creates a temporary disharmony in universal being. The immortality of Brahman is "strained" by human mortality. It is man's business to win release from the strain. Brahman is in man as well as man's consciousness. Conscious man has the 'freedom' to deny, or be ignorant of Brahman. Hence the struggle, the apparent opposition of 'good' and 'evil', and the passing sorrows and joys of man's life. But when man frees his consciousness of the delusion of separate individuality, he is aware of Brahman and he is aligned with Reality. So he wins immortality and knows bliss here and now. And after death, personal consciousness, a function of the individual, is no more, even as the person is no more.

The Upanishadic thinkers could not fail to produce ethical ideas which, whilst agreeing with the highest moral code accepted by the age, also transcended the dualism of good and evil.

Three divisions are discernible: the law of the good life for a man of the world; the stricter code of the ascetic, or of the forest hermit; the law of life for the perfected or liberated man. The first lies in the sphere of society and orthodox religion; the second carries this to its highest point, and is the link between the first and third; the third is beyond good and evil. The first is in terms of obedience, the second of self-responsibility, the third of freedom.

The Chāndogya Upanishad utters this denunciation:

> The plunderer of gold, the liquor-drinker,
> The invader of the teacher's bed, the brāhman-
> killer—
> These four sink downward in the scale,
> And, fifth, he who consorts with them.
>
> V.10.9.

The prohibitions are against murder, theft, adultery, drunkenness and, significantly, against keeping evil company. In III.17.4. are extolled austerity, almsgiving, uprightness, harmlessness and truthfulness. The Bṛihadāraṇyaka Upanishad presents three cardinal virtues: self-restraint (V.2.1.), giving, or liberality (V.2.2.); and compassion, or mercy (V.2.3.) The Taittirīya Upanishad (I.9.) enumerates righteousness, truth, austerity (which in these contexts may be associated with abstemiousness, prudence, temperance, non-assertiveness, and the ordinary decencies that go with a quiet, dignified life), self-control, tranquillity, due observance of religious rites, hospitality, humanity or kindliness, considerateness towards other members of the family, 'begetting and procreating' in the text implying not neglecting to give one's wife love's happiness and fulfilment.

It is noteworthy that positive statements of virtues are more numerous than prohibitions against vice. Taken in conjunction with Aśvapati Kaikeya's appreciation of his people's goodness, quoted at the beginning of this chapter, it may be inferred that the prevalent ethical standard of the people was high. Had it been otherwise, kings would have had their hands full with punishing culprits and preserving law and order in the state, instead of having the leisure to indulge in philosophical discourses. Attendance by royalty at prescribed religious rituals is a part of state duties; but the personal pursuit of truth by royalty is a consequence of favourable conditions offering the right opportunity for natural interest.

India evolved a concept of four stages in the life of a brāhman: the student; the householder; the philosopher-hermit living in quiet seclusion devoted to the realization of truth; and the homeless saint, a wandering mendicant blessing mankind with his teachings and inspiring men with the example of the blameless, dedicated life. Deussen, in his *Philosophy of the Upanishads* (p. 367), declares that "the entire history of mankind does not produce much that approaches in grandeur to this thought".

The ethical views in the Upanishads are consonant with this conception of life. The prohibitions or exhortations of the Ṛig Veda are absolute. Heaven's lord is unquestioningly accepted as unchallengeable sovereign by man, whose redemption depends upon his coining favour with an external God. Ṛig-vedic ethic derives from divine sanction. Brahman of the Upanishads is in man. Man is growing, evolving, into the realization of himself as Brahman. Upanishadic ethic is the law of this evolution, is inherent in the psyche of man himself according to his stage of development, and is the imperative from within his being in answer to the attraction of the infinite call of the transcendent reality. Upanishadic ethic consists of leading ideas on conduct, not commands from an autocratic authority. Man is a self-responsible adult now, the framer of his own laws which he desires to fulfil (rather than obey) of his own free will.

The Bṛihadāraṇyaka Upanishad gives at least two revealing passages :

> Verily, this soul is Brahman, made of knowledge, of mind, of breath, of seeing, of hearing, of earth, of water, of wind, of ākāśa, of energy and of non-energy, of desire and of non-desire, of virtuousness and of non-virtuousness. It is made of everything. This is what is meant by the saying " made of this, made of that ".
>
> IV.4.5.

Each living body is a physico-chemical system, to use a modern phrase. The physico-chemical activity of the body, especially perhaps the activity of the ductless glands, is the source of the " drive " of the psycho-physical organism. Let this drive, which is whole and single, be described in two ways : one material, the other psychological. If " physical energy " be accepted as the material descriptive term, let " passion-energy " be the psychological term.

(Indian thought has regarded mind as " material ". The apposition is not between mind and matter, but between Spirit, Soul, Person, Absolute or Pure Consciousness on the one hand, and Manifestation, the Universe on the other ; between Purusha and Prakṛiti in the terms of the Sāṁkhya philosophy. Physical and psychical, identical at root, are, however, convenient distinguishing categories.)

Passion-energy is the person's psychical voltage so to say. The higher this voltage, the greater are the possibilities for good or ill. No question of morality is involved at this stage.

This energy emerges into consciousness. In certain cases, one is aware only of an undefined passion, a vague diffused feeling, however strong, that he would :—"like some excitement", " do something grand or heroic ", " wish something nice would happen but he doesn't know exactly what ", and so on. In other cases, depending upon the acting stimuli (external, such as the sight of a person, or internal such as the memory of a particular experience), this energy emerges into consciousness in precise, specific forms—desires.

When passion-energy manifests as a particular desire, morality is often involved. Desires range through the entire gamut of passion expressed, tread all the rungs comprising virtuousness and non-virtuousness, as Yājñavalkya might say.

In a given framework of circumstance, a person behaves in a certain way. According to an accepted standard, a qualitative description of this behaviour is given. This qualitative description is the name of a virtue or a vice. If in diverse circumstances, a particular man's behaviour is fairly consistently characterized by the performance of kind acts, then that man is justifiably said to possess the virtue of kindness. And yet, given a sufficiently provocative set of circumstances, that same man could go to the same limit of cruelty as his limit of kindness ; or, on account of an honest error in judgment, he may unwittingly slide into such extreme of cruelty. In either case his passion-energy will have swung the " wrong " way. But if that were the whole story, man is only an automaton. Not so, for his conscious will plays its part. It is far from likely that circumstances so very provocative will arise as will defeat his conscious will and induce him to perform cruel instead of kind action. In this connection, however, there arises another point, namely the corruption of the conscious will, which is a source of even greater danger than misdirected zeal. Grief and frustration, or a superior intellect which is undiscerning in certain respects, or lack of proper discipline, or some other cause, wears down moral reserves. So deeply does the poison seep into the soul, that the very core of being is diseased and on the verge of disintegration. Who in the world really understands the laceration of soul and spirit some go through ? Who but he who has himself hung over the abyss, yet by inner strength has set his feet again on the narrow pathway of right living ? But whilst one is in that bitter loneliness, distraught, the conscious will can be corrupted. Then it is possible for passion-energy to swing to the same limit of evil, unobstructed by any moral will on the man's part, as previously it swung to good. And thus, if caught in a sufficiently provocative circumstance a man can become a willing co-operator with evil as previously he was a willing co-operator with good. The extent of the swing is a measure of the power of the individual's passion-energy, of his psychical voltage.

Now the heart of ethical development lies in the understanding and control of the springs of action, namely, desire. And so Yājñavalkya says:

> As is his desire, such is his resolve ; as is his resolve, such the action he performs ; according to his action is he correspondingly changed.
>
> IV.4.5.

Between this statement and the previous one that "Man is made of everything", comes this statement :

> According as one acts, according as one conducts himself, so does he become. The doer of good becomes good. The doer of evil becomes evil. One becomes virtuous by virtuous action, bad by bad action.
>
> IV.4.5.

That desire is a main root of action, a primal dynamic power determining the pattern of man's life, is a fundamental fact which must first be grasped before any ethical code or system of morality is devised. Morality is not flouted when desire finds harmonious expression ; whereas immorality follows in the wake of the sweeping tide of evil or of frustrated desire. But in order to release harmonious expression and avert the catastrophe of frustration, the understanding of desire and of the circumstance, together with the subsequent control, shaping and directing of desire, are all necessary.

In the Upanishadic ethic, the whole moral life was related to the fact of desire as it is as well as desire transcended ; and the flowering of the moral life was the attainment of freedom from bondage to desire.

That the ancient sages understood that desire could not be extirpated but should be rightly directed, and thereafter satisfied, is indicated in various statements:

Muṇḍaka Upanishad:

> What That (Brahman) is, know as Being and
> Non-Being,
> As the object of desire . . .
>
> II.2.1.

> He who in fancy forms desires
> Because of his desires is born (again) here and there.
> But of him whose desire is satisfied (in Brahman
> as the object of desire), who is a perfected soul,
> All (other) desires (whilst living) even here on earth
> vanish away.
>
> III.2.2.

Bṛihadāraṇyaka Upanishad:

> He who is freed from desire, whose desire is
> satisfied, whose desire is the Soul . . .
> Being very Brahman, he goes to Brahman.
>
> IV.4.6.

In that single section of three short paragraphs in IV.4.5. of the Bṛihadāraṇyaka Upanishad, Yājñavalkya presents a philosophy of ethics based on psychological insight. Psychology in the Upanishads is inferential and implicit, and not a systematic exposition. Scientific psychology is conspicuous by its absence, whereas psychological insight, by contrast, is profound. The transcendental philosophy of the Upanishads could never have emerged unless there was sufficient psychological insight, for man knows God only to the extent he knows himself, and the Immanent is a revelation of the Transcendent only to the extent man perceives the revelation.

The ethical practice of the first stage as a good family man and citizen is the preliminary to the second stage. Having developed the power to discriminate between wrong and right in the social context, to avoid wrongdoing and strive after right doing in the world of affairs, the next step is to make the good and true more powerfully operative, to enrich its content, to deepen its significance. The central feature of the new ethic is the control of desire, the spring of human resolve, planning and action.

The Chāndogya Upanishad says that " in the real city of Brahman, desires are contained. That (the real city) is the Soul, free from evil, ageless, deathless, sorrowless, hungerless, thirstless, whose desire is the Real, whose conception is the Real " (VIII.1.5). The next section, VIII.2., enumerates desires, and VIII.3.1. states " These same are real desires (or true desires, satya kāma) with a covering of what is false. Although they are real, there is a covering that is false ". The ultimate desire is really the dynamic driving power which restores the non-duality between man and Brahman. It is the power working for the removal of ignorance on the part of the separative " I-am-I "-consciousness of the fact that Brahman is the All (or that " I am Brahman "). This power, operating in the objective world of variety and diversity, is consciously apprehended by man in various forms, all of which hide (or cover) the true nature of the fundamental drive. All the different desires man has, are part of these forms. So also are his perceptions and observations, which, like his desires, are bound up with the senses. Desiring and perceiving are related functions of one living complex.

Desires themselves may be classed broadly as true and untrue desires, the latter involving unethical action such as desiring another's property or life. True desires, such as desiring to help neighbours, heal the sick, enlighten the ignorant, serve God and country, need not involve unethical action. But they are only the one ultimate desire—the desire for Brahman, the Beloved—in charming garbs. Howsoever charming, these coverings nevertheless hide the reality.

At this point enter the conscious control of the senses and the deliberate sacrifice of all the different desires which influence man. The Muṇḍaka Upanishad says:

> That subtile Soul is to be known by thought
> Wherein the senses fivefoldly have entered.
> The whole of men's thinking is interwoven with
>   the senses.
> When that is purified, the Soul shines forth.

> Whatever world a man of purified nature makes
> clear in mind,
> And whatever desires he desires for himself—
> That world he wins, those desires too.
> Therefore he who is desirous of welfare should
> praise the knower of the Soul.
>
> III.1.9 & 10.

The pursuit of all objects of sense is relinquished. A strict self-discipline is imposed. Constant vigilance and an alert mind are necessary. Continence in every respect, not only sexually, is observed, for intelligent continence is essential for launching that concentrated, skilful effort which will win the prize. Continence means the conservation of energy, physical and mental, which otherwise is dissipated like a stream in a desert. Self-denial means the deliberate turning aside of all that perpetuates the delusion of separateness from Brahman. A dietetic discipline too is necessary. The Chāndogya Upanishad says:

> "In pure nourishment there is a pure nature . . .
> (leading to) release from all the knots of
> the heart".
>
> VII.26.2.

The dietetic discipline may go even to the extent of fasting (but not starving: fasting is scientifically regulated abstinence from food to an extent which promotes health; starving is the unscientific deprivation of food to an extent which produces decrepitude, disease and death).

All this is the greater austerity. Through such concentrated discipline, self-less-ness is gradually attained, the highlight of the ethic of this second stage. The Maitri Upanishad says:

> Because of selflessness, one becomes a non-
> experiencer of pleasure and pain.
>
> VI.21.

True selflessness is effortlessly maintained when one is unattached to, and stands balanced in, pleasure and pain, the ephemeral consequences of life's activities. He who is effortlessly master of pleasure and pain has mastered desire, and is free from thraldom to desire. The Real Desire—the desire for Brahman—is fulfilled.

And then?

The Muṇḍaka Upanishad says:

1. He knows that Supreme Brahman-abode,
Founded on which the whole world shines radiantly.
They who, being without desire, worship the Person
And are wise, pass beyond the seed of rebirth here.

4. This Soul is not to be obtained by one destitute of fortitude,
Nor through heedlessness, nor through a false notion of austerity.
But he who strives by these means, provided he knows—
Into his Brahman-abode this Soul enters.

5. Attaining Him, the seers who are satisfied with knowledge,
Who are perfected souls, from passion free, tranquil—
Attaining Him who is universally omnipresent, those wise,
Devout souls into the All itself do enter.

6. They who have ascertained the meaning of the Vedānta-knowledge,
Ascetics with nature purified through the application of renunciation—
They in the Brahman worlds at the end of time
Are all liberated beyond death.

III.2.

The Taittirīya:

Wherefrom words turn back,
Together with the mind, not having attained—
the bliss of Brahman he who knows,
Fears not from anything at all.

Such a one, verily, the thought does not torment:
"Why have I not done the good? Why have I

> done the evil ?" He who knows this, delivers himself from these two (thoughts). For truly, from both of these he delivers himself—he who knows this !

Such is the mystic doctrine.

II.9.

The Chāndogya :

> Those who go hence without here having found the Soul and those real (true) desires—for them in all the worlds there is no freedom. But those who go hence having found here the Soul and those real desires—for them in all worlds there is freedom.
>
> VIII.1.6

The Bṛihadāraṇyaka :

> He (the Soul) does not become greater by good action or inferior by bad action.
>
> On knowing him (the Soul), in truth, one becomes an ascetic. Desiring him only as their home, mendicants wander forth.
>
> Verily, because they know this, the ancients desired not offspring, saying : " What shall we do with offspring, we whose is this Soul, this world ?" They, verily, rising above the desire for sons and the desire for wealth and the desire for worlds, lived the life of a mendicant. For the desire for sons is the desire for wealth, and the desire for wealth is the desire for worlds ; for both these are desires.
>
> That Soul is not this, it is not that. It is unseizable, for it cannot be seized. It is indestructible, for it cannot be destroyed. It is unattached, for it does not attach itself. It is unbound. It does not tremble. It is not injured.
>
> Him (who knows this) these two do not overcome neither the thought " Hence I did wrong ", nor the thought " Hence I did right ". Verily, he overcomes them both. What he had done and what he has not done do not affect him.

This very (doctrine) has been declared in the verse :—

This eternal greatness of a brāhman
Is not increased by deeds, nor diminished.
One should be familiar with it. By knowing it,
One is not stained by evil action.

Therefore, having this knowledge, having become calm, subdued, quiet, patiently enduring, and collected, one sees the Soul just in the soul. One sees everything as the Soul. Evil does not overcome him ; he overcomes all evil. Evil does not burn him ; he burns all evil. Free from evil, free from impurity, free from doubt, he becomes a brāhman.
This is the Brahman-world, O king (Janaka), said Yājñavalkya.

IV.4.22 & 23.

With the transcending of desire, and with the realization of the Ātman, man transcends good and evil. This crowning ethic, characterizing the liberated man, means that the very morality of the earlier stages is observed in the highest degree. But more significant is the fact that the morality of the liberated has a sure foundation to it, and involves a different psychology. Ordinary man strives to act morally in order to win freedom. Success and failure, joy and sorrow, right and wrong, hold him in their grasp. Liberated man acts effortlessly. He is a creator. Looking at his creation, he sees, like God, that it is good. There is no problem of success and failure, joy and sorrow, right and wrong, involved in his action. The standard of ordinary morality has the limitation as well as the inspiration of man's duality—his strength and weakness, wisdom and folly, ability and incompetence, and above all, what he considers desirable and worthy, and undesirable and unworthy. The liberated man has transcended this duality. Ordinary man achieves a goal and finds satisfaction in moral victory. Liberated man, through his inevitably moral action, is free of the vanity of achievement, victory and satisfaction. Not achievement but being, not victory but naturalness, not satisfaction but bliss, characterize this transcendent ethic. It is beyond man's good and evil because it has grown out of the world of the relative into the world of the absolute. It is the difference between science and omniscience, between the young Beethoven proving his mastery in musical creation and the liberated genius revealing transcendent Beauty in the last quartets. Like the old Beethoven, liberated man is law unto himself, without disturbing Law, is the creator of his own forms of expression (his actions) without reducing the old order to chaos.

Liberated man is free from pursuing security, love, happiness, well-being and success, the objectives of ordinary man. When an unseasonable frost blights the crop, it is evil, and when the sun shines on picnic day, it is good, for ordinary man. When his employer dismisses a young man from a good post, it is evil, and when the queen of his heart answers yes to his question, it is good, for ordinary man. But blight and devastation, pain and injustice, folly and crime, are not evil, and plenty and peace, health and equity, good sense and construction, are not good, for the liberated man. They all ARE. He accepts the whole, without personal reaction, which would only make confusion worse confounded since personal reaction introduces all personal limitations. In whole acceptance is holiness. But action must go on. So the holy, liberated man, acts impersonally, without desire, without seeking any fruit of action. He is the instrument of Universal Process—and who shall presume to criticize Universal Process ? — and his action is whole action, not mere re-action. It is beyond good and evil. How significant it is that in the Upanishads, it is stated again and again[1] that the liberated man has crossed beyond sin, that evil falls away from him.

For the liberated man, rights and privileges, duties and responsibilities all disappear. All petty busy-ness ceases. Instead, life is filled with creative thought and action, emanating as the simple and natural expression in Beauty of the ineffable consciousness of the Eternal. An intense, ever-active life which is the very soul of goodness, truth and love.

The discipline of the whole personality, the mastery of desire, the transcending of the limitations of the " I-am-I " consciousness

[1] Bṛihadāraṇyaka IV.3.22; IV.4.23; V.14.8; Taittirīya II.5 & 9; Kena 34 (=IV.9); Muṇḍaka III.2.9; Praśna V.5; Maitri VI.18; Chāndogya I.2.8; IV.14.3; etc.

of narrow individuality, so transform the whole nature of man, that he knows blissful eternity in every moment. Complete self-renunciation spells the realization of absolute freedom, the inmost core of man's spiritual being.

* * *

The Upaniṣhads do not present, or even attempt to present, a complete system of thought. In fact there were sufficient contradictions in them to give rise to philosophies as divergent as the Sāṁkhya and the Vedānta. They do not formulate any universal Law of causation, nor do they explain how the universe came out of Brahman, apart from asserting that Brahman created the universe and entered it as Soul (Ātman), nor do they revolt whole-heartedly against the old established polytheism and sacrificial rites, against the rigours of the caste system, but accommodate themselves very far, to their own detriment, to the lesser conceptions. The Greater Upanishads do not develop the doctrines of karma and transmigration much beyond the stage they had reached in the Brāhmaṇas.

The Upanishads exercised a paramount influence over the subsequent development of Indian religious thought. A religious system cannot be based on a Brahman-Ātman concept which altogether transcends religious orthodoxy. The supreme object of orthodox worship has to be something over and against man and the world. Now the monotheism emerging in the later Upanishads did not develop out of Vedic polytheism, in which the gods are " devas ". The personal god of the Upanishads is usually referred to as Īś, Īśa, Īśāna, Īśvara, meaning the Lord, and later on as parameśvara, the Supreme Lord. The individual Soul is regarded as the shadow of this Supreme Soul.

The Kaṭha Upanishad says:

> There are two that drink of righteousness in the world of good deeds;
> Both are entered into the secret place (of the heart), and in the highest upper sphere.
> Brahman-knowers speak of them as ' light ' and ' shade ',

And so do householders who maintain the five
sacrificial fires and those too who perform
the triple Naciketas-fire.
III.1.

This Soul (Ātman) is not to be obtained by
instruction,
Nor by intellect, nor by much learning.
He is to be obtained only by the one whom
he chooses;
To such a one that Soul (Ātman) reveals his
own person.
II.23.

The Śvetāśvatara:

That which is joined together as perishable
and imperishable,
As manifest and unmanifest—the Lord (īśa)
supports it all.
Now, without the Lord the soul (Ātman) is
bound, because of being an enjoyer;
By knowing God (deva) one is released from
all fetters.
I.8.

There are two unborn ones: the knowing (Lord)
and the unknowing (individual soul), the
Omnipotent and the impotent.
I.9.

On the self-same tree a person, sunken,
Grieves for his impotence, deluded;
When he sees the other, the Lord (īś), contented,
and his greatness, he becomes freed from sorrow.
IV.7.

The Śvetāśvatara Upanishad is not, however, solely theistic, pantheistic conceptions being placed side by side with theistic, as also idealistic conceptions which regard only the Ātman as real, all else being unreal. The above quotations shew, nevertheless, that the concept of the Lord originates in the Upanishads.

To a critical mind the Upanishads are not a tidy garden. But if this critical mind is wisely sympathetic, æsthetically sensitive and truly discerning, some of the rarest blossoms of the human mind and spirit can be culled from this same garden.

Chapter IV

THE BUDDHA AND HIS TEACHINGS

"Dwell ye therefore with Self for island, with Self for refuge, with no other refuge; with Dhamma for island, with Dhamma for refuge, with no other refuge."

D.II.100.

"Whatever is liable to uprising, all that is liable to stopping."

"Come now, Bhikkhus, I exhort you, saying: Strive on with diligence."

Mahā-Parinibbāna Sutta
D.II.120.

"From the time, Kassapa, that a Bhikkhu has developed a mind of loving-kindness that is without enmity, without ill-will, and when, by the destruction of the cankers (āsavas), having realized here-now the freedom of mind, the freedom through wisdom that is without the āsavas (sensuality, longing for life, speculation and ignorance), entering in them (the states of loving-kindness and freedom) he abides in them—it is then, Kassapa, that this Bhikkhu is called a samaṇa, is called a brāhmaṇa."

Kassapa-Sīhanāda Sutta
D.I.170.

Chapter IV

THE BUDDHA AND HIS TEACHINGS

The land of marvels can claim uniqueness without immodesty: the Hindu social organization, called caste by the self-invited Portuguese guests of the early fifteenth century of the Christian era, unparalleled in world history, both for its excellences and its defects; the ancient self-contained village polity embodying principles anticipating modern democracy; the rise of a religion, Hinduism, without a personal founder, but emerging as the socio-political order became invested with religious sanctions, to which were added mystical, philosophical and religious ideas, and religious rituals; the rise of Vedic speculation and Upanishadic philosophy, and of that most significant teaching that the mind and spirit of man, through inherent strength and courage and steady self-discipline, can achieve complete emancipation; and last, but not least, a positive tolerance and honest appreciation of other and new philosophies and cults, and an earnest, high-minded search for the Truth wheresoever it may be found.

Then came the Buddha and the rise of Buddhism.

And other evidence of uniqueness followed the age of the Buddha: Aśoka Maurya, the only successful philosopher-king (king on a large scale, for he ruled the largest Indian Empire of all the different Indian Empires); the absorption of, and healthy re-emergence from the shocks of many foreign conquests and cultures, especially of Islam and Christianity, because of the unusual character of the Hindu social system, and of the absorbing and transforming power of Hinduism; the formulation and practical use of a technique of non-violence and soul-force to attain political freedom. The evidence needs no further piling.

Of the peaks in this range of uniqueness, the austere mount

scaled by the Buddha stands prominent. An original thinker, the Buddha founded a world-religion, characterized, surprisingly, by the absence of God, soul and survival, fundamental articles of faith of all the other great religions. Nevertheless, his teaching is religion in the real sense of the word.

Over and above a natural urge to discover the truth, an ineluctable passion to solve the problem of Ill as he saw it and to bring deliverance to mankind—this was the primary inspiration animating the Buddha.

Valuable clues for understanding him, his life and his teachings, are afforded by his extraordinary reaction to the discovery of the suffering of those around him, and by his evaluation of the speculative and religious thought and practice of his day.

The legendary or popular account of his life need not be accepted at face value. Though the symbolism in it is instructive, the exaggerations ill become one of the greatest figures in all history. Certain reasonable assumptions concerning the probable actual course of his life may be made, stripping the popular account of its fancies.

Siddhattha Gotama, the son of Suddhodana, a chieftain of the Sakya clan, was born at Kapilavastu on the southern border of Nepal, approximately in 563 B.C. His mother died seven days after his birth. An aged hermit, Asita, felt inspired to prophesy that he would become either a great king or a great spiritual teacher.

Practical Suddhodana naturally wished his darling would follow in his footsteps, maintain the traditions of his ancestors and rule worthily. He did not turn a deaf ear to Asita's prophecy. With paternal solicitude, as well as the usual over-indulgence of an elderly father for a long desired child, he surrounded young Siddhattha with all possible happiness, and did much to prevent him from living a natural, normal life. Especially was the boy guarded from coming to know pain or sorrow. The father wished to eliminate the possibility of any experience which might induce his son to think deeply.

In fact, however, Siddhattha must have known the pain of at least some physical sickness: fever, cold, stomach-ache, measles, mumps, and all the other ailments of childhood offer rich variety.

He must have known boredom, fits of temper, rebellion against external control when he wanted to do something naughty. It is healthy to be naughty! It is difficult to believe he never experienced some sort of punishment, or escaped the inward misery of feeling he was unfairly or unkindly treated sometimes. In short, he must have gone through a boy's life, set in a background which was somewhat unusual.

Not improbably he was surrounded by women, perhaps quite young women. On reaching puberty, his foster-mother who was also his aunt, or some other woman, or more likely a male instructor, or, most likely some boy friend, may have given him information regarding the sex functions. He was married quite young to princess Yasodharā, and their only child, the boy Rāhula, was born some thirteen years later. A strange coincidence that his son was born so many years after his marriage, just as he himself was born when his own mother and father were ageing!

Siddhattha must have been an unusually sensitive child. It is not difficult to picture him growing up into a hypersensitive young man, experiencing deep inner loneliness, torn with doubts, perchance mistrusting the world around him. It is incredible that he never witnessed, as the legend suggests, other people's pain and suffering until after the first two and a half decades of his life! Under the circumstances he must have been the victim of bitter conflicts. Unresolved discords must have blocked his soul in his later teens and twenties. He was ripe for extremist behaviour.

It is said he was altogether happy with his wife. Impossible. No man who really knows love's happiness can move, or be moved to become a fervent seeker of the solution of human misery, leave alone attain the supreme exaltation of Buddhahood. A hyper-sensitive, or even sensitive young man was sure to have known many an upheaval in his sex life: ardent longings unfulfilled, anticipations and hopes blighted in part, unsatisfactory sex relations at times, and at other times—bliss. The background of the heir-apparent's life was such that a surfeit of delight was his to command, and the loveliest damsel could be his for a mere glance. And then the natural difficulty with

Yasodharā in consequence! If a woman knows she is not the one and only temple of a man's total love, holiness and bliss have gone out of sexual love. Her chamber of delight tends to close the doors against the man. And then? Rending violence in the depths of the soul, ready to surge out in disruptive action when the appropriate external conditions are presented.

It must be accounted the world's supreme good fortune that in all likelihood this was the case. No good can come to fruition without the creative stress of conflict with evil. God is god only by virtue of the Devil, and the Devil is devil only by the unmeasured wisdom and grace of God. The more devilish the Devil the more godlike is God. His Glory shines all the more refulgent the blacker be the reflecting object, the Devil. Man, in his empirical life, experiences the objective blackness reflecting the Truth; if he has grown wise, he closes his eyes and sees, by inward Reason, by spiritual insight, the ineffable Light and Glory of Reality.

In the Buddha and his teachings, the light is apparent. The darkness must be deduced. And in Siddhattha's case, this darkness must have been wonderful and deep beyond compare. For unquestionably Siddhattha was exceptionally gifted. The conditions of his times were favourable for the emergence of a Buddha. The rest was a question of what Siddhattha himself would achieve.

The storm precipitated itself. Siddhattha did come to know of the misery and suffering of his fellow human beings. Simultaneously, all his own pent-up conflicts burst out. Where in hell were the gods, and what were they about that such suffering should be? What use was the ceremonial mummery of fat, sleek priests? Life as it was, for him, for mankind, was unendurable. All the majesty of his soul rose in might to the occasion. Strength and courage, fear and horror, compassion for man and resentment against life, against impotent gods and preposterous priests, all over-flowed in a torrential flood. It was war. Heaven and hell were ranged in grim conflict. His, Siddhattha's, was the dread responsibility for establishing Peace, effortless, self-sustaining, healing Peace, not the rigid, artificial stillness between two deadly wars.

In immemorially correct manner he first retreated; and retreated and retreated, shedding all supports, liabilities in the end, till at the edge of the world be met and found the truth in himself. Alone, he overcame Māra the Evil One, the Prince of Death, and won the last battle. He had become the Buddha, the Enlightened One. Humanity had gained a Great Exemplar. Nearly six centuries later, in Palestine, humanity gained another Great Exemplar.

At the age of twenty-nine, soon after Rāhula's birth (a time when a new mother tends to be wholly wrapped up in the magic she has done and so be incapable of normal attention to her husband), Siddhattha Gotama left wife and child and home, and went away into the forest in search of the solution of the problem of suffering. The orthodox account styles this the Great Renunciation. The cynical may call it the Great Flight. The foolish may say that the unbalanced young man shirked his duties to his family, his responsibilities as heir to the chieftaincy, and was guilty of thoughtless cruelty to his wife. In fairness, his action was not improper. It was the accepted canon of the age that whoso sincerely sought the Truth, whoso desired spiritual salvation in earnest, was entitled to renounce the world and follow his inner urge. Yasodharā was not left unprovided. Siddhattha wanted to kiss his child goodbye before he went out into the night. But seeing him asleep with his mother, and fearing that if Yasodharā awoke his resolve would be shaken, he left without a farewell kiss. And Yasodharā awoke next morning to loneliness, and grief! And what grief must Siddhattha have felt!

Gotama first went to Rājagriha the capital of Magadha, ruled by powerful king Bimbisāra; and thence to nearby caves where under Āḷāra, and next under Uddaka, both brāhmans, he learned what they had to teach. But he who was seeking "the unexcelled highest path to peace", the "unoriginated, Nirvāṇa", left them, dissatisfied, and retired to the woods near Uruvelā. There he practised the extreme of self-mortification and penance, widely believed to be the means for receiving illumination. He nearly perished. This experience taught him the futility of extreme mortification, as his experience of worldly life had already taught him the vanity of pleasure. He gave up his severe discipline, which had attracted five other ascetics. He took to a more balanced mode of life, which the ascetics disapproved.

Alone, he sought deliverance within himself. One night, at the end of the third watch as the legend says, enlightenment came. He understood the cause of suffering, and saw what was the path which brought suffering to an end, to so complete an end that the unchanging bliss of Nirvāṇa was realized.

What did Gotama do when he was alone? He had already learned what others taught, and had practised penance. He had undergone intellectual discipline, and physical discipline whose keynote was forcible repression with extreme severity. The former does not necessarily mean the growth of deep understanding, though it may train intellect, a necessary step. The latter spells no moral advance or development of character, though it may train the will and subjugate the body, also necessary. But through reflection in loneliness, the underlying desires motivating action, and the effects of such desire and action upon oneself and upon others around one, are clearly seen. Thus one of the main bases for moral discipline, as well as the method of such discipline, is discovered. Further, reflection spells the growth of discrimination between the true and the false, of logic, and of sound judgment.

True evaluation, and clear perception of animating motives are essential for self-chosen and self-imposed discipline, externally imposed discipline having little value by comparison. Self-discipline brings order into life, releases inner harmony, teaches one how to apply knowledge correctly, and makes one wise. Through self-discipline man grows in psychological insight, indispensable for understanding and loving others, and in spiritual insight, indispensable for realizing (not merely perceiving) Truth. Self-discipline effects that transformation of the mind and heart which prepares man for the experience of enlightenment.

A man who is "told the Truth" may believe he knows the Truth. This is but the shadow of knowledge. But when a man immediately recognizes the truth of what he is told or shewn, because it is part of his personal experience, he knows the truth. This is real knowledge. Having real knowledge of the truth is thus in quite a different category of experience from having information about the truth. The expectant adolescent knows love is wonderful; the fulfilled adult KNOWS love is wonderful. But even real knowledge of the truth is still in the realm of knowledge. Realization of Truth is the culminating point through a different kind of experience.

Just as in all conscious experience, awareness of what is happening is slight or great as the case may be, so in ordinary thinking, awareness is not profound. By concentrating attention, as taught in Indian systems of meditation, awareness becomes greater and greater with increasing intensity of concentration. When consciousness functions with utmost intensity, it is, as it were, concentrated into a glowing point, and at that moment he who meditates attains complete awareness of the truth of the subject of meditation. The "problem" is "solved", the "matter in hand" has "yielded up its secret"; and the experience is one of knowing the truth by "becoming" the truth. The identification of oneself with the essence of the "other" thing is as complete as it can ever be. An intellectual nuptial has been consummated! This is realization of Truth. It is sudden illumination.

Again, through intense ego-centred feeling-reaction to life, thought, especially introspective thought, is stimulated to the highest degree. This, too, is conducive to the functioning of consciousness at deeper and deeper levels. In the ecstasy of happiness, in the unendurable limit of pain, and in the event of total reaction, a sort of "all-out" response to an external stimulus, sudden realization comes like a flash of lightning, stands still a moment or so, and vanishes. Slowly, the mind reconstructs the flash. If successful, the revelation of the Truth could be embodied in a suitable intellectual frame.

Lastly, he who has grown to an extent sufficient to recognize the event when it occurs, when at ease in himself, relaxed, open to influence either rising up from within or affecting him from without, suddenly becomes intensely aware of what he already knew. But this awareness is so full in content, so illuminating that there is a realization of Truth, such that both the world-outlook and the personal relationship to the everyday environment is utterly changed, and there is no difficulty in living the new kind of life because of the change. This experience comes to many human beings some time or other in their lives. " Conversion " is one of its manifestations.

Bliss is experienced in all these cases. Bliss is ultimate intensity of consciousness. That is why pain and pleasure equally end in the spaceless and timeless depth of bliss. The supreme pain is martyrdom, culminating in bliss before extinction ; often so long before extinction, that the " joyous " martyr is literally unconscious of his pain as he " sings the praises of the Lord." The supreme pleasure is love's consummation in sexual union, culminating in the blissful awareness of non-duality as the ultimate truth of human inter-relationship, spiritual, mental and physical.

Bliss is associated with Nirvāṇa. The consciousness of Nirvāṇa is here-now, not hereafter and beyond, because in truth, eternity is embodied in the unmeasured, but totally experienced, immediate present. Nirvāṇic consciousness is temporarily experienced by many, throughout the ages. But consciousness does not function permanently at that level, or depth, except perhaps in the case of a Buddha or a Christ. Nirvāṇic consciousness may be blissfully experienced for months, and then it may disappear. It may again be won, and again lost. But living continuously in Nirvāṇa as one's natural abode is not an impossibility, as the Buddha taught, if man first establishes himself on a foundation of strength and poise through self-discipline.

The landmarks of the process leading to the Buddha's Enlightenment and Nirvāṇa can now be pictured ; the conditions in boyhood and adolescence ; the experience of frustration and sorrow, as well as worldly success and happiness ; the " divine discontent " ; the innate possibilities ; the withdrawal from the everyday world ; the study and self-mortification, and the dissatisfaction therewith ; the new approach of searching within oneself for the truth, and self-discipline ; the final battle and conquest ; enlightenment and the bliss of freedom.

It is said that on the final night of deliverance, Gotama experienced the last great battle, won his victory, and suddenly understood the cause of suffering and how it may be ended. In all likelihood, nothing happened suddenly. Through the long years of search, Gotama gradually came to understand all that he embodied in his teaching. The battle of the night of deliverance was an oft repeated ancient battle taking place for the last time and which disappeared for ever from Gotama's life after that fateful night. His victory, unlike the little victories of lesser personages, was final.

Gotama retreated into the jungle near Uruvelā, just as One Other in later centuries retired into the wilderness, and looked within himself and practised self-discipline, just as that Other One prayed and fasted. The wilderness, the jungle, is man's own mind and heart. How untidy, how wild, how rank, how poisonous, how full of deadly conflict between plant and plant, insect and insect, animal and animal is the jungle! Man's instincts, passions, thoughts and feelings, constitute the teeming life of this jungle, or the dreariness of the wilderness: good and bad, lesser and greater, stronger and weaker, blindly struggle with each other, without sense, without meaning, yet somehow, unconsciously, by wild trial and error, they try to produce order and reveal significance. How constantly man murders, thieves, destroys; is envious, jealous, malicious; sustains, nurtures, creates; is generous, kind and sacrificing in his daily psychical life! His soul is the battleground of all the opposites, of right and wrong. He is God and Devil embodied. So man fasts and prays, that is, refuses nourishment to evil states of mind and heart, practises self-discipline and looks within. The plants are pruned, the wild beasts are tamed, the stocks are improved; the evil is transformed into the good. The jungle becomes a garden; in the wilderness bloom the flowers of Love, of Wisdom, of Peace.

Man prepares himself. But egoism is there; the natural urges are there because the living organism never loses its organic characteristics; the possibility of wrong judgment, of faint-heartedness, of turn-tail flight, of succumbing to temptation is all there. This battle was fought again and again yesterday, and it will be repeated again and again to-morrow till there is a final battle.

Real knowledge has been gained; discipline has given strength. The powers are arrayed. The evening, red and beautiful, fades into a deathly still night. And the battle starts.

"I know the Truth; I know the path of Righteousness; I am one with God. I want you to know my truth, tread my path, be united with my God." Thus does Māra, the Evil One, Satan, present the first temptation—that of Sovereignty, or Power or ego-assertion. (How easily Satan can ride his docile donkey, the missionary!) Satan is egoism, individuality asserting separateness from the All, finite power aspiring to equality with infinite Might. Māra is Ahaṁkāra, "I-am-ness". Man, functioning in space-time as if separate from the Eternal, is himself Māra or Satan.

In the earlier battles, the first temptation ends with man bruising himself against the facts of life. No one listens to him or wants to enter his heaven and worship his god (himself by identification—tragic delusion). In the last battle, the first temptation ends because there is clear perception that Sovereignty of the world is the wrong way. Service, and living the Truth, is the better way. Truth is not hidden by him who knows from him who seeks salvation. But the Truth is not to be, indeed can not be, published by oppressive force. Nor must man even be persuaded to drink of MY living waters, for that will deprive him of THE Truth since he imbibes only my Truth. But he who comes of his own sweet will hungering and thirsting for Truth can be freely offered all that he can take, for such food and drink will be healthfully converted in his own spiritual body.

In the earlier battles the end of the first temptation sees man in despair and bitterness, frustrated, while the mocking laughter of Māra echoes down the alleys of the soul. Most bitter is the discovery of the incredible folly of believing that to succumb to the temptation of sovereignty would bring success at the price of selling one's soul to the devil. Whether man succumbs or succeeds, sovereignty over this world is a chimaera. If he succumbs, sovereignty is snatched away. His true triumph consists in having nothing to do with sovereignty.

Māra stands in front enticing man with the first temptation. Sovereignty or Power is concerned with the conscious ego. To conjure up the second temptation, Māra runs behind—the conscious I-am sinks out of prominence—and he places one hand on the back of man's head with his thumb on the nape of the neck, and the other on his secret places, and starts up the magic of organic life, life-energy from the hidden depths coursing through the channels of sense delight. The frustrated, despairing and bitter one gives way because he has knowledge, knowledge which tells him that in the context of the Absolute there is no constraining moral code. Moreover, after death there is no consciousness. Therefore, let self-conscious man enjoy here and now. No one need be wronged; and it is possible quietly to enjoy the delights of sense. Since what was imagined as the true vocation in life—to lead man by the scruff of the neck to heaven—was denied, there is nothing which makes life worthwhile. Only now, here, is the chance of sensual happiness—only now, here. Such is the temptation. But if he succumbs, Māra snatches away all his delights, plunges him into another set of circumstances where he is isolated from "happiness", turns his partner into a faithless deceiver, deprives him of limb or faculty, sanity or life.

But he who is fighting the battle for the last time is safely established on the rock of self-discipline. He cannot be put in thrall by the senses; he uses them. Blind life-energy cannot sweep him away; he knows how to hold the flood, and taking advantage of the high tide, to steer himself clear of the rocks of sense-objects and entanglements, on to the peaceful shore of holy living. He wins the final victory.

I am Māra, Satan. Brahman, God, also am I. To-night, after final victory, there will be no more "I". The agelong conflict will be over, all delusions of ego destroyed, and the dualism of God and Devil will be transcended in the realization of the Imperishable. Nirvāṇa, the kingdom of Heaven, is here-now. Man liberated is the Buddha, is the Christ.

The demons and devils of hell are no other than the pricks of conscience and the unresolved conflicts in man's soul, tormenting him all the more cruelly the deeper they have been thrust into the subconscious.

The angels of heaven are no other than the inspiration, strength, wisdom and constructive faculties of the soul, born of the self-discipline practised in thought, speech and action—Milton's Thrones, Dominations, Princedoms, Virtues, Powers, in " Paradise Lost ".

The discipline of looking within is a searching exploration of the whole psyche. No tendency, predisposition or conformation, no cause, influence or power, is destroyed; no tangled knot is cut, no unhealthy growth is knifed out. Everything is transformed, for everything is a particular pattern of the eternal that-which-is. The pattern is made beautiful.

Gotama had done all this through the anxious years. That it was still possible for him to be tempted was due to the fact that organic existence itself is impossible without the different organs and senses which have their own proper activity. There is always a final residue of tendencies and predispositions associated with these organs whilst the body is alive. If discipline has flowered in true control, freedom from illusions and delusions, and understanding, the final battle must end in final victory, and the realization of Truth must attend that final Illumination which is Enlightenment and Nirvāṇa. So it was with Gotama, who became the Buddha.

The Buddha's teachings emerged out of his own life and attainment. They are based on his own concrete experience and judgment, study and analysis, observation and inference, personal discipline and ultimate fulfilment. This, and not the blind acceptance of external authority, is what he would have for every man: the knowledge born of personal realization, which is real faith. So he declares:

> " Now look you, Kāḷāmas. Do not be misled by report, tradition or hearsay. Do not be misled by proficiency in the Piṭakas (the baskets of Sayings on Discipline and the Dhamma), nor by mere logic and inference, nor after considering reasons, nor after reflection on some view and approval of it, nor because it fits becoming, nor because the recluse (who holds it) is your teacher. But when you know for yourselves: These things are not good, these things are faulty, these things are censured by the intelligent, these things, when performed and undertaken, conduce to loss and sorrow—then do you reject them . . . "

". . . but if you yourselves understand that this is so, good and blameless, and when accepted, is for benefit and happiness, then you may accept it."

Anguttara Nikāya
I.189 and 190.

The Buddha had, and taught, the scientific approach. Free from bias and preconception, man must observe with an open mind. Only when " you know for yourselves " should there be rejection of what is discovered to be faulty, acceptance of what is right and good. Man must accept personal responsibility for his beliefs. Liberation is the consequence of individual realization only. In the Buddha's last hours, Ānanda, the faithful, loving disciple, says :

". . . yet notwithstanding I took some little comfort from the thought that the Exalted One would not pass away until at least he had left instructions concerning the Sangha (the Order of Bhikkhus, or monks)."

The Buddha :

"What, then, Ānanda ? Does the Order expect that of me ? I have preached the Dhamma without making any distinction between exoteric and esoteric doctrine ; for in respect of the dhammā,[1] Ānanda, the Tathāgata (he who has found the Truth) has no such thing as the closed fist of a teacher who keeps something back . . .

"Therefore, O Ānanda, dwell ye with the Self for island, with Self for refuge, with no other refuge, with Dhamma for island, with Dhamma for refuge, with no other refuge . . .

"And whosoever, Ānanda, either now or after I am dead, shall dwell with Self for island, Self for refuge, and no other refuge, with Dhamma for island, Dhamma for refuge and no other refuge—these Bhikkhus of mine—those who are willing to train—will be at the topmost height."

Mahāparinibbāna Sutta
D.II.99–101.

[1] Dhamma, singular, may be translated as Truth, Law, Doctrine.
Dhammā, plural, has many meanings : things, phenomena ; mental objects or ideas ; principles of action or procedure ; principles and techniques for mental development or training ; etc.
See also, under dhammā, in *The Pāli Text Society's Pāli-English dictionary*, edited by T. W. Rhys-Davids, F.B.A., D.Sc., Ph.D., LL.D., D.Litt, and William Stede, Ph.D. published by the Pāli Text Society.

The truth is for all. Each man can reach the topmost height. But he must be anxious to learn. Here is the lesson of freedom won through self-responsibility and constant personal effort.

In no uncertain terms does the Buddha denounce priestcraft and all that was wrong with it, and corrupt priests. In a dialogue about brāhman priests and their sacred knowledge, the Buddha expounds to Vāseṭṭha five things leading to lust, called, in the Discipline of the Arahants, a chain and a bond. Four of them are " forms, sounds, odours, tastes ", which are " desirable, agreeable, pleasant, attractive, that are accompanied by lust and cause delight ". The fifth consists of " substances of the same kind perceptible to the body by touch ".

Then he expounds the five Hindrances (or veils or obstacles or entanglements), of Worldly lusts, Ill will, Torpor and Sloth of heart and mind, Restlessness and Worry, Perplexity.

In the course of the dialogue the Buddha elicits the conclusions that the talk of the brāhman priests, versed though they be in the Vedas, is idle talk, for they have not seen or known Brahmā ; nor can the priests show the way to union with what they have neither seen nor known ; nor themselves, after death, be united with Brahmā. Further, the priests possess wives and wealth, have minds not free from anger, malice, impurity of heart, lack of self-mastery. Further, they are caught in the toils of the five Fetters and five Hindrances.

> " Therefore," says the Buddha, " the brāhman priests, versed though they be in the three Vedas, while they sit down (in confidence), are sinking down (in the mire) ; and so sinking they are arriving only at despair, thinking the while that they are crossing over into some happier land.
>
> " Therefore is it that the threefold wisdom of the brāhmans, wise in their three Vedas, is called a waterless desert, their threefold wisdom is called a pathless jungle, their threefold wisdom is called perdition."

Tevijja Sutta,
D.I.248.

This is strong criticism. But the Buddha has no intolerance, no reaction against any who deprecate, or in favour of any who appreciate, him and his teaching. One day Suppiya and his pupil Brahmadatta are respectively speaking against and for the Buddha, the Dhamma (the Doctrine), and the Sangha (the Order). The members of the Order are perturbed. Says the Buddha :

> " Bhikkhus, if others should speak dispraise of me, or against the Doctrine, or against the Order, you should not on that account either bear malice, or suffer heart-burning, or feel ill-will. If you, on that account, should be angry and displeased, that would be a stumbling-block for you. If, when others speak against us, you feel angry at that, and displeased, would you then be able to judge how far that speech of theirs is well said or ill ? "
>
> " That would not be so, Sir ".
>
> " But when outsiders speak in dispraise of me . . . the Doctrine . . . the Order, you should unravel what is not the fact and point it out as not the fact, saying : ' For this or that reason this is not the fact, that is not so, such a thing is not found among us, is not in us '.
>
> " But also, Bhikkhus, if outsiders should speak in praise of me . . . the Doctrine . . . the Order, you should not on that account be filled with pleasure or gladness, or be lifted up in heart. Were you to be so, that also would be a stumbling-block for you. When outsiders speak in praise of me . . . the Doctrine . . . the Order, you should acknowledge what is the fact to be the fact, saying ' For this or that reason this is the fact that is so, such a thing is found among us is in us ! ' "
>
> Brahmajāla Sutta,
> D.I.2 and 3.

The years spent in " looking within himself." had certainly borne fruit in his psychological insight, and taught him the most constructive way in which man should deal with man : like the ideal judge, unbiased towards either party as the evidence accumulates, dispassionate, clearly perceiving the truth, without fear or favour, he should form a correct judgment ; and then, reasonableness not argumentativeness, patient consideration not insistent dogmatism.

The Buddha's manners were probably the model of good manners for all time. When the Master lay dying, Subhadda the Wanderer, approached Ānanda, earnestly desiring to speak with the Buddha in order to have a doubt dissipated. Ānanda said: "The Exalted One is weary; do not trouble him!" But the Lord of Compassion overheard him, and desired that Subhadda should have access to him, for he received whosoever came to him. Subhadda was the last disciple to be converted. All the dialogues bear witness to the exchange of courtesies between the Buddha and his visitors. The usual form runs thus:

> "And when they (the visitors) had come there (where the Buddha was, usually; sometimes the Buddha went to them) they exchanged with the Exalted One the greetings and compliments of politeness and courtesy, and sat down beside him."

When the conversation is over, the visitors rise, and keeping the Buddha on their right hand side, they depart. Whenever the Buddha receives an invitation to dine (the morning meal always, for the Buddha took no other meal), he always gives his consent unless prevented by a previous engagement. After dining, he "gladdens the hearts of his hosts with religious discourse".

Always dignified and courteous, he dealt with conceit or discourtesy on the part of his visitor with complete candour, sparing no detail in revealing the truth of his conduct to him, yet with such perfect equanimity, devoid of anger and ill-will, that he healed his visitor's malady. One day, Pokkharasādi the brāhman sends his disciple Ambaṭṭha, also a brāhman, to visit the Buddha and find out whether he was all that he was reputed to be. Ambaṭṭha goes, accompanied by other brāhmans. The Buddha himself opens the door. The brāhmans accompanying Ambaṭṭha exchange the greetings and compliments of politeness and courtesy with the Blessed One, but Ambaṭṭha himself displays unusual rudeness. Then follows a long conversation in which the Buddha holds up a mirror to Ambaṭṭha's conduct, and points out the vanity of pride of birth as a brāhman, summed up in these words:

> "In the supreme perfection of knowledge and righteousness, Ambaṭṭha, there is no reference to the question either of birth, or of lineage, or of the pride which says: 'You are as worthy as I', or, 'You are not as worthy as I'. It is where the talk is of marrying or giving in marriage, that reference is made to such things as that. For whosoever, Ambaṭṭha, are in bondage to the

notions of birth or of lineage, or to the pride of social position, or of connection by marriage, they are far from the supreme perfection of knowledge and righteousness. It is only by having got rid of all such bondage that one can realize for himself that supreme perfection of knowledge and righteousness."

" But what, Gotama, is that conduct, and what that wisdom ? "

Ambaṭṭha Sutta,
D.I.99 and 100.

And the Buddha expounds to him exactly as he expounds to the courteous and well-behaved ones.

Ambaṭṭha reports everything to Pokkharasādi on his return. Pokkharasādi calls on the Buddha and apologizes for Ambaṭṭha. The Buddha says : " Let him (Ambaṭṭha) be quite happy ". Then Pokkharasādi invites the Buddha to dinner next day; and after dinner, sits on a low stool beside him ; and then :

" The Blessed One gave a discourse which was a graduated talk ; that is to say, he spake to him of generosity, of right conduct, of heaven, of the danger, the vanity, and the defilement of lusts, of the advantages of renunciation. And when the Blessed One saw that Pokkharasādi the brāhman had become prepared, softened, unprejudiced, upraised, and believing in heart, then he proclaimed the doctrine the Buddhas alone have won ; that is to say the doctrine of sorrow, of its origin, of its cessation, and of the Path, And just as a clean cloth from which all stain has been washed away will readily take the dye, even so did Pokkharasādi the brāhman obtain, even while sitting there, the pure and spotless vision of Dhamma, and he knew ' Whatsoever is liable to uprising, all that is liable to stopping ' ".

Ambaṭṭha Sutta,
D.I.110.

And Pokkharasādi the brāhman became his disciple.

The Buddha had no use for any of the brāhman rituals and blood sacrifices, as the Kūṭadanta Sutta shows. To him, living the holy life was the supreme ritual and sacrifice. In the course of the exposition to Kūṭadanta the brāhman, when the Buddha observes that Kūṭadanta has " become prepared, softened, unprejudiced, upraised and believing in heart ", he imparts the supreme teaching : sorrow ; its origin ; its cessation ; and the Path. The Buddha's patience and considerateness, his unsentimental love, a love which had attained absoluteness because he was free of any possibility of any reaction of anger, ill-will or malice, his skill as an educator, his unfathomable understanding of man, and his spotless personal purity need no exposition or panegyric. He who can see the sun in the clear sky needs no discourse on glorious light.

The Buddha's attitude to fantastic metaphysical speculations is an eloquent criticism of the intellectual chaos smothering true philosophy in his day. The people of India have always had a leaning towards philosophizing; but not many had a love for the discipline of philosophy. The Upanishads, and the worthy thought of India, was the creation of the few, and the treasured wisdom of a slightly larger circle of sound students. Just as there are few musical geniuses, but innumerable sense-titillators who cannot help lifting fragments from works of genius and rehashing them as popularly worshipped cacophony, so, too, in connection with philosophers and philosophists!

Wrangling disputations were undermining moral order. Absurd theories, rituals and sacrifices, spiritual authoritarianism, and the disabilities due to an iron bound social system (though its good points must not be forgotten), led to widespread misery. Truth was being loaded in chains and the Spirit of Religion was fading into a dark shade. So the Buddha, concerned with a true philosophy of life, was averse from mere metaphysics. For the mass of men, the knowable lies within the purview of reason—the reason, be it noted, possessed by him who lives a pure life with senses under control. The philosophy of life must emerge out of the knowable. Provided its roots are sound, it can be made as lofty and as idealistic as lies within the power of the sense-controlled man of reason. This bears fruit in the practice of a pure and noble ethic. The self becomes the living example of self-less-ness.

Beyond, lies the unknown. In those rare instances where a man is ready to transcend dualistic intellect and bridge the gulf between the known and the unknown, he may, and will, do so, and realize the All-Truth by conscious at-one-ment. The Mystery is never " known " by him, but it is experienced. And he is unable to " tell " another that experience, because the experience is formless, nameless, timeless and beyond cognizing consciousness but within convinced awareness. This unanalyzable character of the Mystery is experienced by many, though it is not sufficiently treasured because man knows not how to treasure it. If and when he does, he knows what Religion means. And he will also know, as the Buddha did, that whatever metaphysics obfuscates the mind is to be discarded, for it shuts the door of the mind and cuts off the light of Religion.

Now the Buddha had penetrated the Mystery. He had experienced Nirvāṇa, and he lived in Nirvāṇa, that highest state of sublime peace, the unoriginated, the deathless, until the day he passed away forty-five years after his attainment. That he lived the life and taught the Doctrine for nearly half a century, unwaveringly, he with his moral perfection and possessed of his giant intellect, is meaningful. Moreover, since he himself gave convincing hints that he did understand what was beyond ordinary comprehension, it is of no little significance that he held the attitude he did to that intellectual debauchery practised behind the name-plate of metaphysics.

In the Brahmajāla Sutta, after enumerating the "minor details of mere morality," he says:

> "There are, bhikkhus, things profound, difficult to realize, hard to understand, tranquillising, sweet, not to be grasped by mere logic, subtle, comprehensible by the wise. These things the Tathāgata, having himself realized them by his own super-knowing, hath set forth; and it is of them that they, who would rightly praise the Tathāgata in accordance with the truth, should speak".
>
> D.I.12.

Here the Buddha assures the brethren that there are those things which he himself has realized, by his own super-knowing, and set forth.

Then he deals with the metaphysicians:

> "There are recluses and brāhmans, O Bhikkhus, who reconstruct the ultimate beginnings of things, whose speculations are concerned with the ultimate past, and who on eighteen grounds put forward various assertions regarding it. And about what, with reference to what, do these good sirs do so?
>
> D.I.12, 13.

The groups he deals with are the Eternalists, the Semi-Eternalists, the Extensionists, the Eel-Wrigglers (or Equivocators), the Fortuitous Originists; the After-Deathers or those who maintained that after death the Soul is (*a*) conscious, (*b*) unconscious, (*c*) both conscious and unconscious, (*d*) neither conscious nor unconscious; the Annihilationists, and the Happy-Lifers (through free sense indulgence).

First, the Buddha states the theory. For example:

> "There are, Bhikkhus, some recluses and brāhmans who are Eternalists, and who on four grounds proclaim that both the self and the world are eternal."
>
> D.I.13.

He then proceeds to say how the theory arose; and the form of presentation is such that the theory stands self-condemned. Occasionally, he utters strictures on those who originally propounded the theory.

> ". . . some recluse or brāhman is addicted to logic and reasoning. He gives utterance to the following conclusions of his own, beaten out by his argumentations and based on his sophistry . . ."
>
> D.I.23.

> "In this case, Bhikkhus, some recluse or brāhman is dull, stupid. And it is by reason of his dullness, his stupidity, that when a question on this or that is put to him, he resorts to equivocation, to wriggling like an eel—'If you ask me whether there is another world,—well, if I thought there were, I would say so. But I don't say so. And I don't think it is thus or thus. And I don't think it is otherwise. And I don't deny it. And I don't say there neither is, nor is not, another world'. Thus does he equivocate, and in like manner about (all other questions)".
>
> D.I.27.

According to the Buddha's presentation, these theories spring up in the minds of men who think hard and then suddenly "get an idea"; and they are so seized by the idea, so enamoured of it, that they are convinced this must be the truth. The Buddha did not approve of 'a bee in a bonnet'. After presenting each theory, he says:

> "Now of these, Bhikkhus, the Tathāgata knows that these speculations thus arrived at, thus insisted on, will have such and such a result, such and such an effect on the future condition of those who

trust in them. That does he know, and he knows also other things far beyond (far better than those speculations); and having that knowledge he is not puffed up, and being thus not puffed up, peace is known to him of himself; and having known as they really are the arising and setting of feelings, their satisfaction and peril, and the escape from them, the Tathāgata, Bhikkhus, is freed without substrate (remaining for rebirth).

"(But), Bhikkhus, there are those things profound, difficult to realize, hard to understand, tranquillising, sweet, not to be grasped by mere logic, subtle, comprehensible by the wise. These things the Tathāgata, having himself realized them by his own super-knowing hath set forth, and it is of them that they, who would rightly praise the Tathāgata in accordance with the truth, should speak."

D.I.12.

Finally, he lists the different groups of thinkers categorically, and sums up thus:

"That opinion of theirs is based only on the personal feelings, on the worry and writhing consequent thereon, of those venerable recluses and brāhmans who know not, neither perceive, and are subject to all kinds of craving.

These opinions are therefore based upon contact (through the senses). That they should experience those sensations without such contact, such a thing could not be.

They, all of them, receive those sensations through continual contact in the spheres of touch. To them on account of the sensations arises craving, on account of the craving arises the fuel (that is, the necessary condition, or the basis of future lives,) from the fuel results becoming, from the tendency to become arises rebirth, and from rebirth comes death and grief, lamentation, pain, sorrow and despair. It is, O Bhikkhus, when a Bhikkhu understands, as they really are, the origin and the end, the attraction, the danger and the escape from the six realms of contact,[1] that he gets to know what is above, beyond them all.

For whosoever, Bhikkhus, whether recluses or brāhmans, are thus reconstructors of the past or arrangers of the future, or who are both, whose speculations are concerned with both, who put forward various propositions with regard to the past and to the future, they, all of them, are entrapped in the net of these sixty-two modes; this way and that they may flounder, but they are included in it, caught in it.

[1] The realms of the five senses and of the mind.

Just, Bhikkhus, as when a skilful fisherman or fisher-lad should drag a tiny pool of water with a fine-meshed net he might fairly think: 'Whatever fish of size may be in this pond, every one will be in this net; flounder about as they may, they will be included in it, and caught'—just so it is with these speculators about the past and the future, in this net, flounder as they may, they are included and caught.

The outward form, Bhikkhus, of him who has won the truth (the Tathāgata), stands before you, but that which binds it to rebirth is cut in twain. So long as his body shall last, so long will gods and men behold him. On the dissolution of the body, beyond the end of his life, neither gods nor men shall see him.

Just, Bhikkhus, as when the stalk of a bunch of mangoes has been cut, all the mangoes that were hanging on that stalk go with it, just so, Bhikkhus, though the outward form of him who has won the truth . . . neither gods nor men shall see him.

D.I.40–46.

Such speculations are thus the mental writhings of the slaves of craving. But he who understands the origin and end, the attraction and danger, and the escape from the six realms of contact, he is the one who gets to know what is above and beyond them all.

There were ten questions, dubbed the Ten Indeterminates, which the Buddha refused to discuss:

1, 2. Whether the world is eternal or not.

3, 4. Whether the world is infinite or not.

5, 6. Whether the jīva[1] is the same as or distinct from the body.

7–10. Whether a man who has attained to the truth,
a Tathāgata, exists or not after death,
or both exists and not exists,
or neither exists nor not exists.

In the Udāna (VI.4), the lovely story of the elephant is put in the Buddha's mouth. Various non-Buddhist teachers were expressing strong opinions on the Indeterminates. They came to blows! Then Gotama tells a story how once upon a time when a similar riot took place, the king had the blind men of the place, together with an elephant, brought in. The king

[1] Life-principle.

asked each of them to touch the elephant, and describe it. He who felt the head called it a water-pot, the ear a winnowing basket, the tusk a ploughshare, the body a granary, the leg a pillar, the back a mortar, the tail a pestle and the bristles a broom. Each one was convinced of his own rightness. They came to blows! The Buddhist moral is:

> O how they cling and wrangle, some who claim
> of brāhman and recluse the honoured name!
> For, quarrelling, each to his view they cling,
> Such folk see only one side of a thing.

And in many a dialogue (see Majjhima Nikāya, I. 486, for instance) it is pointed out that the Ten Indeterminates are "the jungle, the desert, the puppet show, the writhing, the entanglement of speculation—accompanied by sorrow, by wrangling, by resentment, by the fever (of excitement); they conduce neither to turning away, nor to dispassion, nor to cessation (of craving), nor to peace, nor to super-knowledge, nor to awakening, nor to Nirvāṇa."

So the Buddha discouraged all speculations on first origins or ultimates. No one, except the liberated man, could come to know the truth about what was above and beyond the realm of the five senses and the mind. He himself knew this truth by his own super-knowledge. But if any man questioned him on these subjects, as did Vacchagotta and Mālunkyāputta, he either maintained silence, or made it clear that such questions should not be asked. Some of his disciples, having themselves attained Arahantship, knew. Like their Master, they maintained silence, knowing that their super-knowledge could not be put into words.

There is no Heaven, regarded as an eternal resting place for the good, nor any personal God in the Buddha's teaching. But,

> "There is, O Bhikkhus, that plane of consciousness (āyatana) where there is neither extension (pathavī) nor cohesion (āpo) nor heat (tejo) nor motion (vāyo), nor the plane of infinite ākāśa, nor of infinite consciousness (viññāṇa), nor of no-thing-ness, nor of neither perception nor non-perception, nor this world nor another world nor both nor moon-and-sun. In that plane, Bhikkhus, I say there is no coming, no going, no standing still, no deceasing, no arising

(in rebirth). It is not grounded (on anything), it rolls not on (in saṁsāra), it is without objects (of sense or mind). It is itself the end of Ill.

Udāna, VIII.1.

Side by side with this must be considered what are called the Eight Deliverances, attained through meditation:

1. Having one's self external form, one sees (these) forms.
2. Unaware of one's own external form, one sees forms external to oneself.
3. " Lovely "—with this thought one becomes intent.
4. Passing wholly byond perception of form, all perceptions of sense-reaction dying away, heedless of all perceptions of the manifold, thinking of ākāśa as infinite, one enters into and abides in the sphere of ākāśa as infinite.
5. Passing wholly beyond ākāśa regarded as infinite, thinking of viññāṇa as infinite, one enters into and abides in the sphere of consciousness regarded as infinite.
6. Passing wholly beyond consciousness regarded as infinite, thinking of there being no-thing whatever, one enters into and abides in the sphere of no-thing-ness.
7. Passing wholly beyond the sphere of no-thing-ness, one enters into and abides in the sphere of neither-perception-nor-non-perception.
8. Passing wholly beyond neither-perception-nor-non-perception, one enters into and abides in a state of suspended perception and feeling.

And then the Buddha adds:

" When a Bhikkhu enters upon these eight deliverances in forward order and in reverse order, and in forward-reverse order, and also enters upon (them) and emerges from (them) where he likes, when he likes and for as long as he likes, and by the destruction of the āsavas (cankers, of sensuality, becoming, speculative views and ignorance), he, having entered upon, dwells in that freedom of mind and freedom through wisdom which are without the cankers and which he by himself, here in this present world has come to know and realize,—then such a Bhikkhu, Ānanda, is called ' Freed-in-both-ways '. And Ānanda, any other Freedom-in-both-ways higher and loftier than this Freedom-in-both-ways there is not."

Mahā Nidāna Sutta, D.II.70,71

The states of entering into and abiding in no-thing-ness, in neither-conciousness-nor-unconsciousness and in suspended perception and feeling, are very difficult, if not impossible to conceive. It is not unnatural, therefore, that even eminent scholars have interpreted them to mean vacuity, or the nothingness which is annihilation, whilst others have dismissed them as nonsense. But judgement, without sufficient grounds for judgement, should be suspended, or at least cautiously pronounced, with appropriate reservations. Only those who have long practised, and successfully practised, the yoga or Buddhist or any similar system of meditation, are in a position to speak with authority. Taking into account that part of the Buddha's observations, logic, sound judgement and insight which is obvious to all, the likelihood is that he understood what he was talking about on these deep questions, and it is improbable that he would have been guilty of committing himself to nonsense.

The practice of meditation develops, among other things, the power so to concentrate on any particular image (of an object) or on any particular idea, that nothing else can intrude into the field of awareness. When such concentration attains a peak, that residue of awareness of one's self, the perceiving subject, becomes so small, that it is practically lost in the awareness of the object or the idea on which attention is focused. This is different from the not uncommon experience of being so enthralled by an event which one observes, or in which one participates, that one becomes quite oblivious of oneself, since the attractiveness, or fascination, or extremity of horror of the event makes a deliberate act of concentration unnecessary. Moreover, such an experience is not an act of mental concentration on a single idea, but is an un-selfconscious participation in a series of sensations and ideas.

In the state of deliberate concentration, the mind becomes aware of the inner nature of that upon which it concentrates. It is not necessarily an analytical awareness. It is often a "feeling" awareness. All men can hold an idea—a string of words. But the conscious content or "body" in each man's mind will be different from that in every other mind. Concentratoin strengthens or intensifies this content, while reflection enriches it. Concentration and reflection are different aspects of meditation.

The claim made that the yogi can make himself as minute or as large as he likes, can raise himself and fly through space, can go to the moon or sun, visit the demons in hell or converse with the angels in heaven, is best regarded as a meaningful fantasy, and is not to be taken literally and objectively. The meaning it hides is that by the discipline of meditation certain latent faculties of the mind can be developed, certain fields of awareness can be opened up to the practisant, the yogi. The question should be viewed as one for scientific research, and not as one for superstitious belief in the supernatural, or as the butt of jibes by the thoughtless.

Now the deliverances set forth by the Buddha consist partly in being in the infinity of consciousness or in suspended perception and feeling, and partly in developing the power to make the mind function as required. The Buddha had good reasons for suggesting his particular technique. Up to the eighth deliverance leads in the direction of abstraction ; down to the first in that of concretion. The former leads into the subjective world, the latter into the objective. And the Buddha tells Ānanda that when a bhikkhu can go in one direction, and in the reverse, and also in forward-reverse order, and has also achieved emancipation of heart and mind by rooting out the cankers, then he is 'Freed-in-both-ways', than which there is no higher freedom. Whether he views the world subjectively or objectively, he will be equally free.

This training of the mind will enable one the better to understand the fragment quoted from the Udāna, which the Buddha calls "the end of Ill". Like Yājñavalkya's "it is not this, it is not that", is this particular statement about Nirvāṇa. Its special significance is that the term Nirvāṇa signifies something very different from ordinary mental comprehension. Everyday life does not usually train the mind to grasp unusual conditions, or the un-conditioned. The eight deliverances are the Buddha's own suggested mental discipline for preparing for Nirvāṇa.

The discipline of the eight deliverances gives freedom-in-both-ways here-now whilst alive, as a preparation for Nirvāṇa here-now whilst alive, and not in any hereafter. In the Brahmajāla Sutta quoted above, the Buddha ends the great discourse by saying that after the death of his body, since he had attained the truth and destroyed the possibility of rebirth, neither gods nor men would ever see him again: there could never again be another aggregate of mental and material elements which would constitute another "him".

If the more abstract-sounding deliverances appear to mean nothing, consider how difficult it is, sometimes impossible, to understand the meaning of the more abstruse concepts of the modern physicist. Consider also the attitude of the physicist who says: "Study the subject; come and see for yourself." A just attitude. Furthermore, he does not say: "This is the absolute truth and there is no other." So, too, the Buddha says: "This I have found to be true. But do you, sir, come and see for yourself."

Now the Upanishads speak of four states of consciousness: the waking state; the dream state; the deep sleep state, in which one's consciousness is in its real home, the Brahma-world, unremembered on awakening again; and a fourth state, the Turīya. This fourth state, attainable in waking consciousness, is over and above all the other states. In the Māṇḍūkya Upanishad, the third or deep sleep state is described as

5. "unified, just a cognition-mass, consisting of bliss,
enjoying bliss, whose mouth is thought, the cognitional."

and,

11. "He, verily, indeed, erects this whole world, and
he becomes its immerging—he who knows this."

The fourth, or Turīya state is thus described:

6. "This is the lord of all, this is the all-knowing.
This is the inner controller. This is the source
of all, for this is the origin and end of beings.

7. "Not inwardly cognitive, not outwardly cognitive,
not both-wise cognitive, not a cognition-mass,
not cognitive, not non-cognitive, unseen, with
which there can be no dealing, ungraspable, having
no distinctive mark, non-thinkable, that cannot be
designated, the essence of the assurance of which is

> the state of being one with the Self, the cessation
> of development, tranquil, benign, without a second—
> (such) they think is the fourth (state). He is
> the Self (Ātman). He should be discerned."

In the Maitri Upanishad, the Turīya state is described as

> " That which is non-thought, (yet) which stands
> in the midst of thought,
> The unthinkable, supreme mystery !—
> Thereon let one concentrate his thought."
> VI.19.

The Upanishadic thinkers and the Buddha equally refer, then, to this indescribable, intense, blissful awareness which is beyond ordinary, analytical consciousness. It is unwise to regard these as vague, unreal abstractions, because they cannot be reached by ordinary thought, however penetrating. It may, indeed, be true to say that they are definitely rooted in the concrete real of everyday experience. The snowclad giants of the Himālayas hold their heads so high that they sometimes seem to be self-poised in space. Yet they are undeniably rooted in the solid soil of everyday Asia !

The Upanishads presented Ātman ; the Buddha, Nirvāṇa. The Upanishads made an absolutist approach ; the Buddha, dynamic. The Upanishads, intuitive ; the Buddha, psychological ; and common to both Upanishadic sage and the Buddha was the sure development and spiritual attainment born of steady discipline. Whilst the Buddha resolutely set his face against foolish speculation, he just as resolutely presented the Transcendent where necessary, even as the Upanishads did.

Lastly, in this connection, the four Jhānas, or states of Rapture reached in meditation, must be considered. After the "fourfold setting up of mindfulness ", aloof from sensual appetites, aloof from evil ideas, a Bhikkhu enters into and abides in

> The First Jhāna, wherein there is cogitation and deliberation born of solitude . . . and wherein he is full of joy and ease. Suppressing cogitation and deliberation, he enters into and abides in
>
> The Second Jhāna, which is self-evoked, born of concentration, full of joy and ease, the mind calm and sure, dwelling-on-high. Disenchanted with joy, he enters into and abides in

The Third Jhāna, calmly contemplative, mindful and self-possessed, and feels ease in his body. Putting aside both ease and malaise, and by the passing away of happiness and melancholy, he enters into and abides in

The Fourth Jhāna, in which there is the rapture of utter purity of mindfulness and equanimity, and wherein is felt neither ease nor Ill.

Mahā Satipaṭṭhāna Sutta (abbreviated),
D.II.313.

A sense of ease in the body, joy and calm in mind, are common factors in the first three Jhānas—a point of no little interest to those who observe the correlation of mental states and bodily ease or disease. In the fourth Jhāna there is only rapture. The Buddha's description is not ecstatic. The words are simple, unexciting, like a calm stream flowing placidly through a peaceful plain. But dive into the stream, and see if bottom can be touched.

In his own quiet way, the Buddha gives unqualified assurance of joy and happiness as a permanent state[1] associated with attainment, and also with living the life of the Bhikkhu :

" Being one who has gone forth thus (into the Order of Bhikkhus), he dwells restrained by the restraint of the Pātimokkha (rules) ; he is endowed with right conduct and pasturage (or, the right places to go for alms, etc.) ; he beholds peril in the slightest faults ; undertaking them, he trains himself in the rules of training ; he is possessed of (right) action of body and of speech ; through skill, his way of living is utterly pure ; he is endowed with moral habit ; guarded are the doors of the sense organs ; possessed of mindfulness and clear consciousness,[2] he is of good cheer.

. . . endowed with the ariyan control of the sense organs, he experiences an inner, unsullied (by the defilements) happiness . . .

To the Bhikkhu in whom the five Hindrances have been put away, realizing that himself, joy is born ; rapture is born in him who is joyful ; the body of him whose mind is rapturous is impassible ; with the body impassible he experiences happiness ; the mind of him who is happy is concentrated."

Sāmañña Phala Sutta,
D.I.63, 70, 73.

[1] Cf. Ātmabodha Upanishad: Just as in a wealthy person the desire for poverty does not arise, so in Me who am immersed in Brahmic bliss, the desire for sensual happiness cannot arise . . . Just as an owl sees darkness only in the sun, so a fool sees only darkness in the self-shining Supreme Bliss.

[2] Of whatever he is doing, saying or thinking at each and every moment.

"Now it may well be, Poṭṭhapāda, that you may think: 'Mental objects that have stains will be put away, purifying mental objects will grow much, and entering in, he will abide in the completeness and maturity of wisdom, which he by himself, here in this present world has come to know and realize—but the abiding is sad.' But this is not to be understood in this way, Poṭṭhapāda. When such conditions are fulfilled, then there will be joy and rapture and peace, and continued mindfulness and clear consciousness—and the abiding is happy."

Poṭṭhapāda Sutta, D.I.196.

In the ascent from living the good life to the peak of attainment, the aspirant makes the grades, here in this life, from joy and peace to the indescribable sublimity of Nirvāṇa.

There is another fragment which says:

Bhikkhus, there is a not-born, a not-become, a not-made, a not-compounded.

Bhikkhus, if that unborn, not-become, not-made, not-compounded were not, there would be apparent no escape from this here that is born, become, made, compounded.

But since, Bhikkhus, there is an unborn . . . therefore the escape from this here that is born . . . is apparent.

Udāna, VIII.3.

and an apothegm:

Cut through the stream (of saṁsāra), be energetic, drive away sensual pleasures, O brāhman. Knowing the destruction of the elements of existence (saṁkhārā), thou art a knower of the Uncreated, O brāhman.

Dhammapada, 383.

Such statements recall the Brahman of the Upanishads. It surely is untenable that the Buddha was unacquainted with, indeed was not deeply versed in Upanishadic thought. Siddhattha Gotama learned the lore of his day. Then came the decision to find out the origin and cure for suffering. West of Kapilavastu lay Kurukshetra; Pañcāla to the south; Videha, immortal land of Janaka and Yājñavalkya to the southeast; and farthest of all, also south-eastwards, lay Rājagriha, the capital of Magadha. Siddhattha had no car to rush to Rājagriha. Nor his horse. Nor even an ass. He walked. Through woods and forests he walked seeking hermits and brāhman teachers. He bore no letter of introduction to Āḷāra and Uddaka, no appointment which he would have to keep punctually. So he must have taken a long time, traversing the two hundred and fifty miles or so, if measured in a straight line, between Kapilavastu and Rājagriha. And his path lay through Videha.

Brahman and Ātman, mouthed by minor prophets and pseudo-sages, had degenerated, for many, into the manikin soul of popular belief. The manikin had become the everlasting, transmigrating soul, the special property of the bundle of aggregates called a man, safely locked up in its cardiac house. Each man's little ātman had supplanted the Ātman. Here was something, felt Gotama, which must be remedied.

On the other hand, it is also possible that he met sages who really knew the Upanishadic doctrine. But Gotama was in search of the origin of Ill, and of the way to end it. His goal was the deathless (amata), the Immortal. He discovered that the extravagances of self-mortification led him nowhere except towards the grave. By the time he realized the Truth and attained Nirvāṇa, he had discovered that only at the end of complete self-discipline was man capable of maintaining Nirvāṇic consciousness permanently. It was the permanent end of Ill which he sought, the permanent abiding in Nirvāṇa.

So for the Buddha—and he realized this was true for all mankind—that particular self-discipline which he taught was the indispensable foundation, and the doctrinal concepts of an Absolute or a First Cause could well be left alone. It happened, as indeed it was not possible for it not to happen, that at least once he did make a pronouncement that there is an unborn, unoriginated, unconditioned and unformed, though the statement is not of special practical importance where the daily religious life is concerned.

* * *

Certain threads of teaching from various religions may now be drawn together.

In the fourfold setting up of mindfulness,[1] all feelings, re-

[1] See below, pp. 236, 237.

actions and behaviour pass under review. One's own specific resentments, repressions, prevarications, falsehoods, fears and aversions, together with the causes which gave rise to them, are calmly and fully examined, without censure or praise, like a judge who impartially considers all the evidence produced by each side in the case.

This quiet, dispassionate self-observation acts psycho-therapeutically. When the process has progressed far enough, the mind becomes more tranquil and the body more relaxed. Next, through the cogitation and deliberation beginning with the first Jhāna, the realization of truths becomes intenser, the understanding of their significance and application becomes deeper, and the relationship of one truth with another clearer. From experience of such meditation, one knows that when some truth really goes home and there is a vivid enlightenment, the whole body noticeably relaxes, breathing becomes deeper and calmer, and, as the Buddha says, one experiences greater ease physically. Muscular co-ordination and control over bodily movement increases, and there is an improvement in one's general health. Finally, in the fourth Jhāna, not only malaise, but also ease is transcended.

Again, cogitation and deliberation pass on to concentration, to contemplation, and finally to the rapture of utter purity of mindfulness, wherein is neither ease nor ill.

The fourfold mindfulness, the aloofness from sensual appetites and evil ideas, and the four Jhānas have some correspondence to the methods of Yoga. In the Sāṇḍilya Upanishad, Sāṇḍilya says to Atharvan:

> "Please tell me about the eight aṅgas (parts) of Yoga, which is the means of attaining Ātman."

Atharvan says:

> "The eight are yama, niyama, āsana, prāṇāyāma, pratyāhāra, dhāraṇā, dhyāna and samādhi."

Yama consists in harmlessness, truthfulness, non-covetousness, kindliness, etc. Niyama consists in austerity, contentment, charity, study, faith, etc. Āsana and prāṇāyāma consist of bodily postures and breath control for the purpose of establishing physical health, and also as part of the preparation for effective meditation.

Pratyāhāra is the withdrawal from attachment to the objects of sense. Dhāraṇā, dhyāna[1] and samādhi are the stages of meditation proper leading to union with Ātman or Brahman.

When freed from the sense functions and impressions, speech and discursive thought both cease. In this silence[2] the mind " perishes ", or " mindlessness " is attained, as stated in the Adhyātma and other Upanishads. The Maitri, VI. 34, says:

> By making mind all motionless,
> From sloth and from distraction freed,
> When unto mindlessness one comes,
> Then that is the supreme estate.

Mindlessness is the state in which—and also before achieving this state, when experiencing a temporary illumination—with heightened consciousness, one consciously realizes, not merely logically infers, what the Buddha called the fourth deliverance, the infinity of ākāśa, that is, the one-ness of the eternal " that-which-is " in terms of its all-pervasive, fundamental "material", and then in terms of the infinity of consciousness, or all-pervasive root-mind. Next comes the realm of the No-thing, not to be regarded as that out of which the emergence of any manifestation is impossible, but rather, indeed, as that out of which all manifestation does emerge.

The culminating stage, which is possible only after attaining the true silence, and which is called samādhi, is represented in the Buddha's eighth deliverance. Here, the Upanishadic sages declared, was the union of Pratygātman with Paramātman,[3] which represents the Yogi's realization of Brahman. This, too, is the Buddha's supreme Nirvāṇa, here-now whilst alive in this world.

In this state the round of births and deaths, saṁsāra, is utterly done away with. Never again another " rebirth ", another

[1] In the Maitreya Upanishad, Adhyāya II, abstracting the mind from the objects of sense is called dhyāna.

[2] See also, above, p. 104.

[3] In Christian teaching: "I and my Father are one"—John, X. 30.

uprising and passing away. Avidyā, "ignorance", is utterly transformed into Vidyā, "knowledge", and the triumph over Māra, the Tempter, the Evil One who is Lord of Death, is complete.

Here may be seen the truly significant meaning of the "round of births and deaths", of the Lord of Death, and of certain other teachings.

The Maitri Upanishad, VI. 34, says:

> Saṁsāra is just one's own thought;
> With effort one should cleanse it then.

And the next two lines:

> What is one's thought, that one becomes;
> This is the eternal mystery.

are echoed in the Dhammapada, I. 1 and 2:

> All our tendencies of character are the offspring of mind, dominated by mind and made up of mind. If a man speaks or acts with a sullied mind, then suffering follows him, even as the wheel of the wagon follows the hoof of the bullock.
>
> . . . If a man speaks or acts with an unsullied mind, then happiness follows him ever, just as his shadow.

Again in Maitri, VI. 34, we have:

> For by tranquillity of thought,
> Karman, good and evil, one destroys.
> With soul serene, stayed on the Soul,
> Delight eternal one enjoys!

The Maitreya Upanishad, Adhyāya I, says:

> It is citta (mind) alone which is saṁsāra. It should be cleansed with effort. Whatever be a person's citta, of that nature he becomes. This is an ancient mystery. With the purifying of citta one makes both good and bad karma perish.

In the Muktikopanishad, Adhyāya II, Shri Rāma teaches:

> The Munis know as vāsana, that which is manifested through the consciousness of objects, which is of the nature of the object itself, and which is the cause of the origination and absorption (or fluctuations) of citta.

> This excessively fluctuating citta is the cause of birth, dotage and death, due to its determined and constant identification of itself with objects.
>
> Like the analogy of the seed and the tree, vāsana arises through bodily living in the sense world, and bodily living in its turn through vāsana . . . and this is the seed of citta. To the tree of citta there are two seeds : prāṇa (life) and vāsana. Should either of them perish, both perish soon.
>
> Through the actions of the world being done without attachment,[1] through abandoning the (thought of the) reality of the universe, and through the conviction of the destructibility of the body (or the manifested), vāsana does not arise.
>
> Through the complete giving up of vāsana, citta becomes non-citta . . . then dawns the state of mindlessness which confers the great peace.

This mindlessness simply means stilling the mind : being able to stop the unbidden flow of discursive thought (mental chatter); of deliberately abstracting one's mind from participation in the sense world ; and thus being free to be conscious of, turn attention to, a " new life "[2] in an " inner world ". Further on, Shri Rāma teaches :

> It is manas (mind—particularly that aspect of it termed saṁkalpa) that is the root of the tree of saṁsāra. In order that the tree of saṁsāra may wither soon, dry up its root through the quiescence of saṁkalpa.[3]

Throughout all the Upanishads it is taught that speech and mind (discursive thought) turn back from IT, Brahman, not having found. But in the Bṛihadāraṇyaka, IV. 4. 19, there is this :

> By the mind alone is IT to be perceived.

and in the Maitri, VI. 34, it is said :

> The mind, in truth, is for mankind
> the means of bondage and release.
> For bondage, if to objects bound ;
> From objects free, that's called release.

[1] This is also the Buddhist non-association of self with the transient actions' feelings and ideas of everyday life.

[2] The first resurrection, in Revelation, XX. 5.

[3] Saṁkalpa: resolve of the mind; will; purpose; definite intention.

The Buddha himself precisely declares :

> As soon, Bhikkhus, as my knowledge and insight concerning these Four Noble Truths . . . were pure, I knew that I had attained supreme and full enlightenment . . . The vision of knowledge arose in me : ' Freedom of mind is for me unshakable ; this is the last jāti ; there is not now again-becoming."
>
> Mahā Vagga, I.6.

Throughout the everyday psycho-physical life, the person associates his self with the objects of the sense world, and expresses personal attachment to, or aversion from them. The self-association with the stream of transient experiences, physical or mental, of everyday life, means that I am " born " in the moment of self-association with the stimulating source, that is, of desiring it for myself or attempting to grasp it ; I " live " through the cycle of experience consequent upon the birth associated with that stimulating source ; this cycle may be purely mental, as in the fantasy life, or both mental and physical; and finally I " die " as the cycle of experience comes to an end. The cycle may be pleasant, successful and exciting, or it may be one of frustration, misery and horror. In either case, being unawakened to Reality, I remain in bondage : pleasantly if enjoying "heaven" (a fool's paradise), or unpleasantly if "struggling for existence ", " failing to win through ", in short, suffering hell.

This is the continual uprising and passing away, the "endless" *round* of births and deaths, the stream of saṁsāra, here and now in this very life. This is a real meaning of the doctrine of rebirth. Birth, death, rebirth, redeath, rebirth, redeath . . . is a process which goes on within the lifetime of the single self-conscious individual, who, as officially registered by the local registrar of births and deaths, is born on a certain date, and dies on a certain date.

In this stream of saṁsāra, the repeated objective act, line of thought, or fantasy, sets up a habit, induces a tendency, makes a " natural slope " as the sage Nāgasena said to King Milinda,[1] down which the actor, associating his self with the act and all its psychical and value concomitants, tends to slide.

[1] Milinda Pañha, I. 89.

By far the greater part of everyday worldly life is concerned with preservation, speci-al and individual. In all the elements composing this life, objective, as well as in fancy and thought, the person is born and dies, is born and dies. The habitual tendencies set up make the process go " round and round "—saṁsāra, the unbearable round of births and deaths—a process in which human lives are crushed, souls are frustrated, spirits broken, in which men and women and children know misery and torture, and fight like snarling beasts for personal survival, security, success, self-assertion and self-satisfaction, only to be dust-ground under the relentless wheels of the car of Jagannātha. Safely seated in the car is the brāhman, typifying him who knows Brahman. The rest, because of their self-association with worldliness and with mortality, doom themselves to be mangled by the round-turning wheels. The ignorant themselves turn the wheels.

Hence the necessity for pratyāhāra, the withdrawal from worldly objects and objectives, the disentangling from the sensual life, the cessation of self-association with the fleeting, the mortal.

The " I " which responds to the objects of the world, which entangles itself in the sense life, and which persuades or impels the existential person—the " me " as an object which you are dispassionately observing—is that aspect of the existential ego which is the root of self-ishness, of egoism, which is Māra, Satan, the Tempter, the Evil One, the Prince of Darkness, the Lord of Death.

He cannot be slain. Nothing can be slain in the sense of being annihilated. But it can be, and it has to be transformed, and finally, transmuted. There is most significant teaching in this connection. In Khaṇḍas XI, XIII and XV of the Subāla Upanishad, the Lord Himself, answering Raikva's questions, says that " for him who has attained Ātman . . . Ātman splits open or burns up[1] (among other things) mṛityu (Death) ", and He adds immediately afterwards, " then mṛityu becomes one with the supreme God . . . one with the Supreme . . . one with the great Lord."

[1] Cf. "Death is swallowed up in victory"—I Corinthians, XV. 54; see also Revelation, XX. 14.

One begins to have a dim glimmering then, a distant glimpse through a dark glass, of the indescribable sublimity of the teaching, "I am Brahman." One feels the certitude of the triumphant cry, "O Death where is thy sting, O grave where is thy victory?"[1] A beam of transcendent light illumines the seeker who reads or hears the Buddha's statements, Udāna VIII, 1 and 3, quoted above.[2]

Clearly, that aspect of manifested, personal existence which is brought into being by the activity of Māra or Satan within oneself, and which constitutes the continuous round of births and deaths, the endless saṁsāra, is the domain of the Lord of Death.[3] Therefore the Buddha in his omniscience—and in this context the word omniscience is profoundly significant—declared that existence is Ill (evil), existence is but Suffering. Therefore also, Naciketas[4] said to the Lord of Death: "Keep your girls and your dancing. How can I be happy, know the peace which is the peace of God, with Thee, the Ender, in sight?" Therefore also, there is deep meaning to the Christian teaching that man is born in sin, or into a condition that is sinful.

And how kind is the Lord of Death! For he himself, who is only a manifestation of Brahman, and ultimately becomes one with Brahman through man's redemptive achievement, gives Naciketas the teaching which transmutes the Ender into one of the means for attaining Eternal Life!

Is it any wonder that the Turīya state, in which the Yogi "knows" Brahman, is spoken of in the Māṇḍūkya Upanishad[5] in entirely negative terms, making an apparently meaningless statement? Or that the words in which the Buddha talks of the four Jhānas appear so unimpressive at a cursory glance? At the same time one can well appreciate the awesome meaning of the ascription of Authority, of Divine Authority, to a Kṛishṇa, a Parameṣṭhin, a Yājñavalkya, a Jesus, a Zarathustra, a Buddha.

In the garden of Eden, Satan the Tempter, taking on the form of the serpent, successfully seduces Eve into eating the fruit of

[1] I Corinthians, XV. 55.
[2] See above, pp. 168, 175.
[3] In the manifested universe, Time, the Ender, is the bringer of natural death.
[4] Kaṭha Upanishad.
[5] See above, p. 172.

the tree of knowledge of good and evil: the knowledge of the nature and experiences of the manifested world and of personal life in it; the knowledge of the existent. This is the apara-vidyā, the "mere name", of Indian teachings.

Again, Moses and Aaron contend with Egypt's magician-priests. Aaron's rod becomes a serpent which eats up the serpents born of the Egyptians' rods!

The serpent has typified both wisdom and what is evil, the dark passions. There is also that other symbol: the serpent holding his tail in his mouth.

In the account of the Buddha's trials before his enlightenment, Kālanāgarāja, the serpent king, is one of the powers that aids him.

Kuṇḍalini, the mysterious energy Yogis talk of, sleeps coiled up like a serpent at the base of the spine as some say, in the navel say others. If aroused, Kuṇḍalini destroys if it travels "downwards through the centres controlling the genitals, etc.", or unites a man with Brahman, in samādhi, if it operates through the "centre at the top of the head", which is the real Brahmaloka of the Upanishads, and reaching which the seer becomes "immortal" here-now whilst alive in the body, though at the appointed time, the body yields to natural death.

The serpent represents the total Life-force in its contrasting manifestations. In moments of supreme peril, the peril of even one so advanced that he was to become, if successful in his present trial, a Buddha, a saviour of mankind, Kālanāgarāja himself turns protector. This means that the inherent drive in the living existent is towards the Eternal, Brahman, towards that which is Nirvāṇa, which is the kingdom of God.

When the seeker of Nirvāṇa, or the Yogi, triumphantly emerges out of the trial, and has won his victory over Māra the Tempter, the first resurrection has taken place. He has "overcome the world",[1] the "world" being no other than the realm of his own sense life and discursive thought. Then indeed, there is good reason to "be of good cheer".[2]

At this stage the serpent holds his tail in his mouth.

[1] John, XVI. 33.
[2] See above, Sāmañña Phala & Poṭṭhapāda Suttas; see also John, XVI. 33.

Henceforth, all the energy of the Life-force, harmonious, under the "divine guidance" of the Buddha-become, the Christ-become, the Yogi, the Paramahaṁsa, finds expression as the life and deeds in this world for the period of the ministry —three years in the case of the Christ, forty-five in the case of the Buddha—during which the Pratyagātman united with the Paramātman, the I and my Father in heaven, holds lordship over saṁsāra and over the Lord of Death, Mṛityu, the Prince of Darkness, Māra or Satan. At the end of such a life comes the yielding up of the body to natural death, after which, as the Buddha said, "neither gods nor men shall ever behold this form again."

The serpent, which stands for the Life-force (Brahman as Prāṇa in the Upanishads), also symbolizes, more generally, the manifested universe, and for man particularly, his sense and mind life. Unless there is the serpent, the victory over the serpent and the realization of the Transcendent (wherein is the "consciousness" to be attained yet) which is the Good and the True and the Loving, is impossible. Said the Buddha:

> "For I lay down that the world, its uprising, its passing away, and the course leading to its passing away, are in this fathom-long body itself, with its perceptions and ideas."
>
> Anguttara Nikāya, II.48.

Hence the intense emphasis laid by the great spiritual teachers upon living the holy life here and now. Hence also, of the living person's body, the psycho-physical organism, the opposites are stated, and both are true:

1. The body . . . is impure, being the seat of happiness and misery (the pleasure-pain saṁsāra of worldly existence).

2a. The body is said to be a temple. The Jīva in it is Śiva alone.
Maitreya Upanishad,
Adhyāya II.

2b. The body is said to be the divine temple.
The Śiva (in the body) is the God Sadāśiva[1] (in the temple).
Skanda Upanishad.

Whatsoever transforms the "impure body" into the "pure temple" is Religion.

[1] Literally, Eternal Bliss, or The Ever Auspicious.

Now the Buddha had a profound concern for Religion, not mere religion. He said at the Mahāvana, at the Kūṭāgāra Hall:

> " Therefore, Bhikkhus, ye who have been taught by me the dhammā which I have fully understood, having thoroughly made yourselves masters of them, practise them, meditate upon them, and spread them abroad in order that Brahma-faring may last long and be perpetuated, in order that it may continue to be for the good and happiness of the great multitudes, out of compassion for the world, and for the good and gain and happiness of gods and men ! "
>
> Mahā Parinibbāna Sutta,
> D.II.119.

The Buddha desired no personal worship or adulation. During his last days, he lies down to rest between twin sāla trees on the farther side of the Hiranyavatī river by Kusinārā. The trees are a mass of bloom out of season falling over his body. So, too, heavenly Mandārava flowers and sandalwood powder fall out of the skies. Heavenly music and heavenly songs are heard. And he says:

> " Now it is not thus, Ānanda, that the Tathāgata is rightly honoured, reverenced, venerated, held sacred or revered. But the Bhikkhu or the Bhikkhuni, the devout man or the devout woman who continually fulfils all the lesser and greater duties, who is correct in life, walking according to the precepts—it is he (or she) who rightly honours, reverences, venerates, holds sacred or reveres the Tathāgata with the worthiest homage. Therefore, Ānanda, be ye constant in the fulfilment of the greater and of the lesser duties, and be ye correct in life, walking according to the precepts ; and thus, Ānanda, should it be taught."
>
> Mahā Parinibbāna Sutta,
> D.II.138.

But Religion as propounded by the Buddha is so original, that it is startlingly different from all the other great religions. The Dhamma, and not a Divine Person or Absolute, is the fountain-head. Constant self-discipline, the understanding of man, the knowledge of the Four Noble Truths, becoming morally perfect and living the good life take the place of rituals and ceremonies. Devotion to the Dhamma, and loving service, take the place of worship. Reason, experience and reflection lead to vision, and to that faith of which knowledge is the stuff. The goal is self-less-ness, the cessation from being a source of suffering and evil, and the realization of the Deathless, of Nirvāṇa, which is the triumph of Goodness, of Wisdom and of Love.

The Buddha often speaks of the Dhamma in these terms:

> " The Dhamma, lovely in origin, lovely in its progress, lovely in its consummation, doth he (Gotama) proclaim; both with the spirit and the letter, the Brahma-faring doth he make known in all its fulness and purity."
>
> Sāmañña Phala Sutta, and in many other contexts.

Right from the beginning, after the enlightenment, the Buddha is fully sensitive to the difficulty of imparting the truth. Alone and quiet, he reflects:

> I have attained to this Dhamma, deep, difficult to see, hard to understand, tranquillizing, excellent, beyond argumentation, subtle, to be known by the wise. This generation on the other hand enjoys, is satisfied with and delights in attachments. For this generation . . . causality (idappaccayatā), dependent origination (paṭicca-samuppāda) would be difficult to see, and hardest for them to see would be the pacification of all individuality (sabba-saṁkhāra-samatho) . . . peace (nibbāna)."
>
> Mahā Vagga, I.5.2.

Were he to explain the Dhamma and others did not understand it, he would suffer weariness, vexation. But·

> " Because of compassion for living beings, I gazed over the world and I saw the scarcely tainted, the much tainted, those with keen faculties, with dull faculties, the well-disposed, the ill-disposed, the docile and the indocile, and a few who lived perceiving . . . sin and danger."
>
> Majjhima Nikāya, Sutta 26.

To whom, then, shall he impart this supreme wisdom? He " sees " that Āḷāra and Uddaka were both dead within the week. But there are the Five in the deer park of Isipatana, who had attended on him in the recent past. To Benares, then, he wends his way, and first proclaims the Gospel with the ringing words:

> " The Tathāgata, O Bhikkhus, is the Arahant, all-enlightened. Hearken, Bhikkhus! the Deathless has been gained. I teach, I

> make plain the Truth. If you walk as I teach, you will, ere long and in the present life, learn fully for yourselves, realize (make it come true), and having attained, abide in the supreme fulfilment of Brahma-faring, for the sake of which the clansmen rightly go forth from home into the houseless life."
>
> Majjhima Nikāya, Sutta 26.

The ministry of the Blessed Lord opens like a divine symphony with the arresting chords of Authority, of the Attainment, and of the unequivocally assured Hope of the supreme fulfilment. The Authority is challenged by the Five. The symphony moves momentarily into a minor key, only to return swiftly into the major as the Five are soon convinced of the Authority.

The Buddha straightway proceeds to his main themes: who seeks the Deathless must fully understand the whole body of Ill, Dukkha, which constitutes the deathful; he must avoid the extremes, or dead-ends, and tread the Middle Way. The Buddha's immediate plunge "in medias res" almost sounds as if he were continuing from where he left off when he last discussed the Immortal with the Five ascetics not so long ago:

> These two extremes, (dead-ends), Bhikkhus, are not to be followed by one who has gone forth.[1] Which two? That which is linked and connected with lust through the sense-pleasures, low, of the villager, of the average man, unariyan, not connected with the goal; and that which is addiction to self-torment, painful, not connected with the goal. Now, Bhikkhus, without adopting either of the two dead-ends, there is a middle course, fully awakened to by the Tathāgata, making for vision, making for knowledge, which conduces to calming, to super-knowledge, to awakening, to Nirvāṇa.
>
> And, Bhikkhus, what is the middle course . . . that leads to Nirvāṇa? It is indeed this Noble Eightfold Path, namely, right views, right aspirations, right speech, right action, right mode of living, right endeavour, right mindfulness, right samādhi. This middle road, Bhikkhus . . . leads to Nirvāṇa.
>
> *First Truth.* Now again, Bhikkhus, this is the Noble Truth as to Dukkha (Ill; Sorrow; Suffering): jāti (birth; worldly existence) indeed is sorrowful; old age . . . disease . . . death . . . union with the unpleasing . . . separation from the pleasing . . . the unfulfilled

[1] i.e. entered the religious life, forsaking home in search of the Truth.

wish, is (each) sorrowful. In brief, the grasping fivefold aggregate (i.e. body, feelings, ideas, mental dispositions and consciousness) is sorrowful.

Second Truth. Again, Bhikkhus, this is the Noble Truth as to the origin of Dukkha : it is that craving (taṇhā) which is associated with again-becoming, accompanied by delight and attachment, finding much delight in this and that ; (it is) namely, the craving for sense pleasures . . . for individual existence . . . for super-existence.

Third Truth. Again, Bhikkhus, this is the Noble Truth as to the stopping of Dukkha : it is the utter and passionless stopping of that very craving, its renunciation, surrender, release, the lack of pleasure in it.

Fourth Truth. And this is the Noble Truth as to the course leading to the stopping of Dukkha : it is indeed that Noble Eightfold Path, namely, right views, right aspiration, right speech, right action, right mode of living, right endeavour, right mindfulness, right samādhi.

Freedom . . . As soon, Bhikkhus, as my knowledge and insight concerning these Four Noble Truths . . . were pure, I knew that I had attained supreme and full awakening . . . The knowledge of what was seen arose in me : " Freedom of mind is for me unshakeable ; this is the last jāti ; there is not now for me recurrent becoming." Thus spoke the Blessed One. The Five Bhikkhus, rejoicing, welcomed the word of the Blessed One.

Mahā Vagga, I.6.17–29.

Significantly, announcing the First Noble Truth, the Buddha presents Ill in terms of the personal suffering of Everyman. But what was the point of telling the Five that disease, decay, death, not obtaining heart's desire, being bound to the undesirable (perhaps a locality, a job, a relative, etc.) were sorrowful, for surely they could well be credited with knowing that already, and with being wise enough to remain poised in face of the petty ills of worldly life ? One point is that sickness, decay, death, frustration and circumstantial bondage which characterize individual existence, are in fact derived from the very nature of that fivefold aggregate which the individual is. And another point is that the Buddha's gospel of salvation is addressed, and is applicable to all mankind, though his teaching in its profounder aspects, would necessarily be realized in its fulness only by the capable ones.

After the enlightenment, the Buddha proceeds[1] to the "Goatherd's banyan-tree". After seven days of meditation, he breathes forth this cry:

> The brāhman whose nature is unsinful, not harsh, unstained, self-restrained,
> Who has mastered knowledge and fully traversed the Brahma-Path, he rightly, a brāhman, ought to announce the Brahma-word—(he) who has no self-obtrusiveness in the world.

He next proceeds to the Mucalinda (serpent-king's) tree, and after seven days of meditation he breathes forth this cry:

> Blissful is the solitude of the happy one who has learnt the Law and comprehends;
> Blissful is unhurtfulness in the world, self-restraint towards living things;
> Blissful is non-desire in the world, the transcending of sense pleasures,
> The putting away of the conceit 'I am'—this indeed is the highest bliss.

He next proceeds to the Rājāyatana (the king's seat, or royal abode) tree, and meditates for seven days.

Then he returns to the Goatherd's banyan-tree.

The Goatherd's banyan-tree symbolizes the everyday world of men and women. To men and women in the world, the Enlightened One, by virtue of having become the all-enlightened Arahant, is under obligation to speak the Brahma-word. In this meditation under the Goatherd's banyan-tree, he constructs the appropriate pattern in which his teaching should be cast before presenting it to the clansmen who hear it for the first time; and he decides upon the language in which the truth should be presented, so that Everyman, with his simple intelligence, could grasp it. It is hard to believe that the Buddha did not ponder over this problem with the utmost care, considering how deeply aware he was of the great difficulty[2] the ordinary man would experience in understanding the truth.

[1] Mahā-vagga, I.2.1.-I.4.1.

[2] See above, p. 187.

The Mucalinda tree symbolizes Life manifesting as each individual person, in whom the ego-centred " I "-consciousness is paramount. So the meditation under the Mucalinda tree reveals to him that in addressing the Brahma-word to the individual self, it must be so couched, that the Law is comprehended, sense pleasures are transcended, and the liberation from the conceit of the separate, fixed-ego, " I am ", is realized as indeed being the highest bliss.

The Rājāyatana tree symbolizes that " inner world " which is entered in deep meditation (samādhi) after abstracting attention from all sense-world disturbances or impressions, and the flow of discursive thought, mental chatter, has ceased. In this state of consciousness, the truth realized through the enlightenment has no verbal expression. In that state the Yogi is in the noumenal world—if one may use that term—the world of Plato's Archetypal Ideas. In this connection it is well to recall the Buddha's own words in the Brahmajāla Sutta,[1] that " there are things profound, difficult to realize, hard to understand, . . . *not to be grasped by mere logic*, subtle, comprehensible only by the wise. These things the Tathāgata, having himself realized them *by his own super-knowing* . . . ", and also, " It is, O Bhikkhus, when a Bhikkhu understands as they really are, the origin and the end, the attraction and the danger, and the escape from the six realms of contact (the five sense fields and discursive thought), that he gets to know *what is above, beyond them all*." In this realm of consciousness, the realm of " knowing " Brahman, there is direct knowing by " being " the truth known—a statement which sounds apparently meaningless in any human sphere of communication where language effectively holds sway. But the statement is made, even as such statements have been made through the ages, as witness to a reality so beyond the bounds of usual experience, that language still fails to serve as an adequate means for communicating the experience of that reality.

The Sāṇḍilya Upanishad, chapter I, says:

> Samādhi is the union of the Jivātman (individual Self) and the Paramātman (Supreme Self) without the threefold state (of the

[1] See above, pp. 164–166.

> knower, the known and the knowing). It is of the nature of extreme bliss and pure consciousness.

and the Paiṅgala Upanishad, Adhyāya III, says:

> Samādhi is that state in which citta (the discursive mind) having given up (the conception of the difference between) the meditator and meditation, becomes of the form of the meditated . . . Then arise the modifications pertaining to Ātman. Such modifications cannot be known (in the usual sense of the word "known"): they can only be "inferred" through " memory " of the samādhi state.

The last two sentences suggest that the realm touched by consciousness in samādhi is the original home of those inspirations, or flashes of illumination which mark the genius. A Buddha, a Christ, a Yogi can enter that realm at will by going into samādhi, by communing with God or praying unto the Father (immeasurably different from praying in the ordinary sense of the word). That realm is of the Eternal, timeless and dimensionless, the realm of the deathless Immortal. On returning to the space-time-mind world, forms come present to the mind for conveying the Immortal in verbal teaching to men and women. It is as if, on returning, consciousness becomes prism-like and splits up the ineffable One-Truth into sense-mind, perceivable truth-forms.

The meditation under the Rājāyatana tree, then, is the " Divine " source of inspiration for the methods of work in teaching and spreading the Gospel for the rest of the Buddha's days.

But after the Rājāyatana meditation it is the Goatherd's banyan-tree to which he returns.

Clearly, his teaching is to be for all who come to him weary with the burden of Ill, of sin and sorrow, and he will show them the way to Rest, to Nirvāṇa, here-now in this life.

To the Five, who were soon to become his first and amongst his greatest disciples, he clothes the teaching in the language right for Everyman. Not the profound, philosophical meaning of the Ill wrapped up in all manifestation, the domain of the Lord of Death, but Ill as disease, decay, emotional distress and misfortune was what Everyman could understand.[1]

[1] How well the Buddha realized this, is clearly shown in the Mahā-Dukkhakkhandha Sutta, no. 13 of the Majjhima Nikāya.

Truth the first is addressed to the existential person, then, somewhat in this fashion:

> You, so-and-so, are sick. You, poor dear, have been cruelly jilted. You, hard lines old fellow, have had your beloved, whom you utterly trusted and adored, treacherously desert you without explanation, to satisfy her lust with another. You, given the sack, are destitute and stricken with anxiety. You, oh horror! know the anguish of an absent son languishing, tortured, helpless in an enemy camp. You, unhappy old man, have a pension of two coppers a week to live on, in an age when a single meal costs a whole silver.

Such is the empirical real which any man thoroughly understands. So a Buddha can carry on a sensible discussion, based on a common understanding, from that starting point. The first step in wisdom, teaches the Buddha, is to understand the First Noble Truth, that worldly existence is fraught with Ill. With that preliminary, simple understanding, one proceeds to the next consideration, namely, the nature of the fivefold aggregate, the individual. The teaching concerning this, addressed to the individual is the fruit of the meditation under the Mucalinda tree.

According to the Mahā-vagga, I. 6. 38–46, the Buddha teaches the Five that material-form (rūpa), or "body", is not the permanent-self, the Atta (the Ātman of the Upanishads). If it were, it would not be liable to deterioration, and if it simply willed itself to be thus or thus, it would indeed be thus or thus. Such is not the case, for material-form is not the permanent-self. Similarly, not sensation (vedanā), nor perception (saññā), nor pattern of being or character (saṁkhāra), nor self-consciousness (viññāṇa), is each the permanent-self.

Should the impermanent be regarded as the Ill or the Well? As the Ill, say the Five. Is it, then, proper to regard the impermanent, suffering (or Ill), and the changeable in such terms as: "This is mine; I am this; this is my permanent-self?" No, say the Five.

> "And so," says the Buddha, "all material-form, whether past, present or future, whether within us or external, whether gross or subtle . . . is to be regarded through right wisdom as it really is, thus: 'This is not mine; I am not this; this is not the permanent-self of me.' All sensation . . . perception . . . character-pattern . . . consciousness . . . is to be regarded through right

wisdom as it really is, thus: 'This is not mine; I am not this; this is not the permanent-self of me'."

Thus the *entire* sense-perceived and/or mind-inferred or conceived man—the existential person—is anicca and anattā, that is impermanent and devoid of an unchanging, abiding principle, or, in other words, not atta.

The Buddha makes no positive assertion about the Atta, nor does he attempt to describe it. For the Atta is so other than the nature of the entire manifested universe as we perceive and understand it, that even to say "It is" or "It is not", or "It is and also is not", or "It neither is nor is not", is misleading, or at least partly misleading. For the everyday person, "it is" or "it is not" has meaning only within the framework of his existential being and the phenomenal universe. But every perceived and known element constituting this being and universe is impermanent, mortal. Everyman's entire range of comprehension is enclosed within the limits of the universal mortal. How then, can he, unawakened as he is, comprehend the Immortal, the Infinite, the Atta? Every means of conception and of expression he possesses can be utilized by him only in relation to the finite and mortal. So the Buddha does not discuss the Atta.

Appearing within a century or so of the golden age of Yājñavalkya, Uddālaka, King Janaka and others, the Buddha found strange distortions of the Ātman teaching, and fantastic, worthless and unmoral philosophies springing up. Smitten to the quick with the ubiquity of sorrow in man's life, the scarcity of holy living and the prevalence of evil, he sought deliverance, and found it. Himself having gained the Immortal, himself knowing through his super-knowledge what was above and beyond the six fields, he saw that what was necessary as a practical concern for man in order to make an end of Ill, was that he should tread the path of holiness. This required, among other things, that he should cease from mistaking the transient for the Eternal, the Atta.

Man's actual life is evidence of his ignorance of the fact that none of the khandhas of the fivefold aggregate is the Atta. As long as there is such ignorance, personal existence in the world is a source of Ill. Hence the necessity for right views:

and one right view consists in seeing that the sense-contacted and mind-perceived universe is characterized by impermanence (anicca) and by the absence of abiding entity (anattā).

In the Mahā-Sudassana Jātaka, King Mahā-Sudassana is consoling his Queen, weeping bitterly on account of his approaching death. He explains how all component things are transient: the moment a thing is born, or has a discrete, separate existence, there is a state. The moment there is a state, the process of disintegration is at work. Thus, any "coming into being" inherently contains within it "going out of being". All component things, therefore, are impermanent, momentary . . . unstable . . . sure to depart, only for a time, without substance —as temporary as a phantom, as the mirage, or as foam! "How then in these, dear lady (Queen) Subhaddā, can you feel any satisfaction? Understand rather 'to bring them into subjection, that is bliss.' For to bring them into subjection, since it involves mastery over the whole circle of saṁsāra, is the same as Nirvāṇa . . . And there is no other bliss than that."

In the discourse on anicca and anattā, the Buddha concludes his teaching thus:

> Regarding them (the five aggregates composing the person) thus, O Bhikkhus, an instructed disciple of the Noble turns away from (nibbindati) rūpa . . . vedanā . . . saññā . . . saṁkhāra . . . viññāṇa. Becoming turned away from (these), he becomes free from desire; through non-desire he is liberated.
>
> *Release.* When he is liberated, there arises in him the knowledge 'I am liberated.' He knows that 'jāti is ended; the brahmacariya has been lived; what ought to be done has been done; there is nothing (to be achieved as far as the existential life is concerned) beyond (higher or nobler than) this state'.

In what manner, now, does this impermanent universe undergo change?

After the Buddha's discourse on anicca and anattā, Koṇḍañña is the first amongst the Five to obtain the clear, stainless vision of the Law:

> Everything that has by nature an origin,
> has also by nature a cessation.

He begs:

> "Reverend Sir, let me receive from the Blessed One ordination as one who has gone forth, and receive admission."

In this context, "gone forth" may well mean that Aññāta Koṇḍañña, Koṇḍañña the Perceiver, who had already gone forth from the householder's life into the homeless life, now goes forth out of a state of ignorance into a realized consciousness of the truth. The "poor", "blinded" child of mortality finds what he sought so long, immortality. The Blessed One answers:

> Come, O Bhikkhu, well-proclaimed is the doctrine. Tread the Brahma-walk (Brahmacariya) for making a complete end of Ill.

These words are amongst the most significant the Buddha ever uttered. Not the individual's selfish well-being and escape from sorrow, but making a complete end of all Ill is the goal of individual endeavour.

Now in that early springtime of the ministry, Sāriputta and Moggallāna, seeking the Deathless, were staying near Rājagriha. Sāriputta sees the elder Assaji set forth on his begging round. Struck by his demeanour and his personal appearance, Sāriputta draws nigh and enquires, "Who is thy teacher? Whose doctrine dost thou profess?" Assaji tells him that he follows Gotama the Sakyan. "And what, venerable Sir, does thy teacher declare, what does he announce?" Assaji, newly ordained, only recently come to the doctrine, modestly disclaims any ability to expound it fully; but its pith, he suggests, could be put thus:

> "Whatsoever things are produced from a cause,
> of these the Tathāgata tells the cause,
> and that which is the cessation of these;
> thus the Great Recluse declares."

Mahā-vagga, I.23.5.

"If this, indeed, be the Dhamma (doctrine)," says Sāriputta, "ye have reached even now to the griefless state, unseen in the past during many vast numbers of ages." And he and Moggallāna move on to the Blessed One, and become two of his greatest disciples.

Sāriputta sees that any one thing has an origin by way of a cause; the thing, a consequence of a cause, in its own turn is the cause of a consequence. A thing in its arising is a consequence; in its passing away, it is a cause.

But the conception, far from being static and confined to the mechanical, is dynamic, is "evolutionary" or "emergent" (to use a modern term, without necessarily reading the present into the past) in its "feel". The Buddha himself clothes it in the best terms available in his day:

"There being this, that comes to be."

This *becomes* that. This grows, or is transformed, into that. The Buddha constantly reiterates that whatever arises, of necessity passes away. Nothing in the manifested world ever stands still, or merely moves unchanged in space and time, but undergoes continuous change in the endless movement of the cosmic process. But the change is by way of cause.

For many millennia, men, observing an event, believed that it happened because of the will of a fickle, capricious God, or because of the influence of malign or friendly spirits, or by chance. Now, for the first time in human history, *circa* 528 B.C., came One with insight who taught: this, prevailing at any one instant, changing continuously, becomes that at some subsequent moment. The nature of the change wholly depends upon the nature of the conditions and forces operating at the previous moment. Men, beasts, gods, things, all are included in this all-embracing conception. Whatever holds at this moment is the resultant emerging out of the interaction of all the forces and conditions, physical and mental, which held good at an antecedent moment.

If for no other conception than this, the Buddha has an assured, honoured place among the greatest intellects of all time. He hurled one of the mightiest thunderbolts against irrational, superstitious fear, which chilled men's hearts and emasculated their minds with a devastating sense of impotence against omnipotent caprice, whether of god or demon or nature. He enthroned Law everywhere, Law in highest heaven as in hindmost hell, on earth and in space, over man and through all nature. Whilst the Vedic poet-seers had exalted Law by right of unquestioning faith, and the Upanishadic spiritual geniuses by right of transcendent vision, the Buddha enthroned it by right of emancipated Reason.

Gotama the Buddha is the true father of the scientific spirit. After him, the Indian mind becomes firmly imbued with the conviction of the permanence and universality of Law.

This profound insight of the Buddha is represented by the word karma, which literally means action. The process of the whole universe of form (rūpa), mind and consciousness is the karmic process: self-adjusting, because all change proceeds by way of cause: a continuous becoming which is not fortuitous, haphazard or "lawless". Karma is inadequately conceived if it is regarded as an abstract law controlling process, and altogether wrongly if merely as a law of retribution meting out rewards and punishments through a series of lives. If universal process is understood as that seen-as-a-whole activity, displaying the continuously new integration emerging through the interaction of matter and force and mind and will and consciousness, then such universal process is the karmic process. Karma covers the changing shape of universal process together with the forces and conditions involved in that changing. The event is whole. The mind of man is such that it splits up the whole event into inert substance being moved by an invisible, mysterious, active energy or force. Karma means whole-event. Karma is existential.

Within karma are contained determinism and indeterminacy, freedom and necessity. According to the nature of the observed situation, karma may be seen to operate as natural law—apples falling earthwards; or as human law—offenders being punished, the meritorious being rewarded; or as divine law—Jesus on the Cross. In complex situations where "natural", "human" and "divine" impinge upon, interfere with or merge into each other, it becomes impossible to see justice manifest—justice as conceived by mortals. But if these situations, or events, are seen as resultants of all the forces and conditions involved, then the problem of justice or injustice does not arise, and one sees that which happens for what it truly is.

Action-reaction, reward-punishment, retribution-forgiveness, expiation-redemption are all in their own special contexts part of the universal process. How each of these is related to the other, or how each is integrated into the whole, is not always easy to see. But they are all subsumed within karma.

This knowledge of the nature of the universal process—that whatsoever has an origin has it by way of cause, and that it must of necessity pass out of its present state and become transformed into another state—is a ground for Faith. Faith, in all the Great Teachings of India, has knowledge born of experience, observation and inference as its stuff. Like other Great Indians, the Buddha imposes no blind belief—the source of terrible misconceptions and foul deeds, as all too amply attested by history—but teaches, and himself perfectly exemplifies, that Faith is the fair daughter of knowledge, the knowledge obtained by experience, and by study, and by revelation. He himself exemplifies in his own methods the appropriate use of the principle of verification.

Faith born of the "stainless, clear perception of the Law" is the assurance of stability, the ground on which to base that action which leads to liberation. The Buddha points out[1] that "Nothing is to be got by mere wishing . . . ", but it is to be obtained by constant exertion[2] in the method (naya), the Law (dhamma) and what is skilled (kusala). "Seeking after what is skilled, he had been a pilgrim through the realm of naya and dhamma, outside of which no victory can be won."[3] It is strange, then, to hear it said by some that the Buddha taught inaction, or that his teachings are negative. The Buddha did teach

> Abstention from all evil, doing of what is skilled, purification of one's thought—this is the doctrine of the Buddhas.
>
> Dhammapada, 183.

He exhorts his aged father thus:

> One must rise, one must not be slothful;
> One must follow the law of good conduct.
> Who follows the Dhamma lies down in bliss
> in this world and that beyond.
>
> Nidāna Kathā

The Buddha's whole teaching is essentially religious. The foremost place is occupied by his ethics, the second by psychology and logic, and the last by an irreducible minimum of metaphysics

[1] Mahā-Satipaṭṭhāna Sutta, D.II. 307.
[2] Majjhima Nikāya, II. 181, 197.
[3] Mahā-Parinibbāna Sutta, D.II. 151.

His ethics and his philosophy are based on psychology and logic.

By virtue of the nature of the Law, one may legitimately proceed from Faith to Hope. Ill is not the consequence of malicious or vengeful caprice. All dukkha comes by way of cause. Useless are sacrifices and supplications to non-existent or impotent deities or spirits. It is for each individual man to perceive the cause of suffering, and to remove it. He alone can tackle the cause. He alone, and no external person or power on his behalf, must tackle it, or else freedom were a mockery. His is the basic decision. Afterward, there may come aid, from on high, from the teacher, from anywhere. But it is absolutely for the person himself to accept the implication of individuality: self-responsibility. If he does not, he continues to be a perpetuator of evil and suffering in the world, and for himself.

Suffering has a cause. Can man do anything about it? Yes, says the Buddha, man can extinguish suffering. Though subject to the working out of preceding forces and conditions, man has the power to bring new forces into play, which can change for the worse or better, disintegrate or intensify, what is already present. By completely uprooting the causes of dukkha, man can utterly extinguish sorrow and evil, and can win, and abide here-now in the deathless Immortal.

In the Mahā-Satipaṭṭhāna Sutta, D. II. 308–311, the second and the third Truths are presented by the Buddha in detail. Summarized:

> The coming to be of Ill is due to Craving, potent for rebirth, accompanied by lust and self-indulgence, seeking satisfaction, now here, now there, to wit, the craving for the life of sense, for becoming, and (also) for super-becoming . . .
> Craving arises out of the senses (including imagination), the objects of sense, thoughts, feelings, perceptions, intentions, memories, preoccupation, and deliberation arising out of the use of the senses and objects of sense . . .
>
> The cessation of Ill is brought about by the utter cessation of and disenchantment about that very craving, giving it up, renouncing it, emancipation from it, detachment from it, by putting away material things, the use of the senses, the objects of sense; and by putting away thoughts, stimuli, feelings, perceptions, inten-

tions, memories, preoccupation, and deliberation arising out of the senses and sense objects.

The Upanishadic philosophers knew that "this-all", the manifested universe, was impermanent. From Brahman it emerged; to Brahman it returned. Brahman was "the Constant among the inconstant" (Hume's translation), "the Eternal among things that pass away" (Mascaró's translation).[1] But the mass of men, possessing only a confused understanding, clung fondly to their belief in a permanent personal self. The Buddha showed that the constituents of the manifested world and of man were not the Atta (Ātman), that whatsoever was an object of thought, including thought and consciousness itself, was impermanent.

Now here comes the tragedy. Man seeks permanent peace, freedom, happiness, fulfilment, in the impermanent realm of "this-all". With the inevitable passing away of "this-all", whatever peace or happiness he found in it also disappears. Sorrow supervenes.

What makes man seek peace, happiness, freedom and fulfilment in the sphere of "this-all"?

First, ignorance: ignorance of the truth that whatsoever has by nature an origin must of necessity pass away, and of the fact that personal existence is characterized by the absence of abiding entity in it, and by pain.

Out of ignorance arises the delusion of a distinct, permanent "you" as being wholly separate from a distinct, permanent "I". The delusion of a separate, permanent "I" is the source of selfishness. This deep-rooted, devilish selfishness, which makes man seek continuously to gather for himself, leads to the other great cause of evil and sorrow, namely, craving.

For out of ignorance man seeks happiness in the transient. What fleeting pleasure he obtains, he stores in his memory. To this fleeting pleasure, which he mistakes for true happiness, he attaches a value. This precisely is his mistake. He considers it worth his while to strive for the fleeting pleasure, imagining that thereby he will achieve fulfilment, and establish lasting happiness for himself. So he attempts to fix or to perpetuate

[1] Kaṭha Upanishad, V. 13.

the external pattern of the particular experience which brought him temporary pleasure; or he bends his efforts to ensure the continual repetition of that experience for which he thirsts, for which he is consumed with longing—the wearisome, senseless round of uprising and passing away, of births and deaths, of saṁsāra. Thus he becomes the slave of quenchless craving, craving for sensations, possessions, power, and the maintenance of separate selfhood in perpetuity. In other words, he is the slave of lust and egoism. Ignorance and craving, then, are the main elements of the cause of sorrow and evil.

Ignorance and craving are two out of the twelve elements of the causative process expounded by the Buddha and known as the Paṭicca-Samuppāda, the Law of Dependent Origination, which has ever proved difficult to understand.

After becoming all-enlightened, at the end of seven days, the Buddha is still sitting in meditation:

> Then the Blessed One during the first watch of the night thought over the causative process forward and reversed . . . 'Thus there is origination of this whole aggregation of Ill' . . . 'Thus there is cessation of this whole aggregation of Ill'. Then indeed the Blessed One, having understood its essential meaning at that time, breathed forth this cry:
>
> When things become clear to the strenuous,
> contemplative brāhman,
> Then all his doubts vanish because he
> understands thing-with-cause.
>
> Then again the Blessed One during the middle watch of the night thought over the causative process . . . breathed forth this cry:
>
> When things become clear to the strenuous
> contemplative brāhman,
> Then all his doubts vanish because he
> discerns destruction of cause.
>
> Then indeed the Blessed One during the third watch of the night thought over the causative process . . . breathed forth this cry:
>
> When things become clear to the strenuous,
> contemplative brāhman,
> Scattering the army of Māra, he stands
> even as the sun lighting the heavens.
>
> Mahā-vagga, I.1.2–7.

It is stated in various texts, such as the Majjhima Nikāya, Sutta IV, M. I. 22, and the Sāmañña-Phala Sutta, D. I. 81, that after the enlightenment the Buddha recalled his previous existences:

> " One, two, three . . . a hundred thousand births, many an aeon of disintegration of the world, many an aeon of its redintegration . . . In this or that former existence I remembered such and such was my name, my sept, my class . . . and my term of life. When I passed thence, I came by such and such subsequent existence, wherein such and such was my name, and so forth. Thence I passed to this life. Thus did I call to mind my diverse existences of the past in all their details and features. This, O brāhman, was the first knowledge attained by me in the first watch of the night . . ."

In the Mahā-Sudassana Sutta, D.II.196, the Buddha says:

> " Now it may be, Ānanda, that you may think ' The Great king of Glory (Mahā-Sudassana) of that time was another person.' But, Ānanda, you should not view the matter thus. I, at that time, was the Great King of Glory."

In the Kūṭadanta Sutta, D.I.143, Kūṭadanta asks:

> " Does the venerable Gotama admit that he who celebrates such a sacrifice, or causes it to be celebrated, is reborn at the dissolution of the body after death into some state of happiness in heaven ? "

The Buddha answers:

> " Yes, O brāhman, that I admit. And at that time I was the brāhman who, as chaplain, had that sacrifice performed."

In the Kassapa-Sīhanāda Sutta, D.I.162, the Buddha says:

> " Herein, O Kassapa, I am wont to be aware with purified deva-vision surpassing that of men, how some men, given to mortification, living a hard life, are born, on the dissolution of the body, into some unhappy, fallen state of misery and woe, while others, living just so, are reborn into some happy state or into a heavenly world."

In the Sankhāruppati Sutta, M. III 99, the Buddha talks of one of the ways in which the force leading to rebirth is generated: a man cherishes the thought of being reborn in a princely family; the predispositions thus set up lead to rebirth in that family.

In the face of all the above, the popular fancy naturally pictured rebirth as a process in which a permanent entity, a soul or ego, left one body after its death and entered a new one, left that one at death and entered a new one, and so on through a succession of lives. But what the Buddha meant by jāti is not what the mass of people understood, and still understand by that word. This difficult subject has been well treated by Mrs. Rhys Davids in the chapter entitled "The Norm as Moral Law" in her book *Buddhism: A Study of the Buddhist Norm.*[1] Especially to-day, when individualistic self-consciousness is stronger, perhaps, than it has ever been in the past, it is difficult to free one's thinking from the effects of the notions of identity and mechanical causation. From the Buddha's point of view:

> To say one (person) acts, but another reaps the fruit of those acts, is not true. And to say one and the same both acts and is affected by the result is (also) not true.[2]

The Buddha rejects the static view that either everything is or nothing is. One should see, therefore, that one thing or situation is the cause of, and becomes transformed or is taken up into another. *That* fellow in relation to *this* fellow is neither the same fellow nor a different fellow. Nevertheless, the phenomenon of jāti (rebirth) is manifest. If one looks at a river, the water flowing past is continuously different although the river is continuously the same. (This is comparable to looking at *that* fellow and attesting quite truly, 'He, indeed, is that fellow.') Now a change of climate takes place and the river completely dries up. (This is comparable to the death of the existential *that* fellow.) The waters of the sea into which the old river used to flow, continually evaporate, forming rain-bearing clouds. A thousand years pass by. The climate again changes, rain falls, even the solid landscape has altered slightly. Again there stands one on the bank and looks at a river. No map or historical record of the past is available to this onlooker. He does not know that the river he is looking at is a jāti of the river that was looked at a thousand years ago. But you, the reader, see jāti manifest; you see a demonstration of "becoming, by way of cause." (This river, of a thousand years later, is comparable to the jāti of *that* fellow of a thousand years ago—neither a different person nor one persisting identity.) It is

[1] Published by Williams & Norgate, in the Home University Library Series.
[2] Saṁyutta Nikāya, II. 20.

not surprising that the Buddha was so keenly aware of the difficulty which would be experienced in understanding what he had perceived through his enlightenment, a difficulty which will be even more weightily appreciated when considering the Paṭicca-samuppāda. The preliminary consideration of jāti is necessary before proceeding to the causative process, and should be kept in mind side by side with the discussion, and explanation offered earlier of the round of births and deaths.

What value the Buddha himself attaches to the understanding of the causative process is indicated by what he uttered during the watches of the night as he meditated upon it.[1]

The Paṭicca-samuppāda is expounded in short as well as in full form, in differing arrangements, and with slight variations in explanation. One short form runs thus:

> Depending on both the eye and material forms, there arises visual consciousness (cakkhu-viññāṇam); the meeting of (these) three is (called) impression or contact (phassa); because of phassa there is sensation (vedanā); because of vedanā there is craving (taṇhā). With the cessation of this very craving, so that no remnant or trace of it remains, there is cessation of grasping (upādāna); with the cessation of upādāna there is cessation of becoming (bhava); with the cessation of bhava there is cessation of jāti; with the cessation of jāti, cease decay and death, grief, lamentation, sorrow, dejection and despair.
>
> Thus there is origination and cessation of this whole aggregation of sorrow.
>
> Depending on both the ear . . . nose . . . tongue . . . body . . . mind (as the source of memories, anticipations, fantasies) . . . and material-forms (or any external stimuli), there arises hearing-consciousness . . . smelling-consciousness . . . (as above) . . .
>
> Thus there is origination and cessation of this whole aggregation of sorrow.
>
> Saṁyutta Nikāya, Nidāna-vagga, Nidāna Saṁyutta (Saṁ.12) Sutta 45, (Nātikā) (P.T.S. II.74).

In Sutta 60 (Nidāna) of the Saṁyutta Nikāya, the Blessed One says to Ānanda:

> Through not understanding this Law . . . mankind cannot get . . . beyond saṁsāra (the ceaseless round).

[1] See above, p. 202.

In one who sees enjoyment in notions (dhammesu) of grasping and abides therein, craving increases.
Because of craving there is grasping (upādāna); because of upādāna there is becoming (bhava); because of bhava, jāti; because of jāti there is decay and death, grief, lamentation, sorrow, dejection and despair.
Thus there is origination of this whole aggregation of sorrow.

The slight difference in presentation between Suttas 60 and 45 may be noted. Sutta 66 (Sammasa) of the Saṁyutta Nikāya shows that what is lovely and pleasant, interacting with the six sense fields, is the origin of craving:

The Blessed One spoke thus:

"Scrutinize now with an inward scrutiny (sam-masaṁ), O Bhikkhus . . . In this regard, a Bhikkhu . . . with an inward scrutiny . . . (sees that) this various and manifold Ill, this decay and death which arises in the world . . . is based upon supports (upadhinidānam), has its origin . . . its birth . . . its production from supports.
When there is support there is decay and death; when there is no support decay and death are not . . .
Support is based upon craving, has its origin . . . birth . . . production in craving.
When there is craving there is support; when there is no craving support is not . . .
Whatsoever in the world is lovely and pleasant, here this craving, should it arise, arises; should it abide, it abides here . . .
Sight . . . hearing . . . smell . . . taste . . . body (touch) . . . mind . . . here this craving, should it arise, arises . . . abides . . .
Those who in past ages, whether devotees or brāhmans, viewing what is lovely and pleasant in the world, have seen it as permanent (niccato) . . . as happiness . . . as reality (attha) . . . as health . . . as peace (khemato), they made craving to increase . . . (thereby) support to increase . . . (thereby) dukkha to increase; and making dukkha to increase they had no release from jāti, decay, death . . . they had no release, I say, from sorrow . . ."

Significant is the fact that in the above discourses, the causative process is presented as contained here and now within one's lifetime.

As in the Sammasa Sutta above, so too in the Mahā-Satipaṭṭhāna Sutta[1] the Buddha traces the uprising of craving to sense experience and certain mental processes.

The Mahā-Nidāna Sutta[2] presents the Paṭicca-samuppāda

[1] D. II. 308 & 309.
[2] D. II. 55-64.

more fully, as schematically shown below, to which the Mahāpadāna adds one more step, namely, the six fields of sense, saḷāyatana, inserting it between name-and-form (nāma-rūpa) and contact (phassa) :

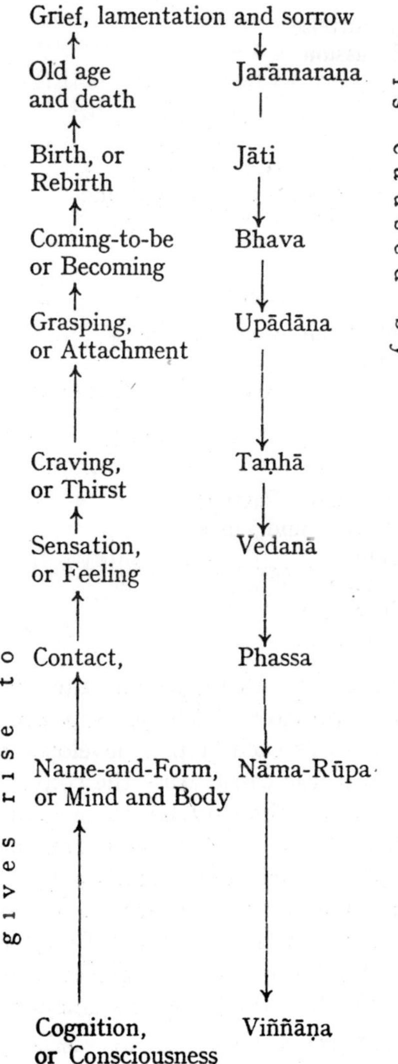

at the things of sense; attachment through speculative opinions, through soul theories; grasping after mere rule and ritual.

for sights, sounds, odours, tastes, tangibles and ideas.

born of impressions through sight, hearing, smell, taste, touch and mental object.

reaction of sight, hearing etc. to stimuli in the shape of objects, events, memories etc.

those modes, features, characters and exponents by which the aggregate called 'Name' manifests itself. If all were absent, there would be no manifestation of a corresponding verbal designation of the aggregate called (bodily) 'Form'.

In the same Sutta, a sub-section of the Paṭicca-samuppāda is worked out as follows :

Sensation gives rise to Craving
which gives rise to Pursuit
which gives rise to Gain
which gives rise to Decision or Purpose
which gives rise to Desire and Passion
which gives rise to Tenacity
which gives rise to Possession
which gives rise to Avarice
which gives rise to Watch and Ward over Possessions
which gives rise to Blows and Wounds, Strife, Retorts and Contradictions, Quarrelling, Lies and Slander.

From this point the cycle is traced backwards :

Blows and Wounds, Strife, Retorts and Contradictions, Quarrelling, Lies and Slander are
caused by Watch and Ward over Possessions
which is caused by Avarice
which is caused by Possession
which is caused by Tenacity
which is caused by Desire and Passion
which is caused by Decision and Purpose
which is caused by Gain
which is caused by Pursuit
which is caused by Craving
which is caused by Sensation.

In the Mahāpadāna presentation, the Blessed One puts the exposition into the mouth of a previous Buddha, Vipassin. This sentence is constantly repeated as each step is developed : " Then, Bhikkhus, from attention to the cause arose the conviction through reason . . . ." For Gotama the Buddha, there could be no such thing as faith contrary to, or even straining reason.

In the Mahā-Nidāna, more explicitly than in the Mahāpadāna, the Buddha says that nāma-rūpa and viññāṇa are each the " cause " of the other. The essence of it is that the Buddha regarded an individual as a psycho-physical organism. In Rhys Davids's words[1] : " Barely stated, the summary amounts

[1] *Sacred Books of the Buddhists*, Vol. II I,p. 61 ,footnote 2. See also Sāmañña-Phala Sutta, D. I. 76.

to this—' only through cognition, language and bodily form do we live and express ourselves'."

The Mahā-vagga, I. 1. 2, presents the causative process in its full form:

1. Because of Avijjā (ignorance)	there are	Conformations Predispositions Tendencies	Saṁkhārā
2. Because of Saṁkhārā	there is	Cognition Consciousness	Viññāṇa
3. Because of Viññāṇa	there is	Name-and-Form Mind and Body	Nāma-rūpa
4. Because of Nāma-rūpa	there are	the six sense-fields	Saḷ-āyatana
5. Because of Saḷ-āyatana	there is	Contact Impression	Phassa
6. Because of Phassa	there is	Sensation	Vedanā
7. Because of Vedanā	there is	Craving	Taṇhā
8. Because of Taṇhā	there is	Grasping	Upādāna
9. Because of Upādāna	there is	Becoming	Bhava
10. Because of Bhava	there is	Birth Rebirth	Jāti
11. Because of Jāti	there are	Decay and death, grief, lamentation, sorrow, dejection and despair.	Jarāmaraṇa

Thus there is origination of this whole aggregation of Ill, dukkha.

1. By the extinction of Avijjā there is extinction of Saṁkhārā
2. By the extinction of Saṁkhārā there is extinction of Viññāṇa
3. By the extinction of Viññāṇa there is extinction of Nāma-rūpa
4. By the extinction of Nāma-rūpa there is extinction of Saḷ-āyatana
5. By the extinction of Saḷ-āyatana there is extinction of Phassa
6. By the extinction of Phassa there is extinction of Vedanā
7. By the extinction of Vedanā there is extinction of Taṇhā
8. By the extinction of Taṇhā there is extinction of Upādāna
9. By the extinction of Upādāna there is extinction of Bhava
10. By the extinction of Bhava there is extinction of Jāti
11. By the extinction of Jāti there is extinction of Jarāmaraṇa

Thus there is extinction of the whole aggregation of dukkha.

If the Paṭicca-samuppāda as stated above is taken literally, then the extinction of viññāṇa-nāmarūpa, which stands, according to the Mahā-Nidāna Sutta, for the psycho-physical person, can only mean the extinction of the man himself. So it is necessary to look at the twelve-nidāna form of the causative process in a different way.

Avijjā means ignorance. Ignorance of what? Sāriputta the beloved, the honoured disciple of the Buddha, says:

Not to know the truth of Dukkha, friend,
Not to know the truth of the origin of Ill
Not to know the truth of the stopping of Ill
Not to know the truth of the Path that leads
to the stopping of Ill,
This, O friend, is Avijjā.

Sammādiṭṭhi Sutta, Majjhima Nikāya, I.54.

As shown earlier (p. 201), man's belief in separate, permanent ego, the source of selfishness, perpetuates the gulf between "you" and "me", and the distinction between "thine" and "mine". In the Mahā-Govinda Sutta, D. II. 241, Govinda asks: "Wherein proficient, training in what, can mortal reach the immortal world of Brahm?" Comes the answer from Brahmā Himself: "He among men who eschews 'me' and 'mine',[1] who is one-pointed on Brahman, intent on compassion, with no delight in unchastity."

The belief in a separate ego makes a man bend all his energy towards acquiring for himself, towards flattering, pleasing and feeding that ego. This belief, together with craving, perpetuates ignorance. Now the knowledge born of the mere experience of suffering, common to all mankind, must be distinguished from the knowledge of the truth of suffering. In the former case, man still holds fast to the ego and constantly tries to "dodge" suffering, or to insure against it; and he continues to live and act in the belief that the pursuit of the

[1] Cf. There are two causes, one leading to bondage, the other to emancipation. They are "mine" and "not-mine". Through "mine", creatures are bound; whereas through "not-mine" they are released from bondage.

Paiṅgala Upanishad, Adhyāya IV.

The wise, through the practice of deep meditation on Brahman, leave off the conceptions of "I" and "mine" in the body and the senses.

Adhyātma Upanishad.

satisfactions of his cravings will bring him true happiness and permanent peace. But this merely piles up evil. In the latter case, man perceives that evil and suffering are rooted in his belief in his separate selfhood and are part of the very fabric of his sentient existence. If, therefore, man wants a real release from suffering, from " this whole body of Ill ", he must first see this truth of dukkha.

There is another, and a profounder meaning in certain contexts, of the word avijjā. In Sutta 36 of the Majjhima Nikāya, the Buddha, relating the enlightenment, says: " This was the third vijjā which I gained . . . thus it is with one who abides diligent, ardent and firm."

Vijjā means Awakening; the intense, all-alive, concentrated, glowing, profound Awakening in the deeps of consciousness; something more than, and qualitatively different from knowledge, however wide, great, sound. He who has vijjā is the Awakened One, the Enlightened One.

Avijjā marks the unawakened one. This unawakened state is the ill-state, the suffering state, the state wherein one is ignorant of the truth that dukkha characterizes individual existence, and the manifested world.

Saṁkhāra is a word with several meanings. According to its derivation from the verb which means to arrange, to adorn, to prepare, saṁkhāra means both the preparing and the thing prepared. It means, also, confections or conformations; and the actual conformation or pattern in being at the moment predisposes towards the next pattern. Saṁkhāra also means predispositions and tendencies; also actions, but actions in the inclusive sense of will (or desire)-thought-physical expression, all in one.

Jāti means birth or rebirth, in the sense of a creature being born. Let it also be understood as a having come into concrete manifestation or being, as distinct from com-ing into being (bhava). For instance: a child shows musical promise; his parent, desiring to give him a good instrument, looks around in a shop and says, " I will have that one " (upādāna); he pays his cheque, and the instrument is coming home in the van (bhava); it is placed, with great glee, in the place of pride in the drawing room (jāti).

Now, the causative process may be considered thus: the starting point, as the Buddha shows in the Mahā-Nidāna Sutta, is the psycho-physical person, the nāmarūpa-viññāṇa, beginning in the mother's womb. He is ignorant, unawakened—although the author of the Garbha Upanishad seems to think otherwise. He is born, the product of all the influences that made him, such as hereditary factors, and circumstantial factors like the food and drink, exercise and fresh air, excitement or peace, sensible or riotous living, happiness or misery and anxiety of the mother, and so on. So there are certain saṁkhārā.

At birth, then, the starting point is this single complex of nāmarūpa-viññāṇa-avijjā-saṁkhārā.

Phassa begins within the womb itself in part, and in all its aspects after birth.

The infant is subject to the external world, and to its internal processes of digestion and breathing, and to painful and pleasant sensations. It is a "child of Fate". It cannot choose or control or convey specific desires, apart from its fundamental needs for existence and avoidance of pain.

In its daily life, innumerable external influences such as sights, sounds, pressures, temperatures, cuddling, rough-handling and so on, all play upon it. In short, it is conditioned. The capacity for response is slowly evoked from it, controls are taught, and self-consciousness is encouraged and developed along the usual separative, permanent ego lines. Thus new saṁkhārā come into being, affect the child, and continuously transform into fresh saṁkhārā as life goes on and the child becomes the adult.

Avijjā remains the all-affecting cause for Ill in the whole process. Ordinary religious or secular education does not get rid of avijjā. The person's own strenuous and unremitting effort, if crowned with success, removes avijjā.

The other steps of the causative process up to jāti are perfectly clear.

Now, these steps from phassa to jāti must be seen in relation to each and every specific activity or process, successively, in the life of this single complex of nāmarūpa-viññāṇa-avijjā-saṁkhārā. At jāti, heart's desire is realized. The maintenance of this realization to which one is bound by one's craving, by one's self-association with the object of desire, is attended with effort. There is nothing wrong with effort which is pure or perfect. But in this situation of bondage through craving, all effort is fraught with strain and anxiety, is poisoned with fear, jealousy and envy, hate, strife and war.

Sooner or later there is a wearing down ; there is decrepitude, decay and death. Heart's desire is dead, and jarāmaraṇa is the end of that cycle. If the effort (taṇhā-upādāna-bhava) is frustrated, then one reaches maraṇa without realizing heart's desire, without a proper jāti.

This cycle from phassa to jarāmaraṇa is endlessly repeated in the course of one's lifetime. The stream of saṁsāra is kept flowing, the wheels of Jagannātha's car are kept turning, and the draught of sorrow is constantly quaffed, illusions and delusions are obstinately preserved, and Ill is maintained. Therefore man knows hell, self-decreed. Because the self-decree is made out of ignorance, infinite Compassion is evoked from a Buddha, infinite Love from a Christ,[1] and infinite, tender Mercy from God.

Meanwhile, the person, the single complex of nāmarūpa-viññāṇa-avijjā-saṁkhārā, is steadily moving towards the end of his life-span. The Lord of Death, sovereign over saṁsāra and dukkha, has already exacted heavy toll from him. And then, Father Time gives him sweet release. The man lays down his burden, and " yields his soul to God ", whilst the Glory is unto God. (Indeed, the Glory is always unto God—the Glory so tragically bedimmed in poor, suffering, existential man, the sorrowful, mortal bundle of impermanent aggregates. The extinction by Time of the illusory, separate-ego consciousness which was so potent a source of Ill, is one meaning, and evidence, of the Mercy of God). Time the father, a supporter, sustainer and bringer to fruition, is gentle and friendly, and brings the end happily and naturally, comfortingly and sweetly. Time is the external, and universal Ender. He is like Grandfather smiling at peaceful Baby. Death, he of dreadful mien and lurid eyes, with a bloody scythe in his hand, is an executioner, a slayer,

[1] "Jesus wept."—Luke, XIX. 41.

the fiendish agent of the self-imposed " vengeance of God "—for Law cannot be flouted. He is the internal and specific, and violent Ender, bomb-like.

Where there is holiness, Time folds Death in his arms. Together they bring peace to him who has run his course, like fading sunset glory, and immortality to his Name. Previous to the realization of that supreme consummation, the bundle of aggregates of material-form, feelings, ideas, saṁkhārā and viññāṇa which made up the person, vanishes from human sight when death comes. Unexhausted taṇhā impels to a future re-forming, and eventually there is a jāti, a rebirth. But, the born and the reborn, in the reincarnational sense, are neither two different persons nor one and the same person.

Not always is the cycle from phassa to jarāmaraṇa a deadly ill. There are those beautiful, selfless deeds and thoughts and creations by men and women, which are the lightnings of the Eternal, reminders to man to look at all worldly loveliness with calm clear-sightedness, and, unensnared, to become awakened within. And for this same end do the Great Messengers appear as Redeemers or as Tathāgatas, Exemplars to sufferers caught in the meshes of Ill, or of worldly existence under the sway of worldly values.

But now, whilst many will acknowledge that much in this world is evil, the counterstatement will be made, neither unreasonably nor unjustifiably, that surely life also holds a million delights, and that every person, though he knows some sorrows, also enjoys many pleasures.

Here one comes to a critical point in the whole range of Indian Religion and Philosophy. If a man is prepared to accept the stream of all passing experiences undiscriminatingly and uncreatively, and if he is content to accept worldly values and live by the principle, " This is how it is, and I must do what I can to get along and make good somehow ", then he may ignore Indian thought, or stifle any stirrings of divine discontent. But if he is not, then he enquires: What is the worth-while, the good, the real, the true ?

For Indian thought, the true, good, real and worth-while as a goal of endeavour is man's realization of the peaceful, free and eternal, whereas the unreal, the not worth-while, as the objective fact of each person's actual life, is brought about by attachment to, and by the impassioned effort to crystallize or to fixate the transient, fevered, bound, mortal. It must be clearly understood that it is not the objective universe—the transient, the dual, the round-turning—which is Ill. The objective universe is the objective universe, and as such is marvellous and wonderful, terrifying and awful, beautiful and inspiring to us. That this is the true Indian view is irrefutably evidenced by the entire range of Indian Art. But manifestation becomes an ill for man, because of his very own ignorance and misperceptions, his attachments and his misdeeds. Otherwise, manifestation is verily Eden Garden. Therefore, whilst pain or suffering is obvious Ill (though it is a blessed instructor in the long run), pleasure also is Ill, because not only does pleasure undergo inevitable decease, which is sorrowful loss, but also the pleasure seeker is left the slave of his recurring craving. Moreover, all the world's antagonisms and wars, anxieties, jealousies, hatreds and other ills, the whole world's Evil, spring almost entirely out of the pursuit of pleasure, the pleasure of the senses and of egoistic self-assertion.

Not transient pleasure but permanent bliss, not a little piece of knowledge but the supreme enlightenment, not the petty goodness of the respectable citizen but the divine perfection of the holy man-become-God, not merely the fulfilment of human ideals but the realization of the purpose of existence, of the Will of the Eternal, is the worth-while, the real, the true, for Indian Religion and Philosophy.

And in that light the whole of ego-circumscribed personal existence is Ill, because it is the domain of the Lord of Death, of Māra, tempter and sin-maker. " You " and " I ", swept along in the poisoned stream of saṁsāra, the round of births and deaths, must escape and reach the safety of the other shore. But escape can never mean a running away, or a release for one's " self ". *Escape* from Ill and Sorrow means this, and only this, that each person so disciplines himself that he *ceases to be a producer* of evil and suffering, by himself ceasing to sin, and simultaneously himself constantly doing good. This is achieved through the extinction of that type of I-consciousness which is the source of selfishness and egoism. This extinction is part of the " dying out " which is Nirvāṇa ; and its inevitable concomitant (rather than consequence) is that blissful, inward peace which is also called Nirvāṇa.

And also : " you " and " I " are absolutely prevented from escaping sorrow, even though " you " and " I " have realized Nirvāṇa. " Self " extinction has no meaning whatever in terms of a selfish Nirvāṇa ! " I " am altogether incapacitated by virtue of the real nature of the manifested universe from cutting myself off from all mankind, indeed from this-All. " I ", out of the infinite Love characterizing him who has touched Nirvāṇa, will suffer infinite pity, feel infinite compassion and tender mercy, for my brother man bound to the round-turning wheel.

But it is impossible to save a brother without being the Lord of Salvation myself. I, myself, even here and now as the existential person, must make " my " Nirvāṇa come true. For how can I give what I do not possess ? How easily I behave like a fool and a hypocrite strutting on the world stage doing " good " to others when I myself am empty of the substance of goodness, saving " you " when it is I myself who am perishing of malaise of spirit !

So, the individual effort has the double result : one, of benefiting " me ", a person, and " you ", any person who is my neighbour at the moment ; and next, of making an end of Ill. He who treads the Middle Way is the conqueror of Māra ; he is the spiritual alchemist who transmutes the Ill into the Well ; he is the healer who reduces the fever caused by ignorance and craving to the blissful, healthy cool of Nirvāṇa, the fruit of Wisdom.

Theoretically, the Paṭicca-samuppāda presents the extinction of ignorance as the first step leading to the extinction of Ill. In practice, the Buddha singles out the extinction of craving as the preliminary step in the extinction of all Ill. Ignorance, here, cannot be removed by being told the truth, or by mere study, or by sitting down, in the moral and mental condition in which one is at the moment, and " thinking it out ".

The Muṇḍaka Upanishad says :

> The whole of men's thinking is interwoven with the senses.
> When that is purified, the Ātman shines forth.
>
> III. I. 9.

In all Indian Religious practice, moral and intellectual development, the purification of heart and mind, are indissolubly linked together. Avijjā cannot be directly tackled by any and every man. But any and every man is only too aware, painfully aware, of what he craves for, of what he believes is pleasant for himself. Hence the Buddha, who was concerned with Everyman's fulfilment, with "Deliverance from this entire body of Ill", struck his mightiest hammer blow at taṇhā, the central bastion of the citadel of all evil. This is a charming contrast to the Upanishadic "he who knows Brahman . . ." The Upanishadic circle was an elite one; the Upanishadic wisdom was not broadcast; and the Upanishadic sages were not missionaries but seers, perfect in saintly wisdom, to whom came the few who sought the radiance that lights all Eternity.

Hence the Buddha, propounding the third Noble Truth, recommends the utter extirpation of all craving. As presented in the Mahā-Satipaṭṭhāna Sutta,[1] not only is craving, the slave-maker, to be extirpated, but all desire, and also material things, the use of the senses (a strange teaching at first glance) and the objects of sense are all to be put away.

Can this really be put into practice? The Buddha says:

> It is in respect only of trifling things, of matters of little value, of mere morality, that an unconverted man when praising the Tathāgata, would speak. And what are such trifling, minor details of mere morality that he would praise?
>
> Putting away the killing of living things, Gotama the recluse holds aloof from the destruction of life. He has laid the cudgel and the sword aside; he lives scrupulous and full of mercy, friendly and compassionate to all creatures that have life.
>
> Putting away the taking of what is not given, abstaining from taking what is not given, Gotama the recluse lives as one who takes (only) what is given, who waits for what is given; and by not stealing he lives with a self become pure.
>
> Putting away unchastity, Gotama the recluse is chaste. He holds himself aloof, far off, from the vulgar practice (gāma-dhamma), from the sexual act.
>
> Putting away lying words, Gotama the recluse holds himself aloof from falsehood. He speaks truth, from the truth he never swerves; faithful and trustworthy, he breaks not his word to the world.

[1] See above, p. 200.

> Putting away slander, Gotama the recluse holds himself aloof from calumny. What he hears here he repeats not elsewhere to raise a quarrel against the people here; what he hears elsewhere he repeats not here to raise a quarrel against the people there. Thus does he live as a binder together of those who are divided, an encourager of those who are friends, a peacemaker, a lover of peace, impassioned for peace, a speaker of words that make for peace.
> Putting away harshness of speech, Gotama the recluse holds himself aloof from harsh language. Whatsoever word is blameless, pleasant to the ear, lovely, reaching to the heart, urbane, pleasing to the people, agreeable to the people—such are the words he speaks.
> Putting away frivolous talk, Gotama the recluse holds himself aloof from vain conversation. In season he speaks, in accordance with fact, a speaker on the goal, a speaker on Dhamma, a speaker on discipline, he speaks words that are worth treasuring, with similes at the right time, that are discriminating, and connected with the goal.
> He abstains from wearing, adorning or ornamenting himself with garlands, scents and unguents, from the use of large and lofty beds, from accepting silver or gold, uncooked grain, raw meats, women and girls, bondmen or bondwomen, sheep, goats, fowls, swine, elephants, cattle, horses, mares, cultivated fields or waste, from acting as a go-between or messenger, buying and selling, cheating with scales or bronzes or measures, the crooked ways of bribery, cheating and fraud, maiming, murder, putting in bonds, highway robbery, dacoity and violence.
> Such are the things, O Bhikkhus, which an unconverted man, when speaking in praise of the Tathāgata, might say.
>
> Brahmajāla Sutta,
> D.I.3–5.

Nor does the above complete the list. For there follows a list of all the sports, amusements, music, dancing, low arts (like foretelling, augury, etc.), all that appertains to comfortable living, and in short, almost everything which is comprised in everyday worldly life. One more list is of some interest—the Buddha's conception of " low conversation ":

> Talk about kings, robbers, ministers of state; war, terrors, battles; foods, drinks, clothes, beds, garlands, perfumes; relatives and relationships; equipages, villages, towns, cities, countries; tales about women and heroes; gossip at street corners or wells; ghost stories; desultory talk; speculations about the land and sea, about becoming and not becoming thus or thus.

This gives a remarkable insight into the Buddha's views and personal standard of life. This is what he called "the mere details of minor morality." It is a particularly interesting revelation of what he meant in practice by his teaching concerning the Middle Way, and avoiding the extremes of self-indulgence and mortification. This mode of life was austere in the highest degree. The lesson is that perfect attainment necessitates the complete rejection of whatsoever is unessential. In other spheres, some of the finest examples of this principle in the modern world are seen in the manufacture of precision instruments and in the creations of genius in the fine arts.

All observation necessitates the use of the senses. In fact, the Buddha's very technique of purification and development makes the senses more reliable instruments of apprehension. Only through keener sense perception can there be accurate observation. Again, the Buddha repeatedly emphasizes the necessity for health, energy, joy and application. His own experience taught him that the misuse of the body brings only ill in its train. Physical health, therefore, is indispensable; and what meaning has physical health but that, among other things, the senses function better than ever? But a vital, energetic person is quite naturally moved by lusty life (the serpent's tail). How thrilling, exciting, pleasant, how "good" it is to enjoy one's body and mind, to express one's self, to be happy now, extracting the last drop of delirious delight whilst one can and letting decay and death look after themselves! Since they will come inevitably, why forgo the honey of the moment?

The question, as well as the attitude, expresses the folly of the immature. Rejecting it, and far from teaching unintelligent repression, the Buddha points out that the extirpation of craving and ignorance leads to permanent happiness, not to a trumpery, momentary pleasure.

The Buddha does mean what he teaches, namely, actually putting away material things to the limit, actually not using the senses for making unnecessary observations, but concentrating wholly upon the supreme aim in view, the winning of the deathless Immortal. If a drink addict is seeking to free himself from his miserable slavery to drink, it is not exactly unhelpful to him to refuse the following:—to go into a drinking place; to look at bottles containing drink; to listen to others' talk about drink (either for or against); to stand outside a drinking place for the sake of a mere sniff of the drink; or to conjure up in his imagination anything connected with drink.

Through intensive training alone can craving be extirpated. Since the Buddha's personal example, and his method, are the embodiment of the highest austerity, what did he mean in his very first discourse to the Five by the term Majjhima Paṭipadā? In which sense is this Way the Middle Way?

Earlier (p. 92) it was shown that the Manifest, lying between the infinities of the point and the boundless sphere, is the Medium; it is that which is in the middle. Nirvāṇa, the deathless Immortal, is the Infinity to which the Infinity which is "oneself" here, proceeds. This proceeding is by way of the Medium in which oneself manifests. The procession to the Perfect, Nirvāṇa, can only be a Perfect Way. The Middle Way, the Way through the Medium to the Infinite Nirvāṇa, can be no other than the Perfect Way, altogether antithetical to the two extreme ways of indulgence and mortification. But ordinary man confusedly believes, because his standpoint and criterion are of the realm of dukkha, of the wilderness, of the jungle, that a middle way is a compromise between indulgence and mortification. In practice, he interprets this as lusting without being found out. Unfortunately for this view,

> The mighty Ruler of the worlds beholds as though
> from close at hand
> The man who thinks he acts by stealth: all this
> the gods perceive and know.
> If a man stands or walks or moves in secret, goes
> to his lying down or uprising,
> What two men whisper as they sit together, King
> Varuṇa knows: he as the third is present.
>
> Atharva Veda, IV.16.1, 2.

The Buddha announces that the eight elements composing the eightfold path are sammā-diṭṭhi, sammā-sankapo, and so on, using the prefix sammā for each element. Sammā is usually translated by the word "right". Sensitive discernment shows that merely right views or right actions hardly express all that the Buddha had in mind. By sammā, he undoubtedly meant " perfect "[1]. It was the Perfect Life which he himself lived and which he taught his followers to live. The Middle Way of the Buddha is no sour-milk-and-water compromise between indulgence and denial here at this earthly level of ordinary life, but the radiant apex in heaven of the triangle whose base line joins the earthly extremes. The Middle Way is nothing less than the Perfect Way.

The teaching of the Majjhima Paṭipadā, which is for the instruction of the masses, and which is addressed to the individual, and which is, above all, for the earnest aspirant to realize more and more profoundly through constant practice, is the fruit of the meditation under the Rājāyatana tree, subsequently related to the conclusions drawn from the meditations under the Mucalinda and Ajapāla trees.

Of the eight elements of the Perfect Way, samādhi has been already discussed in these pages. Sammā-Sati, perfect mindfulness, the equivalent of " watch " in the Christian admonition " watch and pray ",[2] one of the most important elements from the practical point of view, is treated below (see pp. 236, 237).

The fifth element, sammā-ājivo, means perfect mode of living, which includes the idea of making a livelihood by right means. If everyone spent five minutes each night before retiring to rest, in a calm, dispassionate survey of the day's mode of living, and if each person tried to abide each successive day in the light of the conclusions reached in such a survey, a revolution for enduring good and human happiness would take place.

The prohibitionary side of sammā-vācā, perfect speech, is well expressed in the Brahmajāla Sutta (above). Sammā-diṭṭhi, perfect views, is expounded by Sāriputta, when the Blessed One was once staying in Jeta's grove in Anāthapiṇḍika's pleasaunce :

> When the disciple of the Noble comprehends that which is wrong and the root from which it springs, when he comprehends that which is right and the root from which it springs, thereby he becomes right in his views . . .

[1] See also *Buddhism* by Mrs. Rhys Davids, Home University Library, p. 150 & p. 218.

[2] Mark, XIII. 33.

> Killing is wrong, theft . . . sensuality, etc . . . is wrong. Its roots are greed, hate and delusion.
> Not killing . . . thieving . . . etc . . . is right. Its roots are freedom from greed, hate and delusion.
> . . . by putting away every tendency to passion . . . repugnance . . . the idea and conceit " I am " . . . that is how he is right in his views . . :
> . . . (is right in his views) when he understands becoming, its origin, its cessation and the course which leads to its cessation. Now what are these ? There are three kinds of becoming—sensuous, corporeal and incorporeal. From the arising of attachment, becoming takes its rise ; from attachment's cessation comes the cessation of becoming, the course whereto is just the Noble Eightfold Path . . .
> There are four graspings—after sensuous pleasures, after speculative ideas, after good-works, and after soul-theories . . .
>
> Majjhima Nikāya,
> I.46–51.

Soul theories ! The Buddha's teaching of soullessness, anattā, as characterizing all existential manifestation, and his silence, or rather non-exposition, in connection with the Atta, has been a source of tribulation to many. How could a religion explicitly teach anattā, completely deny any possibility of the survival of a personality or soul or self-consciousness after the death of the body ? A religion of abysmal despair ! Of inconceivable hopelessness ! A religion of pessimism which touched the very nadir of perdition !

Not so. The Buddha pointed out that the popular meanings of words like " soul " or " self " were misconceptions of the truth. Inability to understand the illimitable, indefinable Ātman led some to misconceive it as a separate, personal ego—a misappropriation for oneself of the universal which cannot be appropriated. Others, ignorant of the Upanishadic teaching of the Ātman, and having a naively animistic outlook, also thought in terms of this Frankenstein, the permanent ego. The Buddha knew for himself the " not-born, not-become, not-made, not-compounded ", the plane of consciousness which was " the end of Ill ". He knew the Uncreated, or the Transcendent. Thus knowing, he hurled his thunderbolt at the view which regarded any or all of the elements constituting the existential person as the Atta.

This doctrine of the absence of any abiding limited entity in the existential person, is one of the outstanding achievements of the Buddha. Until man clearly understands this truth, he will never rid himself of selfishness, and of evil and suffering.

Man is made up, according to Buddhist analysis, of five aggregates (khandhas) :

1. Material attributes (rūpa)—the stuff of the body ; sense organs ; gesture and speech ; male or female sex ; qualities like buoyancy, elasticity, etc.
2. Sensations or Feelings (vedanā)
3. Abstract Ideas or Perceptions (saññā)
4. Mental Dispositions and Will (saṁkhāra)
5. Consciousness (viññāṇa)

All the khandhas undergo continual change, there being no abiding entity in any of them or in the person as a whole. Here, one must recall the Upanishadic teaching that Brahman, which is identical with Ātman, is the Eternal among the things that pass away. The Ātman is inconceivable, that is, its reality cannot be represented through discursive thought and speech. But the things that pass away, such as the khandhas composing existential man, can be represented through discursive thought and speech. So the Buddha, confining his talk or description to the conceivable, shows that the whole of the existential is mortal. And yet, he also unequivocally repudiates annihilation. The equal repudiation of both survival and annihilation means the repudiation, not of The Eternal, of The Atta, but of the idea of eternal entity, an idea expressed in self-contradictory terms, since entity means defined, limited manifestation, or that which is non-eternal. In this connection, it should also be noted that certain questions have hitherto remained unanswerable : How does God create heaven and earth and all therein ? How does Ātman become, or create, this-All ? How, and even more cogently why, does the Eternal, the Perfect, the Immortal, become, or create, the temporal, the imperfect and the mortal, full of pain, evil and sorrow ? It is in man's nature to ask such questions. Strictly speaking they should not be asked. That fact, and the unanswerability of such questions make for part of the dukkha of life. Yet the answer, the perfect answer, is achievable by the individual, through realizing the

Immortal. Thereby, speech and thought are transcended, thus immobilizing the means for human discussion and communication. But the achieved answer is the sure ground for the authoritative repudiation of annihilation, and also of such a misconception as eternal entity abiding in existential manifestation.

In the Mahā-Nidāna Sutta, the Buddha deals with four declarations concerning the soul, namely that the atta

> has form and is minute ; has form and is boundless ;
> is formless and minute ; is formless and boundless.

Each of these declarations is made with regard to the present life or the next life ; or the person resolves that he will refashion the atta into the likeness of a selected one of those four modes.

Next, the atta is regarded as

1. Feeling, sentience. 2. Not-feeling, non-sentience.
3. Some " thing " which is itself neither sentience nor non-sentience, but has feelings and has the property of sentience.

1. To this, one answers :
   Feeling is (a) happy, (b) painful, (c) neutral.
   Which do you consider your atta ?
   Moreover, (a), (b) and (c) are impermanent states ; they are the product of a cause or causes, and become extinct in course of time.
   Therefore, " My atta is feeling " does not commend itself.
2. To this, one answers :
   Where there is no feeling of anything, can you say, ' I am ' ?
   No.
   Therefore (2) is not commendable.
3. To this, one answers :
   Were feeling of every sort to cease absolutely, then there being, owing to the cessation thereof, no feeling whatever, could one then say, ' I myself am ' ?
   No.
   Therefore (3) is not commendable.

And then the Buddha says :

> Now when a Bhikkhu, O Ānanda, does not regard the atta under these aspects—either as feeling, or as non-sentient, or as having feeling—then he, thus refraining from such views, grasps at nothing in the world ; and not grasping, he trembles not ; and trembling not, he by himself attains to perfect peace. And he knows that

birth is at an end, that the higher life has been fulfilled, that what has to be done has been accomplished, and that after this present world, there is no more of being such and such.
And of such a Bhikkhu, O Ānanda, whose heart is thus set free, if anyone should say, 'His creed is that an Arahant goes on after death'—that were absurd—or, 'His creed is that an Arahant does not go on . . . or does, and yet does not go on . . . or, neither goes on nor goes not on after death'—all that were absurd.
And why is that?
Because, O Ānanda, whatever verbal expression there is and whatever system of verbal expression, whatever explanation there may be and whatever system of explanation, whatever communication is possible and whatever system of communication, whatever knowledge there is and whatever sphere of knowledge, whatever round of life and how far the round is traversed—
by mastery over all this that Bhikkhu is set free.
But to say of a Bhikkhu who has been so set free by insight, 'He knows not, he sees not'—that were absurd.

D.II.66–68, abbreviated.

The current views of the atta are shown to be not commendable. By refraining from such views, a man grasps at nothing in the world. At least one powerful source of selfishness is removed. "Not grasping" means that all the hopes, fears, anxieties and struggles involved in obtaining things for this atta or self disappear. Naturally, there is peace, there is serenity.

Rebirth is at an end. The purpose of existence is fulfilled. And after death, "there is no more of being such and such."

At the end of the Brahmajāla Sutta, the Buddha says of himself that

> On the dissolution of the body, beyond the end
> of his life, neither gods nor men shall see him.

Yājñavalkya says to his beloved wife, Maitreyī:

> After death, there is no consciousness.

After fulfilling the purpose of existence, after attaining freedom of mind, after realizing Nirvāṇa, and after the destruction of Ill, there is complete cessation of the rūpa-vedanā-saññā-saṁkhāra-viññāṇa complex, or, the existential person. This is the truth which the majority of human beings cannot accept, and against which they fight tooth and nail. Not the blind acceptance of credulity nor the blind rejection through incredulity, but the real acceptance born of clear-sightedness, is required. Those who blindly accept will merely continue to do evil, because they have not rid themselves of this illusion of " self ". Those who blindly reject will equally continue to do evil, and also shut the door on understanding. But those who will extinguish craving will find wisdom, obtain the vision, and realize Nirvāṇa.

But let the further teaching be noted. First, Yājñavalkya's exposition of immortality after saying, " After death there is no consciousness." Next, the Buddha's own statement that if anyone should say of an Arahant, that after death " he goes on, or does not go on, or . . . ", all that he says is absurd. What, then, does happen after death ? Translate jāti by the term further-become (not new-become or re-become), instead of birth or rebirth. In the case of the unliberated, the force leading to an existential again-become, namely the force of upādāna, the grasping which is the fuel for the flame of sentient existence, does give rise to a jāti. In the case of the Arahant, since the khandhas, dissolving in death, are dispossessed of upādāna by the previous extirpation of craving during the Arahant's lifetime, there can be no further bhava and no further jāti. In this case, the Atta has successfully demonstrated[1] in existential terms the meaning of Perfected Man, and Perfected Man has fulfilled the purpose of existential manifestation. Thereby, Perfected Man is a Tathāgata, a Redeemer, and after the death of the body, He is the non-existential deathless Immortal, the Eternal, which is devoid of parts but is only the Whole.

Until liberation is realized, jāti after jāti arises. Exactly how the Buddha pictured the process is impossible to say, for he gave no explanation of its rationale. Buddhist teaching gives the analogy of the one flame which is transmitted from torch to torch : craving and grasping supply the fuel by which the flame of life is kept burning from one existence to another.

In trying to understand rebirth, most people word their enquiry thus : since there is no permanent entity, no ' who ', then ' what ' is reborn ? And they argue thus : it is said that the karmic force generated in one life must work itself out because of the law of causality, and so the character pattern of one grouping of

[1] This is a demonstration of "The Grace of God."

khandhas, the person A, reappears in another grouping of khandhas, B. In that sense, in Buddhist teaching, B is a reincarnation of A. But no explanation whatever is given of the mechanism of transmission. Analogies like the flame transmitted from torch to torch, or like the momentum of one billiard ball being transmitted to another on impact, are bad. One flaming torch is actually put into contact with another flaming torch; one billiard ball having momentum, physically touches another ball without momentum. If the analogy is to hold, then one pattern of khandhas 'flaming' with life should 'fire' a non-living pattern of khandhas. In other words, the 'flame' should 'fire' a new non-living pattern by actual contact. But the first flaming pattern dies out. To say that the predispositions, the saṁkhārā, persist after bodily death and give rise to another body, or to say that consciousness, viññāṇa, survives and enters another body, is hardly tenable, for it is clearly taught that consciousness on the one hand, and name-and-form on the other, are reciprocally dependent upon each other.

The concept of karma, the idea that every force, physical (and energetic as the scientist would say), or moral or mental (and non-energetic as the physicist might affirm), must work itself out, may feel acceptable. But in the application of this concept to the life of man, the idea of rebirth, however garbed, does not stand critical examination.

So runs the critic's argument. Both his enquiry and argument show that he is thinking atomistically, that is, in terms of discrete, unchanging ultimates of rūpa, or vedanā, or viññāṇa, etc. But the Buddha points out that nothing whatever in all manifestation is unchanging. Again, karma is not like a judge who punishes to-day a particular man who committed a crime a year ago. In practical life, that man today is regarded and treated as the identical man who committed a crime in the past. But in the actual, universal process, there is no unchanging identity. The two views —one and the same individual; two different individuals—are both inadequate. The more adequate view is that one thing, or situation, is the cause of, and becomes transformed, or is taken up into another.[1] If, as suggested above, the term jāti is translated

[1] See above, p. 204.

as further-become (not new-become—new individual therefore, nor again-become or re-become—same individual therefore), or by fresh-become or fresh-transformed, it might prove easier to master the conception of jāti. There is much in ordinary life which dims, or even blots out the awareness of continuous change as underlying all process. A dynamic view is inhibited by observing, say, such an atomistic event as an instantaneous death. Such observations so condition the mind, that it becomes difficult to grasp the Buddha's presentation of karma and jāti.

To return now to the Paṭicca-samuppāda.

The eradiction of taṇhā (craving) leads to the cessation of upādāna (grasping), of bhava (becoming), of jāti, and of decay, death, despair and misery. The daily activities go on, but with this difference, that one no longer hankers after or identifies oneself with anything. So life ceases to be the wretched stream of saṁsāra. It now consists of pure action, that is, action which is a well considered, skilful[1] or creative response to life, instead of a helpless, automatic reaction to sense stimuli. Thus there is the end of the whole aggregation of sorrow, the extinction of Ill and the establishment of the Well.

The person, that single complex of nāmarūpa-viññāṇa, attains this through the discipline of the Eightfold Path. In the attainment, the state of avijjā is completely transformed into vijjā. As long as the enlightened individual is alive, there is a distinct recognizable nāmarūpa-viññāṇa complex before one's eyes, namely, the Arahant himself. With the extinction of avijjā, dukkha is utterly shattered and the light of Nirvāṇa wholly suffuses the dhamma-become, the Brahma-become Arahant.

Thus the complex composing the existential person of the Arahant is not extinguished, as one may be led to deduce from the statement of the Paṭicca-samuppāda as it stands in the Mahā-vagga. Instead, having ceased to be a producer of Ill and sorrow, and " escaped " from dukkha, he is now a creator and maintainer of the Well, and abides permanently in Nirvāṇa.

Henceforth, the twelve steps of the Paṭicca-samuppāda in the order given in the Mahā-vagga apply in relation to each and every experience, and especially to each and every mental state—there

[1] Cf. "Skill in action is yoga, (O Arjuna)"—Bhagavad-Gītā, II. 50.

is no fantasy life in the Arahant's mind. The erstwhile ignorant individual has now extinguished avijjā. Therefore, during the remainder of his life, his positive effort as he goes through each experience is directed towards the maintenance of the awakened state. Therefore, only those saṁkhārā which are the tendencies and dispositions to Brahma-faring, which constitute the pattern characterizing holy living, and freedom, remain active; necessarily so, for no experience is shapeless and bodiless. Therefore, the state of consciousness associated with each single experience is pure. Therefore, there is no taṇhā generated out of the experience. There is only pure and skilled thought, word and deed. Therefore, when the inevitable end of the experience comes through the objective activity of Father Time, there is no decease of an illusory " I ", and there is no despair, misery, grief, lamentation and suffering. There is but freedom and peace, the upekkhā, the calm and silent but transmutatively active watching by him who has extinguished all Ill. Thus the Arahant moves unstained[1] through all the experiences of the rest of his life. He moulds those experiences; he is master of environment; he is " lord of the world ".

If some cause brings about a temporary avijjā in an Arahant, he can directly extinguish it, as well as the other nidānas, up to jarāmaraṇa.

Again, if one who is far advanced on the Path comes into touch with a sufficiently powerful source of inspiration—a Vision, or the Dhamma, or an Arahant or Buddha in person—he might suddenly become enlightened himself. There would then be an extinction of all the nidānas up to jarāmaraṇa.

There is another form in which the twelve-nidāna Paṭiccasamuppāda could be expressed:

	Because of
Avijjā	Ignorance, there is the
Saṁkhāra	Predisposition to that kind of
Viññāṇa	Awareness of any
Nāmarūpa	Object, or situation, or train of thought or fantasy, which (awareness), operating through the appropriate
Saḷāyatana	Field(s) of sense, leads to those
Phassa	Contacts which produce those

[1] See also, Bṛihadāraṇyaka Upanishad, IV. 4. 22 & 23, quoted above, pp. 140, 141.

Vedanā	Sensations, out of which, as a hard core, arises the
Taṇhā	Craving which impels one to
Upādāna	Grasp at the desired objects, physical or mental, thus giving rise to the
Bhava	Formative process culminating in (frustration, for various reasons, thus ending directly in jarāmaraṇa, or in)
Jāti	Obtaining the object of craving, which, because of the Law—whatever uprises, of necessity deceases—ends in
Jarāmaraṇa	Loss, suffering, dissolution, death, Ill.

But if avijjā gives place to vijjā, there is no predisposition to that kind of awareness of any object . . . which . . . (could lead to) . . . loss, suffering, Ill.

Thus, in various ways, one may read rightly the twelve nidānas composing the Paṭicca-samuppāda.

When the Arahant who has shattered the circle of avijjā dies, there is no more of mortality for him. Never again will any saṁkhārā recombine into a pattern of separate being, for the fuel for such becoming is no more. The Awakened is one with Nirvāṇa, beyond the pale of avijjā.

But when the unliberated one dies, the forces for recombination into another pattern of being, enclosed within the prison walls of avijjā, give rise to another jāti. Again there is manifest a person, before whom lies the task of crossing the stream of saṁsāra, of finding release from avijjā into vijjā, of realizing the deathless Immortal, here-now, whilst existent in the nāmarūpa-viññāṇa complex.

In this manner one may understand the Paṭicca-samuppāda, both in terms of a single life-span and in terms of a series of jātis.

It should be noted that whilst it is not incorrect to derive the uprising of the whole aggregation of dukkha from avijjā as the starting point, and to proceed step by step as presented in the Mahā-vagga, the extinction of Ill for the ordinary person still in the unawakened condition does not start with the extinction, first of avijjā, and then, successively, of saṁkhāra, viññāṇa, etc., but with the extirpation of taṇhā. For avijjā, the unenlightened state or the unawakened consciousness, apart from being every person's natural inheritance, is the inevitable consequence and concomitant of taṇhā and of self-association with the fleeting, transient world and its objects. Hence the necessity for the extirpation, first, of taṇhā, through the discipline of the Noble Eightfold Path.

* * *

> " How are we to conduct ourselves, Lord, with regard to womankind ? "
> " As not seeing them, Ānanda."
> " But if we should see them, what are we to do ? "
> " Not talk, Ānanda."
> " But if they should speak to us, Lord, what are we to do ? "
> " Keep wide awake, Ānanda."
>
> D.II.141.

Not an altogether unwise admonition ! For Ānanda was an attractive, handsome man, possessed of tact and charming manners, a trifle susceptible to feminine charms, and blessed with the ability to make everyone feel at home. In the last year of his life, the Buddha freely consented to dine with the courtesan Ambapālī. Because of this engagement, he excused himself from the invitation by the Vajjian nobles to dine on the same day.

Several texts show that the Buddha tends not to regard womankind with favour, although he holds certain exceptional characters in high esteem. He regards sexual love as lust, a bringer of sorrow. He exhorts wise men not to fall into the hell of the married state ; and if men could not keep away from marriage, not to commit adultery (Dhammika Sutta, 21). On the whole he thinks woman is definitely the weaker vessel.

* * *

In his exhortation to his disciples at the Mahāvana at the Kūṭāgāra Hall (see above, p. 186), the Buddha mentions the " dhammā which I have fully understood." These dhammā, categorically stated, are as follows :

1. The four earnest applications of mindfulness on the body ; sensations ; mind ; dhammā.
2. The fourfold struggle against evil ; to
   (a) prevent evil states from arising
   (b) put away evil states which have arisen

(c) produce good states not previously existing
(d) make good states grow when they have arisen.

3. The four roads to psychic power or to Iddhi, through will; effort; thought; investigation.

   Each is to be united to earnest thought and the struggle against evil.
4. The five moral powers, balāni, which are identical with
5. The five organs of spiritual sense: faith; energy; mindfulness; concentration; wisdom.
6. The seven branches of enlightenment: energy; mindfulness; concentration; investigation; rapture; calm; upekkhā.
7. The Noble (Ariyan) Eightfold Path.

The Buddha laid the first emphasis on the mind and on contemplation. All activity, sinful or good, had deep roots in the mind. No wrong could be effectively righted without putting the mind right. So he says, in connection with upright conduct, earnest concentration and intelligence:

> Great is the fruit, great the advantage of earnest concentration, when it is set round with upright conduct.
> Great is the fruit, great the advantage of intellect, when it is set round with earnest concentration.
> The mind set round with intelligence is set quite free from the cankers of sensuality, becoming (the thirst for continued existence), delusion and ignorance.
>
> Mahā-Parinibbāna Sutta,
> D.II.123.

The Buddha had full sympathy and understanding for the layman too. The following is in the Mahā-mangala Sutta:

(A deva speaks) 1. Many devas and men
Have held various things blessings
When they were yearning for happiness.
Do thou declare to us the greatest blessing.

(The Buddha) 2. Not to serve the foolish
But to serve the wise;
To honour those worthy of honour;
This is the greatest blessing.
(This refrain ends every verse.)

3. To dwell in a pleasant land
Good works done in a former birth,
Right desires in the heart.

4. Much insight and education,
Self-control and pleasant speech,
And whatever word be well spoken.
5. To support father and mother,
To cherish wife and child,
To follow a peaceful calling.
6. To bestow alms and live righteously,
To give help to kindred,
Deeds which cannot be blamed.
7. To abhor, and cease from sin,
Abstinence from strong drink,
Not to be weary in well-doing.
8. Reverence and lowliness,
Contentment and gratitude,
The hearing of the Law at due seasons.
9. To be long-suffering and meek,
To associate with the tranquil,
Religious talk at due seasons.
10. Self-restraint and purity,
The knowledge of the Noble Truths,
The realization of Nirvāṇa.
11. Beneath the stroke of life's changes,
The mind that shaketh not,
Without grief or passion, and secure.
12. On every side are invincible
They who do acts like these,
On every side they walk in safety,
And theirs is the chief good.

A detailed exposition of the method of self-purification and training is given by the Buddha in his answer to the question put by the son of his old friend King Bimbisāra. One night in mid-autumn, when the water-lily blooms, King Ajātasattu of Magadha is enthralled by the beauty of the full moon. He expresses a yearning to hear religious discourse. Jīvaka, his physician, recommends him to visit the Buddha. He tells the monarch the good report noised abroad of the Buddha: "An Arahant, fully awakened, is the Exalted One, abounding in goodness, happy, with knowledge of the worlds, unsurpassed as a guide to mortals willing to be led, the teacher of gods and men, a blessed Buddha." The king goes with an enormous retinue, with his elephants bearing his women, himself mounted on the state elephant, to the Mango

Grove which sheltered the Buddha together with twelve hundred and fifty of his Bhikkhus. Fear seizes the king. "How can there be such unearthly peace with twelve hundred and fifty men present?" Doctor Jīvaka reassures him. The King completes his journey on foot, and stands respectfully and sees the Blessed One and his assembly, calm as a lake, seated in perfect silence. Deeply moved by what he sees before him, the powerful ruler of Magadha says:

> "Would that my son, Udāyi Bhadda, might have such calm as this assembly of the Bhikkhus now has!"
> "Do your thoughts then go where love guides them?"
> "I love the boy, and wish that he might enjoy such calm as this assembly has."

The King bows with joined palms stretched out in salutation to the Blessed One, sits down, and wants to know what is the immediate fruit, visible in this life, of the life of a Bhikkhu. The Buddha asks him what has he already learned. The King tells him of the doctrines expounded by various thinkers, and expresses his dissatisfaction with them all. Then the Buddha points out the advantages of the life of a Bhikkhu: that he is shown honour and respect by all; that he is trained in all the minor moralities (as stated in the Brahmajāla Sutta); that the consciousness of right-doing results in confidence and fearlessness; and then,

> "How is a Bhikkhu guarded as to the doors of his senses?
> "When, O King, he sees an object with his eye, he is not entranced with the general appearance or the details. He sets himself to restrain that which might give occasion for evil states, covetousness and dejection, to flow in over him so long as he remains unrestrained as to his sense of sight. He keeps watch on his faculty of sight, and he attains to mastery over it. So with the other senses, hearing . . . and with the representative faculty. And endowed with this self-restraint, so worthy of honour, as regards the senses, he experiences within himself a sense of ease into which no evil state can enter. Thus the Bhikkhu becomes guarded as to the doors of the senses.
> "And how, O King, is the Bhikkhu mindful and self-possessed?
> "In this matter, O King, the Bhikkhu on going out (on his alms-round) or returning, acts with clear consciousness.[1] And so (too)

[1] That is, being fully aware of exactly what he is doing.

on looking forward . . . drawing in or stretching out (his arm) . . . carrying his outer cloak, bowl, robes ... eating, drinking, chewing, savouring . . . obeying the calls of nature . . . walking, standing, sitting, asleep, awake, talking, silent . . . Thus it is, O King, that the Bhikkhu becomes mindful and self-possessed.

" And how, O King, is the Bhikkhu content ?

" In this matter, O King, the Bhikkhu is content with sufficient robes to cover his body, with sufficient food to keep his stomach going. Whithersoever he may set out, these he takes with him as he goes—just as a bird with his wings, O King, whithersoever he may fly, carries his wings with him as he flies. Thus it is, O King, that the Bhikkhu becomes content."

A Bhikkhu's meditation is then described by the Buddha :

1. " Putting away hankering after the world, he remains with a heart that hankers not, and he purifies his mind of hankering.
2. " Putting away the stain of malevolence, he remains with a heart set free from malevolence ; he purifies his mind from the stain of malevolence, (and is) compassionate and kind towards all breathing creatures.
3. " Putting away sloth and torpor, keeping his ideas alight, mindful and clearly conscious, he purifies his mind of sloth and torpor.
4. " Putting away restlessness and worry, he remains free from them, and with heart serene within, he purifies himself of restlessness and worry.
5. " Putting away perplexity he remains as one passed beyond perplexity, and no longer in suspense as to what is skilled, he purifies his mind of perplexity."

D.I.70, 71.

" The Bhikkhu, so long as these five hindrances are not put away from him, looks upon himself as in debt, diseased, in prison, in slavery, lost on a desert road. But when these five hindrances have been put away from him, he looks upon himself as freed from debt, rid of disease, out of jail, a free man and secure.

" To the Bhikkhu in whom the five hindrances have been put away, realizing that himself, joy is born ; rapture is born in him who is joyful ; the body of him whose mind is rapturous is impassible ; with the body impassible he experiences happiness ; the mind of him who is happy is concentrated (in samādhi)."

D.I.73.

In this important dialogue, the Sāmañña-Phala Sutta, the Buddha proceeds with other points, and ends with the assurance that the purified life and heart of the Bhikkhu enables him to understand the Four Noble Truths, to become free of the cankers of lust, becoming, delusion and ignorance. And then :

" In him thus set free, arises the knowledge of his emancipation, and he knows : ' Rebirth has been destroyed. The higher life has been fulfilled. What had to be done has been done. There is not now any more of being such and such '."

D.I.84

King Ajātasattu, profoundly impressed, asks the Buddha to accept him as his disciple. He expresses deep contrition for having murdered his father, King Bimbisāra, the great friend of the Buddha. The Blessed Lord accepts the King's acknowledgement of his misdeed :

" Verily, O King, it was transgression that overcame you in acting thus. But inasmuch as you look on it as transgression, and make acknowledgment according to rule, we accept your acknowledgement as to that. For that, O King, is custom in the discipline of the noble ones, that whosoever looks upon his fault as a fault, and acknowledges it, shall attain to self-restraint in the future."

D.I.85.

In Kammāssadhamma, a city of the Kurus, the Buddha says :

" The one and only path, Bhikkhus, leading to the purification of beings, to passing far beyond grief and lamentation, to the dying out of ill and misery, to the attainment of right method, to the realization of Nirvāṇa, is that of the Fourfold Setting up of Mindfulness.

" Which are the Four ? Herein, O Bhikkhus, let a Bhikkhu, as to the body, continue to look upon the body in such manner, that he remains ardent, self-possessed and mindful, having overcome both the hankering and the dejection in the world. And in the same way as to feelings, thoughts and mental objects, let him so look upon each that he remains ardent, self-possessed and mindful, having overcome both the hankering and the dejection in the world."

D.II.290.

The point is then set out in detail, first in relation to the body :

The Bhikkhu thinks how it comes to be, and how it passes away.

> He makes himself aware of every activity of the body, such as lifting an arm, or walking, or eating, and so on—acting with ' clear consciousness ' as it is called. His vigilance is pure observation. So he develops the power never to be caught unawares or to be swept into wrong or indeliberate action. He himself ' abides independent, grasping after nothing whatever in the world.'

Similarly, in relation to the feelings :

> How they come to be and pass away ; whether they are pleasant, painful or neutral ; whether they concern material or spiritual things. ' And he abides independent, grasping after nothing whatever in the world.'

Similarly with thoughts :

> Their origination and decease ; whether they are full of lust and hate, whether they are dull or intelligent, or exalted, and so on. " Or again, with the consciousness, ' There is a thought ', mindfulness thereof becomes established far enough for the purposes of knowledge and self-possession, And he abides independent, grasping at nothing whatever in the world."

Similarly with mental objects.

The whole technique revealed above, and in the discourse to King Ajātasattu, is remarkable. It is a discipline which releases self-knowledge, teaches control without repression, reveals the nature of one's own psyche and of the hidden springs of action, and slowly and surely purifies one's whole being and leads to liberation through self-less-ness. At first sight it appears to promote self-centredness. But in fact, this type of pure self-observation, without praise or censure, without emotional reactions, without being bound by ideals or values, is the royal road to self-less-ness. This technique of the Fourfold Setting up of Mindfulness is described in detail in the Mahā-Satipaṭṭhāna Sutta.

At Bhaṇḍagāma, the Buddha says :

> It is through not awakening to, not penetrating four conditions, O Bhikkhus, that there has been this long, long running-on and faring-on (in saṁsāra) both for me and for you. And what are the four ? The ariyan virtue (moral habit, or sīla), the ariyan concentration (samādhi), the ariyan wisdom (paññā), the ariyan freedom.
>
> D.II.122.

The main elements concerning these four have been set forth in these pages.

There is another formulation of the stages to final liberation:

1. "Entering the stream." This follows the acceptance of the Buddha, the Doctrine and the Order. It may be the result of the practice of virtue, hearing the Doctrine being preached, enlightened reflection, or companionship with the faithful and good. Freedom from the delusion of the ego, from doubt regarding the Buddha and his teachings, and from reliance on the efficacy of rites and ceremonies, is attained in this stage.
2. This stage marks him who will return but once more. Lust, resentment, and falling under the spell of worldly or spiritual glamour are reduced to a minimum.
3. At this stage the disciple is safe. He will not fall back; he will achieve in this life. Lust and resentment are destroyed in this stage.
4. The final stage is Arahantship, the stage of him who has attained the supreme "worthiness." The Arahant is free from pride, self-righteousness, ignorance and the desire for rebirth.

It is sometimes said that the Buddha's teaching is mainly negative. Evil and suffering are brought into the forefront. Man's life is to be spent in a struggle against evil, and the ethical code is quite often, but not always, worded in terms of abstention from evil. Concentrated mental activity is emphasized, and little is said about "doing things."

There is some truth in the criticism. For example, this oft quoted verse from the Dhammapada gives the teaching of love in negative form:

> Never in this world can hatred be stilled by hatred;
> It will be stilled only by non-hatred—this is the law eternal.

But side by side with this consider the teaching of love as presented in the Mahā-Sudassana Sutta. The Buddha tells the story of the Great King of Glory, who, at one stage, enters a chamber, and, strongly feeling what he says, cries out: "Stay here, O thoughts of lust, ill-will and hatred. Thus far only, O thoughts of lust, ill-will and hatred." Then the Great King enters the Four Raptures. Then he goes out of that chamber into another, and he lets his mind pervade the four quarters of the world with Love, grown far-reaching and great, free from the least trace of anger or ill-will. Similarly, he lets his mind pervade the four quarters of the world with compassion, sympathy and equanimity.

> Love, grown far-reaching and great, free
> from the least trace of anger or ill-will.

There is the secret. The opposites exist together in man. The Buddha's psychological insight showed him that Love could not wholly be Love, unless, first, man purified his nature to such an extent, that he became incapable of reacting with malice or hate under any circumstances, however provocative. Only those who have rich experience, together with the requisite perception to understand the significance of their experience, can see how profoundly right the Buddha was. Through the ages man has failed to fulfil Love because he has not first cleansed his heart of that which can poison Love. The Buddha's psychological basis, namely the heart cleansed of anger and ill-will and hatred, enables transcendent Love to triumph.

"Lets his mind pervade the four quarters of the world with Love . . . Compassion . . ." This teaching of the four Brahmavihāras (literally God-residences or Divine-residences) is one of the most remarkable in the entire range of all religion.

The young brāhman, Subha, asks the Buddha for his opinion on one point; the brāhmans teach that a householder achieves method, law and meritorious action, whereas one who goes forth into the homeless life does not. The Buddha says:

> "On this point, young sir, my opinion is conditional . . . I have not a rigid opinion . . . Both the householder and one who goes forth, acting rightly, because and on account of right action, achieves method, law and what is skilled."

As the conversation proceeds, Subha says:

> ". . . it would be well should the respected Gotama show to me the path to union with the Brahmās."
>
> "Then, young sir, listen well," says the Buddha. "Pay attention . . . Here, a Bhikkhu with a mind of loving-kindness (mettā) abides suffusing one world-quarter, then a second . . . a third . . . a fourth.

"Thus he stays whilst he suffuses the whole world above, below, across, on all sides, in all completeness with a mind of loving-kindness, wide, extended, immeasurable, without enmity, without ill-will; with the liberation of the mind through loving-kindness thus developed, he will not stay, he will not stop at what is finite . . .

"And again . . . with a mind of compassion (karuṇā) . . .

"And again with a mind of sympathetic joy (muditā) . . .

"And again with a mind of serenity (or unperturbedness, upekkhā) . . . wide, extended . . . not stop at what is finite . . ."

Majjhima Nikāya,
Subha Sutta, no: 99.

Again, it is taught:

Be thou unequalled in loving-kindness

Buddha-vaṁsa, II.158.

So also do thou suffuse friend and foe with loving-kindness.

ibid. II 160.

As a mother even with her life protects her child, her one and only son, so let one cultivate (a loving) heart without measure towards all living creatures.

Khuddaka Nikāya, Metta Sutta.

This was said by the Exalted One . . .

"Bhikkhus, whatsoever grounds there be for good works undertaken with a view to rebirth, all of them are not worth one-sixteenth part of that love which is the heart's release; love alone which is the heart's release, shines and burns and flashes forth in surpassing them."

Itivuttaka, I.3.7.

Like Yājñavalkya before him, and Jesus after him, the Buddha gives the supreme teaching, and is himself the embodiment of transcendent Love. Each teacher presented Love in his own unique way. The Buddha's uniqueness consisted, partly, in his unrivalled psychological insight, and in his practical technique by which, stripping oneself of all obstructing evil, such Love could be realized. This Love has no limitation, no bondage, no sentimentality; no reservations, no conditions, no requirement or dependence upon reciprocity. It is pure, beyond mortality, absolute, transcendent and divine, of the nature of Eternal God.

The discipline enjoined in the Upanishads, the Yoga system, and the Buddha's teachings, would be incomplete without the discipline of love. The form in which the Buddha presents it is of unique interest : mettā, or loving-kindness ; karuṇā, or compassion ; muditā, or sympathetic joy, that is, delighting in the happiness of others ; upekkhā, or serenity, the poise that knows no shaking. Discipline which leads to one's moral perfection and the liberation of the mind, and to those states in samādhi of at-one-ment with the Transcendent, might conceivably tend to make one indifferent to this world's creatures, to their follies and sufferings. Freed of the illusion of separateness, freed of egocentric personality, one might become less able to enter into congenial inter-relationship with the egocentric man of the world. And further, having transcended worldly values, one might become not only unappreciative and aloof, but also unsympathetic to him with worldly values, him with the petty woes and cares, the little sorrows and joys of everyday life.

Expressed in another way, he who lives in the deathless Immortal may be unable to bridge the gulf between himself and the ordinary man. In order to talk the language of existential man, without which it would be hardly possible to help mortal to be reborn—and reborn as immortal—the Arahant, out of infinite love and understanding, must have whole acceptance of the other man at his own valuation, even though that valuation is inaccurate. For out of love, the Arahant transmutes the false into the true.

Thought and wisdom lead to the Impersonal, to the Void ; to processes, to the becoming-stream ; to Vision. Love leads to persons, to beings ; to selves, to individuals ; to the understanding which is intelligent compassion, to clear-seeing sympathy or loving clearsightedness. Thought and love creatively integrate in selfless action by the actor who is wholly moral and free from all delusion.

Through right-regarding, one achieves impersonal altruism. " No-self ", as seen by intellect, revealed by spiritual insight and accepted out of wisdom, when adopted as a standard for dealing with myself, makes me self-less, and just and fair to others. And " person ", distinct and individual, as obvious to sense perception, revealed by spiritual insight and accepted out of love, when adopted as a standard for dealing with others, makes me unselfish, considerate and sympathetic to them. Right-doing towards them through personal love is the result.

By nay-saying to worldliness in life in myself and yea-saying to life in others, the harmony of wisdom and love establishes the norm for individual action. Hence the Brahma-vihāras build, maintain and sanctify the truest and purest links between mortal man, enmeshed in Ill, and the man made God, the Saviour, the Tathāgata.

There are too many, who, criticizing Indian Religion as cold, negative, impersonal, a selfish seeking after personal salvation, take pride in rushing about doing good deeds, and are self-satisfied with their love for man, and for God. Only a Buddha, a Christ, knows fully how to love, and to do good. The rest can love only partially, and do good only in limited measure. Until the lover and doer has become a Buddha or a Christ, a part, too big a part sometimes, of his loving and his good deeds is an expression of lust and egoism.

This is not to suggest that one must wait for the day of Perfection. On the contrary, as the Buddha himself emphasizes (Dhammapada, 183), " doing of what is skilled " is necessary. But one must clearly understand that good is wholly good only when evil has been rooted out. Does a good gardener clear out weeds?

So it is that whilst the forms in which the greatest teachings are clothed may be negative, the actions entailed and the results achieved are positive. And it was action above all, the heroic action in which man wages incessant battle, single-handed, unyielding, against the very source of evil, the ego, and craving, for which the Buddha stands. An uncompromising iconoclast, a ruthless dispeller of illusions, a preacher who preached only what he himself fulfilled to perfection, a teacher who taught only what was his own realization of truth, the Buddha stands out as one of the overtowering intellectual and spiritual giants of all history. And it may be, that his teaching, example and influence will come to be increasingly recognized as one of the most remarkable that ever emanated from a single being, whether he be called son of man or son of God, lawgiver or prophet, redeemer or saviour.

To this day the Buddha stands as the greatest apostle and exponent of freedom: the freedom which is absolute release from the fetters of self, from the false kind of dependence upon man or saviour or God, and from every taint of character that darkens the life of man and makes him a blot upon fair nature; the freedom which is complete at-one-ment with the immutable law that governs all process; the freedom which only he who attains knows is the utter fulfilment of the purpose of human existence, and which not only leads to, but itself is the Peace that passes understanding. In the Buddha were incarnate the Truth and Goodness and Love that man can ever envision.

The Buddha ushered in a new age. Intuitive transcendentalism was not enough. Here and now was the need for clear vision by each individual for himself, for a reasonable, constructive and practical approach to the problems of life, solving such problems through continuous personal effort for moral perfection and intellectual clarity. If the Buddha's austere and awful perfection demanded the life of a Bhikkhu, if it necessitated a life not intimate with the crowd, it is well to pause and consider that the creative artist, the scientific genius, the leader of a nation, the business magnate, the householder, the lover, all of them without exception go into retreat in studio, laboratory, cabinet room, office, study and secret trysting place. Can anyone say that at any time in history, the life which perfectly fulfilled the True and the Good was compatible with living in the world of affairs?

The secluded life, slightly distant from the turmoil and evil of everyday existence, was a source of inspiration to man at large. This pure way of life preserved in practice the tradition and knowledge of that which culminated in the supreme worthiness, Arahantship. It is indeed well that the sun lightens and warms the earth from a great distance.

Greatest among the great ones who lived in that wonderful age—Parmenides, Xenophanes, Pythagoras, Isaiah, Job, Mahāvira, Lao Tze and Confucius—the Buddha lit a flame of spiritual splendour which only in the years to come will be seen at its brightest. For his is the teaching which will show the best solutions to the age-long conflict between individual and society, between self-assertion and self-realization, between "thou" and "I".

For five and forty years after his enlightenment, the Buddha travelled, spreading his teachings, ministering to the spiritual needs of man. At last the time came when his old body, eighty years of age was nearing its final sleep. Ānanda, his faithful and loving disciple, feels the stress of the approaching end. The Master gives him quiet counsel: " But now, Ānanda, have I not formerly declared to you that it is in the very nature of all things, near and dear unto us, that we must divide ourselves from them? . . . Anything whatsoever that is born, brought into being, and organized, contains within itself the inherent necessity of dissolution." Lying on his deathbed, he asks his beloved disciples if they have any doubts, any questions. To the end he gives himself in loving service.

" Behold now, Bhikkhus, I exhort you, saying:
' Decay is inherent in all component things!
Strive on with diligence!' "

Those were the last words of the Tathāgata. He entered into meditation, into Nirvāṇa, the deathless Immortal. And when he breathed his last, the elder of the two greatest teachers of humanity passed to his eternal rest.

CHAPTER V

THE BHAGAVAD-GĪTĀ

" Yield not to unmanliness, O Pārtha !
It doth not befit thee.
Abandon base faintheartedness !
Stand up, Parantapa ! "

II.3.

" Whoso forsaketh all desires and goeth onwards free from yearnings, without the thought of mine or " I ", attains to Peace."

II.71.

" O son of Pṛithā, neither here nor in the next world is there destruction for him (who worketh righteousness) ; for no one who does good, O my son, goes an evil way."

VI.40.

" Thy business is with the action only, never with its fruits ; so let not the fruit of action be thy motive, nor be thou to inaction attached."

II.47.

" Without attachment, constantly perform action that should be done ; for, by performing action without attachment, man verily reacheth the Supreme."

III.19.

" I am the abode of Brahman, the Immortal, the Inexhaustible, of eternal righteousness, and of unending bliss."

XIV.27.

Chapter V

THE BHAGAVAD-GĪTĀ

Arjuna cried:

" . . . Between the two armies,
stay my chariot, O Acyuta,

" That I may behold these standing, longing for
battle, with whom I must strive in this outbreaking war;

" And gaze on these here gathered together, ready to fight,
desirous of pleasing in battle the evil-minded son of
Dhṛitarāshṭra."

Bringing the chariot to a standstill, Kṛishṇa said:

" O Pārtha, behold these Kurus gathered together."

I.21, 22, 23, 25.

It is difficult to excel the Hindu sense of the dramatic in religion. Here on the field where mighty armies were gathered, the battle hangs, like petrified thunderclouds withholding the storm, whilst the Lord of the Universe, incarnate in Shri Kṛishṇa, is about to utter the supreme truths which will dissipate the doubts clouding the mind of Arjuna. The poet-author of the Gītā could hardly have chosen a more arresting opening scene for his philosophical song.

The Great War is the theme of the Hindu epic, the Mahābhārata, euphemistically called a poem, in fact, an encyclopedia of Hindu philosophy, ethics, religion, legends, law and political science. The epic also contains some lyrics of touching beauty, and—the Gītā.

Arjuna, peerless archer, is one of the five Pāṇḍava brothers who are fighting to recover their kingdom, of which they were deprived by their Kaurava cousins, the sons of Dhṛitarāshṭra. Kṛishṇa is Arjuna's charioteer.

When Kṛishṇa stays the chariot, Arjuna gazes upon the embattled hosts, and gives vent to the anguish in his soul. For he sees that on both sides stand his relatives and kinsmen, teachers, friends and comrades. Deeply moved to pity, he utters in sadness :

> " Seeing these, my kinsmen, O Kṛishṇa, arrayed eager to fight, My limbs fail and my mouth is parched, my body quivers, and my hair stands on end ;
>
> " Gāṇḍīva (the bow) slips from my hand, and my skin burns ; I am not able to stand, and my mind is whirling ;
>
> " And I see adverse omens, O Keśava ; nor do I foresee any advantage from slaying kinsmen in battle.
>
> " For I desire not victory, O Kṛishṇa, nor kingship, nor pleasures. What is kingship to us, O Govinda ? What are enjoyments, or even life ? "
>
> I.28–32.

And the victor of a hundred battles goes on to say that all who stood before him were the very people for whose sake the war was being waged ! What pleasure could there be in slaying relatives ? Families would be destroyed, and therefore the traditional way of family life, the bedrock on which Hindu society and the Hindu state were founded, would disappear. Lawlessness, corruption and confusion would arise. Slayer and slain would equally end in hell.

> " Alas ! in committing a great sin are we engaged,
> we who are endeavouring to kill our kindred
> from greed of the pleasures of kingship.
>
> " If the sons of Dhṛitarāshṭra, weapon in hand,
> should slay me unresisting, unarmed, in the
> battle, that would for me be the better."
>
> I.45, 46.

Arjuna sinks down on the seat of his chariot, casting away his bow and arrow, his mind overborne by grief. For more than twenty centuries since the day the Gītā was penned, many a soul has known the same anguish.

The answer of the Gītā is in the finest Hindu traditions. It is primarily a philosophy of action : action performed without attachment to the fruits of action, as a sacrifice to Brahman, with knowledge of Brahman, with devotion to the Lord, with one's self freed from passion, fear and anger, from lust, greed and hate ; action performed with precise knowledge of what exactly is one's duty, which is determined by one's own nature or pattern of being. The author of the Gītā resourcefully uses all his material to support his philosophy of action. Brahman and Ātman of the Upanishads, some of the teachings of the Buddha, and the Sāṁkhya and Yoga philosophies, and the way of life as enjoined by the Vedas, all appear in the Gītā. The doctrine of Avatāras or Incarnations of Deity, is used with striking effect.

Whilst the Upanishads are for the few, the Gītā is the treasured scripture of the multitude. Men feel the need of a personal God, the embodiment of their highest ideals, whom they can conceive of in familiar, personal terms—a Being—to whom they can confide what cannot or must not be communicated to fellow men, on whom they can lavish all the love-longing which otherwise remains pent up within, or which has already found frustration here, to whom they can aspire with fervent devotion, and whom they can reverently worship. Such a God is the magnet that irresistibly draws the millions; the profounder concepts are too austere, too deep for them. In the person of Kṛishṇa as the Lord incarnate, the Hindu ideal conception is embodied.

When Kṛishṇa vouchsafes the vision of the Divine Form, Arjuna, overpowered, with joined palms says:

" Rightly, O Hṛishīkeśa, at thy praises
The universe is gladdened and rejoices;
The rakshasas in terror flee to all quarters,
And all the hosts of siddhas do thee reverence.

" And wherefore should they not to thee do reverence,
Great-souled one, greater than Brahmā, first creator?
O infinite Lord of gods, the world's home art thou,
The imperishable, being, non-being, and beyond them.

" Thou art the primal God, the ancient Person,
Thou of this all the supreme place of treasure,
Knower and knowable, the supreme dwelling,
Boundless of form, by thee is all created.

" Vāyu and Varuṇa, fire, moon, and Yama,
Prajāpati art thou, the father's father;
Reverence, reverence to thee a thousandfold,
And yet again to thee be reverence, reverence.

" Reverence before thee, reverence behind thee,
O All, to thee be reverence from all sides;

O endless in thy strength, boundless in vigour,
All thou envelopest, all therefore art thou.

"Deeming thee friend, whate'er I have uttered roughly,
Calling thee Kṛishṇa, Yādava, or comrade,
Whate'er, not knowing aught of this thy greatness,
Speaking in carelessness or in affection,

"Whate'er in jest I have spoken with irreverence,
When in our sports, or resting, or in eating,
Alone, in other's presence, O firm fixed,
For that I crave thee pardon, boundless one.

"Father of all the world that moves and moves not
Art thou, and worshipful most reverend teacher;
None is like thee, much less is there a greater
In the three worlds; thy glory has no equal.

"Therefore I bow, and casting down my body
I seek thy favour, Lord adorable;
As father spares his son, comrade his comrade,
As friend his friend, so do thou deign to spare me.

"With ecstacy have I beheld what no one
Has seen before; with fear my mind is shaken;
Therefore, O God, show me thy other body;
Be gracious, Lord of gods, the world's one refuge.

"Holding the diadem, the mace, the discus,
As erst thou wert, so do I wish to see thee.
That very form, four-armed, take upon thee,
O thousand-armed, O figure universal."

XI.36–46.

Power is the aspect revealed in this vision of the Form. Manifestation is power in action. In the world of endless change, all things come into being, and pass away, ruled by the law underlying process. Viewed objectively as stark fact, the active process of the universe can be terrifying and awe-inspiring, making one's hair stand on end.

What, then, was revealed in the vision? In the body of Kṛishṇa, Arjuna beheld the Supreme, with many mouths and eyes, wearing divine vestures, all-marvellous and boundless, with face turned everywhere. The whole universe, divided into manifold parts, stood in the body of the Lord of gods. An unbounded form, within which were Brahmā upon his lotus throne, the Rudras,

Vasus, Ādityas, Aśvins, Maruts and all the celestial host. No source, no midst, no end. The sun and moon his eyes, he alone filling earth and heaven and all the regions between. This awful majesty the worlds behold terror-struck :

" Touching the clouds, blazing with many colours,
Thy open mouths I see, thy wide eyes blazing ;
Beholding thee my inner being trembles,
No firmness do I find, no rest, O Viṣṇu.

" Thy mouths with many dreadful fangs beholding,
Like to Time's universal conflagration,
I know the quarters not, I find no shelter,
Be gracious, Lord of gods, the world's protection."

XI.24, 25.

Into those gaping, tremendous-toothed mouths, rush the great heroes, the Kurus and Pāṇḍavas and all the armed hosts, and are pulverized :

" Thou lickest up and swallowest entirely
The worlds around, with blazing mouths devouring ;
The entire universe with light thou fillest ;
The dreadful rays of thine blaze forth, O Viṣṇu.

" Tell me, O thou of dreadful form, who art thou ?
Reverence to thee, O best of gods, be gracious ;
I fain would understand thy primal nature,
For thy appearing thus I know not."

XI.30, 31.

The Lord says :

" Know I am Time, that makes the worlds to perish,
When ripe, and come to bring on them destruction ;
Even without thee they all shall cease their being,
Who stand arrayed in hostile ranks as warriors.

" Therefore arise, stand up, and win thou glory,
Defeat thy foes ; enjoy successful kingship ;
Even by me these men are slain already ;
Be but the means, right and left-handed archer."

XI.32, 33.

Life and death are part of the universal process, which is but the incessant activity of the Lord of the universe. Stars and planets, forces, creatures and beings are but His tools. He gives life; He is also the Reaper. No one need question why or when; the process of the universe in terms of action which makes and breaks all forms, is implacable. Let man act, then, according to his duty.

What is the nature, or character of the Lord?

> "I the sapidity in waters, the radiance in sun and moon, the word of Power in all the Vedas, virility in men;
> "The pure fragrance of earth and brilliance in fire, life in all beings, and austerity in ascetics,
> "The Buddhi of the Buddhi-endowed, the splendour of splendid things am I;
> "And I the strength of the strong, devoid of desire and passion. In beings, I am desire not contrary to duty, O best of Bharatas."
>
> VII.8–11.

In fresh detail Arjuna wants to hear of Kṛishṇa's glory. And the Lord declares:

> "I am victory, I am resolution, I am the goodness of the good.
> "I am the rod of them that subdue, the statecraft of them that desire victory; I am the silence of secrets, the knowledge of knowers.
> "Whatever is vast, good, auspicious, or mighty, understand thou that it exists as a portion of my splendour."

And also, very significantly:

> "I am the gambling of the cheat, and the splendour of splendid things am I."
>
> X.36, 38, 41.

Further, the Lord declares:

> "I am the origin and likewise the dissolution of the whole world.
> "There is nothing higher than I, O Dhananjaya; on me all this is strung like jewels on a thread."
>
> VII.6, 7.

> "By me in the form of the unmanifested has all this universe been created; all beings abide in me, but I abide not in them.
> "Yet beings abide not in me; behold the Yoga of me the Lord. I bear these beings, yet I abide not in beings; my own self is the abode of beings.
> "As the great vāyu, ever established in ākāśa, goes everywhere, so all beings abide in me: thus understand it."
>
> IX.4, 5, 6.

The identity of the One and the Many is declared :

> " Others also . . . worship me as the one and the manifold everywhere present."

Again :

> " I the oblation, the sacrifice, the herb, the sacred formula, the fire, the burnt offering ;
> " I the father of this universe, the mother, the supporter, the one to be known, the purifier, OM, the Vedas,
> " The path, supporter, Lord, witness, abode, shelter, friend, origin, dissolution, foundation, treasure-house, seed imperishable.
> " I give heat ; I hold back and send forth rain ; immortality and also death, being and non-being am I, O Arjuna."
>
> IX.16–19, (abbreviated).

Here, the Lord Himself, like Brahman, is the source of everything. He categorically declares that He is " the origin and likewise the dissolution of the whole world " (VII.6.) He affirms : " I am the source of all ; from me everything arises ; so deeming the wise worship me endowed with my nature " (X.8) ; and, " All beings enter my nature at the end of a world-age ; at the beginning of a world-age again I emanate them " (IX.7).

But the entire universe does not exhaust him :

> " Having established this whole universe with a fragment of myself, I remain."
>
> X.42.

Further,

> " I am the Self (Ātman) seated in the heart of all beings ; I am the beginning, the middle and also the end of all beings."
>
> X.20.

and he also speaks of himself as the most perfect and representative in all things :

> " Of the Ādityas I am Viṣṇu ; of radiances the sun ; among the constellations the moon ;
> " Of the Vedas the Sāma-veda ; of the senses, the mind ;
> " Of mountains, Meru ; of lakes, the ocean ; of immovable things, the Himālaya ; of men, the monarch ; of weapons, the thunderbolt ; of calculators, Time ; of wild animals, the lion ; of sciences, the science of the Self.
> " And all-devouring death am I, and the origin of all to come."
>
> X.21–34, (abbreviated)

The poet-author of the Gītā is not wholly consistent. He does not hesitate to use the monism of the early Upanishads, the dualism of the Sāṁkhya, and the theistic tendency of the later Upanishads to support his inspiration and illustrate his point. Nevertheless, the Gītā achieves a strange unity through its underlying single purpose, its author's fervour, and its unquestioned beauty. It is a song of songs.

The Gītā presents God as a Being, transcendent and immanent, the abode of Brahman, the Indestructible. God is the father, the mother, the way, the friend and the Lord. Arjuna addresses Kṛishṇa as the " supreme Brahman, primeval deity, omnipresent Lord ", and as " supreme spirit " (X. 12 and 15 ; and VIII.1). He is the maker of heaven and earth, the supporter. He is the creator, preserver, and destroyer-regenerator. He is truth, goodness and beauty. He avows his love for Arjuna and for all his devotees. In these terms, characteristic of the Indian outlook and way of life, God as Love finds expression in the Gītā.

* * *

Right from the beginning the Lord exhorts Arjuna to shake himself out of his dejection and to perform his duty. In the last discourse, he once again drives home the teaching of duty and action. In between, philosophical and religious teachings are given, in answer to Arjuna's questions. At the crucial moment, the hero cannot bear the thought of shedding his kinsmen's blood. He turns to his comrade in arms, his charioteer Kṛishṇa, whom he does not yet know as the supreme Lord incarnate, and says :

> " My nature is overcome with the fault of meanness ; my mind is confused as to duty . . . I am thy disciple, teach me, who have come to thee.
>
> " For I see not what would drive away the sorrow that dries up my senses, if I should attain unrivalled, prosperous kingship on earth, or even sovereignty among the gods."
>
> II. 7, 8.

Arjuna is in need of spiritual teaching. Smiling, as it were, the Lord says :

"Thou grievest for those that should not be grieved for, yet speakest wise-sounding words. The wise grieve neither for the living nor for the dead.

"Nor at any time verily was I not, nor thou, nor these princes of men, nor verily shall we ever cease to be hereafter.

"As the dweller in the body experienceth, in the body, childhood, youth and old age, so passeth he on to another body; the steadfast one is not perplexed thereat."

II.11–13.

Death is part of a universal cyclic process. Man, if wise, does not grieve on account of it. The Real is eternal:

"Know That to be indestructible by whom all this (the universe) is pervaded. Nor can any work the destruction of that imperishable One.

"These bodies of the embodied One, who is eternal, indestructible and boundless, are known as finite. Therefore fight, O Bhārata.

"He who regardeth this as a slayer, and he who thinketh he is slain, both of them are ignorant. He slayeth not, nor is he slain.

"He is not born, nor doth he die; nor having been, ceaseth he any more to be; unborn, perpetual, eternal and ancient, he is not slain when the body is slaughtered."

II.17–20.

Arjuna thinks that the killing of relatives and friends is horrible. So Kṛishṇa first draws attention to the subject of death generally, and then tries to help Arjuna to re-evaluate death. He introduces the idea of the imperishable One, for he wants Arjuna to look at the question from this standpoint and not from any other. Confusion of mind and faintness of heart are experienced when the transient is valued at the expense of the eternal. But if the situation is viewed from the standpoint of the eternal, death is seen in right perspective. So:

"Who knoweth him indestructible, perpetual, unborn, unchanging, how can that man slay, O Pārtha, or cause to be slain?"

II.21.

Looking at it from another angle:

"For certain is death for the born, and certain is birth for the dead; therefore over the inevitable thou shouldst not grieve."

II.27.

Further arguments are adduced to show why Arjuna should not grieve. Then Kṛishṇa touches the problem of faintness of heart :

> "Further, looking to thine own duty, thou shouldst not tremble ; for there is nothing more welcome to a Kshatriya than righteous war."
> II.31.

If Arjuna will not carry on this righteous warfare he will incur sin by casting away duty and honour. His name will be dishonoured, and that will be worse than death. On the other hand :

> "Slain, thou wilt obtain heaven ; victorious, thou wilt enjoy the earth ; therefore stand up, O son of Kuntī, resolute to fight."
> II.37.

So far, the conversation is a straightforward exhortation to Arjuna to cast off despondency, regard death from a different point of view, and do his duty as a warrior. The argument has followed the Sāṁkhyan line that That is the real, whereas the body belongs to the transient world of phenomena. Hence the wise base themselves on the real.

The same teaching is next set forth according to the Yoga doctrine, which, if heard with the ear of wisdom, would enable Arjuna to "cast away the bonds of action" (II.39). Freedom from the bonds of action is the new note struck. For Kṛishṇa sees that Arjuna is seeking peace in his soul, and he seizes the opportunity, not only to solve the little problem of despondency and faintheartedness, but also to put him in possession of the means for liberation. If not for this aspect, the Gītā need have been no more than a pep talk, in poetic language, to urge Arjuna to soldierly behaviour.

The determined soul is one-pointed in its objective, whereas the irresolute one branches off into endless byways of thought. The foolish cling to pleasure and lordship. But,

> "The Vedas deal with the three attributes.[1] Be thou above these three attributes, O Arjuna, beyond the pairs of opposites, ever steadfast in purity, careless of possessions, full of the Self (Ātman).
> "All the Vedas are as useful to an enlightened brāhman as is a tank in a place covered over with water."
> II.45, 46.

[1] The three guṇas, or qualities of nature: sattva, rhythm or harmony; rajas, motion or passion; tamas, inertia or darkness.

Arjuna's attention is then brought back to the main point, together with the teaching which will free him from the bonds of action. This remains the dominant note to the very end of the last discourse :

> " Thy business is with the action only, never with its fruits ; so let not the fruit of action be thy motive, nor be thou to inaction attached."
>
> II.47

This is the most important statement, reiterated often, in the whole of the Gītā.

Kṛishṇa continues :

> " Perform action, O Dhananjaya, fixed in yoga, renouncing attachments, and balanced evenly in success and failure ; inner poise is called yoga."
>
> II.48

But in the next breath he points out something higher than action and at the same time enjoins action :

> " Far lower than the discipline of Buddhi is action, O Dhananjaya. Take thou refuge in Buddhi ; pitiable are they who work for fruit.
>
> " United with Buddhi, one abandoneth here both good and evil deeds ; therefore train thyself in yoga ; yoga is skill in action.
>
> " The sages, united to Buddhi, renounce the fruit which action yieldeth, and liberated from the bonds of birth, they go to the sorrowless abode.
>
> " When thy mind shall escape from this tangle of delusion, then thou shalt rise to indifference as to what has been heard and shall be heard.
>
> " When thy mind, bewildered by what has been heard (the Vedic texts), shall stand immovable, fixed in concentration (samādhi), then shalt thou attain unto yoga."
>
> II.49–53.

The scene can be pictured. Arjuna's anguish is fierce ; his mood is one of pained despair. Kṛishṇa's opening exhortation has little or no effect upon him. He is still sitting in the same position in his chariot, downcast. When Kṛishṇa introduces the subject of yoga, Arjuna shows the first sign of interest. Kṛishṇa goads him on with an exhortation to action, which is inconsistent with his extolling of knowledge as superior to action. But when the new interest of yoga comes uppermost, Arjuna's attitude is partly that of an enquirer, and partly debative. One secret, inner longing, namely, to regain his mental balance, befitting a hero, has been touched, and so he enquires :

> " What is the description of him who is stable in mind, steadfast in contemplation, O Keśava ? How doth the stable-minded talk, how doth he sit, how walk ? "

The Blessed Lord answers :

> " When a man abandoneth, O Pārtha, all the desires of the heart, and is satisfied in the Self (Ātman) by the Self, then he is called stable in mind.
>
> " He whose mind is not agitated amid pains, has no longings amid pleasures, loosed from passion, fear and anger, he is called a sage of stable mind.
>
> " He who on every side is without attachments, whatever hap of fair and foul, who neither likes nor dislikes, of such a one the understanding is well-poised.
>
> " When again, as a tortoise draws in on all sides its limbs, he withdraws his senses from the objects of sense, then is his understanding well-poised.
>
> " The objects of sense, but not the relish for them, turn away from an abstemious dweller in the body ; and even relish turneth away from him after the Supreme is seen."
>
> II.54–59.

Exactly as taught by the Buddha, and by the Upanishads, Shri Kṛishṇa teaches that control of the senses and freedom from bondage to desire lead to mental poise. But the task is by no means easy, for,

> " The excited senses of even a wise man, though he be striving, impetuously carry away his mind.
>
> " Having restrained them all, he should sit harmonised, I his supreme goal."
>
> II.60, 61.

Like a bolt out of the blue the charioteer declares himself to be the supreme goal. The earnest mood of caution is immediately followed by the assertion of authority. Before Arjuna quite recovers from this, Kṛishṇa gives him a psychological analysis :

"Man, musing on the objects of sense, conceiveth an attachment to these; from attachment ariseth desire; from desire cometh forth anger;

"From anger proceedeth delusion; from delusion confused memory; from confused memory the destruction of Buddhi; from destruction of Buddhi he perishes."

II.62, 63.

If that is the fate of the thrall of sense, who shall find salvation? Kṛishṇa says:

"But the disciplined self, moving among sense-objects, with senses free from attraction and repulsion, mastered by the Self, goeth to peace.

"In that peace, the extinction of all pains ariseth for him; for of him whose heart is peaceful, Buddhi soon attaineth equilibrium."

II.64, 65.

There is the secret: in that peace, Arjuna's anguish will be no more; and the path to that peace is the control of the senses and freedom from desire.

"He attaineth peace, unto whom all desires flow as waters flow into the ocean, which, though full, remaineth unmoved—not he who desireth desires.

"Whoso forsaketh all desires and goeth onwards free from yearnings, selfless and without egoism, he goeth to peace.

"This is the Brahma-state, O son of Pṛithā.
Having attained thereto, none is bewildered.
Who, even at the death-hour, is established
therein, he goeth to the Nirvāṇa of Brahman."

II.70–72.

Immediately Arjuna poses the question:

"If it be thought by thee that knowledge is superior to action, why dost thou, O Keśava, enjoin on me this terrible action?

"With these perplexing words thou only confusest my understanding. Therefore tell me with certainty the one way by which I may attain the greater good."

III.1, 2.

"Attain the greater good." In some form or other, that is the fundamental urge in all life. Hence the eager longing to know the secret of such attainment. Hence, also, the ease with which many men follow any will o' the wisp if only boundless happiness is promised them by any misguided or unscrupulous leader or exploiter. Hence, too, the turning away from religion, the bitter medicine which says : discipline ; renunciation ; transcendence of the need, the thirst for happiness, love, security and success, and then, perhaps, one will find "the greater good." Alas ! The only path to bliss, to Nirvāṇa, is the one path most men will not tread. For the one thing they will not give up is the impassioned pursuit of personal desires, stemming from the egoistic "I"-consciousness of separate selfhood, the last stronghold to fall before the advance of Truth. Men die before Truth wins.

Kṛishṇa knows this well. He does not answer Arjuna's question immediately. With the sure touch of the perfect Master, he slowly educates his disciple. He says :

> "In this world there is a twofold path, as I said before, O sinless one, that of yoga by knowledge of the Sāṁkhyas, and that of yoga by action of the yogis."
>
> III.3.

Strange and significant epithet—sinless one—does the Lord bestow on Arjuna. Only a little while ago Arjuna felt sharply conscious that he was about to engage in sin by killing relatives and friends. The Lord reassures him. He calls out a new awareness in him that a sinless man is the one who can be a true yogi. He proceeds :

> "Man winneth not freedom from action by abstaining from activity, nor by mere renunciation doth he rise to perfection.
>
> "Nor can anyone, even for an instant, remain really actionless ; for helplessly is everyone driven to action by the qualities born of nature.
>
> "Who sitteth, controlling the organs of action, but dwelling in his mind on the objects of the senses, that bewildered man is called a hypocrite.
>
> "But who, controlling the senses by the mind, O Arjuna, with the organs of action, without attachment, performeth yoga by action, he is worthy.
>
> "Perform thou right action, for action is superior to inaction, and inactive, even the maintenance of thy body would not be possible.
>
> "The world is bound by action, unless performed for the sake of sacrifice ; for that sake, free from attachment, O son of Kuntī, perform thou action."
>
> III.4–9.

Having set forth the philosophy of action, extolled action as superior to inaction, laid stress upon freedom from attachment when performing action, Kṛishṇa asserts that

> "From food creatures become; from rain is the production of food; rain proceedeth from sacrifice; sacrifice ariseth out of action.
>
> "Action from brahma (the Vedic magical formula, or prayer) groweth, know thou, and brahma from the Imperishable cometh. Therefore brahma, the all-permeating, is ever present in sacrifice."
>
> III.14, 15.

All action is traced back to the Imperishable. Only by action performed as a sacrifice, devoid of all selfishness, can man win freedom. Kṛishṇa stresses the need for action:

> "He who on earth doth not follow the wheel thus revolving, sinful of life and rejoicing in the senses, he, O son of Pṛithā, liveth in vain."
>
> III.16.

Yet in the very next verses he says:

> "But the man who rejoiceth in the Self (Ātman), with the Self is satisfied, and is content in the Self, for him verily there is nothing to do.
>
> "For him there is no advancement through things done in this world, nor any through things not done, nor does any advancement of his depend upon any being."
>
> III.17, 18.

If so, how is the man who rejoices in the Ātman to act, if at all? Kṛishṇa says:

> "Therefore, without attachment constantly perform action which is duty, for by performing action without attachment, man verily reacheth the Supreme."
>
> III.19.

For the liberated man, there are no objectives, worldly or unworldly, to be pursued for the sake of his personal advancement. There is no planning for the future, but only a living in the moment, like the lily in the field. There are no ideals to strive after, because here and now he naturally fulfils all that is required of him.

But far from becoming a liability to society, he constantly performs action which is duty, without being personally attached, without desiring the fruits of action, knowing that the karmic process inevitably brings results. Therefore he maintains the inner freedom he has won, by preserving his attitude of detachment. Thus, constantly fulfilling duty, he reaches the Supreme, which is bliss.

Indeed it is impossible not to engage in action. The supreme Lord Himself mingles in action, or else the worlds would fall in ruin, as Kṛishṇa teaches :

> "There is nothing in the three worlds, O Pārtha, that should be done by me, nor anything unattained that might be attained ; yet I engage in action.
> "For if ever I did not engage in action, unwearied, men all around would follow my path, O son of Pṛithā.
> "These worlds would fall into ruin, if I did not perform action ; I should be the author of confusion, and should destroy these creatures."
>
> III.22–24.

Unweariedly, the Lord engages in action. No room for sloth and torpor, qualities which the Buddha called hindrances to attainment.

Now there are two verses in this discourse which illustrate the considerateness of the Lord for those who are not Arjunas :

> "Let not the trained wise man unsettle the mind of ignorant people attached to action ; let him so act himself that all his actions are liked by others.
> "Those deluded by the qualities of nature are attached to the functions of the qualities. The man of perfect knowledge should not unsettle the foolish whose knowledge is imperfect."
>
> III.26, 29.

Not all those who long to lead the higher life wish, or are able, or are allowed by circumstance and obligation, to leave the world of affairs and become recluses. Such men have to live the higher life amidst people who live differently. Their views and actions would conflict with those around them. Who should be considered, those seeking the Supreme, or the others ? Kṛishṇa's answer covers both the mental and physical aspects of the problem: do not upset other people's faith and beliefs, on which the peaceful order of their lives depends, by imposing your new or higher knowledge upon them, but act in harmony with the Lord with such skill, as to make such action attractive to the multitude. Such teaching is typically Hindu, representative of that artistry which makes Hinduism all-comprehensive, and the Hindus such practical exponents of tolerance.

Is it possible to act thus always? And what if the immediate circumstance—the imminent battle—allows a somewhat cramped scope for attractive action? The Blessed Lord says:

> "Surrendering all actions to me, with thy thoughts resting on the Supreme Self, from hope and egoism freed, and of (mental) fever cured, engage in battle.
> "Who abide ever in this teaching of mine, full of faith and free from cavilling, they, too, are released from actions (i.e. the bond of actions).
> "Who carp at my teaching and act not thereon, know them to be blind to all wisdom, lost and senseless.
> "Even the man of knowledge behaves in conformity with his own nature; beings follow nature, what shall constraint avail?
> "Affection and aversion for the objects of sense abide in the senses; let none come under the dominion of these two; they are obstructors of the path.
> "Better one's own duty though destitute of merit, than the duty of another well discharged,
> Better death in the discharge of one's own duty; the duty of another is full of danger."
>
> III.30–35.

Each man has an individual pattern of being—a framework of innate abilities and character, or his "inner nature". Interacting with circumstances, favourable or obstructive, this individual pattern of being always affects the shape of all that happens to him. A born poet always bursts out in song. His life bears the impress of his poetic nature. A man born to be an agent of destruction gets involved in destructive activity—not necessarily an evil always, for destruction precedes regeneration. So, beings follow nature. Constraint or repression is of little or no avail.

Happy is the one who understands the inner pattern of his being. It happens, all too often, that a man lives his conscious life in little conformity with his inner nature. Perhaps he is too versatile, and he has too many interests which obstruct his perception of the outstanding ability that is his, and which he ought to cultivate and express above all others. " Affection and aversion for the objects of sense " are two of his greatest enemies. It is his business to pause ; to control the " I wish, I like, I want " and enquire : " I being what I am, and placed in this situation, what is the right course of action ? " Then he will discover a little more of his inner pattern of being. He will see more clearly what is his proper task, his true vocation in life. And he will understand that it is better to do his own duty by following his true vocation, even though destitute of merit, that is, unproductive of what is held estimable by those without insight, than attempt to do what is proper for a man with a different pattern of being. In short, the teaching is, " Be true to yourself." If by nature one is a soldier, better death fulfilling a soldier's duty than organizing a health campaign to save a million lives.

Again and again the Lord pronounces the central teaching : perform action which is duty, true to one's own nature, as a sacrifice to Brahman, without hope or egoism, without attachment, without desire for the fruits of action. Arjuna being a soldier, the Lord exhorts him imperatively to stand up and fight. If the disciple had been a pacifist in his inner nature, the Lord would have said : " Endure the insult and calumny, the loneliness and torture that may be inflicted on you by the deluded ignorant. Give love to those who hate you. Speak the word of Peace and Brotherhood, and let all thy ways be the ways of Peace for that is thy duty born of thy inner nature."

The Lord's teaching concerning the philosophy of action is clear. There is, however, a practical difficulty. Every man experiences it. Many men are bitterly frustrated by it time and again. In spite of the sincere passion to live the good life, in spite of unquestionable ability to do right,

> " Dragged on by what does a man commit sin, reluctantly indeed, as it were by force constrained ? " asks Arjuna.

And the Lord answers :

> "It is desire, it is wrath, begotten by the quality of rajas (the passionate quality) ; all-consuming, all-polluting, know thou this as our foe here on earth."
>
> III.36, 37.

No blaming of others, no self-excusing on the grounds of circumstance, but going straight to the heart of the matter, the Lord answers straightly Arjuna's honest question. Kṛishṇa is in agreement with the Upanishads and the Buḍdha. Man's desires, too often, are not the pure awareness of life-energy seeking the necessary means for everyday existence—the real needs of life and not the petty, innumerable wants and likes, wishes and fancies—but are pure awareness distorted by separative, limiting, and sometimes destructive ego-consciousness. Such desire is the master producer of the fantastic tragedy of life. It is the all too prolific parent of frustration, grief and evil. Frustration and grief give rise to self-pity and anger, wrath as Shri Kṛishṇa says. The quality of rajas is called all-consuming and all-polluting, for who, in the feverish pursuit of undisciplined desire, pauses to consider the nature of the desire and the ethics involved in fulfilling it, or to foresee its consequence to oneself and to others ?

> "Therefore, O best of the Bharatas," says Kṛishṇa, "mastering first the senses, do thou slay this thing of sin, destructive of wisdom and knowledge.
>
> "It is said that the senses are great ; greater than the senses is the mind ; greater than the mind is Buddhi ; but what is greater than Buddhi is He (the Supreme).[1]
>
> "Thus understanding Him as greater than Buddhi, restraining the self (the personal ego) by the Self (Ātman), slay, O mighty-armed, the enemy in the form of desire, difficult to approach."
>
> III.41–43.

Suddenly the Lord confronts Arjuna with an irrelevant statement. Before the echo of his previous words have died away, he says :

> "This imperishable yoga I declared to Vivasvān ; Vivasvān taught it to Manu ; Manu to Ikshvāku told it.

[1] Cf. Kaṭha Upanishad, III. 10.

"This, handed on down the line, the king-sages knew. This yoga, by great efflux of time decayed in the world, O Parantapa.

"This same ancient yoga hath been today declared to thee by me, for thou art my devotee and my friend. It is the supreme secret."

To this the astonished Arjuna rejoins:

"Later was thy birth, earlier the birth of Vivasvān. How then am I to understand that thou declaredst it in the beginning?"

And the Blessed Lord answers:

"Many births have been left behind by me and by thee, O Arjuna. I know them all, but thou knowest not thine, O Parantapa.

"Though unborn, the imperishable Self, and also the Lord of all beings, yet, establishing myself in nature, which is mine own, I am born through my own māyāvic power.

"Whenever there is decay of righteousness, O Bhārata, and there is exaltation of unrighteousness, then I myself come forth;

"For the protection of the good, for the destruction of evil-doers, for the sake of establishing righteousness, I am born from age to age.

"He who thus knoweth my divine birth and action in its essence, having abandoned the body, cometh not to birth again but cometh unto me, O Arjuna.

"Freed from passion, fear and anger, at one with me, taking refuge in me, purified in the austerity of wisdom, many have entered into my being.

"However men approach me, even so do I welcome them, for the path men take from every side is mine, O Pārtha."

IV.1–11.

The Lord's purpose is to introduce the doctrine of Avatāras (the divine incarnations). In the past, the Lord Himself descended to earth, incarnated in flesh, and spoke the Word, the imperishable yoga, to Vivasvān. The sacred teaching is transmitted down the line.[1] This is a treasured Hindu tradition. Whilst India extolled the king who was a sage, her sister civilization of China lauded the king who was an artist, a man of letters. That the oldest surviving civilizations, richest in the wisdom of life, should have extolled sage and artist above conqueror and administrator, is deeply significant.

But the tradition decays with the passage of time. Again the Lord must descend to save mankind. When the world comes to

[1] See also, below, p. 370 et seq.

a great crisis, the hour must produce the man, or else the Dark Ages descend.

The historical fact in the lives of nations has its religious counterpart. Woe to the nation whose religious life receives no new stimulus ! For the nation dies. Recent centuries have witnessed the passing away of the last few descendants of very ancient peoples, their life-force spent, their spirit become a pale shade. The poet-author of the Gītā had both knowledge and insight. The Buddha's influence had administered a severe shock to orthodox Brāhmanism. The prestige of priests and the existence of the sacrificial system of worship were in jeopardy as never before. The unparalleled reformer from Kapilavastu had numbed the warm-blooded priestly system with the icy Himālayan blast of truth and freedom. Brāhmanism, however, absorbed the shock, and re-emerged, incorporating several of the finest elements of the Buddha's teachings, especially his ethics. What emerged became the foundation of Hinduism to this day. The Gītā, one of the rarest blossoms of the human spirit, is a key to understand the vitality and the secret of survival of Hindu India.

So the Lord comes again as Kṛishṇa, and teaches Arjuna, his " devotee and friend ", the supreme secret. Arjuna is at once made aware of two facts : he is one of a small company ; and on his shoulders rests a solemn responsibility. For no man may dare even to ask for, leave alone receive, the truth, unless he has the strength to bear it, the resolution to fulfil it and the fortitude to accept its consequences. Greece had a story ; Daedalus could fly ; he taught his son Icarus ; but Icarus did not prove quite worthy of the secret ; he flew too close to the Sun (Truth), and met his destruction. And also, there is the story of Prometheus : whoso steals the fire from heaven (or whoso storms the kingdom of Heaven by sheer might of intellect without sufficient moral discipline as a foundation), will be condemned to be chained to the rock (of earthly experience) while the vulture (of frustrated ego or desire) eats out (or deprives him of) his liver (the ability to digest and assimilate the heavenly truth), until Hercules (the son by mortal woman of the divine lord of Olympus—in a sense, therefore, the divine made flesh, and representing the grace of the Most High) liberates the chained Titan. Might—the might of Power or of Conquest—is of no avail against Right. The Truth, hidden, subtle, infinitely pliant, realized through Love which is complete self-surrender, is Lord of the universe, and ultimately triumphant. The Truth, then, is Might.

So the Lord gives his pledge of love and acceptance : " for thou art my devotee and my friend."

Each man, in the dark night of his soul, can call upon the Divine Charioteer. And if He gives his pledge of love and acceptance, there is nothing whatever to fear. Whoso knows in its essence the birth and action of the Divine Charioteer reaches the Eternal.

Shri Kṛishṇa assures Arjuna that many, freed from passion, fear and anger, with no interest other than the Lord filling their lives, have entered His Being. It matters not on which road a man approaches Him—be it the path of wisdom, devotion or action—He will meet him on that road. The promise of redemption and salvation is as large in its generosity and inclusiveness as it is reassuring in its certainty of fulfilment.

A new question comes up :

> " 'What is action, what inaction ?' Even the wise are herein perplexed. Therefore I will declare to thee the action by knowing which thou shalt be loosed from all evil."
>
> IV.16.

Kṛishṇa teaches Arjuna that he must distinguish between action, unlawful action and inaction. He reiterates much that he has already said, and then introduces a thought-provoking idea : " He who sees inaction in action, and action in inaction, he is wise among men." So much action is futile. It is equivalent to inaction. Indeed, there are times when the wisest action is to deliberately refrain from action. A deliberate omission, productive of good, is a mark of wisdom. For instance, so much energy is wasted like a stream in the desert under the excuse of earning a living. Like all the Great Teachers of India, the Blessed Lord says :

> " Content with whatsoever he obtaineth without expectation, free from the pairs of opposites, without envy, balanced in success and failure, though acting, he is not bound."
>
> IV.22.

Where the wise are concerned, who is the actor, and what is the action ? Here, the Upanishadic view is upheld :

> " Brahman the act of offering, Brahman the oblation, are offered in Brahman the fire, by Brahman ; unto Brahman verily shall he go who in his action meditateth on Brahman."
>
> IV.24.

It is the age old teaching that man must dedicate his whole life to God. Every action of his must be freely rendered as willing service to the Highest. Such action is sacrifice, a making sacred ; and such a man is a saint. In the fearful, ignorant, spiritual childhood of the very early days, man gave up something which he treasured, as a propitiatory gift to the gods. Man in his maturity knows that there is no god to propitiate. All that is necessary is to live inspired by the overriding awareness that Brahman is the All. Animated by that consciousness, all life is one continuous sacrifice, a sacrifice which is not a losing but an enriching, not an abject slavery but an exalted glorification. Not separate man, but Eternal God, is the one and only actor. So Kṛishṇa teaches :

> " Better than the sacrifice of objects is the sacrifice of wisdom. All actions in their entirety, O Pārtha, culminate in wisdom.
>
> " Learn thou by discipleship, by questioning and by service. The wise, the seers of the truth, will instruct thee in wisdom.
>
> " And having known this, thou shalt not again fall into this confusion, O Pāṇḍava ; for by this thou wilt see all beings without exception in the Self, and thus in me.
>
> " Even if thou art the most sinful of all sinners, yet shalt thou cross over all sin by the raft of wisdom.
>
> " As the burning fire reduces fuel to ashes, O Arjuna, so doth the fire of wisdom reduce all actions to ashes.
>
> " Verily, there is no purifier in this world like wisdom ; he that is perfected in yoga finds it in the Self in due season.
>
> " The man of faith obtaineth wisdom, intent on it, with mastery over his senses ; and, having obtained wisdom, he goeth to the supreme peace.
>
> " But the ignorant, faithless, doubting self goeth to destruction ; nor this world, nor that beyond, nor happiness is there for the doubting self.
>
> " He who hath renounced action by yoga, who hath cloven asunder doubt by wisdom, who is Self-possessed, actions do not bind him, O Dhananjaya.

"Therefore, with the sword of the wisdom of the Self, cleaving asunder this ignorance-born doubt dwelling in thy heart, be established in yoga.
Stand up, O Bhārata."

IV.33-42.

Like the Buddha, Kṛishṇa extols wisdom, praises faith and denounces doubt. He recommends discipleship, investigation not blind faith, and service.

But Arjuna is still sunken on his chariot, still the thrall of delusion and uncertainty. His standing up will be the sign that his delusion is destroyed and that he will fight. The command of the Lord is insufficient by itself. Man can co-operate with God only when his delusion is destroyed, and his ability for right action has flowered through wisdom.

Arjuna is still down because of a new perplexity:

"Renunciation of actions thou praisest, O Kṛishṇa, and then also yoga. Of the two, which one is the better? That tell me conclusively."

V.1.

Shri Kṛishṇa answers:

"Renunciation and yoga by action both lead to the highest state; of the two, yoga by action is verily better than renunciation of action."

V.2.

"But without Yoga, O mighty-armed, renunciation is hard to attain to; the yoga harmonized Muni swiftly goeth to Brahman."

V.6.

"For a sage who is seeking yoga, action is called the means; for the same sage, when he is enthroned in yoga, serenity (consequent upon renunciation) is called the means."

VI.3.

Thus does Kṛishṇa steadfastly uphold action.

In the fifth discourse he points out that the Sāmkhya and Yoga are not really different from each other, and they lead to the same goal. The sense-subdued, harmonized yogi is not affected by actions. He understands that all his sense activities and all that happens are but matter or nature in action. If he were not a yogi he would react to this, and experience pleasure and pain.

He would be bound by actions and by events. As a yogi, he is conscious of the Self, or of Purusha who is the onlooker only, not participating in the activities born of matter. In other words, the yogi's consciousness is centred not in the transitory and unreal, but in the permanent and real. Therefore :

> " He who acteth placing all actions in Brahman, abandoning attachment, is unaffected by sin as a lotus leaf by the waters."
>
> V.10.
>
> " Thinking on That, merged in That, established in That, solely devoted to That, they go whence there is no return, their sins dispelled by wisdom.
>
> " Sages look equally on a brāhman adorned with learning and humility, a cow, an elephant, and even a dog and an outcaste."
>
> V.17, 18.

The mind of the sage is balanced. He can be one with Brahman, and maintain equanimity under all conditions. The delights that are contact-born spell pain, for they have beginning and ending :

> " He who is able to endure here on earth, ere he be liberated from the body, the force born from desire and anger, he is harmonized, he is a happy man.
>
> " He who is happy within, who rejoiceth within, who is illuminated within, that yogi, becoming Brahman, goeth to the peace of Brahman."
>
> V.23, 24.
>
> " Having known me as the enjoyer of sacrifice and of austerity, the mighty Ruler of all the worlds, and the friend of all beings, he goeth to peace."
>
> V.29.

The Lord specifically calls himself the friend of all beings. He identifies himself with Brahman, with the Self of the universe. Then he proceeds to point out that the Self is the friend of the self, that is, the person who tries to reach the Supreme, but the enemy of him who is unsubdued and seeks to glorify his little self. The subdued one, the harmonized yogi, is satisfied with wisdom. A lump of earth, a stone and gold are the same to him. He is impartial to all without exception. The yogi goes to " Peace, to the supreme bliss that abideth in me " (VI.15). But yoga is not for him who eats too much or who abstains too much, who is addicted to sleep or to wakefulness. Kṛishṇa says:

> " When his subdued thought is fixed on the Self, free from longing after the objects of desire, then he is said to be disciplined."
>
> VI.18.

What is the object of search of the yogi? What does it bring in its train? How does the would-be yogi set about it?

> " That in which the mind finds rest, quieted by the practice of yoga; that in which he, seeing the Self by the Self, in the Self is satisfied;
>
> " That in which he findeth the supreme delight which Buddhi can grasp beyond the senses, wherein established he moveth not from the reality;
>
> " Which, having obtained, he thinketh there is no greater gain beyond it; wherein established, he is not shaken even by heavy sorrow;
>
> " That should be known by the name of yoga, this disconnection from the union with pain. This yoga must be clung to with a firm conviction and with undesponding mind.
>
> " Abandoning without reserve all desires born of the imagination, by the mind curbing in the aggregate of the senses on every side,
>
> " Little by little let him gain tranquillity by means of Buddhi controlled by steadiness; having made the mind abide in the Self, let him not think of anything.
>
> " As often as the wavering and unsteady mind runneth away, so often reining it in, let him bring it under the control of the Self.
>
> " Supreme joy comes to this yogi whose mind is peaceful, whose passion nature is calmed, who is sinless and is Brahman-become.
>
> " The yogi who thus, ever disciplining the self, hath put away sin, he easily enjoyeth the infinite bliss of contact with Brahman.
>
> " His self trained by yoga, he seeth the Self abiding in all beings, all beings in the Self; everywhere he seeth the same.
>
> " He who seeth me everywhere, and seeth everything in me, of him will I never lose hold, and he shall never lose hold of me.
>
> " He who, established in unity, worshippeth me abiding in all beings, that yogi liveth in me, whatever his mode of living."
>
> VI.20–31.

Yoga is " the disconnection from the union with pain ", and it leads to the enjoyment of the infinite bliss of Brahman. And the road is the royal road of self-control, of converting ego-centred consciousness into god-absorbed awareness. With true psychological insight, Kṛishṇa teaches Arjuna to abandon without reserve all desires born of the imagination (VI.24). What a world of sorrow ceases to crush the heart of him who can abandon without reserve all desires born of the imagination !

Is it possible for man, with the kind of mind he has, to attain yoga by equanimity ? Arjuna voices the difficulty :

> " This yoga which thou hast declared to be by equanimity, O Madhusūdana, I see not a stable foundation for it owing to restlessness ;
>
> " For the mind is verily restless, O Kṛishṇa ; it is impetuous, strong and obstinate ; I deem it as hard to curb as the wind."
>
> VI.33, 34.

Which earnest seeker has not known despair on this account ? The Lord appreciates the difficulty, and answers :

> " Without doubt, O mighty-armed, the mind is hard to curb and restless ; but it may be curbed by constant practice and dispassion.
>
> " Yoga is hard to attain, methinks, by a self that is uncontrolled ; but by the Self-controlled it is attainable by the right means."
>
> VI.35, 36.

Constant practice and dispassion. There are no short cuts to the Highest. Perfection demands the uttermost from us, unreservedly. The concert artist practising all day and every day perfecting his art, the dancer, the acrobat, the craftsman, the student, the philosopher and the mystic, all know what constancy of purpose and practice means, and how indispensable is such constancy. And so also with respect to dispassion. For passion distorts the truth, " covers the real with a layer that is false ". Passion binds man to an egoistic view. But truth, bliss and freedom are universal in scope and quality. They need to be realized by a free consciousness, the consciousness of the universal-minded, for which dispassion is indispensable.

One last question born of uncertainty does Arjuna ask :

> " He who is unsubdued but who possesseth faith, with the mind wandering away from yoga, failing to attain perfection in yoga, what path doth he tread, O Kṛishṇa ?
>
> " Fallen from both, is he destroyed like a rent cloud, unsteadfast, O mighty-armed, deluded in the path of Brahman ?

" Deign, O Kṛishṇa, to completely dispel this doubt of mine ; for there is none to be found save thyself able to destroy this doubt."

VI.37–39

" O son of Pṛithā, neither in this world nor in the life to come is there destruction for him ; never doth any who worketh righteousness, O my son, tread the path of woe."

VI.40.

So answered the Lord.

How changed is the situation now ! The despondent Arjuna has been slowly awakened. The resistance in his soul has been skilfully met. His secret longings have been understood, his questions answered, his perception deepened. The hitherto unconquered victor, who has been stricken by a malady of the soul so terrible, that his subsequent weakness and refusal to fight could not have failed to humiliate him to the depths, was in no condition to place his trust in another, or to dare to hope that the future held any promise of fulfilment. Eternal God Himself incarnate in Kṛishṇa the charioteer has had to use divine patience and skill in dealing with the low-sunken warrior, a mighty person, a tremendous ego. He has used His wisdom, His authority as the Blessed Lord, His promise that the end would be well and His assurance that He regarded Arjuna as His devotee and friend.

Inwardly, Arjuna has awakened. Eagerness is manifest for the first time. And at last he unreservedly expresses his confidence and trust in Kṛishṇa ; " for there is none to be found save thyself able to destroy this doubt." Passionate is the outcry of his heart as he begs Kṛishṇa to completely dispel this doubt.

It is the critical moment of the Kṛishṇa-Arjuna drama ! One mistake and all would be lost. Arjuna would know shipwreck of the soul. How evil beyond imagination this is, only he who has known the death of the soul while still alive in the body can understand. But should Kṛishṇa give the right answer, the end was sure. All would be well.

And Kṛishṇa does give the right answer. For where man, calling upon God, is fit to receive the answer, that answer is always exactly right. So are the ways of God fulfilled in man. Therefore, too, the Lord exercises infinite patience and loving care as he " brings up " this delicate, sick child, man, to healthy maturity, in order that he may enjoy his divine heritage, and exercise dominion over the world which is his. For the world belongs to him who knows; and knowing, understands; and understanding, loves and nurtures. Loving and nurturing—that is dominion.

Like all the great scriptures of the world, the Gītā tells of the stark, wonderful drama that is enacted in the soul of man, in which good and evil, God and the Devil, right and wrong, are locked in stressful conflict. The sense of right is inherent in the living organism. The natural choice of the organism, blind and instinctive, of what is " good " for itself, is the gift of the universe. The knowledge of what is right is a question of growth, of becoming consciously aware and consciously practising what the inherent sense of right vaguely prompts one to do. The " rules of the game " today are different from those of the days of Neanderthal man, but the innate sense today is the same as it was then, even if other influences suppress it today as they did then. Religion is that by which the sense of right, the sense for the true, is brought to flower in man as a conscious, purposive, controlling power in life. Without it, no true fulfilment is possible. The relative right of ego-centred man is transformed into the absolute Right of liberated man, in whom no relative, circumstantial conditions either darken or diminish the clear flame of the spiritual value, the Right.

It is Religion which ushers man into this sphere. But the process is awful. Its dimensions are the dimensions of the universe itself. A thousand million light years' extent is taken in but one stride of the soul! Viṣṇu takes his famous three strides. One covers the manifested universe. Only one! Another covers all heaven—Father, Son and Holy Ghost, or Brahmā-Viṣṇu-Śiva, together with all the celestial realm! And the third stride—why, no one can either see or imagine it! He alone who has taken it, " knows " it. For it is the stride which spells the transcendence of all limiting dualistic consciousness by the realization of IT, Brahman. But before this stride can be taken, the previous two, covering the known and knowable totality must first be taken. And the third is possible only after equilibrium, or inner poise (which is yoga) has been reached with the first two strides. And then it is a soaring rather than a stepping into Brahman. Long before equilibrium is reached, man explores and traverses the entire universe in his soul, fights the battle of the universe, for each part of the universe (material or spiritual, God or the Devil) claims man as its whole property. First, this battle; only afterwards, dawns the understanding of what it means. That is the source of tribulation—the battle is fought blind, a losing battle for most, with the powers arrayed against lonely, single man, when he is down and out, ripe to be crushed and despoiled.

Here, he calls upon God.

But he must first be prepared to die completely to the old life, or else God never answers the call, for man himself, by clinging to ego, prevents God from answering. Man must first prove his love for God by being willing to die—the chrysalis cannot become a butterfly and still remain a chrysalis! He must prove his sincerity and readiness for the new life by really being prepared, in addition to being willing, to die to the old. Then when he cries out, " Deign to completely dispel my doubt, for there is none other than Thyself who can do it ", Eternal God rises in majesty and power and says: " O My Son, never is there death for him who worketh righteousness."

" My Son! "

There indeed is the pledge of safety. Not alone now, but as a team, an invincible team of two, whose mutual love and co-operation will give birth to a new heaven and a new earth! And no puny strength of the deluded, demon-haunted enemies of Right can even scratch the citadel of Love and Truth built by immortal hands.

In almost every man's life comes a crisis. For some, several crises. On the stepping stones of his old dead selves, man liberates himself into IT.

Thus did Arjuna's sincere interest in realizing Truth, in becoming one with Brahman, bring forth the Lord's pledge of Love and deathlessness. Mere despondency and faintheartedness do not merit the attention of the Divine Healer.

Man, the child, calls upon God for trivial things. Everything is trivial except one thing: to be united to God. Sickness, grief, soul-torment, everything is trivial. It should be dealt with by man alone. It arises out of the dualism caused by his egoic outlook, " thou and I, thine and mine." No child learned to walk without stumbling. But God is no indulgent nurse. God demands perfection from man. Without the slightest, sentimental hesitation God lets foolish, ignorant, deluded man destroy himself. Which creative genius hesitates to destroy what is not perfection in his eyes ?

So God makes no answer to any call whatsoever in man's life except to the one call for union with Him. Yet any and every call will be answered if subservient to the call of Love, which is the irresistible call. Whoso denies Love, whoso betrays Love, in any and every sphere, in any and every appropriate form, receives the wages of sin. Sin means that which attempts to deny or hurt or mar the eternal unity of the universe. The call of Love is the one compelling power which commands Almighty God to act, and act in meek obedience to the behest of Love. Love is the absolute Ṛta of universal Being and its activity.

Arjuna made the call. And the Lord answered.

The poet-author of the Gītā was one of the world's supreme artists.

* * *

Consonant with Indian thought, Kṛishṇa tells Arjuna that if he fails to achieve yoga in this life, he will obtain, as a reward for his attempt now, better conditions and opportunities in succeeding lives to fulfil this worthy aim. The yogi is held in high esteem :

> " The yogi is greater than the ascetics ; he is thought to be even greater than the wise ; the yogi is greater than the men of action ; therefore become thou a yogi, O Arjuna.
>
> " And among all yogis, he who, full of faith, with the inner Self abiding in me, adoreth me, he is considered by me to be the best trained."
>
> VI.46, 47.

Henceforth, the Lord holds nothing back from Arjuna. Full revelation follows. Kṛishṇa promises :

> " With the mind clinging to me, O Pārtha, performing yoga, refuged in me, how thou shalt without doubt know me to the uttermost, that hear thou.

> "I will declare to thee this knowledge and wisdom in its completeness, which, having known, there is nothing more here needeth to be known."
>
> VII.1, 2.
>
> "Earth, water, fire, air, ākāśa, mind and Buddhi also, and egoism (consciousness of separate selfhood), these are the eightfold division of my nature.
>
> "This is the inferior. Know my other nature, the higher, the life-principle, O mighty-armed, by which this universe is upheld."
>
> VII.4, 5.

The Lord then reveals his nature, his character, his excellences and his powers, and finally grants Arjuna the vision of the Divine Form (see above, pp. 248–252).

In the seventh discourse, Kṛishṇa says that all this world deluded by the natures (harmonious, active, slothful) born of the three guṇas, does not know him, above the qualities, imperishable. Those who succeed in piercing the illusion of the qualities do reach him. But not so, the evil-doers.

He then mentions the four groups of righteous ones who worship him: the suffering; the seekers of knowledge; the desirous of worldly objectives; the wise. Of these, the wise are dearest to him. He next makes a statement about himself and his own nature:

> "Those devoid of understanding think of me, the unmanifest, as having manifestation, knowing not my higher nature, changeless and supreme.
>
> "Nor am I of all discovered, enveloped in my creation-illusion. This deluded world knoweth me not, the unborn, the unchanging."
>
> VII.24, 25.

He knows all beings, past and present, and those to come. But beings do not know him, for they become bewildered, on being born, by the pairs of opposites in the world, by attraction and repulsion. Only the sinless, acting virtuously, are released from bewilderment. They worship him, the Lord. They strive for release from "old age and death" (jarāmaraṇa), and they come to understand what is action, what is manifestation, and what is the inner Self. They know Brahman.

At last Arjuna asks the deepest questions:

> "What is that Brahman? What is that inner Self? What is action, O most excellent Person? What is declared as Nature, and what is called the chief God (God regarded as a personal being)?
> "What is the supreme sacrificial rite here in this body, and how performed, O Madhusūdana? And how art thou to be known at the time of death, by the Self-controlled?
>
> VIII.1, 2.

The Lord answers:

> "Brahman, supreme, is the indestructible. Its innate nature is called inner Self (Creative Spirit, or Paramātman). The producing power which brings all (beings and things) into existence—understand that as action.
> "Manifestation is the perishable part of everything. Purusha[1] is the essential deity. I myself am present in the great sacrificial rite here in the body, O best of beings wearing the body.
> "And he who, casting off the body, goeth forth thinking upon me only at the time of the end, he entereth into my being; there is no doubt of that."
>
> VIII.3–5.

For the first time Arjuna addresses Shri Kṛishṇa as Purushottama, as most excellent Person, or Supreme Being. It is the moment of acceptance of the Lord and the confession of faith—"Thou art the Lord my God." Only after the acceptance can the question, "Who (or what) art Thou?", be asked without irreverence, and receive a reply. When man and woman are first introduced to each other, they learn each other's names—mere labels. When love flashes between them and binds their hearts, mystified, thrilled, they ask each other with inner yearning, "Who are you?" And she reveals her beauty, and he gives of all his strength. But first comes the acceptance born of love. So too, man first touches God, then opens his eyes and beholds the wonder, and then with the fullness of love-longing he asks, "Who art Thou, O Lord?"

[1] In the Sāṁkhya teachings there are two fundamentals: Matter, and an infinitely large number of Souls; or Prakṛiti, and Purushas. Each Soul plunges into material manifestation, and through successive incarnations liberates itself. The Soul, which is always pure and unsullied, merely "looks on" while the drama of life is enacted, in which the actors and actions, the senses and sense-objects, are all matter-born.
Purusha also represents the male creative energy. The supreme Purusha is the Divine Man, the manifested, personal God.

Having answered Arjuna's questions, Kṛishṇa declares that whoso reaches him returns not to earth, the transient abode of pain. Once again he exhorts Arjuna to become a yogi :

> " Knowing these paths, O Pārtha, the yogi is nowise perplexed. Therefore at all times be firm in yoga, O Arjuna.
> " The fruit of meritorious deeds, attached in the Vedas to sacrifices, to austerities and also to almsgiving, the yogi passeth all these by, having known this, and goeth to the supreme and acient abode."
>
> VIII.27, 28.

In the ninth and tenth discourses, Kṛishṇa proceeds with the revelation of his nature (see above, pp. 251, 252). Arjuna's conviction that he is indeed the Lord becomes absolute (X.12–14). He is now enthralled. He is enthusiastic—literally god-intoxicated. Only one thing interests him—God :

> " Deign to tell without reserve of thine own divine glories, by which glories thou remainest, pervading these worlds.
> " How may I know thee, O Yogi, by constant meditation ? In what aspects art thou to be thought of by me, O Blessed Lord ?
> " In detail tell me again of thy yoga and glory, O Janārdana ; for me there is never satiety in hearing thy life-giving words."
>
> X.16–18.

Even as the simple " I love you ", endlessly repeated millennium after millennium, has never failed to work its magic with true lovers, just so there never is satiety for the devotee in hearing the life-giving words of the Lord. So once again does the Lord detail his glories.

And now comes the question, the answer to which will decide whether the great discourses have fulfilled their purpose or not :

> " But what is the knowledge of all these details to thee, O Arjuna ? Having established this whole universe with a fragment of myself, I remain."
>
> X.42.

Arjuna answers :

> " This word of the supreme Secret concerning the Self, which thou hast spoken out of compassion for me, by this my delusion has been taken away."
>
> XI.1.

Yes, the Lord has triumphed ! Triumphed in the ultimate sense, because he answered no call other than the one call, Love's call to know him, the supreme, to know IT, Brahman. And Arjuna acknowledges it. This indeed is the love and mercy of God; nothing sentimental; absolute. The old teaching that just as a parent fondles and also punishes the child, out of love, even so the " Lord chasteneth those whom he loveth ", is true. Let man endure the stripes and chastisement of the Lord, or else there is no salvation. He who tries to dodge karma, he who, a coward, seeks to escape the stern, loving hand of the Lord, will indeed be lost. Out of full acceptance alone comes vision. And without vision, what liberation can there be ? If the Lord were not all-wise and all-loving, he would be a tribal idol foolish enough to prevent necessary suffering. It is the Divine Compassion which demands absolute self-surrender and absolute endurance in order that the Divine Love can flow through the purified and redeemed channel, liberated man.

Now that his delusion has been taken away, Arjuna asks to see the Divine Form. The mental aspect has been grasped. Now for the concrete experience. The Lord grants the request. Prostrate, with hair upstanding, Arjuna, having seen the almost unbearable truth of the nature of universal process, asks the Lord to revert to his gentle, familiar form ! And the Lord stands before him again as Kṛishṇa the charioteer. What imagination !

The Lord says :

> " This form of mine beholden by thee is very hard to see. Even the gods ever long to behọld this form.
>
> " Nor can I be seen as thou hast seen me by (study of) the Vedas, nor by austerity, nor by alms, nor by offerings.
>
> " But by devotion to me alone I may thus be perceived, Arjuna, and known and seen in essence, and entered, O Parantapa.
>
> " He who doeth actions for me, whose supreme good I am, my devotee, freed from attachment, without hatred of any being, he cometh unto me, O Pāṇḍava."
>
> XI.52–55.

Repeatedly, Kṛishṇa emphasizes the necessity for one-pointedness, for unswerving devotion to the Supreme alone. He, the Lord, is the supreme good. Whoso performs every action as unto the Lord, freed from attachment, at peace with all mankind, will surely know his Lord.

It was realized in India that few could soar to the peaks of the Upanishads. Wisdom and spiritual food are all men's needs. That which was the creation of the few had to be conveyed in appropriate form to the many. The Buddha made his contribution, the special characteristics of which were psychological insight and ethical idealism. He was the first and most powerful democratizing force. But it was clear that for the masses, an austere ethic, however sublime and true, could make little headway unless backed by the spiritual sanction of a personal God, who would also be the object of devotion. The poet-author of the Gītā makes Kṛishṇa the embodied God. But in the course of his teachings, he has presented the Supreme both as Brahman of the Upanishads and also as the personal Lord of the universe incarnate in Kṛishṇa. In truth, there is no discrepancy. The only difference made is that the ordinary man's task is made easier through the use of the personal Lord concept. He need not wrack his brains too much. Instead of making transcendental flights into a rarefied spiritual atmosphere, he could simply pour out his heart's devotion before the Lord his God.

But in each case—the Upanishads, the Buddha, the Gītā—the demand made on man is absolute: perfection, one-pointedness and self-surrender. As far as the practice of virtue is concerned there is no difference. But as far as the extent of the intellectual grasp is concerned there are differences. In which case, which is more acceptable to the Lord? The point is brought out in Arjuna's question:

> "Those devotees who ever disciplined worship thee, and those who worship the Indestructible, the Unmanifested—which of these is the more learned in yoga?"

The Lord answers:

> "They who with mind fixed on me, ever disciplined, worship me, with faith supreme endowed, these, in my opinion, are best in yoga."
>
> XII.1, 2.

The Gītā is thus mainly a scripture of devotion. In all religions in which a personal God occupies the supreme position, the next most important factor is the worship of that God. To that God, then, his devotee is necessarily the best.

Kṛishṇa then points out that those who worship the Indestructible also come to him. But these worshippers follow a more difficult path than the devotees who worship the Lord. Again he exhorts Arjuna, and explains the lesser steps he could take if the greater ones were beyond his powers :

> " Place thy mind in me, into me let thy Buddhi enter ; then without doubt thou shalt abide in me hereafter.
>
> " But if thou art not able firmly to fix thy mind on me, then by the yoga of (patient and assiduous) study, seek to reach me, O Dhananjaya.
>
> " If also thou art not equal to constant study, be intent on my service ; performing actions for my sake, thou shalt attain perfection.
>
> " If even to do this thou hast not strength, then taking refuge in my yoga, renounce all fruit of action, with self-control.
>
> " Better indeed is knowledge than constant study ; than knowledge meditation is better ; than meditation renunciation of the fruit of action ; on renunciation follows peace."
>
> XII.8–12.

The Lord proceeds to describe the characteristics of those who are dear to him :

> " He who beareth no ill-will to any being, friendly and compassionate, without attachment and egoism, balanced in pleasure and pain, and patient,
>
> " The yogi who is ever content, with the self controlled, resolute, with mind and Buddhi dedicated to me, he, my devotee, is dear to me.
>
> " He from whom the world does not shrink and who does not shrink from the world, freed from joy and anger, fear and agitation, he is dear to me.
>
> " He who wants nothing, is pure, expert, impartial, untroubled, renouncing every undertaking, he, my devotee, is dear to me.
>
> " He who neither liketh nor disliketh, nor grieveth, nor desireth, renouncing good and evil, full of devotion, he is dear to me.
>
> " Alike to foe and friend, and also in fame and ignominy, alike in cold and heat, pleasures and pains, destitute of attachment,
>
> " Taking equally praise and reproach, silent, wholly content with what cometh, homeless, firm in mind, full of devotion, that man is dear to me.

"They verily who worship this life-giving wisdom as taught herein, endued with faith, I their supreme object, devotees, they are surpassingly dear to me."

XII.13–20.

It will be clearly seen by now that there is no difference between the saṁnyāsin of the Upanishads, the bhikkhu of the Buddha, and the devotee of Shri Kṛishṇa. India has been quite consistent in its conception of the holy man, in its exaltation of virtue, and in its teaching of the path to liberation.

Arjuna now wishes to learn the philosophy underlying the religious teaching, and he says :[1]

"Matter and spirit, also the field and the knower of the field, wisdom and that which ought to be known, these I fain would learn, O Keśava."

Kṛishṇa tells him :

"This body, O son of Kuntī, is called the field ; that which knoweth it is called the knower of the field by the sages.

"Understand me as the knower of the field in all fields, O Bhārata. Knowledge as to the field and the knower of the field, that in my opinion is wisdom."

XIII.1, 2.

As regards the field :

"The great elements (fire, air, earth, water and ākāśa), the ego-sense, Buddhi, and also the Unmanifested, the ten senses and the one, and the five pastures of the senses ;

"Desire, aversion, pleasure, pain, organism, intelligence, firmness, these, briefly described, constitute the field and its transformation."

XIII. 5, 6.

As regards wisdom :

"Humility, honesty, harmlessness, patience, rectitude, service of the teacher, purity, steadfastness, self-control,

"Indifference to the objects of the senses, and also absence of egoism, insight into the pain and evil of birth, death, old age and sickness,

"Unattachment, absence of clinging to son, wife or home, and constant balance of mind in wished-for and unwished-for events,

[1] This verse is omitted in several editions.

> "Unflinching devotion to me by yoga, without other object, resort to sequestered places, dislike of crowds,
> "Constancy in the wisdom of the Self, understanding of the object of essential wisdom—that is declared to be the wisdom; all against it is ignorance."
>
> XIII.7–11.

Here, wisdom overflows the bounds set by the ordinary meaning of wisdom, and includes the possession and practice of virtue, and the life of the devotee. What ought to be known? The Blessed Lord gives the great Upanishadic teaching:

> "I will declare that which ought to be known, that which, being known, immortality is enjoyed—the beginningless supreme Brahman, which can be called neither being nor non-being.
> "Everywhere That hath hands and feet, everywhere eyes, heads and mouths; all-hearing, He dwelleth in the world, enveloping all;
> "Possessed of all sense-faculties, (yet) without any senses, unattached, supporting everything, free from qualities and enjoying qualities;
> "Without and within all beings, immovable and also movable; by reason of His subtlety imperceptible; at hand and far away is That.
> "Not divided amid beings, and yet seated distributively; That is to be known as the supporter of beings; He devours and He generates.
> "That, the Light of all lights, is said to be beyond darkness; wisdom, the object of wisdom, by wisdom to be reached, seated in the hearts of all.
> "Thus the field, the wisdom and the object of wisdom have been briefly told. My devotee, thus knowing, enters into my being."
>
> XIII.12–18.

The philosophy of matter and spirit is presented along Sāṁkhyan lines:

> "Know thou that Nature and the Person are both without beginning; and know also that modifications and qualities all arise from Nature.
> "Nature is called the causer in the production of causes and effects; the Person is called the causer of the experience of pleasure and pain.
> "The Person seated in Nature tasteth the modes born of Nature; attachment to the modes is the cause of his birth in good and evil wombs.

"Supervisor and permitter, supporter, enjoyer, great Lord (Maheśvar) and also the supreme Self (Paramātman); thus is styled in this body the supreme Person (Purusha).

XIII.19–22.

"Seated equally in all beings, the supreme Lord, unperishing within the perishing—he who seeth Him, he seeth."

XIII.27.

"He who seeth that Nature (Prakṛiti) verily performeth all actions, and that Self (Ātman) is actionless, he seeth.

"When he perceiveth the diversified existence of beings as rooted in the One, and spreading forth from it, then he reacheth Brahman,

"Being beginningless and without qualities, the imperishable supreme Self (Paramātman), though seated in the body, O Kaunteya, worketh not nor is affected."

XII.29–31.

Ethics is based on psychology and a philosophy of life. Good and evil, and the practice of virtue, are related to one's world-view. How do things happen? How does the mind and heart of man work? No intelligent practice of virtue is possible without some self-knowledge and without a grasp of the nature of the environment.

In the thirteenth and fourteenth discourses, the Sāṁkyan view is unfolded by Kṛishṇa. Sattva (harmony or rhythm), rajas (restless activity or passion) and tamas (inertia or darkness or delusion) are the three guṇas (qualities or constituents) of the world of Nature, of non-eternal manifestation, of ever-changing process. The guṇas bind the indestructible Dweller (Purusha) in the body. Harmony binds by attachment to bliss and to wisdom; passion is the source of attachment and thirst for life, and binds by action; inertia, born of unwisdom, is the deluder, and binds by heedlessness, indolence and sloth. All three guṇas function simultaneously, one particular guṇa being uppermost in a given situation. Whoso is established in harmony progresses; the active dwells in the mid-region; the inert goes down, enveloped in vile qualities. Kṛishṇa teaches that

"When the seer perceiveth no agent other than the qualities, and knoweth that which is higher than the qualities, he entereth into my nature.

> "When the dweller in the body hath crossed over these three qualities, whence all bodies have been produced, liberated from birth, death, old age and sorrow, he enjoys the immortal."
>
> XIV.19, 20.

Arjuna asks:

> "What are the marks of him who hath crossed over the three qualities, O Lord? How acteth he, and how doth he go beyond these three qualities?"
>
> XIV.21.

He who is in equilibrium, and remains unattached, answers the Lord. He neither likes nor dislikes any and every quality; in his inner self he stands apart from the guṇas, just watching them at work; he is balanced in pleasure and pain, self-reliant; rock, gold, love, hate, praise or blame bestowed on him, honour, ignominy, friendship or enmity are all the same to him. What is important, again, is single-minded devotion to the Lord:

> "And he who serveth me exclusively by the yoga of devotion he, crossing beyond the qualities, is fit to become Brahman.
>
> "For I am the abode of Brahman, the Immortal, the Inexhaustible, of eternal righteousness and of unending bliss."
>
> XIV.26, 27.

Twice in this discourse, the Lord mentions the immortal. The form in which the Gītā presents its teachings introduces a difference from the teachings of the Upanishads and of the Buddha, with regard to the questions of personal survival after death, and of immortality. What the Gītā means by liberation may be deduced, for instance, from XIV, 2, in which the Lord declares: "Having taken refuge in this wisdom, and being assimilated to my own nature, they are not reborn even in the emanation of a universe, nor are disquieted in its dissolution."

Purusha, the attributeless dweller in the body, exists through all eternity, unaffected by time, space, causation and nature. Kṛishṇa says:

> "A portion of mine own Self transformed in the world of life into a living Spirit, eternal, draweth round itself the senses, of which the mind is the sixth, veiled in matter.

"When the Lord acquireth a body and when he abandoneth it, he seizeth these and goeth with them, as the wind takes fragrances from their retreats."

XV.7, 8.

"The deluded do not perceive him when he departeth or stayeth or enjoyeth, swayed by the qualities; the wisdom-eyed perceive.
"Yogis also, striving, perceive him, established in the Self; but, though struggling, the unintelligent perceive him not, their selves untrained."

XV.10, 11.

"And I am seated in the hearts of all . . ."

XV.15.

"Since I transcend the perishable and am higher also than the imperishable, therefore in the world and in the Veda I am proclaimed the Supreme Spirit.
"He who, undeluded, knoweth me as the Supreme Spirit, he, all-knowing, worshippeth me with his whole being, O Bhārata."

XV.18, 19.

Kṛishṇa then lists the qualities characterizing the man born with the divine properties. Positively: Fearlessness, cleanliness of life, steadfastness in the yoga of wisdom, almsgiving, self-restraint, sacrifice and study of the scriptures, austerity, straightforwardness, harmlessness, truth, renunciation, peacefulness, compassion to living beings, mildness, modesty, vigour, patience, fortitude and purity. Negatively: absence of wrath, crookedness, covetousness, fickleness, envy and pride.

Next, the qualities characterizing those born with demoniacal properties: Hypocrisy, arrogance, conceit, wrath, harshness and unwisdom. Demoniacal men know neither right activity nor right abstinence, nor purity nor propriety. The truth is not in them. They believe the universe is without truth, without moral basis, without a Creator, without a co-ordinating principle, but is merely the product of lust and chance. Such men, says Kṛishṇa, come forth as enemies for the destruction of the world. They blindly pursue insatiable desires. They are held in bondage by a hundred ties of expectation, and are given over to lust and anger. They strive to amass wealth for the sake of sensual pleasures. Self-glorified, obstinate, filled with pride and the intoxication of wealth, they perform lip-sacrifices. They are given over to egoism, power, lust, insolence, wrath and malice, and hate the Self in the bodies of others and in their own. To hell do they go :

> " Triple is the gate of this hell, destructive of the self—lust, hate and greed ; therefore let man renounce these three."

Kṛishṇa then gives his support to the established order :

> " Let the scriptures be thy authority in determining what ought to be done, or what ought not to be done. Knowing what hath been declared by the ordinances of the scriptures, thou oughtest to work in the world."
>
> XVI.21, 24.

Whatever the poet-author of the Gītā may have been professionally, he was a practical-minded man. If the highest teachings were to be brought to the masses only at the expense of orthodox religion and the established order of the land, then the ensuing anarchy and chaos would sweep away both wisdom and less than the highest wisdom. No one can travel by air except from and to the earth as a landing ground. Besides, the scriptural ordinances had played, and did play, a vital part in the life of the nation. When the Lord incarnate supported them, then those amongst the masses who could not take any steps higher than those laid down by the scriptures were reassured. Their inward faith was not threatened ; their minds were at rest. They could peacefully go on playing their part in the national life, and continue to be the fertile soil nourishing the tree of culture which bore the fair fruit of philosophy and spiritual fulfilment.

But Arjuna the disciple, being in a different position, naturally asks :

> " Those that sacrifice full of faith, but casting aside the ordinances of the scriptures, what is verily their condition, O Kṛishṇa ? Is it one of purity, passion or darkness ? "
>
> XVII.1.

The Lord explains that even as a man's faith is, so is his character. At the same time, his faith is shaped to his character. Pure men worship the gods ; the passionate, the gnomes and giants ; the dark, ghosts and spirits. He proceeds at length with the threefold classification. First he denounces self-mortifiers :

> " Men who perform severe austerities unenjoined by the scriptures, filled with hypocrisy and egoism, impelled by lusts and passions and violence,
>
> " Unintelligent, tormenting the aggregated elements forming the body, and me also, seated within the body, know these to be demoniacal in their resolves."
>
> XVII.5, 6.

Next he touches upon food. Foods that augment vitality, energy, vigour, health, joy and cheerfulness, delicious, bland, substantial and agreeable, are dear to the pure—the philosophy and science of dietetics in a nutshell. Food which is bitter, sour, saline, over-hot, pungent, dry and burning, producing pain, sickness and grief is dear to the passionate. Food which is stale and flat, putrid and corrupt, left-over and unclean, is dear to the dark.

There are those who do not appreciate the emphasis on austerity in Indian teachings. On this subject, Shri Kṛishṇa declares:

> " Worship given to the gods, to the twice-born, to the teachers and to the wise, purity, straightforwardness, continence and harmlessness are called the austerity of the body.
>
> " Speech causing no annoyance, truthful, pleasant and beneficial, the practice of the study of the scriptures, are called the austerity of speech.
>
> " Tranquillity of mind, gentleness, silence, self-control, purity of thought—this is called the austerity of the mind.
>
> " This threefold austerity performed by men with the utmost faith, without desire for fruit, harmonized, is said to be pure.
>
> " The austerity which is practised with the object of gaining respect, honour and worship, and for ostentation, is said to be of passion, unstable and fleeting.
>
> " That austerity which is done under a deluded understanding with self-torture, or with the object of outdoing another, that is declared to be of darkness."
>
> XVII.14–19.

* * * * *

There remains the last stage. After the aspirant to the realization of Truth has been through his novitiate, gathered his worldly experience, emerged out of the trials and tribulations of life, reaped a harvest of wisdom, grown in ability to live the life beautiful, the final step is renunciation. No one can start with renunciation, for what is there to renounce? If a boy is heir to a fortune on the death of the previous enjoyer of the fortune, and he just gives it away, he has not renounced but merely cast away his fortune. Only that which is "one's own"—by earning through hard work, by creation, by right use and fulfilment of all responsibility, by arriving at the end of a fully worked out relationship—that alone can be renounced. "God" can renounce. By such renunciation, God sacrifices. The world, and ourselves, are the product. Man fulfilled, having attained, having gained and utilized to the full, is in a position to renounce. Man perfected, is God. Perfected man, by renunciation, is liberated. Thus the final self-less-ness which is freedom, the peace which passes understanding—not a mere figure of speech but the infinite, most real bliss, here-now—is attained.

Arjuna has now arrived at the last stage. One final request:

> "I desire, O mighty-armed, to know severally the essence of renunciation, and of relinquishment."

And the Blessed Lord answers:

> "Sages have known as renunciation the renouncing of desire-prompted works; the relinquishing of the fruit of all actions is called relinquishment by the wise."
>
> XVIII.1, 2.

In detail, Shri Kṛishṇa explains that all that ought to be done, one's own proper duty, should be done. If it is done without attachment, without desire for the fruit of action, then that is true renunciation. Kṛishṇa gathers up the threads of all the teaching he has given, and comes back to the point from which he started:

> "He who is free from the egoistic notion, whose Buddhi is not affected, though he slay these peoples he slayeth not, nor is he bound."
>
> XVIII.17.

"Though he slay, he slayeth not." Paradoxical, but true. A guilt conscience, or a satisfied conscience, each belongs to the sphere of egoic functioning. So long as the limited self's limited motives are bound up with action, whether right or wrong according to the social ethic, so long is there bondage, so long has one to bear the burden of consequence upon oneself. If a man kills the killer of his father, he is guilty of murder. But when the hangman kills the killer, impersonally carrying out his duty as an agent of the law, without attachment to his action as hangman, without desiring the fruit (satisfaction) of his action, then though the hangman technically kills, he kills not. Even so with a soldier. If a soldier slays with malice, hatred, or in any way which binds him to the act, then he is a slayer. But if he is able to perform his duty purely, then "though he slays, he slayeth not."

So the Lord repeats again what he said in the beginning: beings follow nature; better one's own duty, though destitute of merit, than the duty of another, even well-executed; congenital duty, though defective, should not be abandoned. Thereupon,

> "He whose Buddhi is everywhere unattached, the self subdued, dead to desires, he goeth by renunciation to the supreme perfection of freedom without obligation.
>
> "How he who hath attained perfection obtaineth Brahman, that highest state of wisdom, learn thou from me only succintly, O Kaunteya.
>
> "United to Buddhi, purified, controlling the self by firmness, having abandoned sound and the other objects of the senses, having laid aside passion and malice,
>
> "Dwelling in solitude, abstemious, speech, body and mind subdued, constantly fixed in meditation and yoga, taking refuge in dispassion,
>
> "Having cast aside egoism, violence, arrogance, lust, hate, covetousness, selfless and peaceful—he is fit to become Brahman.
>
> "Becoming Brahman, serene in the Self, he neither grieveth nor desireth; the same to all beings, he obtaineth supreme devotion unto me.
>
> "By devotion he knoweth me in essence, who and what I am; having thus known me in essence, he forthwith entereth into the Supreme.
>
> "Though ever performing all actions, taking refuge in me, by my grace he obtaineth the eternal, changeless abode.

" Renouncing mentally all works in me, intent on me, resorting to the yoga of Buddhi, have thy thought ever on me.

" Thinking on me, thou shalt overcome all obstacles by my grace; but if from egoism thou wilt not listen, thou shalt be destroyed utterly.

" Entrenched in egoism, thou thinkest, 'I will not fight'; to no purpose thy determination; nature will constrain thee.

" O son of Kuntī, bound by thine own duty, born of thine own nature, that which from delusion thou desirest not to do, even that helplessly thou shalt perform.

" The Lord dwelleth in the heart of all beings, O Arjuna, by his illusive power causing all beings to revolve, as though mounted on a machine.

" Flee unto him for shelter with all thy being, O Bhārata; by his grace thou shalt obtain supreme peace, the everlasting dwelling-place.

" Thus has wisdom, more secret than secrecy itself, been declared unto thee by me; having reflected on it fully, then act as thou listest.

" Listen thou again to my supreme word, most secret of all; beloved art thou of me, most surely; therefore will I speak for thy benefit.

" Merge thy mind in me, be my devotee, sacrifice to me, prostrate thyself before me, thou shalt come even unto me. I pledge thee my troth; thou art dear to me.

" Abandoning all (other) modes of religious living, come unto me alone for shelter; sorrow not; I will liberate thee from all sins.

" Never is this to be spoken by thee to anyone who is without austerity, nor to one without devotion, nor to one who desireth not to listen, nor yet to him who speaketh ill of me.

" He who shall declare this supreme secret among my devotees, having shown the highest devotion for me, without doubt he shall come to me.

" Nor is there any among men who performeth dearer service to me than he, nor any other shall be more beloved by me on earth than he.

" And he who shall study this sacred dialogue of ours, by him I shall be worshipped with the sacrifice of wisdom. Such is my mind.

" The man also who, full of faith, merely heareth it, uncavilling, even he, freed from evil, obtaineth the radiant worlds of the righteous.

" Has this been heard by thee, O son of Pṛithā, with one-pointed mind? Has thy delusion, caused by unwisdom, been destroyed, O Dhananjaya?"

XVIII.49–72.

Arjuna declares:

"Destroyed is my delusion. I have gained knowledge through thy grace, O immutable One. I am firm, my doubts have fled. I will do according to thy word."

XVIII.73.

And the warrior rises up in strength as Kṛishṇa whips the horses into action. Swift and thick his arrows fly. Everywhere the foeman falls. The battle rages and the dust is laid with streams of blood. Invincible, the hero and his great brothers fulfil the behest of the Law that operates in the universe. The great hosts of Kurus and Pāṇḍavas are almost exterminated. An old order goes crashing into ruin, making way for the slow and painful birth of the new. The Mahābhārata, the great battle, is fought. Vanquished and victor both suffer—a lesson through the ages for all mankind. Kṛishṇa returns home. He has fulfilled his mission.

But the Divine Charioteer, who was also the Divine Lover, lives enshrined in the heart of Hindu India. As long as there are Hindu lips, the name of Kṛishṇa will be heard, and will never fail to evoke the profoundest response a true Hindu is capable of making. Kṛishṇa's great discourses will ever live as the Lord's Ṣong, the Bhagavad-Gītā, the beautiful song of Truth, embodying the religious ideals and teachings, the insight and devotion of Hindu India.

Scrutable are the ways of the Lord, when expounded by a Kṛishṇa.

Part Two

ESSAY

Section A

HINDUISM AND THE BUDDHA

Bewildered by the infinitely varied religious practices of the people of India, an ordinary observer might conclude that the different religions flourishing in the subcontinent are irreconcilable. Yet in truth it may well be that these distinctive religions are integral developments out of a single core which is RELIGION, and that to regard them as irreconcilable may only betray one's dimness of vision.

The early religious thought of India emerged out of the cultural interaction of Negritos and Proto-australoids, Sumerians and Armenians, alpine groups from north of Irān, Āryan speaking peoples, and Austro-asiatic and Mongoloid groups ; whilst later thought was influenced by the advent of Greeks, Scythians, Chinese, Huns, Arabians, Afghans, Turks, Mughals and modern Europeans. They carve out seven thousand years of prehistory and history! Well might the peoples of India have ranged through the gamut of emotion and thought involved in searching the eternal verities, devising disciplines to enable them to shatter the veil of darkness, and embodying the fruit of their effort and realization in their philosophies and religions.

Not only must one take into account the time span and the diversity of races, but also the influence of the land itself—its extremes of quiet and storm, of dry and wet ; its long, languid rivers and monsoon-swollen, short-lived torrents ; its majestic mountains ; its endless plains, so monotonous in the dry season, so magical when the rains come ; and the sublime splendour of its starlit nights, especially the bright nights over the great white solitudes where snow-headed giants gleam upwards into the sky. No one who has not lived in that land, and having lived there, has attuned himself and yielded himself to it, can quite savour the inmost spirit of Indian religions.

In that land arose the Indian way of life, which displayed certain elements common to most if not all of the racial groups in the subcontinent. Subsistence agriculture was the basis for all. Industry, frugality, peaceful settlement, division of labour, control from above, and the general objectives of stable government, prosperous economy, and a secure and contented society, were common elements. The land itself was responsible for this, and indeed the land was the great unifier. Although new immigrants behaved intolerantly towards already settled peoples, in conformity with the principle of avoidance, they identified themselves in due time with the land of their settlement and adopted its essential, old established way of life.

In the old established order there was caste. The hierarchical principle prevailed, and the inequality of man was accepted, the individual being regarded as the instrument of a social function. Out of singularly heterogenous elements, the Āryans reared a stable order; and for twenty-five centuries Hindu civilization flourished until the devastating inroads of Mahmud of Ghazni preluded the approaching Muslim supremacy over northern India. The caste system differentiated one socio-economic group from another. But the religious sanction of the Ṛig Veda unified mankind by declaring that each and every man, according as he belonged to one or other of the four main castes, emanated from one part or another of the single body of Purusha.[1] Thus the Āryans fully recognized the spiritual unity of mankind, and also frankly acknowledged outer differences in status and duty. Within the caste circle, practical brotherhood was strongly marked; and inside each joint family, the unity of the family circle quite swamped distinctive individuality and individual rights as understood to-day. Not the individual but the family was the unit on which Indian society was always based, and the organic wholeness of society was maintained through co-operation achieved by meticulous fulfilment of allotted individual duty.

This caste system, so uniquely characteristic of Hindu culture, was the focal point, and an integrating factor, of all aspects of life, for religion, politics and economics were intimately related

[1] Ṛig Veda, X. 90.

to it. Collectivism and rigid adherence to established custom hardly allowed personal liberty in the modern sense. For the masses, daily duty as laid down by caste rules covered the field of one's life as a citizen, a breadwinner, a member of a family, and an emanation from Purusha. Duties, consisting of rituals and ceremonies, to the fathers, the gods, and the host of other spirits, and observance of the simple, ethical precepts, constituted the religious life as far as the practice of the masses was concerned.

But where religious philosophy was concerned, and the pursuit of the holy life, individual freedom found play as in no other civilization then or since. And no obstruction could stand long in the path of the earnest seeker of Brahmavidyā.

Thus the people, their way of life, and the nature of the land, were responsible for the unique and phenomenal development of religions and religious thought in India, particularly during the millennium and a half before the birth of Christ. Indeed, if one asks what is the most powerful and deeply rooted source of inspiration of all Indian culture, the unequivocal answer is religion. This is as true of India as it is to say that beauty was a keynote of ancient Greece, that Chinese culture displayed an engaging and practical æsthetic sensibility, that respect for law was Rome's great bequest to mankind, and that in the modern world science is regarded by most as the language of truth.

It is of no little significance that India is now, as in the past, the safe home of all the great religions of the world. Vedic religion and the Upanishads, Jainism and Buddhism, Brāhmanism and the theistic Hinduism of the Gītā, Sikhism, and the theistic Hindu religions of devotion, Vaishnavism and Śaivism, are amongst the emergent religions of India, whilst Zarathustrianism, Christianity and Islam are among the main impacts on the subcontinent. Apart from Hindu-Moslem conflicts (specifically as religious conflicts) in the early centuries from Mahmud of Ghazni till the advent of the Mughals, and again under the aegis of the able but ill-starred, fanatic, Aurangzeb, religious tolerance has outstandingly characterized Indian history. Not merely tolerance, but creative interaction between creeds and cults. And above all, the recognition as nowhere else in the world, that Truth, Reality, God, use what name you will, is the single, secondless, Source from which all religions draw sustenance, has distinguished India's sages.

Hinduism begins, as far as can be gathered, as a socio-economic order with a moralistic basis, and a religious sanction underlying every aspect of life. Religion and philosophy, in the stricter sense, emerge out of this Hindu order, a distillate of practical experience on the one hand, and of purely religious realization and spiritual insight on the other. So in Hindu tradition one finds religious motives and principles sanctioning the reasonable dictates and sensible deductions of practical polity and economy—Kauṭilya's Arthaśāstra, however, cannot be cited as a typical representative of this tradition! Through accommodation to the extraordinary variety of the ways of life and age-long customs of diverse peoples at different levels of intelligence and ability, and possessed of their own distinctive traditions and usages, religion became inchoate, like an amoeba so vast, and with pseudopods sprawling so far afield, that a lifetime is insufficient to circumambulate this mass. Hinduism defies definition. Hindus did not want Hinduism to be so, or not so. Hinduism just "happened" like that over the span of millennia, because the land and the people were what they were. The stardust that showered for age after age over this Āryāvarta, this Bhāratavarśha, became just dust, useful things and strange things, horrible things and wonderful things, Peacock Thrones and Koh-i-Noors, just ordinary folk with ordinary stories, and—those who realized Brahman and flung open the gateway to immortality.

So, Hinduism as the practice of innumerable millions of souls is a phenomenon which causes many an observer perplexity, even heartbreak. If and when the observer himself realizes God, he sees truly, and then he sees that Hinduism in essence, like all other faiths in essence, is pure religion.

That essence is not merely the teachings, even the verities, however profound. God, eternity, immortality, redemption, liberation, love, truth, goodness—what heights were not scaled, what depths were not plumbed. But the teaching, the statement of truths, is only about the Truth and not the Truth itself. Any statement, in any system of verbal expression, of any verity pronounced by any religion whatsoever, only re-presents the Truth. When that Truth is realized consciously by a living man, that man is a man-become-Brahman, and that realized Truth is the ineffable essence.

But the primal re-presentation of the ineffable by the Great Teachers—the pure milk of the word—is indispensable for inspiring others to fare on to Brahman, and for administering the Glory of God to man. Hinduism has ministered with a generosity hardly approached by other faiths. This is not to derogate other faiths, but to take notice of the fact that the inchoate, all-inclusiveness of Hinduism, a weakness from certain points of view, is the very source of the richness of the paths ascending to the city of God. Move clear out of the welter of popular beliefs, fancies, superstitions and the fossilized, conventional practice of the masses, some of which are so irreligious, revolting, cruel and stupid, and one finds perfection in the suggested paths along which any man, whatever his type, temperament or capacities, may achieve the supreme realization. For the union with God, or yoga, may be attained through action, or devotion, or wisdom, or spiritual insight and mysticism. There are the Vedas, whose meaning can be extracted through psychological insight. There are the Upanishads. There is the Gītā.

These, the difficult mountain paths for the God-seeker, are, however, only for the elect, the self-elected. This Hinduism is exclusively religious. For the masses, Hinduism caters through a ritual system, social and religious, the secular life (and the acceptance of the secular values of wealth, worldly happiness and well-being) never being divorced from the spiritual life. But in striking its compromise, this section of Hindudom, an all too large section, could not be free of priestly corruption, a round of ceremonial mummery (mummery only because neither low-paid, professional priest nor average man in the street had either ability or desire to penetrate to the meaning underlying ceremony[1]), cruel sacrifices of animals, and fantastic speculations and beliefs.

[1] This is true of all faiths in varying degrees.

The mass of the people therefore knew the misery of the daily grind, the sorrow of loss and deprivation, the fear of death and of the unknown beyond. They also had their full share of the worldly joys common to the race of man. But these pleasures were ephemeral. Could not man, could not all men and all women be shown a way to real happiness, a way by which sorrow and evil were banished?

In answer to this arises Siddhattha Gotama, the supremely enlightened Buddha, whose teachings are exclusively religious, that is, unconcerned with kings as kings and commoners as commoners, but wholly concerned with all persons as persons who longed to be liberated.

The Hindu order prior to the rise of the Buddha was a cut and dried organization, characterized more by rigidity than by elasticity. Peasant and artisan, merchant, shopkeeper, administrator and priest, each had his fixed station. His mode of life and what he could legitimately hope to attain was all mapped out for him. If he achieved this in the present, he would have won the right, and would be given the opportunities for climbing higher in a future existence. Such a system certainly diminished the ravages wrought by personal ambitions, encouraged virtues like patience, contentment and peaceful living, acknowledged the inevitability of gradualness, and made for the security associated with a slow-moving, conventional and complacent order. But it put a brake upon individual initiative and enterprise; and it laid down that the individual, by virtue of his exactly docketted place in the scheme of things, had to live just so, and could attain at best only such and such specific fulfilment, material and spiritual. So the sorrows and frustrations of life not only were to be borne because it was virtue to endure nobly, but also had to be borne out of resignation. Here was cause for despair for millions, and for the degradation of virtues like contentment, calm dispassion and intelligent acceptance into contemptible apathy, social insensitivity and stupid fatalism.

But Siddhattha is the complete reverse of apathetic, insensitive and fatalistic. As a human being, conscious of himself at this stage as a separate person, he cannot endure the misery and frustration of his fellow men. Out into the homeless life he goes, seeking the way by which man can become free of his ills, a way which can be of use not only to those who, as in the brāhmanical tradition, are privileged by their station in life to be shown it and to take advantage of it, but also to the ordinary town-dweller and villager. It must, therefore, be a way which can be understood and practised even by a simple householder, by one who has not the endowment or opportunities for the intellectual training or mystical experience which the privileged ones have.

The search for the way begins with the known and accepted Hindu (brāhmanical) disciplines of the day. In the process, the nature of the search changes. It becomes clear that "I" cannot find a cut and dried technique of deliverance for "you" or for "myself", because the ordinary conceptions of "I", "you" and "myself" are false; and also because deliverance is not deliverance from the sorrowful or painful events of old age, disease, emotional and mental distress and death, but from one's own mis-consciousness of self, bound by the impurity of unawakenedness, which is the producer and perpetuator of evil and sorrow. So the way of deliverance, basically, is not a political and economic system, not social and economic progress and security, not an educational method, not the ushering in of a technological millennium, not a systematized philosophy of life, not a set of beliefs however pious, or true, not an observance of ceremonies and rituals, not even a wearisome round of good deeds, of plain living and high thinking, or even of worshipping God. Expedients for material relief, which are but temporary, or consolatory doctrines for emotional soothing, which are but cages of illusion, do not, and never can, bring true deliverance. So, what begins as a noble impulse and an altruistic endeavour, according to the world's definition of nobility and of altruism, is seen by Siddhattha to be inefficient. That which is efficient transcends the egoistic altruism and vulgar nobility of unawakened man: it consists in seeking the Immortal and becoming freed of bondage to mortality.

The way is by self-purification, by going within, by a transformation of consciousness. Gotama accepts, first, the teachings of the vanavāsins, the forest-dwelling hermits who produced

Āraṇyaka and Upanishad. He follows their practices of the virtues, the austerities, the studies, and the methods of yoga. Soon he is far, far away from his original search. No longer is he concerned with discovering how to be free of Ill in the worldly sense—to be free of disease, of an unloving husband or a nagging wife. He is not interested in raising the expectation-of-life figure for the community. Instead, he is plumbing the depths of the mystery which is the Self, Brahman or God, the mystery which is man, and the mystery which is the Way, by which, becoming Brahman, man realizes the Deathless, here-now. The release from worldly ill is sought so long as one lives ego-centrically conscious of all beings as separate persons only, and is involved with them in turning the wheel of saṁsāra. When the Immortal is sought, one has already made a rent in the veil of separate ego, and is busy night and day transforming the impure citadel of self into the holy temple of God.

But just here is a problem, a challenge. The Self, or Brahman, or the Immortal, as written or spoken, is but a word, a symbol. What precisely is the Reality which has to be experienced, but is ineffable when realized? That which can be shown by one to another is only the way. The Immortal Itself is realizable only by him who is freed of self, that is, freed from mortality, for limited self and mortality are as much interchangeable terms as are Brahman and immortality.

Gotama treads the way of yoga. Āḷāra Kāḷāma teaches him to reach the plane of no-thing in meditation. This is the sixth deliverance. Uddaka Rāmaputta teaches him to reach the seventh, the plane of neither-consciousness-nor-unconsciousness. Gotama values these achievements, and acknowledges their place in the ascent to the highest freedom, for he incorporates them in his own teachings (see above, pp. 168, 169). Had Gotama not been Gotama, or had his circumstances been such that his teacher was one of those who, like Vāmadeva, "ascended aloft and became immortal," Gotama might have become another star in the Vedic galaxy. As it happens, he is different. He sees that these seven deliverances (as far as he was taught) spell an ecstacy or exaltation whilst one is in meditation. But when one re-enters the common-or-garden consciousness of everyday life, the sensual and mental activities tend to pull one back to the level of the separative egoist, and one can still be buffetted like a slave by the ills of everyday life. The " progress " made is still disappointing. Even the high states of consciousness attained in meditation belong to the realm of mortality. Though they can be brought into being, their effect is not transmutative, and the peace or exaltation experienced does not remain permanent but recedes. Thereafter, given a sufficiently powerful external stimulus, one may again be caught in the whirlpool of worldliness and be tossed about on the stream of saṁsāra.

Hence the Bodhisat is dissatisfied with his attainment under Āḷāra's and Uddaka's tutelage. For Gotama, any state, from the everyday worldly consciousness right up to the exalted level of neither-consciousness-nor-unconsciousness, still meant involvement in the deathful. One more step,[1] and the task would be over. For Gotama, then, the question was: How could one realize the Deathless? How could one win that sublime poise, winning which one is free for ever from the power of Māra, and from the snares of sin, the wages of which is repeated death? How could one be permanently at home in Nirvāṇa, here-now?

Gotama undertakes the Great Effort, the way of extreme physical asceticism, in company with the Five. It is not unlikely that this was combined with entering those states of consciousness in meditation which he had learnt from Āḷāra and Uddaka. When the extreme asceticism does not lead to the goal, but only teaches him that it is the wrong way, he gives it up, and then proceeds to the final effort, a lonely and unique effort, which was crowned with the supreme enlightenment, which made him the Brahman-become, the Dhamma-become, the Perfect Buddha.

The heart of the matter is the extirpation of taṇhā, with which is associated each of the other essential elements of the enlightenment:

1. Putting aside the conceit "I am". This means such complete understanding of the self, that the limited, separative I-consciousness is wholly transcended and God-consciousness is realized. Henceforth, the use of the word " I " by a Buddha

[1] See also, Anguttara Nikāya, IV. 429-434.

is no longer attended with any of the false self-conceptions which inevitably cloud the self-consciousness of the unawakened mortal. The word is but a convenient symbol to denote what is apparent to the unawakened mortal by way of his senses. To the awakened one, not the self but the Self is the real—the reality of the Self is "made to become". And only the awakened one really knows what he is talking about when he says "I". The liberation from false self-conception depends upon 2 and 3 below.

2. The realization that whatever arises, arises by way of cause and passes away; or, the entire, existential universe, including the phenomena of states of consciousness, belongs to the realm of the deathful. This, which is an intellectual perception at first, becomes a realization when

3. the Perfect Way, the Brahmacariya, is trod. The principal implication of this Perfect Way, the Worthy (Ariyan) Eightfold Path, is the recognition that man is fundamentally a religious and ethical being. He is an ethical being with respect to his intellectual and æsthetic life, his actions and his interrelationship with the world. In each sphere—the separation into spheres of what is whole, active living, is only for verbal convenience—his activity must be made perfect. This Perfect Way or the Way of the Golden Mean, rejects the extremes of self-pleasing and self-torturing, and also rejects any despicable compromise between pleasure and pain, or indulgence and denial—"compromise" is a damning misinterpretation of "the Middle Way"—for pleasure, torture and compromise each spell thraldom to the senses and to ignorance, leaving man in the toils of sin and a victim of death. By treading the Perfect Way, a transformation of one's thinking, speaking and acting takes place, associated with a transformation of one's consciousness, of one's whole apprehension of everything. The crowning point is a transmutation of consciousness, for an integrative principle, universally operative, works the miracle of taking one out of the deadly state of sorrow-dealing oscillations between ignoble indulgence and profitless denial into that self-transcendence wherein the human is lifted into unity with the Godhead. Here, in the eighth deliverance, is "the stopping (transcending) of

perception, knowing and feeling." Here, as well as in the "purity of rapture of utter mindfulness, beyond both ease and malaise" of the fourth Jhāna, is the utter ending of Ill, the realization of the Deathless, the permanent abiding in Nirvāṇa.

"Treading the Perfect Way" is not "just another of these perfectionist ideas," doomed, therefore, to failure. The possible, here and now, through evolution, through growth, through creative effort,[1] integrates into, or is transmuted into the altogether more wonderful. This is the perfecting of the here-and-now-possible, and a new, more wonderful possible emerges thereby.

The "stopping of perception, knowing and feeling" is not a blank, a nothingness, an annihilation. On the very contrary, it is the emergence into eternal life, here-now whilst living in the body. But it is "life" altogether removed from the categories attached by mortals to the word life.

Entering into the eighth deliverance, or into the fourth Jhāna, is to become free of the trammelled consciousness of our mortal experience, and to "experience" the true Immortality. Herein Upanishad, Udāna, Gītā and Bible, to mention only a few Revelations, are in complete accord. For instance: Be still, and know that I am God (Psalm XLVI. 10). Being still is the stopping of perception, knowing and feeling. Again: For now we see through a glass, darkly; but then, face to face: now I know in part; but then shall I know even as also I am known (I Corinthians, XIII, 12). "Here", within the compass of the senses and mind (discursive thought), darkly; "there", at the eighth deliverance, face to face.

The Buddha teaches:

> "But again, O brāhmans, a Bhikkhu passing entirely beyond the sphere of neither-perception-nor-non-perception, enters on and abides in the stopping of perception, knowing and feeling. And of one who has seen by wisdom, the cankers come to be utterly destroyed. Brāhmans, this Bhikkhu is called one who, having come to the world's end, abides at the world's end; he has crossed over the entanglement in the world . . . This Bhikkhu is called one who has made Māra blind, trackless, and who, having

[1] The sammā-vāyāmo of the Eightfold Path.

destroyed Māra's vision, goes invisible to the Evil One, and who has crossed over the entanglement of the world."[1]

From this stage there is no returning to common-or-garden consciousness, as from the other stages of deliverance, for this is not a consciousness which can be categorized. Purely for convenience, one calls it Brahman-consciousness, or God-consciousness; it is the butterfly, of which " consciousness " of the sense-mind sphere is the chrysalis. This stage where all Ill is ended, the stage of " I and my Father in heaven are one," of the Jīvanmukta, is the complete fulfilment and goal of individual man. It is the " gaining of the Immortal." Once that has been gained, once the fire of taṇhā is extinguished, then whatever be one's " state of consciousness " here in the sense-mind world, the cooled one (the Nibbāna-d one) remains unentangled, free and at peace, not to be tossed by the storms of saṁsāra. Hence he can effectively utter, " Peace, be still ",[2] when the yet imperfect, frightened disciples wake him up in the " storm ", and behold! there is Peace!

That Immortal is not the mere opposite of the mortal. It is the eternal that-which-is in which the mortal is subsumed,[3] or else the living, existent person here, the man, could never realize that Immortal. Up to the seventh deliverance, development, growth, advance, unfoldment—use what word you like—takes place. All seven deliverances lie within the compass of manifested existence, of universal process. Then occurs the transmutation, the integration, and the Immortal is realized; and the Transcendent which is over and above, and controlling all process, is also realized. This eighth deliverance begins a new octave of consciousness, so to say, and God Transcendent is offered, and utilizes, an habitation of flesh—as Kṛishṇa says in the Gītā, as is declared by Jesus in the New Testament—by one who, erstwhile a mortal, in danger of sin, has become a Saviour. Once the transmutation has taken place, the return to corporeality, to worldly-mindedness, to sinful existence, is rendered impossible.

[1] The Buddha explains earlier that by "world" is meant the sense-life of the body.

[2] Mark, IV. 39.

[3] For ultimately, mṛtyu becomes one with Brahman (see above, p. 182).

Let, now, the contrast between the beginning of the search and the end of the search be well appreciated. Siddhattha Gotama, aged twenty-nine, is a man of this world. Grant him as exceptional qualities and possibilities and abilities, as unusual or remarkable circumstances as desired. Yet he remains mortal man, in a state of avijjā, not truly enlightened. As the Buddha, aged thirty-five, he has gained the Immortal, become fully enlightened, realized Nirvāṇa. Gotama the mortal, seeking release from subjection to Ill, is transformed into the New Man, the all-enlightened Buddha, the Son of God (in non-Buddhistic terminology), the Brahman-become, the Perfect Man who has gained the Immortal.

Thus one is able to appreciate another contrast. Mortal man, however great, advanced and capable, whether philosopher, administrator, doctor, educationist or social reformer, will seek "practical" measures applicable to the limited context of the situation here, *accepting the underlying beliefs, evaluations and criteria*, current now, in order to tackle Ill as he sees it. The Immortals, having fully understood the world (mortal man) and travelled through the universe (the seven deliverances: consider, also, the first and second strides of Viṣṇu, in this connection), know one thing alone to be Ill, namely the state of avijjā, which is sin, which spells bondage to the circle of mortality in which are continual "births" and "deaths". Their solution of the problem is the awakening of man, and their sole business is to be Awakeners. When the Teacher—the Jagadguru, the Buddha, the Messiah—awakens those who are unawakened, He has done the whole work there is to do. This is the complete answer to those busy mortals who impatiently feel, "What *use* is all your mysticism or holiness, all your preaching, when such mountains of social service, political work, economic progress, and healing and educative work still have to be done." But if and when busy mortals seek to be still, then in that state of poise they make the stirring discovery that it is not the Immortals who are useless or unpractical.

For the Buddha, welfare means Brahma-faring, Brahmacariya; well-being means Brahma-becoming. His discovery, and teaching, that to extinguish tanhā and tread the Perfect Way leads to the supreme Well-being, means that for every man, an ethical being essentially, happiness is none other than the Good Life in practice. The Buddha comes to know the mystery which is God, the mystery which is man. And further, by coming to know the mystery which is the Perfect Way, his Noble Eightfold Path, he teaches every man to be in the world but not of the world. The " mystery " of the Way lies in this, that the way is trod, in its earliest stages only, by following the morality and discipline laid down by those who have gone ahead. Later on, the Way consists both in retreating within and also advancing boldly without on one's own responsibility in the light of one's own vision. Finally, the highest morality as recognized by mortal man is left behind as a raft for reaching the other shore, and the Perfected One lives by a transcendental or absolute ethic, beyond the relative good and evil as understood in the sphere of mortality.

The Buddha's practicality lies in integrating (or equating) the psychological, realist " is " with the philosophical, idealist " ought-to-be ", not by making the one fit into the other, either by raising the psychological up to the philosophical or by stepping the philosophical down to the psychological, but by that process of self-purification through which perfection, or the emancipation of heart and mind is realized ; whereupon each of those confused conceptions of mortals, namely the complacent " is " and the aggressive " ought-to-be ", is transcended. Such also is the practicality of Jesus, Kṛishṇa, Lao-Tzu, Zarathustra, and the Vedic and Upanishadic Ṛishis. The practicality of the Great Teachers is the efficient creativity of the Immortal ; the practicality of the social worker, educationist, philosopher, economist or politician (by no means to be discarded or mis-valued), is a temporary makeshift set in the framework of mortality.

Whereas the Buddha's attainment and realization is no different from that of those Vedic and Upanishadic seers who had realized the Immortal, his emphases, and his methods of teaching and training display the highest originality.

His ariyan (noble or worthy) Eightfold Path is an ethical approach, and a practical, ethical treatment of man's

1. Mental life—sammā-diṭṭhi: perfect views, conceptions, philosophy;
   sammā-sankappo: perfect aspirations, yearnings, ideals;
2. Physical life—sammā-kammanto: perfect action;
   sammā-ājīvo: perfect mode of living:
3. Psycho-physical life—sammā-vācā: perfect speech;
   sammā-vāyāmo: perfect endeavour;
   sammā-sati: perfect mindfulness, vigilance, wide-awakeness;
4. Spiritual and transcendent life—sammā-samādhi: perfect communion, "prayer".

This practical ethic sweeps aside beliefs, ceremonials and the worship of God as a personal being—the life of the Exemplar Himself, the Buddha, is the perfect refutation of the idea that ethic, or the ethical life, needs a belief in, and a worship of a Personal God as its basis. No one, whatever his station in life, his caste, is barred from setting his feet on this Way of Deliverance. The Buddha does not—and the reason has already been set forth above—waste his time upon sweeping away caste-distinctions,[1] which characterized the social order of his day. But where the gaining of the Immortal or the deliverance from Ill is concerned, there is no caste or creed to obstruct the earnest seeker. A thief, a barber, to mention only two examples, are amongst the greatest of his Arahants.

Moreover, the Way is such, that high or lowly, wise or of little learning, leisured or toiling, king or commoner, genius or ordinary fellow, he, even he, can tread the Path. The Buddha is the supreme establisher of religious and spiritual democracy. To appreciate the fact that his was no merely intellectualist, doctrinaire position in this respect, one has only to consider his teaching of the Brahma-vihāras.[2] His unflagging insistence upon individual effort and upon individual realization is indicative of his conception of individual worth. Householder and forest hermit alike could utilize this ethical way of life which led to the stage of the Arahant, and the life of the Arahant exemplified the transcendental ethic, the "beyond good and evil" of the Brahman-become.

[1] Or upon any of the multifarious "good works" so highly prized by mortals.
[2] See above, p. 239 et seq.

Thus is witnessed the remarkable fact of a great religion which does not have belief in a personal God, individual soul (of popular conception), and the survival of that imaginary soul among its tenets. This Buddhism, as preached and practised by the Sangha after Gotama's death in 483 B.C., is accepted as part of the life of India with the magnanimous tolerance characteristic of Hinduism. Aśoka, as emperor of India, raises Buddhism to the status of an established religion about the middle of the third century before Christ. But the austere Way of the Buddha cannot be imposed on masses. It is one thing for men out of any and every class to tread the Eightfold Way of their own free choice, but quite another thing to make a formalized religion of it. Whenever the teachings of any Master are formalized and institutionalized, the orthodox church thus formed is thrown into the maelstrom of the events of mortal life, and comes to grips with vested interests. Brāhmanism and Buddhism interact with each other. The masses require a personal God to satisfy their emotional wants. Brāhmanism re-emerges, transformed into the Hinduism of the theistic Bhagavad-Gītā, the Śvetāśvatara and other later Upanishads, and the great monotheisms of Vaiṣnavism and Śaivism. In a monotheistic faith, especially if it is sufficiently simplified, the mass of men can pour out their hearts in a flood of devotion to a personal God. The Dravidian-descended Southerners of India have given expression, in the opinion of reputable scholars, to devotional faith unsurpassed elsewhere.

SECTION B

THE WORD : MĀYĀ : REALITY

ALL FOUNDERS of religions speak with authority, and their utterance is regarded by their followers as the whole and pure truth, the Word of God. Hindus look upon the Vedas as eternal, as the revealed word of the Supreme Being, and upon the Gītā as the word of Viṣṇu embodied in Kṛishṇa. The Buddha breathes forth this cry on the night of the enlightenment: " Who has mastered knowledge and fully traversed the Brahma-path, he rightly, being a brāhman, should announce the Brahma-word." Zarathustrians regard the Gāthās of Zarathustra as revelation from Ahura-Mazda. Christians look upon the Bible as the inspired word of God, and Muslims the Quran as directly inspired by Allāh.

In the Majjhima Nikāya, I. III, it is said of the Buddha that " . . . he has become Brahman . . . giver of the Immortal, Lord of Dhamma." In the Aggañña Sutta, D. III. 84, the Buddha himself says: " Vāseṭṭha, these are names tantamount to Tathāgata: Belonging to the Dhamma, and again, belonging to Brahma: and again Dhamma-become, and again Brahma-become." Shri Kṛishṇa unequivocally declares himself to be the Supreme Spirit. Jesus affirms his unity with the Father. The Ṛishis of the Upanishads are one with Brahman; like Sāṇḍilya, they become immortal. The poet-seers of the Vedas, like Vāmadeva, ascend aloft and become immortal.

The faithful followers of each of the Teachers firmly hold the conviction that they possess the Word of God.

This very Word, so potent for good, is equally potent for destruction. The Truth is uttered in the Word. Yet the Word, when taken in vain, when defiled in the mouths of the unholy, no longer spells Truth and illumines man, but covers the Real with what is false. Then there is confusion, immorality, evil and destruction. Man alone can enthrone God in the cosmos; man alone can be the supreme blot on the universe.

Verily, the Word is God, is the sacred syllable:

> In the beginning was the Word, and the Word was with God, and the Word was God.
>
> John, I, 1.

" Then Śaibya Satyakāma asked him (Pippalāda):

> ' Verily, Sir, if some one among men here should meditate on the syllable *Om* until the end of his life, which world, verily, does he win thereby? '

To him then he said:

> ' Verily, O Satyakāma, that which is the syllable *Om* is both the higher and lower Brahman.' "
>
> Praśna Upanishad, V.1, 2.

He who is become Brahman, who is one with the Father, is indeed the living embodiment of the Word. His life, he himself, is the full explication of the Word. His words are a part unfolding of the Word, which is God or Brahman.

The Word indeed is God's, uttered through the lips of the God-become.

But the interpretation is man's, the not yet God-become, but only God-becoming. And to the extent that he is not the God-become does he inevitably darken the Word, spinning it out into strange and fascinating webs of " mere name ", as Sanatkumāra said to Nārada, webs made iridescent by the cold, glitter of intellect unredeemed by insight. Such intellect, whose domain is the realm of Ill, of the senses and discursive thought only, enclosed within the leaden sphere of avijjā, the unawakened consciousness, holds man a bond-slave to mortality.

Death is lord here, and one deadly deed to which he impels a man, is to make him declare that his is the only true faith, his the only true god, and that all that is not entrapped in his particular web is heathenish, is of the unsalved, to be despised, broken and swept away, or converted to his own. Little does the bigoted converter of others to his own beliefs perceive that what he does is to express his own egotism, his own rapacity for spiritual merit, and his own lust for dominating others.

By all means, freely pour out the waters of life. But who is capable of pouring? Only the Brahman-become, the Immortal Ones. Can the zealot presume to pour? He himself has to struggle to cease to be a producer of Ill, and to escape the web of words. Only after he has escaped, and realized Brahman ("from which Speech and Mind turn back, not having found"), only after he has entered the sea of Nirvāṇa (=" the still waters," Psalm XXIII. 2,—" the Cosmic Ocean " of Hinduism), does he himself become the river of life. Then he may give, and in fact he cannot avoid giving freely of the waters of life, for he is no longer a zealot.

Each of the Great Teachers gives a unique teaching, presented with telling originality; and the Word, each time it is uttered by the Brahman-become, is a new song. Each Great Teacher flings open the doors of immortality, having himself known the Deathless; and each, an Exemplar, is himself the Way, the Truth and the Life. An expositor, or he who is striving to follow in the footsteps of the Master in order to get out of the pit of mortality, can only point towards, but cannot open the gates of immortality, for he is not yet in the kingdom of heaven. After he is enthroned in the realm of light, he too will utter the Word, in his unique way, singing his own new song and not merely churning the words of other Exemplars. And *he* knows that all converting as a professional enterprise, is a persuading or enticing or forcing of others into one's own dull prison of "mere name", a forgery of the living signature of the Immortals.

Each religion as a whole, like any and every whole in all the universe, is unique and incomparable. It is sinful folly for man to quarrel with his brother man, or to hurt or to destroy him, in the name of one incomparable against another.

Wilberforce played no small part in the abolition of slavery. But he himself was not quite free from slavery to his own prejudices, as betrayed in his statement in the British Parliament: " Our Christian religion is sublime, pure and beneficent. The

Indian religious system is mean, licentious and cruel . . . It is one grand abomination ! " Precisely this attitude has been expressed through centuries by too many adherents of each and every religion against any or all religions other than their own, and has proved itself a potent cause of social and national hatreds.

When European scholars began, hardly two centuries ago, to investigate Sanskrit literature, and later on, Pāli, they did the greatest and noblest service which the Christian, Western world has done to the East generally, and to India particularly, and, as time is proving, to the Christian, Western world itself. They made Indian Wisdom available to many Indians outside the closed circle of the privileged. They introduced and established a method of objective, scientific study of the old texts.

These savants were conditioned by their own great traditions and culture. The excellences in their works are obvious. But one discerns in their pages the underlying assumption that whatever is Christian and European is the Olympian standard of judgment. Clerics, and the theologically biased, treat all Indian religious thought from the standpoint that monotheism is the highest form of religion, that an ethical, holy, spiritual god is the one and only true God, and that Christian monotheism and the Christian God is the highest and final revelation by God of Himself.

On the other side, there are authorities of each of the other faiths who display, in relation to faiths other than their own, excellences and defects similar to those displayed by Europeans and Christians. " My family, my nation, my religion and my way of life is the best, the elect, the most perfect and right " represents the unwisdom with which the human race has been afflicted through the ages. But to-day, happily, men are becoming increasingly free of a narrow, sectarian approach.

Enough has been said already to point the difference between whole realization and intellectual knowledge. So all evaluations in terms of superiority-inferiority, better-worse, of one religion in relation to another may be discarded. It is to our own profit to approach all religions, and above all, RELIGION, in the light of whole realization. And in this light must be sought new understanding, where required, of old teachings.

Each of the Great Teachers—the Vedic Seers, the Upanishadic Sages, Zarathustra, Jesus, the Buddha, and others—goes through discipline culminating in union with God. Apostles and disciples, devotees and followers, scholars and students, not one of whom is at the level of the Teacher's enlightenment, afterwards form their own conceptions, build their own orthodoxies, lay down dogmatic teachings and spin systems of belief out of the verbal form in which the Great Teachers expressed their realization, and out of the example of their actions. It is no easy task, therefore, to discover how truly the conceptions and systems of disciple, devotee or scholar correspond with the Truth which is the conscious, quite-at-home realization of Nirvāṇa, or the kingdom of God, of those supreme yogis, the Great Teachers.

Yet the situation is essentially a hopeful one, and the prospect far from bleak. For indeed, every one has some vision, or has at least a partial realization; and who tends the spark may fan it into a flame. Besides, there is no option but to go on—to stumble, to retrace one's steps, to blaze new trails—until there is flowering and fulfilment for each seeker. The Word is an inexhaustible quest for all men; and the earnestness, devotion and reverence marking the humblest quest is worthy of both respect and love.

The Word represents, amongst other things, magic, or the inexplicable, mysterious creative power in the universe. God the Creator "makes heaven and earth and all therein." The Vedas, the Upanishads, the Gāthās, the Bible, the Quran, all agree here. The Creator commands, and lo and behold! there is everything! Man investigates this-All, and within an infinitesimal fraction of time accumulates mountains of knowledge, which crush his head and blind him with their overwhelming immensities. A funny little Atlas is the knowledgeable man! Yet even within the covers of the most explicatory book, the frontiers of Mystery converge swiftly upon the lean fields of knowledge.

Magic everywhere, and incessantly! Just as well, or else boredom would wither all life more effectually than does hellfire; or man would out-vegetate the fallen oak for want of stimulus to pierce the ever-tightening skin of ignorance. Quite rightly, man does not wish for a world without mystery. For then his love, be it for his fellow or for God, would become but a wet squib. He would be deprived of his supreme delight, the exercise of his own magical power of creation. Man delights in the child of his flesh, and also in the child of his imagination, fundamentally because he proves, even if unconsciously, that he too, like God, is lord of mystery. But if and when his child is God, or a God, will the limits of the cosmos be able to contain his delight? Then indeed the Uncreated, that is Nirvāṇa, or the kingdom of God, will have to be his bourn.[1]

All religions, the most "spiritual" as well as the most "reasonable", have magic. The monotheisms have their miracles. Buddhism has its miracles. The Upanishadic sages ascend aloft, and become Brahman.

This is troublesome to a mind conditioned in twentieth-century fashion instead of, say, second or twelfth-century fashion. Man always says he wants to know the facts, and demands that they should be told simply. Thereby he contradicts that other wish he has, the longing for the thrill of mystery and marvel, or magic. But when he wants to be sober, he rebels against magic and mystery, and says that he will not have his intelligence insulted.

He forgets that what he calls intelligence (manas) and factual knowledge (apara vidyā) is to a considerable extent a confusion-making, sorrow-producing agent in his life. His profounder need is to develop that spiritual intelligence (buddhi) which characterizes the illuminated one, freed from avidyā. For the universe manifest to man's senses, and interpreted by his mind, is an empirical real only as long as the generally experienced context of sense-functioning and mind-working is accepted. But if, for instance, a man is climbing Everest, where temperatures and pressures are different from those of the Indian plains, he may see "gremlins"; or else he becomes so strongly aware of "beneficent presences" that he, a sensible, athletic Western European, quietly announces that bare fact of his experience in his broadcast talk over the radio, months later; or else his will becomes quite different from his normal will, and his judgments undergo strange transformation. Again, a sober man

[1] See also, below, pp. 481 et seq.

looking out into space on a clear, sunny day, declares truthfully that there is nothing in sight; but scientific apparatus will convince him that his empty space is crammed full.

What then is Reality? Indian thought affirms Reality IS. Brahman, or Ātman, is Reality. Although Brahman is indescribable, unanalysable, indemonstrable, nevertheless Brahman can be realized by each individual. Is Reality, or Brahman, simply a postulate made by man? A mere word? No, says Indian thought, Reality is not simply a postulate made by man; but Indian man affirms, and bears witness to, Reality. Brahman or Reality is not a mere word but *the* Word. It is the eternal that-which-is.

Whilst a man is awake, a continuous silent chatter goes on in his mind. He is quite unable to stop this unbidden flow of discursive thought. Only with an effort of will, and through deliberate concentration of attention, can he exercise some control over speech-mind; but at no time can any ordinary man hold his mind entirely still.

In sleep, the silent chatter goes on in a modified form. Sometimes, the man becomes aware of it on waking up—his dreams. In this connection, it is well to recollect the Chinese Emperor's question, after he related a very vivid dream he had had: "What is the truth, then? Am I really a butterfly dreaming that I am a man, or am I really a man who dreamt last night that I was a butterfly?"

Dream consciousness is so different from waking consciousness, even contradicting the facts of physical experience. Yet both dream consciousness and waking consciousness form part of man's apprehension of his continuous experience as a living being in the world. But when a man enjoys really deep sleep, he never remembers any dreams. In this third condition, that of deep sleep, the body is completely relaxed, and breathing is perfectly rhythmic. Has the mental chatter become still? Such sleep is characterized, as usually said, by profound unconsciousness. Indian thinkers said that here "the soul goes back to his own home." They appear to have thought that in reality the living person, in sushupti, apprehends the peace or bliss of at-one-ment with universal being. But this apprehension cannot be brought into conscious comprehension on waking up. The known fact is that such sleep is the most refreshing and healing sleep. The sleeper wakes up re-charged, invigorated and vitalized.

What has happened? This much is certain: in such a sleep, the whole person is in a state of harmony, or of perfect peace within himself and in relation with his immediate environment. He and his environment constitute the perfect situation, a single whole, the holy state, and demonstrate one aspect of the "Peace of God", in which there is no intrusive I-consciousness. This is a state in which a-hiṁsa, not-hurting, is manifest.

But this state is one which comes about, in that dreamless sleep which is one of Nature's boons.

It can also be deliberately brought about, and in a strikingly different manner, through one's own endeavour. First note a saying of the Buddha in the Kandaraka Sutta (M.I.342) and again in the Apaṇṇaka Sutta (M.I.412): "If you hurt neither yourself nor others, nor both yourself and others, you dwell with a self become Brahman." This is the reason why love, tenderness, mercy and redemptive forgiveness (not mere, thoughtless brushing aside of hurt received, deluding oneself that one has forgiven, whereas in reality the passion for vengeance has sunk to a deeper, more explosive level of consciousness) are such divine virtues. Throughout the Upanishads, especially the Yoga Upanishads, the Gītā and all the tender range of Indian thought, a-hiṁsa holds prime place.

Any of the major disciplines of Indian Religion, Mysticism, Yoga and Philosophy establishes one in the condition of harmlessness, together with all the moral and intellectual perfections required. Thereafter, pratyāhāra (detachment from the objects of sense), dhāraṇā (concentration of attention), and dhyāna (incessant contemplation[1]) lead to samādhi. In this state, the psycho-physical organism is in perfect repose, there is a complete

[1] Contemplation, here, does not mean merely turning a question over in the mind, or just musing. Dhyāna is that process by which, after concentrating attention on the object of contemplation, one slowly transcends the distinction between observer and observed. It is claimed by the yogi that thus one comes to "know" the observed as the thing in itself, or, one "becomes" that which is observed. Contemplation brings about the union of the seer and the seen, and it is the stage before the final consummation in samādhi.

pacifying of sense functions, and the flow of discursive thought, including all mental pictures and defined or undefined feelings, is completely stilled. It is as if one were most wide awake in deepest sleep. But this state is very different from that of dreamless, deep sleep. Whilst deep sleep is a state of uncontrolled and uncontrollable de-control, samādhi is a state of conscious, perfectly controlled and controllable de-control.

All ordinary consciousness is limited to the sphere of sensation, emotion and speech-thought. In samādhi there is the conscious transcendence of this sphere, the sphere of uprising and passing away, of birth and death, of saṁsāra. In samādhi man enters the realm of the Immortal, of the IS. Mystics have talked of this as the Void, and also the Plenum. Here they " see " the Light of lights, " hear " the Voice of the Silence, " touch " God, " know " Brahman, " enjoy " bliss and " experience " the peace of God which passes understanding.[1]

This consciousness is what is meant by the Upanishadic statements, " He obtains the Brahma-world " and " He realizes the Ātman." This is the Nirvāṇa of the Buddha, the kingdom of Heaven of Jesus.

In this consciousness, Brahman is not " contacted " or, " seen " as an objective Real, or " felt " as a subjective Real but by the transcending of both subjective and objective, Brahman is consciously realized. The pairs of opposites, indispensable for discursive thinking and verbal description, are transcended, and hence the indescribable, but nevertheless statable (that is, affirmed as being, though beyond the possibility of description) is experienced, or rather, made real, in that consciousness.

Brahman is that Real. The conscious individual himself in the samādhi of the Brahman-become, in the communing with God of Jesus, is the sole " touch ", " link ", " communication ", " union "—all words are inept—of the Brahman-become

[1] There are some sincere devotees of all faiths who set aside a daily period for meditation and for practising the "Presence of God." This is realized only in samādhi, as in the Ecstasy of Plotinus, in the *secret* praying of Jesus, the Eighth Deliverance of the Buddha, etc. Impressions, however noble and exalted, which one obtains whilst yet unable to transcend sense-mind disturbance, are not God's messages. God's guidance is of that other sphere, the sphere of the deathless, and not of worldly affairs or conduct which is specifically man's business.

individual, a microcosm, with Brahman Itself (not the Father-God or Mother-Goddess of all monotheisms but something at least one stage profounder, more real), the Infinite, the Eternal, the Absolute, the Godhead. Such an individual in Brahman-consciousness is the true meaning of The Person.

That consciousness is the most intimate intimacy that an individual man-become-Brahman—a Vāmadeva, a Sāṇḍilya, a Yājñavalkya, a Buddha, a Christ, a Kṛishṇa, a Plotinus, but not anyone who cannot still the flow of discursive thought—achieves with Brahman. If not for the ability to reach that state of consciousness, the few Exemplars could not have authoritatively affirmed Brahman or Ātman, could never have uttered the magical Word. Anyone can merely babble that Brahman IS, Brahman IS, in fashion similar to the Udgītha of the dogs in the Chāndogya Upanishad (I.12), but only the Brahman-become can effectively pronounce the Brahmavadam; and here, effectively pronounce means pronounce with that extraordinary influence which completely transforms the listener's outlook, thought and mode of life—the one and only legitimate and true "conversion".

The objects of the world come and go, impermanent. They are discovered to be made up of elements—fire, air, etc. of the ancients, hydrogen, nitrogen, etc. of the moderns—which in turn are made up of the mūlaprakṛiti of the ancients, or "energy" or whatever it is of the moderns. So Indian thinkers, for the sake of making it more convenient to talk about such matters, ascribed Reality to the more and more fundamental, and considered the passing gross forms in which the fundamental garbed itself as less than Reality, as illusory, and in the view of some thinkers, as illusion.

Similarly, in relation to the subjective world, what one was left with was "my consciousness"; and since the yogi in samādhi realized a consciousness wherein both the objective and subjective universe was transcended without a state of unconsciousness or death supervening, Brahman, or Ultimate Reality came to be denominated as Pure, or Absolute Consciousness—*the* fundamental out of which everything was made, in heaven and earth, above the heavens and below the earth;

out of which came Spirit and Matter, Life (Prāṇa) and Form (Nāmarūpa), the worlds of Indra (individuality, self-consciousness), of Prajāpati (integrated wholes), and of Brahmā (creativeness in all its aspects).

Whatever is, receives a name when one is conscious of it. As far as man is concerned, although his unconsciousness of anything does not prevent at least part of its influence from affecting him, its reality for him begins with his conscious perception or recognition of it. After recognition, a name is given. The name is the word. The Name—of God, " recognized ", " realized ", in samādhi—is the Word. All exchanges between man and man, between man and his bond-beast or pet, between man and God, are effectual and produce concrete results through the word, be it a command or a request. The Word represents God. When God "speaks" the Word it is a command, a magic which brings forth the universe out of himself; for God is creativeness, the creative power, the ultimate energy which becomes matter, or the universe which man experiences.

But indeed energy does not become matter! Brahman does not become this-All! Energy is matter, Brahman is this-All, if one had but the " eye " of Brahman with which to see. And in Brahman-consciousness, in samādhi, one does have the Brahman-eye. Hence the magnificent, profound realization, superbly expressed in the Bṛihad-Āraṇyaka Upanishad:

> Looking around, He (Ātman) saw nothing else than himself.
> He said first: " I am."
>
> I.4.1.

Only the Ātman, only God, seeing nothing else than himself, could say that. Only the man-become-Brahman truly understands that. You or I, looking around, need an other, an otherness, to recognize unitary selfhood. Which means that Brahman's "consciousness" is of a dimension wherein integrated wholeness, singleness, is all-sufficient for Self recognition. You and I, by ourselves, are incomplete. Hence Adam had to have Eve. Hence you or I need friend, wife, master, servant, God, and—the Devil. Through creative interaction between self and other-self, emerges Whole Self.

But it is all a matter of consciousness, be it at man-level or at man-become-Brahman-level. And the man-become-Brahman-level consciousness communicates itself, steps down to, returns to the corporeal level, through the special, unique mode of communication which has come into being with man's emergence on the world stage, namely thought-speech, or the word.

The meaning and significance of "meditation on the sacred syllable, AUM", may now be better understood.

Also, one sees why "keeping one's word" is the same as "keeping faith", as fulfilling a sacred trust—the significance of Mitra.

And finally, man, not possessing Brahman's consciousness (to be distinguished from becoming Brahman-conscious), cannot "see" *how* Brahman is this-All, or becomes this-All, *how* God made heaven and earth. Hence, speaking symbolically, man says: "The Word becomes flesh", or "The Word is the creative word"; the process, the rationale, is such a complete mystery, that "magic" is as good a word as any to symbolize it. Science, quite appropriately, observes a self-imposed limitation here—not to talk of the undiscussable.

Indian teaching stresses one point: "What is one's thought, that he becomes; this is the eternal mystery" (Maitri Upanishad, VI.34). Here, "thought" means state of consciousness, and not *any* thought. If man's consciousness of himself is of himself as beast, man or god, as wise, foolish, brave, kind or cruel, he is that, or becomes that. Is-ness is what one's inner consciousness determines, and not what one merely fancies. One may change what is accepted as an external picture of oneself; one may wear it lightly like a suit of clothes. But that which is inner consciousness, the active centre of awareness, is that which is decisive. Hence, for some, "I am a spark of God"; for others, "I am my body"; for others, "I am a psycho-physical organism"; for others, "I am a spiritual and organic whole"; for others, "I am my feelings and thoughts". For some, "I am a good man"; for others, "I am a canny fellow"; for others, "I am my own master", and so on. Whatever be the particular, dominant conception formally representing the inner consciousness of oneself, towards that are all the energies of the person bent. If, then, the conception "I am Brahman" operates, the ultimate attainment possible is Self-realization as

Brahman. One may succeed in establishing one's self-conception as a fact, or one may not. That depends on many factors. Religion recommends union with Brahman, seeking first the kingdom of God, liberation or Nirvāṇa. Whether man-become-Brahman is a senseless fantasy, a delusion of grandeur or a Messianic complex—and it could be so—must be left for each person, as he regards a Buddha or a Christ or a Zarathustra, to decide for himself. But can man's yardstick measure, and can mortal, sinful man regard truly the immortal, pure, man-become-God? Whose eyes can gaze upon the sun?

Brahman, then, or AUM or the Word, represents ultimate Reality. Man's next questions are: "Am I real?" and "Is the universe real?"

"Looking around, Ātman said 'I am'." Ātman never said it! A man in samādhi, realized through experience. Realized what? The incommunicable. His experience was ineffable. He symbolized it in two words, "I am". We, listening to those words, symbols only, immediately start up a pandemonium of neuronal circuits in the brain—thoughts which are strings of words!—and draw various inferences. None of these is *the* truth ("neti, neti," said Yājñavalkya); yet all of them constitute part of the quest which ends with our own individual realization. Hence words need not be unnecessarily despised, nor prematurely discarded.

If I as an individual not merely say, but realize in samādhi, the "I am", the Ātman, then truly I am real. But I, Ātman, as the Real, the fundamental, is that out of which all this emerges. So, My Reality is not spatio-temporal or material. Ātman is the Reality of me rather than my reality is Ātman, and hence is ineffable. IT is real; whereas the affirmation of a described, expressed, recognized, separate "I" is a mis-statement of the Real. Relative to the Real, the entire sphere of sense-mind manifestation is the veil of the Real. Who will, or can, unveil Isis? Only the man-become-Brahman.

Indian thinkers use the term Māyā. This represents the power and the mode by which Brahman becomes this-All. The whole of manifestation is illusory, in so far as man mistakes a part for the whole, the impermanent for the permanent and the temporal for the eternal, like Baka the Brahmā ; but it is not an illusion, for it is Brahman.

The magic by which the Word of God is transformed into that which you and I experience as mortal men, is Māyā. You and I and the universe are Reality, in ineffable truth, but are illusory in the garb of any and every descriptive category. We are, from electron to total cosmos, Reality veiled, and our business, the purpose of our existence, is to unveil Reality, and to reveal Brahman, ourself-become-Brahman being the " final " and " true " Revelation—a universal destiny.

" Behold the universe in the glory of
God : and all that lives and moves
on earth.
Leaving the transient, find joy in
the Eternal : set not your heart on
another's possession."

" The face of truth remains hidden
behind a circle of gold.
Unveil it, O god of light, that I
who love the true may see !"

Īśā Upanishad, 1, 15.

" From the unreal lead me to the real,
From darkness lead me to light,
From death lead me to immortality."

Bṛihad-Āraṇyaka Upanishad, I.3.28.

" May we attain that excellent glory of Savitar the god (the sun by
day as well as by night, symbolizing the whole truth) ;
So may he stimulate our prayers."

Ṛig Veda, III.62.10.

If, now, one could completely return from the evolved man-become-Brahman consciousness to the involved sense-mind human consciousness, then all that universe or experience which comes within the scope of the latter would be the sole Real. But human consciousness is partly evolved and partly involved. Seeing what appear to be two worlds, this one and that beyond as they are called, philosophy attempts to explain their relationship or to fit them into a unitary scheme, whereas religion quite simply accepts them. Man, as at present constituted, is confused because he cannot decide whether one world is real and the other is not, or whether both are real or not. The philosopher, like an artist making a thing of beauty, makes, or tries to make, a consistent system of thought *satisfying to the mind.* The religieux, or mystic, is mainly concerned with that which constitutes perfect living in this world in order that individual men and women may become that which they are " intended to become ", and thus realize here-now that yonder world, *satisfying to the spirit.*

Indian religious thinkers maintain that man's fulfilment consists fundamentally in a transmutation of one state of consciousness, the worldly, belonging to the domain of the Lord of Death, into the perfected, namely the God-consciousness of the liberated one, the Nirvāṇa of the Arahant. This is brought about through discipline, through an intellectual-moral development, till a stage is reached when suddenly a transmutation of consciousness takes place. This transmutation is not simply another rung on the ladder of development. It is not effected solely by Nature, but by self-conscious man's deliberate effort, " graced " by Brahman or God. It is a complete transformation into something new. Just precisely what is the integrative factor which brings the new state into being, or how it operates, is the mystery. It is magic ; it is Māyā.

But without *this, that* could not come into being. Indian religion concerns itself with rightly dealing with *this* in order to realize *that,* and hence it recognizes both worlds, the temporal and the eternal, the māyāvic and the sattvic. Whilst the religieux accepts the teaching that this world is māyāvic, the philosopher will enjoy himself arguing whether this world is only māyāvic, or wholly a māyā in the sense of being a complete illusion.

Factually there is but one world. Its cleavage into *this* world and *that* world is consequent upon man's dimly awakened and grossly unawakened condition. Before " transgression ", man walks with God by day and sleeps in His bosom by night, but with the undiscriminating ignorance of the new-born babe. That is blind bliss. Yet the impression of that bliss remains, after " the Fall ", so unforgettable, that it is the everlasting goad which slowly and surely drives man to regain immortal companionship with God, but as a voluntary and conscious union this time, attained by complete sacrifice (tyāga). The

Fall is indispensable, for without going through the stage of the sundered consciousness—*this* world and *that* world—the voluntary and conscious union with God could not be brought about, and indeed, would not even be sought. Man ends his ignorant, blindly blissful, pre-natal stage violently—with shedding his mother's blood (a " sinful " act), and with a desperate struggle for survival—and independent, self-sustaining and self-responsible, individual (or whole-in-oneself) living is his objective thereafter. What tribulation! Yet if complete fulfilment is sought, and found, man-become-Brahman is the final result here-now, and the confused, worldly consciousness, bound in the realm of sin and mortality, is liberated into the God-consciousness or Ātmic-consciousness of the realm of immortality.

But the entire drama is enacted here and now in the one, factual world.

Once again, then, what is Reality? Brahman, or the factual world? Which is the whole, single Reality? Why surely, the factual world, for Brahman *is* the world, *is* man the existent, the unity which is essence-substance.

To see truly needs pure vision. Where vision is pure, there commonsense, the rarest thing in the world, becomes transformed into omniscience, the sabbaññuta-ñāṇaṁ of the Buddha, and one eats of the fruit of the tree of Life, and knows immortality. But where there is no vision, one perishes. And where there is distorted vision—the vision of fanatics and zealots, and of the ignorant, the thoughtless, the unloving—one drags others also to perdition.

Religion is not the sole means for obtaining vision. Philosophy, Art, Science, Active Beneficence, Daily Duty, are each an avenue leading to the vision of the Supreme, and a wholly valid approach to Reality. Any one of these, *in perfection*, effects that magic which transmutes the sinful into the pure, the mortal into the immortal. Any one of these, in perfection, is a divine revelation of reality which is the truth. The avenue which most appeals to each person is the one which is naturally suitable to his temperament and character. He who is emotional and sensuous may find the Supreme in Art as the symbol and expression of Reality; he who is intellectual and favours logical, compendious description, may find the Supreme in Science as the revelation of Reality. " Howsoever men approach me, even so do I welcome them, for the path men take from every side is mine, O Pārtha." (Bhagavad-Gītā, IV.11.) And also, she who is gifted with that particular type of perfection marking certain women, is a divine revelation of Reality as wife, mother, housekeeper, cook and maid.

SECTION C

REASON : BUDDHI

Interpretations of some Teachings

THERE CAN be no manifestation without coherence. Reason makes for the coherence of thought, and also for its beauty and its influence upon man. Only a section of whole apprehension is illuminated by reason. The remainder, a vast region which is twilit or dark, affects each man as an emotive force which often dominates his life, sometimes making the sway of reason look ridiculously ineffectual by comparison. If one could understand the nature and workings of this emotive force, the full significance of personal experience could be grasped. Through sammā-sati, perfect mindfulness, this dynamic, emotive aspect of whole apprehension is brought into line with reason, giving one a more intimate hold of one's whole inner life. A new kind of understanding grows, the fruit of that discipline of the whole mind which is an essential part of Indian religious practice. It is Buddhi, the Pure Reason of the Arahant, the Reason of the realm of Brahmavidyā as distinguished from the reason of man in the empirical world.

The inspirations of genius and the affirmations of the Great Teachers cohere by virtue of Buddhi. The systems of thought derived from such inspirations or affirmations cohere because of logical reasoning. The former are independent of time and cumulative growth, and beyond the sphere of discursive thought; whereas the latter grow with time, and are cumulative, and within the realm of discursive thought.

The vision of Truth is the personal realization of him who has found the Immortal. It is independent of a laborious study of all the accumulated discursive-thought-and-speech knowledge of the past; but it is never independent of the self-discipline which leads to perfection, or purification (in Plato's sense), or liberation (as the Buddha declared).

These personal realizations find formal expression in the splendid affirmations by the Great Teachers, scattered through the pages of the Vedas, the Upanishads, and the various scriptures of the world. From these affirmations as the fountain-head, various philosophies flow in course of time. Whilst the philosophies belong to history, the affirmations of the eternal verities are timeless, and embryonically embody the whole Truth. In this sense the Vedas or Upanishads or the Gāthās or the books of the Bible are eternal—not every word in them, but the affirmations of those Last Things which are also First Things, affirmations of the Spirit, of which one becomes conscious as and in eternity, beyond qualities, description or limitation.

The realizations of the Great Teachers are conscious experiences, not merely logical deductions from given premises, not merely reasonable inferences from certain observations or experiments. Aspirations become verified by the immediacy of the conscious experience which crowns self-discipline. A youngster may reasonably deduce from what he reads or hears above love that the fulfilment of love is blissful. But only when his personal, conscious experience verifies the logical deduction does he realize that fulfilled love is blissful.

The realizations of the Great Teachers enable them to be constantly at home in God-consciousness, and to live daily in harmony with the eternal verities with the same easy efficiency, the become-second-nature, with which the skilled housewife manages her daily household affairs. These realizations are not merely the first stages of a growing system of thought, but are like Minerva emerging full-fledged from the brain of Jupiter. They are not mere gropings after Reality nor mere guesses at Truth. They are the whole unlimited Truth. They are Revelation.

This conscious, experienced Revelation is put into words in order to teach and to help men and women in the world. That which belongs to the sphere where Buddhi (the Reason of enlightened or awakened consciousness) functions, has to be stepped down to the mortal where reason holds sway in the speech-thought realm of not fully awakened or enlightened consciousness. Since the realm of Buddhi is attained in its fullness only by transcending the confusion or distorted perception of sense-mind consciousness, the difficulty of translating Revelation into words can be well appreciated.

The most effective communication of Revelation is undoubtedly the day to day example of the living Teacher. But all Exemplars die physically, and even in their lifetime they cannot be everywhere. So the recorded word is necessary for preserving the teaching.

The explication of these first words expressing the original Revelation certainly spells the development of a philosophy, or of several philosophies, whereas personal realizations, which are the experiences of a transmuted inner consciousness, undergo no development. When one has crossed over the stream of saṁsāra to the Blessed Haven (saraṇa) of Nirvāṇa, then once and for all there is the felicity of the undisturbed state (upekkhā) of the enlightened consciousness, or moksha, or fellowship with God, the state in which "as it was in the beginning is now and ever shall be," the immortal IS of Brahman wherein "development" has no meaning or place.

Again, unlike a musical note which bears a perfect relationship to the same note in another octave, reason does not bear a similar, perfect relationship to Buddhi. What is perfectly coherent through Buddhi where Brahmavidyā is concerned, is not so coherent through the use of reason, when Brahmavidyā as consciously realized experience is translated into a philosophical system, or into a formal religious teaching. The translator of the experience, the philosopher, has not the consciously experienced Revelation of the Teacher. Often, the philosophical systems, the commentaries and treatises by intellectuals, take one farther away from the original, transcendent light of the Teacher. Mystical and religious teaching, in the forms in which one finds it, is only too often discarded or ignored when "the light of reason" is brought to bear upon it, because it seems incoherent. Of necessity, it appears incoherent. But with growth in understanding, reason can formulate this apparently incoherent teaching in more coherent terms. Reason, however, achieves asymptotically. As one develops through disciplining one's senses and mind, one is able to present in an increasingly reasoned, coherent, verbal structure, the Revelation which is so wholly coherent to Buddhi. But, like an asymptote, reason will not wholly coincide with Buddhi, except at infinity.

How, then, quicken Buddhi, refine reason, and make it continually approach closer to Buddhi ?

The ancients made extensive use of symbols as a means for making one wise. They well understood the predominant influence of feeling. Symbols evoke feelings, apprehensions. Meditating on the symbol gives rise to trains of thought, which, through critical, discriminative examination, become the clear, reasoned core of the original, vague feelings. Express such feelings prematurely, and there is obscurantism, the mystification of which certain forms of mysticism are accused. But express such feelings after carrying the meditation through to a successful conclusion, and the triumph of reason is manifest ; and the prize won is wisdom, and not just a sequence of thought.

If an earnest student sought divine wisdom, the ancient teacher offered him an appropriate aphorism or a suitable symbol as the subject for meditation. If in course of time the student achieved realization and himself became an Enlightened One, he in his turn taught his pupils in similar fashion. The form in which certain teachings were given—for example, ethical teachings—is explicit and literal. But certain subjects necessitated a symbolic, or a poetic or an allegorical presentation. Yājñavalkya's exposition on immortality is as explicit and logical as he can make it, whereas his discourse on the Imperishable is poetic. Teachings concerning Brahman and Ātman, or concerning inner states of consciousness are often presented symbolically ; and the gods of the Ṛig Veda, and much the larger part of the Brāhmaṇas, are presented in the form of mythology.

A symbol is more fecund than a literal statement. It can stir the inner depths of consciousness, and stimulate both feeling and reason. With feeling one grasps the truth. With reason one shapes it. Only in recent times, since the days of

Francis Bacon and the rise of experimental science, has literalism held so much sway. In ancient times, religious teaching in particular was presented in symbolic form, through myth and allegory, through poetry, through ritual and ceremony. In India, deep truths were never scattered indiscriminately.[1] Only when the aspirant proved himself worthy of acceptance as a pupil was he given a few hints. According to his temperament and capacities certain truths in symbolic garb were given him. It was his business to penetrate the inner meaning of these symbols, obtaining elucidation through perception and reason, and final realization through Buddhi. The realization of the eternal verities culminated in the unification of Pratyagātman and Paramātman, in becoming Brahman.

We, to-day, have no profounder realization of those eternal verities merely on account of our vast accumulation of scientific knowledge, or because of philosophical development over the centuries, than that achieved by the Great Teachers—the means for climbing to the top of a mountain may improve a hundred-fold with the passage of time, but the view from the summit is still the view from the summit. Essentially, that realization is Self-realization. The means for its attainment—self-discipline, prayer, samādhi—is the religious life. Man's growth is a continuous process of self-discovery, which gives him greater inward freedom and culminates in the fulfilment of the purpose of his existence, namely God or Self or Brahman realization.

Since Religion is concerned with Self-realization through self-understanding, self-discipline, self-control and self-transcendence, the religious teaching of India includes teaching about one's own self (about " you " and about " me ") in all its aspects, physical, psychical and spiritual. One of the golden keys to unlock the mysteries of this teaching is the psychological; and the psychological and allegorical interpretation of the old teachings, far from doing violence to history as some are inclined to think, is the most important and correct way of understanding these teachings. This is not to suggest that modern psychological science must be read into the past. But it is to suggest that the psychological and intuitive insights of the ancient seers,

[1] Cf. "Cast not your pearls before swine."—Matthew, VII. 6.

which gave them full understanding of man and his nature, are embodied in their symbolic teachings. Our understanding to-day is no deeper than that of the Great Teachers; and the stupendous achievement of Brahman-realization by a Parameṣṭhin, a Pippalāda, a Buddha, a Jesus, a Zarathustra, a Kṛishṇa, should make it clear that we are not capable of reading too much into their teachings, even if we wanted to do so.

If the symbolic cast of the teachings is taken literally, it often reads like jargon, or appears as crude fantastic superstition. The difficulties in the path of correct interpretation must not be underestimated. Besides the psychological there is also a naturalistic, or theological, or cosmological, or physiological, or ritualistic or some other interpretation possible. Again, not one interpretation only, but more than one may fit the context. And further, particularly where mystical teachings are concerned, it is often not easy to draw the line between literal statement and symbolism, between the need for psychological interpretation here and here, and say, cosmological there and there,[1] between a delineation of what appertains to God Immanent, and to God Transcendent.

There is still another difficulty. Our training conditions our minds in those ways which make us accept Aristotelian logic, that a thing or an idea is just this and not that, and that to be precise and concrete, and to give a simple, clear exposition are virtues. All this is not unacceptable, in fact it is necessary and right, within the framework in which it can and should operate. But man's total experience includes much more. Where early Indian mysticism or religious thought is concerned, the neat framework of dualism, the either-or desert-like clearcutness, is inadequate. For example, the simultaneity of the "is" and the "is not" in certain instances, and the view that the eternal is the reality wherein the spatio-temporal is subsumed, are accepted by Great Teachers. Therefore, some of the best minds to-day, unless they have themselves attained the realization of the Great Teachers, are suddenly confronted, after going thus far, with a seeming void, a silence, which spells confusion and misunderstanding.

[1] As for instance in many of the hymns of the Ṛig and Atharva Vedas.

The understanding of religious teaching depends on the understander :

> The threefold offspring of Prajāpati—gods, men and devils—dwelt with their father Prajāpati as students of sacred knowledge. Having lived the life of a student of sacred knowledge, the gods said: 'Speak to us, sir.' To them then he spoke this syllable, 'Da.' 'Did you understand ?' 'We did understand,' said they. 'You said to us, "Restrain (*damyata*) yourselves."' 'Yes !' said he. 'You did understand.'
>
> So then the men said to him : 'Speak to us, sir.' To them then he spoke this syllable, 'Da.' 'Did you understand ?' 'We did understand,' said they. 'You said to us, "Give (*datta*)."' 'Yes !' said he. 'You did understand.'
>
> So then the devils said to him : 'Speak to us, sir.' To them then he spoke this syllable, 'Da.' 'Did you understand ?' 'We did understand,' said they. 'You said to us, "Be compassionate (*dayadhvam*)."' 'Yes !' said he. 'You did understand.' This same thing does the divine voice here, thunder, repeat : Da ! Da ! Da ! that is, restrain yourselves, give, be compassionate. One should practise this same triad : self-restraint, giving, compassion.
>
> Bṛihad-Āraṇyaka Upanishad, V.2.1–3.

* * * * *

Now the Ṛig Veda says :

> We have drunk Soma and become immortal ;
> We have attained the light, the gods discovered.
>
> VIII.48.3.

No one becomes immortal by taking a drink ! Soma, in its profoundest signification, is that inspiration which comes to him who has transcended the sense-mind world and can enter samādhi. Then one is filled (drunk) with that inspiration which is a "modification pertaining to Ātman" (Paiṅgala Upanishad ; see above, p. 192), and one realizes immortality. To drink Soma is to "drink of the waters of eternal life." "We have become immortal" does not mean that any individuals, or any of their aspects, such as "souls" or "spirits", continue to exist endlessly in time, here on earth or in a mythical heaven. It means that the eternal, in which the existent spatio-temporal universe and individuals are subsumed, is realized by the living, existent individual. Such realization is " becoming immortal ". It is the making real, consciously, of "As it was in the beginning is now and ever shall be ", in which consciousness does not function in terms of an uprising or birth, of process, and of passing away or death, which three together constitute the mortal. The time sense and the mortal are transcended, and the immortal is consciously experienced—it is not a mere thought which is but a string of words—wherein there is intensest awareness of the Whole, as an integrated unity and not as of several parts related to each other. The limitation of the movement of awareness, the " stream " of consciousness—past, present, future ; birth, process, death—which characterizes all who have not " become immortal ", is transcended by him who realizes the immortal. He who has " become immortal ", on the death of his body, will " never again be seen by gods or men " as the Buddha said ;[1] but THAT, the Creator, of which this, the living, existent individual is the manifestation, is the Imperishable, as Yājñavalkya said, and knows no annihilation. " We have attained the light, the gods discovered." All the gods, besides their cosmological and other significances, represent aspects of man himself, his faculties and potentialities. When one enters samādhi triumphantly, then indeed, in that supreme God-realization, all the gods are discovered, laid bare, and one becomes immortal.

Brahman, once superconsciously realized, remains as the permanent background and fount of inspiration of the Perfect One for the rest of his days. The light of God shines perpetually on him and through him. And yet, the stress of spatio-temporal suffering can disjoin, for a time, the unity with the Father, or can obscure the light of God-communion. Then, with patient effort, the Suffering One has to restore the perfection of the immortal. So when Bhishma the Teacher lies dying on the battlefield, riddled with Arjuna's shafts, he is asked by the victor what could he, Arjuna, do for him. Bhishma asks him to fix another arrow in such a position that he could rest his head upon it. Arjuna obliges him. Whereupon Bhishma the

[1] See above, p. 167.

yogi maintains his life until the time when the planetary positions are auspicious, and then, merging his consciousness in Brahman, he passes away, immortal.

In chapter four, interpretations of some of the symbolic statements in connection with the Buddha's enlightenment have already been offered. There is another interesting statement to the effect that after the enlightenment, the Buddha spent seven days gazing at the tree-root where he had sat till he became enlightened. Buddhas do not spend seven days gazing at tree-roots even if they have botanical interests! The tree referred to here is the Aśvattha tree, with "roots above and branches below".[1] This tree, associated with the brain, spinal column and nervous system, is mentioned times out of number in Indian teachings. The statement means that the Buddha pondered deeply over the nature of the mind, which is the "slayer of the Real" whilst involved in saṁsāra, but when purified, is the most important instrument for "gaining the Immortal." "By the mind alone is IT to be perceived," says the Bṛihad-Āraṇyaka Upanishad, IV.4.19. The impure mind, that is, the involved in saṁsāra mind, is known to us. But the purified mind is something new and strange. What is its nature? What are its potentialities? That is what the Buddha looked at. For the purified mind means, among other things, one in which the faulty use of reason is overcome, and what is far more significant, one in which Buddhi comes into its own. So the Buddha says that he attains super-knowledge (abhiññā, paññā), and has omniscience (sabbaññuta-ñāṇaṁ): in Christian terms this is the descent of the Holy Spirit, which is Divine Intelligence, the Spirit of Truth, the Comforter. Afterwards, the gospel is taught by the Exalted One, the true Mind-Healer. Rightly, then, does the Buddha carefully examine this tree-root, wherein a miracle of transmutation—the worldly mind being converted into the pure mind—took place.

Significantly, reasoned statement rather than poetic utterance is characteristic of the Buddha's teaching. But the Buddha also uses the language of symbolism. Brahmā Sahampati, the Lord of Self, Sakka, chief of the gods, Māra, the Evil One, and

[1] Bhagavad-Gītā, XV. 1. See also, Ṛig Veda, I. 24. 7.

several other such personages, are all daily familiars of the Buddha. Conversations with them simply stand for the process of question and answer, of enquiry and deliberation, which goes on within the mind, the dignitaries named representing but various aspects of one's own make-up. Often, Māra tempts the Buddha with the suggestion, " Now is the time to pass away into Nirvāṇa." How often man experiences that temptation—the longing to die, or even commit suicide, when frustrated or frightened; or to die this very moment, after experiencing some ecstatic pleasure, or after fulfilling some great aim in life! So, also, in the Upanishads, the sage questions, and is answered by, the Supreme Being, just as in the Ṛig Veda he addresses one or other of the gods, or others of the celestial clan. So, too, the Lord God speaks unto the prophets of Israel; Jesus declares that he is sent by the Father, whose will he does, and that he communes with the Father; Zarathustra speaks with Ahura-Mazda, the One, only God. These are all symbolic expressions of man enquiring of himself, communing with himself, and carrying out the behests of God Immanent in him. But God as a literal " other ", holding literal converse with a " me ", is a pathetic misrepresentation of God, and of the experience of God-communion. The reality intended to be conveyed by the statement, " man communing with God ", is as difficult to understand as " the eternal which transcends all spatio-temporal categories." Reason achieves the status of the right complement of Buddhi only when a man has perfected himself, and at that enlightened stage one says, simply and truly, " Yes, I see."

Religions have their miracles, which are usually regarded as suspensions of natural law by divine intervention. Belief in them as literal facts is natural to those in their spiritual childhood. Man is captivated into the acknowledgment of superior authority by a timely demonstration of power beyond his grasp or understanding. Moreover, such demonstration satisfies one of his longings, namely, to be astonished and overpowered.[1] But if any religion hangs solely, or even principally, on the peg of

[1] Man also has the opposite longing, namely, to astonish and to overpower the other person. "Man is made up of everything"—Bṛihad-Āraṇyaka Upanishad, IV. 4. 5.

miracles, it will fall down on the day that a sufficient number of its adherents reach maturity through the unavoidable process of growing up. What girl still believes in storks after she has borne her own babe? And yet she may unhesitatingly and charmingly spin the same tale to her own inquisitive infant daughters.

It is not intended here either to refute or to prove that miracles either did or did not take place as physical facts. Believing them as physical facts is significant for people at a certain stage of development. At another stage, a different interpretation of miracles illumines and inspires. For instance, Jesus turns water into wine at a marriage feast. For most men and women, marriage is a reciprocal relationship: "I will love, honour, protect and be faithful unto you, and you, in your turn, must likewise love, honour and co-operate with me." The special, unique bond between man and wife is sexual. Thereby, one of nature's great purposes is fulfilled, and the stream of organic life (symbolized by water) keeps flowing. But Jesus comes along and teaches love on a plane transcending (without invariably rejecting) the organic, social, contractual and usual. He shows this couple how this ordinary, creaturely love can be transformed into a non-contractual (unlimited, unbound, free and pure), unchanging, undemanding, all-giving, extraordinary love, which manifests as: "Whatsoever thou doest, howsoever thou behavest, my love shall ever be like the sun radiating light." This love is non-reciprocal. It is absolute. The water of creaturely love is converted into the wine of divine love, the spiritual value called Love. Exactly that Love is taught by Yājñavalkya in his discourse to Maitreyī. Exactly that Love is taught by the Buddha in his Brahma-vihāras, in his teaching of mettā-karuṇā-muditā-upekkhā. Exactly that Love is represented in Zarathustrian teaching in Āramaiti, the divine love of Ahura-Mazda. The key to the interpretation of Christ's miracle is supplied by the fact that it was performed at a marriage feast. A club dinner would have formed the setting for quite a different teaching (miracle).

The idea of the Virgin Birth is associated not only with the Buddha and the Christ, but also with Zarathustra, Lao-Tze,

Plato and the ancient British magician, Merlin. One meaning of this symbolical teaching is that procreation should be holy action, a true act of creation by man and woman.[1] Another meaning is seen in the process and fulfilment of God-realization. Man purifies himself as he proceeds with his discipline. The culminating point is reached through that emancipation of heart and mind when the enlightenment makes him the fully Awakened One, when the yogi enters full samādhi, when the sage " ascends aloft ", when the unity with the Father is established and he becomes the Anointed One, the Christ, when Pratyagātman and Paramātman are united. Herein, the alone—pure, sinless, associateless[2]—is united with the Alone—the single, secondless One. Thus takes place the Immaculate (undefiled by mortal desire) Conception (the " knowing " of God, or Brahman), and the Virgin Birth (virgin, because born of the utterly purified mind and heart, born in peace, and born without any struggle for survival, and so a Prince of Peace) of God the Son, manifest in the world as a Buddha or a Christ or a Paramahaṁsa. God the Son is the Second Person of the Trinity, is Viṣṇu, who is born again and again to re-establish righteousness.[3] The Soul of man aspiring to union, *in full consciousness*, with her Beloved, the Father-God, who also, through His aspect of the Holy Spirit, is seeking union with the Beloved, the Daughter-Soul, on realization, gives birth to God the Son, who is now a concrete reality embodied in man, the Word made flesh, housed in the temple of the body, the psycho-physical individual. The incarnate God the Son, each time he is manifest, is a unique, individual manifestation through man of God the Universal Transcendent. In other words, God the Immanent in man, representing the potentiality of God the Universal Transcendent, on awakening out of sleep into full, active, effective consciousness through individual man's self-purification, is God the Son incarnate.

Since this whole drama is enacted within the single man himself, the Son is the alone-begotten of God. There is no

[1] See below, p. 491 et seq.
[2] "The Ātman is . . . . associateless . . ."—Subāla Upanished, Khaṇḍa VIII.
[3] Bhagavad-Gītā, IV. 8.

" external " God involved in it, nor a spatio-temporal sequence of events. But neither " man " nor " God " must be understood atomistically—as distinct, permanent, separate selves, or as interior or exterior. Nor is there, in reality, a specific, isolable event of enlightenment, although in temporal retrospect there are recognizable landmarks of what is apparent to sense-mind as a process composed of specific events. Enlightenment or God-realization, as the transmutation or integration of the deficient into the efficient, the Less into the More, the Part into the Whole, is of the Eternal. What Buddhi realizes through omniscience of the Eternal, is translated into a more or less reasoned presentation in terms of the spatio-temporal. But since the ordered steps of the spatio-temporal are a mode of expression, the nature of which is so under and below the whole apprehension by Buddhi of the Eternal, some of the logical objections which can be raised against interpretations of mystical teachings may be set aside. For instance, it could be said that since God is already God the Father and Son and Holy Ghost, how can God the Son be born afterwards through man attaining union with God? The question is couched in the separatist, atomistic terms of the spatio-temporal world, which are inadequate in relation to the eternal—you cannot wholly explain water and its properties in terms of hydrogen and oxygen, although water is no other than hydrogen and oxygen in combination. God as the Trinity, or a Triune Unity, is man's conception. It is man's mode of stating the reality which is God, after it is experienced by him. The Transcendent God is " seen ", and postulated, only " after " the Immanent God is realized by the man himself. But the Immanent God is not a small manikin spirit in relation to the Transcendent God as a supermanikin spirit. Immanent God and Transcendent God are one and the same. When mortality-bound man awakens to the truth, he shatters the hell-circle of separative, ego-istic perception. Thus spatio-temporal separateness of immanent and transcendent is swept away through the vision of the Divine. There is then no question of how an " already existing " God the Son can be born " later " through the individual's self-purification and enlightenment.

Man, although he is partly of the death-ful, is given the possibility of experiencing Brahman, of winning the deathless, the Immortal. This is one meaning of " The Grace of God ". This Grace works in each man as an integrative principle, universally operative. The condition for its operation is first and foremost self-purification, which may or may not include a calling upon a Saviour, or upon God directly. To say that the Grace of God cannot rest upon a man through his " unaided " endeavour, but rests only through a particular Saviour, and by his intercession, is to confess ignorance of what man is in his wholeness, and even greater ignorance of God and of the relationship between man and God. It is to deny the unity of the universe, and all its implications in terms of inter-dependence, inter-relation and interaction between the parts constituting the whole, and between the part and the whole. It is also to deny the one-ness of the One.

SECTION D

GOD-CONCEPTION

THE EMERGENCE and development of the God concept, at once the seed and the blossom of all religions, is the clearest index of man's self-discovery and his realization of inner freedom. It epitomizes his fearful gropings, his brave struggles, his victory over self, and his sublime vision and fulfilment of the Truth. The word God, in whatever language it is uttered, is The Word. As long as there is speech, so long will there live this word, which Indian religious thought has spelled with such rich diversity: Deva, Varuṇa, Indra, Viśvakarman, Purusha, Brahman, Ātman, Īśvara, Parameśvara, Brahmā, Viṣṇu, Śiva, Bhagavān, etc. It stands for the final essence, the ultimate reality, the Supreme Being, the highest power, which is the source, cause, creator, mover, maintainer and controller of the universe; for the apotheosis of the good, the final goal of man's aspiration and endeavour; for the holiest Sacred, the supreme object of man's most solemn worship, of his most fervent devotion and of his deepest veneration. Man treasures this word as his most priceless inheritance from the past, and his most worthy legacy to the future. It is the lodestar of his life, the touchstone of his conduct, the supreme inspiration of his best endeavour.

This word is man's answer to questions touching origin and end, creation, life, purpose, fulfilment, significance, immortality and eternity. To-day, as in the past, some men would prefer words like energy or force to God; some, Mind or Divine Mind; some First Principle or Prime Cause; some, the Eternal or the Infinite; some, the Absolute or the Unconditioned; some, Love, and others, Truth. Some would say they do not know the answer, nor feel called upon to answer; and others, that they are not interested in such questions.

The Word expresses man's infrequent, overwhelmingly impressive experience, irresistibly convincing because of its undiscorded wholeness and its unchecked immediacy, of an all-embracing, unitary reality which includes him, the experiencer; or of a Wholly Other, one and only God, the Necessary Being, in relation to whom all nature is contingent, all the universe but the product of His Divine Will. At the other end of the scale, the Word represents that Powerful Sacred in which man believes, and which he worships with propitiatory rites because of his fears and ignorance, his superstition.

Whatever may be the reality which truly corresponds to the Word, God for each ordinary man is either an impersonal force or the personal creature of that man's feeling, reasoning, imagining and experiencing, conditioned by his upbringing and education. For the unique man who has realized God, God is the Supreme Being—Brahman the Self-Existent, Parameśvar, The Lord, Ahura-Mazda, Allah, God the Creator, the Father, Brahmā, Viṣṇu, Śiva, Transcendent God—and also, more profoundly and more truly, Brahman, Ātman, The Godhead, The Absolute, The Eternal, The Infinite (=The Void=The Plenum). For him who has partly realized, that is, who has not quite won the supreme stillness, Nirvāṇa, the Peace that passes understanding, the complete control over the fluctuations of mind, God is only the Supreme Being, the Saguṇa Brahman, whilst the Nirguṇa Brahman, The Godhead, is as yet a conception but not a realization.

Descriptions of God, and the development of God-conceptions, are the explications of the Word; and the Word is the most succinct summarization of God-conceptions and God-experiences. For the individual himself, inwardly, the Word embodies the rich, significant content of all his experience and conception of God; whilst God-conceptions are his and society's attempts, outwardly, to convey to each other what reality the Word holds within itself. God-conceptions, and the Word, are coterminous for society; but an individual member of that society hears the Word from his early days, before he forms any specific conceptions of God.

The Word, and God-conceptions, arise out of living man's

experience, and are immured in speech-thought. There is no revelation of God by God after the fashion of one man introducing himself to another. God is revealed in and through the man-become-God, to himself in terms of realization, if he is Brahman-become, or to his unific understanding if he is not yet Brahman-become. Also, God is revealed-veiled in the man not yet become Brahman, and also in and through all nature, for him who has eyes willing to see and ears glad to hear.

When a man triumphantly enters samādhi, becomes a Mukta, an Enlightened One, an Anointed One, all God-conceptions cease, for here is God-realization, wherein the " Word " has become " flesh ". The God-realized or Brahman-become is the silent. He is also the ever-speaking Voice of God.

In some form or other, the sense of God inheres in man. At all stages, from primitive to Brahman-become, man apprehends God, since he subsists in that which is represented by the Word. The sense of God, at its heart, in its deepest depth, is indescribable, unanalyzable, unperceivable. It is a conviction not born of logic, nor of perception of the external world, though inward response to such perception may support or expand the sense of God. The heart of this sense is the point at which all God-affirmations, whether made by primitive or simple citizen or man-become-God, meet—it is the realm of the Word—however widely God-conceptions, which are explications of the Word by the simple man or the intellectual, the primitive or the beatified, may differ.

The simple person, like the primitive, sometimes experiences a " participation mystique ", a sense of unity with nature. He comes under the spell of the moment under certain circumstances, and he feels with compelling conviction his kinship, in the sense of a real, substantial one-ness, with all that lives, and his interdependence and inter-wovenness with all nature. He senses, too, a supreme Power, conscious and masterful, who is Lord over him and nature. This vague though whole apprehension cannot be clearly comprehended by his untutored mind. He is as one groping in the dark ; he can only touch and hear. So his faith, though intense, is clouded with fear, ignorance and superstition.

With education and civilization, the primitive, emotional

sense of unity recedes, and an intellectual perception of differences becomes more pronounced. The logical, analytical mind of the developed man brings him to grips with difficult problems in connection with God, for his restless intellect wants to know God, and he is not content with blind, emotional faith. But these are problems posed by him himself because of his very development; they do not exist for the simple soul, blissful through ignorance, nor for the mukta, blissful through enlightenment. They are the problems invariably associated with the increasing sense of separate selfhood, which is an unavoidable concomitant of the early steps in the growth of individuality. They arise out of the experiences and stages of progress, and out of the changes in the mind and heart and character of the man himself as he pursues his enquiry into the nature of God. God's nature is itself entirely free of problems.

But when the partly enlightened attains full liberation, then his apprehension of God becomes a perfect, conscious realization, wholly free of fear, ignorance and superstition. Instead of having to grapple with problems, he "knows" God and is at peace in God.

In the primitive there is confusion and fear, and in the developed man, perplexity and self-obtrusiveness. The Arahant is enlightened and at peace.

* * * * *

From the many to the One; from the diversity so obvious to the senses, to the unity which is the fruit of inward realization: such is the general trend in religious thought. Slowly through the millennia, it becomes apparent to a man here and a man there, that the total environment conveyed to him through his senses is a whole, consisting of inter-related parts, which he regards as, and calls, a universe, a turned-into-one. And in the ages when most men worshipped and believed in tree-gods, river-gods, animal-gods and all kinds of gods and ghosts, a man here and a man there, a sensitive, endowed, self-disciplining truth-seeker, was learning to look within himself for the answer to his innermost, secret quest: Who is He? What is IT?

There is little or no ground for assuming that men were

incapable of God-realization before the specific revelations made by the historically known teachers of the great religions. It is a fact that the vision of God has come to certain persons throughout the last three or four millennia. Provided a man is so constituted, he senses the whole truth. Thus prepared, to him can come revelation. The extent to which he himself grasps what he senses depends upon his intelligence and moral development, whilst the extent to which he can convey it to others depends upon his intellectual training and abilities. Many centuries before Moses, Enoch "walked with God: and he was not: for God took him" (Genesis V.24); and for centuries before Enoch, God "spoke" to man, even to Adam, the "first" man. Enoch was one so holy that it was not said of him that he died, but that God took him. Enoch realized God, realized immortality and crossed over death. And Enoch lived in, or at least not far from, the land whence came those who raised the Indus Valley civilization.

What, now, is the significance of the seal representing a deity in a meditative pose, which Sir John Marshall thought represented Śiva? *In a meditative pose.* Far back in the dim past, millennia before the historical Founders of the great religions, there were individuals not inexpert in the practice of meditation and of looking within, not incapable of achieving such holiness that they realized God and transcended death. The transcending of death was not explained openly but was put in symbolical terms, sufficiently compelling in wonder, in "magic", to appeal to the hearts of the untutored and hold their reverence. The story of Abraham and Isaac may indicate to one who can understand its symbolical aspect, how far developed those men were in the art of God-communion through meditation, in Yoga in other words. As Abraham is about to slay his son as a sacrifice in obedience to God's own command, the angel of the Lord stops him. Looking up, Abraham sees a ram caught in a thicket by the horns, and he slays the ram, to complete the sacrifice due to the Lord. He names the place Jehovah-jireh—"As it is said to this day. In the mount of the Lord it shall be seen" (Genesis XXII.14). This "mount of the Lord" is the same as the Zarathustrian "Ushi-darena" and the Hindu "mount Meru" (the abode of Brahman); it is "the thousand-petalled lotus (Sahasrāra) at the top of the head", fully activated when one enters full samādhi and is "in union with God".

God-communion and God-realization are as old as the hills. But God-conceptions, and the extent to which these have permeated the lives of larger and larger numbers of people, have developed through the millennia, and grown into the theologies of the established world religions. The Śiva seal of the Indus Valley people means that at least a few remarkable individuals knew the meaning of "looking within" and the nature and consequence of God-communion. There is nothing to warrant the presumption that those ancients in India did not, or could not attain God-realization, for in this matter the accumulation of mere knowledge has no finally determining influence. Men in that age were constituted by nature like men in subsequent ages; and there is no *a priori* reason why their potentiality for spiritual fulfilment and their capacity for the vision of the Highest need have been less than that of men in historical times.

If the man-become-God was not non-existent in the fifth or sixth millennium before our own day, one wonders: Who were the poet-seers of the Ṛig Veda? What was their cultural level, the quality of their minds? Was their genius comparable to that of later spiritual geniuses of whom we have more intimate knowledge? Was their inner illumination far profounder than what is outwardly apparent in the hymns as they stand? Undoubtedly, the great Ṛishis like Bhāradvāja, Kaśyapa, Gotama, Atri, Vasishṭha, Viśvāmitra, Jamadagni and others had inwardly realized God. This they expressed in symbolic poetry, the Saṁhitā. Less symbolic and more literal expression, philosophic and psychologic, followed later. Inspiration and God-realization are timeless; theology and philosophy and developing God-conceptions belong to history.

Through the ages, then, the written word mirrors the changes that have taken place in man's mode of conceiving and interpreting, expressing and conveying his inner realization. In the very early stages, the ordinary man's observation of the external world is interpreted subjectively in terms of himself, a living creature. Animism flourishes. The prevailing verbal statements of the accepted beliefs offer the literary forms and the intellectual mould in which the man-become-God of that period could convey his realization: hence the unconditionally unitary (or mono-) nature of what was realized could be conveyed only in poly- forms, theistic and daemonic. Later on, with increasing knowledge and manipulation of the physical world, together with the growing capacity for systematization, man observes and interprets more objectively. Philosophy makes its infant bow, and begins, steadily but not wholly, to displace animistic interpretations: hence the form of the Creation hymns, for example, of the Ṛig Veda. Gradually, self-knowledge grows, "looking within" develops into a systematized practice, and objective, intellectual abstraction of truths, laws and principles quite displaces animism and polytheism. The "poly" becomes "mono" when conceptions and interpretations and forms of expression have developed far enough, through man's own development as a thinking human being, to coincide with his inner God-realization, which is always, and necessarily, of a "mono" quality. The verbal statement and intellectual form (or the speech-thought) in which the man-become-God of this later age presents his realization is correspondingly different, therefore, from that of his predecessor: hence, for example, the Brahman-Ātman teachings of the Upanishads.

It is stated by so many of the Great Ones, that they reiterate, or crown or fulfil, in consequence of their own realization, what was taught by their predecessors. For instance, Gotama the Buddha (in a line of twenty-four Buddhas[1]) puts one of his profoundest teachings, the Paṭicca-Samuppāda, into the mouth of a previous Buddha, Vipassin, in the Mahāpadāna Sutta. But this same teaching, given directly on his own authority by himself to Ānanda, in the Mahā-Nidāna Sutta, is slightly different in form, as shown by a comparison of the two discourses. The pantheon of the Vedic Saṁhitās finds its crown in the Brahman-Ātman of the Upanishads. God's holiness as emphasized by Isaiah, His righteous judgements by Amos, His forgiving mercy

[1] Cf. the twenty-four Tīrthankars of Jainism, and the twenty-four Elders of Revelation.

by Hosea, lead to the demonstration of His Fatherhood and His holy sacrificial love in Jesus Christ. The poly-theistic and poly-daemonic host of ancient Irān gives place to Zarathustra's single, spiritual and ethical Ahura-Mazda, as that of Arabia to Muhammad's Allāh.

At whatever period in history a man realizes God, that realization is in terms of himself, and himself alone. Anyone may see God in a Great Teacher: which means, in fact, he sees god-likeness in the Teacher; and he sees it only to the extent to which he, the man, has himself become good. "Blessed are the pure in heart for they shall see God"—and the partly pure one will see only partly. What he sees in the Teacher is an impression he receives, a conception he forms, an interpretation he gives, and an inspiration pressing him forward to personal achievement. But his realization of God is only through and in himself made God. It is a Self-realization, possible only when his self—dim-visioned erring, imprisoned—has through purification and not repression rent the veil and liberated itself into conscious unity with the Supreme Self. This is the full and true knowing of God here-now. When the attempt is made to convey or to show this knowing to another, the showing, as well as the seeing by the onlooker, is in terms of a personal God, of a Supreme Being.

But as soon as inward realization, the constant, here-now, God-being of the man-become-Brahman, is poured into the mould of speech-thought and externalized by the Person who has realized, the terms of description of God arise, and God-conceptions are presented. The forging of these terms is the work of the mind, bound by duality. The terms of description are postulates made by mind—and dualistic mind is human, not divine. So the terms—Transcendent and Immanent God; God the Father, Creator, Preserver; God the Omniscient, Omnipotent, Omnipresent; God who is Love, Truth, Goodness, Justice, Mercy and Forgiveness, Perfection and Immortality—all arise. All are true; and simultaneously, all are slightly other than true. The whole truth is the Brahman-become himself, the Living God made manifest in man; and that truth can never be known in terms of another, but only in terms of oneself through Self-realization.

The Vedic poet-seers understood this, and very succinctly, taught it.

Ancient peoples were spiritist minded. Everything, whether animate or inanimate, was a " thou ". A river was not merely hydrogen oxide containing dissolved salts inevitably impelled by gravity downwards from the mountains to the sea. A river was person-like, indwelt by a goddess; even to-day, some rivers have " personality ", like Father Thames. At least, everything in nature was inhabited or animated by a spiritual being, sacred and either beneficent or maleficent. Overriding this welter of spirit animated Nature in its details, was the feeling—the Kar Nicobarese, for instance, believing vaguely in a supreme God; the Paliyans in a supreme Goddess—of a single World-Spirit animating and controlling all Nature, the whole universe being regarded as organic, living.

Thus the not-self was felt and described in terms of the self animistically, anthropomorphically.

At the same time, it was impossible for man not to see the difference between himself and the universe. The great gods represent not only aspects of himself or the whole of himself, but also of the universe and life as a whole, and of the universe and life in their large fragments—Sky, Sun, Dawn, Fertility, the Elements, Inspiration, Death, and so on. God-conceptions thus become more objective, in their aspect of the universal outside man's individual self. But the gods, objectively, cannot be mere mechanisms. They must be living, that is, conscious, vital, powerful and capable, like man, but in superlative degree. Furthermore, they must have man's virtues *par excellence*. Their objectivity, however, leads man to a conception of their other-than-man aspect to such an extent, that they end up in the single, wholly-other-than both man and Nature, the Transcendent God, who still is spiritual and ethical, or else there would be no link whatever with man—man, the ethical being who is God's true and only conceiver.

The ancients conceived of everything in the cosmos as being correspondingly inter-related: man the microcosm was the miniature of the macrocosm; the elements, forces, qualities and gods of the macrocosm had their correspondences in him.

All the gods—Ādityas, Olympians, Celtic or Teutonic personages —all belong to this world, the manifested and perishable world. The cosmos, conceived theogonically, is then inter-related in all other ways, each theos having his naturalistic or cosmological, his elemental, physiological, psychological and other counterparts. These he inhabits and controls, and he is also other than them. The mass of men being what they were, could accept them as celestial entities and worship them. Varuṇa, Indra, Agni, Soma and others are all great conceptions; peculiarly great, for in each is represented the whole, and yet each is also individual and special. They are the shapes given to Pure God, Very God of Very God, by man. And man perfects and purifies the shapes in his search for Very God, as his capacity for seeing grows, that is, as he becomes increasingly pure in heart and mind, and knows himself better and better. The great gods of civilized communities are projections of man himself, apotheosized and immortalized.

From the Ādityas, and especially from Varuṇa, he moves forward to Viśvakarman and Hiraṇyagarbha. When the ways apparently part, one line leads him to Brahman-Ātman, the other to

> 17. They who in Purusha understand Brahman
> know Him who is supreme.
> He who knows Him who is Supreme, and he
> who knows the Lord of Life,
> These know the loftiest Power Divine, and
> thence know Skambha thoroughly.
>
> Atharva Veda, X.7.[1]

Here, in Purusha, is the unequivocal affirmation of God as the Supreme Being, as the Lord of Life or the Living God. But where, and what, is the Supreme Being? In what manner, or in whom, shall a man see and know the Supreme Being?

> 29. . . . then the gods entered into man.
> 30. All Waters, all the Deities, Virāj with Brahmā at her side: Brahmā into the body passed; Prajāpati is Lord thereof.
> 32. Therefore whoever knoweth man regardeth him as Brahman's self. For all the Deities abide in him as cattle in their pen.
>
> Atharva Veda, XI.8.

[1] The whole of this remarkable hymn will amply repay careful study.

Unequivocally is it stated that in man, and through man, is the Supreme Being seen and known. By what kind of a man is the Supreme Being known?

5. The Brahmacārī, earlier born than Brahmā,
   sprang up through Fervour, robed in hot libation;
From him sprang heavenly lore, the highest Brahmā,
   and all the Gods, with life that lasts for ever.

Atharva Veda, XI.5.

43. Men versed in sacred knowledge know
   that living Being that abides
In the nine-petalled Lotus flower (the body),
   enclosed with triple bands and bonds.
44. Desireless, firm and immortal, self-existent,
   contented with the essence, lacking nothing,
Free from the fear of Death is he who knoweth that
   Soul, courageous, youthful and undecaying.

Atharva Veda, X.8.

Clearly, the Supreme Being is known by the man who through self-discipline and self-transcendence has crossed over sin and death, has become still, or firm as in verse 44, who is self-existent, or self-contained or whole, and has realized God. Only the man become self-existent can know the Living God, Parameśvar, Brahman the Self-Existent, the Svayambhū of the Upanishads (Bṛihad-Āraṇyaka, II.6.3; IV.6.3; VI.5.4; Kaṭha, IV.1.; Īśā, 8).

THAT which is realized in samādhi, in becoming still (Psalm XLVI. 10), in the eighth deliverance where there is "the stopping of consciousness, knowing and feeling" but which is nevertheless a deliberate activity of the Arahant, THAT, embodied, is the Supreme Being, the Living God of any and every faith. It is the immortal Living-Existent, discoverable and knowable as such by mortal, existential man only after he has freed himself utterly from lust, hate, delusion and the ignorant conceit of "I am" of everyday life, and has himself become the perfect expression of the Living-Existent in man's form. In other words, the man has at last, stripped of petty, limiting ego, become the true individual, the undivided from the supreme-All. The Son is one with the Father. He has attained the harmless state, a-hiṁsa, which is comprised within the infinite Love of God.

The Ṛishis who realized, the " men versed in sacred knowledge " of Atharva Veda, X.8.43 above, have appeared on earth through the millennia. But in India the full statement of the realization, or, the perfecting of the God-conception, had to wait for the time of the Atharva Veda, the Upanishads, the Gītā and the Buddha ; in Irān, for the advent of Zarathustra ; in the Eastern Mediterranean lands, for the great prophets up to Jesus. It may seem altogether strange to mention the Buddha in this connection. Yet in actual fact, the Buddha gives one of the most enlightening teachings of the Supreme Being. For the Buddha was fully cognizant of what really happens with man's growing insight. One knows, or can know the Supreme Being, never in manifested wholeness,[1] but only in limited manifestation. The perfect, limited manifestation is oneself-become-God. An other man-become-God is only partly revealed to oneself. His inner life is secret ; his " praying unto the Father ", his samādhi, is in secret, is the Silence.[2] He, a Living-Existent embodying the Supreme Being is only to be inferred by oneself, if one is capable of reading aright the external symbol of the inward and invisible grace. Hence the Buddha puts aside all speech-thought regarding *the* Supreme Being, or the Transcendent or Immanent God. Instead, he draws attention to the actual reality, and without hesitation affirms that he himself is the Brahman-become, the Dhamma-become. Further, in verse after verse of the Dhammapada, canto XXVI, he clearly describes the man-become-God when he says, " Him I call a brāhman who . . . " Brāhman, in the profound sense of the term, is not a social dignity (an ephemeral bubble), but

[1] When Shri Kṛishṇa vouchsafes the divine vision of the Supreme Being as manifested wholeness, Arjuna is so overwhelmed that he begs the Lord Incarnate to reassume his familiar, gentle form again!

[2] It may be objected by some that the Gospels offer no evidence that praying to the Father in secret means the Silence which is the cessation of speech and discursive thought, because the Lord's Prayer as taught by Jesus is given in verbal form, as also his other prayers, as recorded. There are two types of God-communion or samādhi: the saṁprajñāta in which the union with God is still tinged with the obtrusive consciousness of individual self, and can find verbal expression; and the asaṁprajñāta, in which the union with God is complete and the superconsciousness which is the meaning of the term "God-become" is realized, and in which speech and discursive thought are not. This asaṁprajñāta samādhi is the ultimate praying to the Father in secret, of Jesus. It is unrecordable.

represents him who has become Brahman. In the Vajrasūcī Upanishad it is said:

> There are four castes—the brāhman, the kshatriya, the vaiśya and the śūdra . . . the brāhman is the most important of them . . . Who indeed, then , is a brāhman ?
>
> Whoever he may be (that is, whatever caste he may belong to), he who has directly realized the Ātman, who is directly cognizant of the Ātman which is without a second, devoid of class . . . free from faults . . . of the nature of truth, knowledge, bliss, eternity . . . which cannot be reasoned about but is known only by direct cognition . . . he alone is a brāhman.

Only the true individual, who is the full flower of humanity, and who is the incarnate Living God, fully knows what is meant by the term, the Living God. The intellect, or reason, of the ordinary man cannot contain or convey whole-apprehension by the whole-Self. All experience, in truth, is whole; it is an unbroken continuity; it is complete in the sense that the particular in it is fully inter-related with the universal. Any formulation of it by speech-thought, descriptive, or abstractive (that is, conveying the lesson, or essence), is like a line-drawing. All speech-thought is only line-drawing. But experience, substantively, is the whole-living of the whole-apprehending whole-self. The existential mortal, to take, at random, the Buddhist analysis, consists of rūpa-vedanā-saññā-saṁkhāra-viññāṇa. Egocentric self-associations with any one or more of all these are false comprehensions of the Self; they are the product of the sense-mind activity of the unenlightened, whose perception or cognition or intellection is not whole-consciousness, and cannot re-present whole-consciousness. Here and now, in this mortality state, all is shadow-play. But here-now, immortally, having " overcome the world ", one knows by being the Truth, the Self, which is Self-realization. This " being the Self " is the Living Existent, the Living God: " I " am the Truth, the Way and the Life, as the Great Teachers taught.

The individual is like a drop in the ocean. But what exactly is the drop ? It apparently is and simultaneously is not. Arbitrarily, one may delimit a certain quantity of water and say, " that is a drop." Yes. But is it *the* drop ? Small drop, big drop. Become smaller till you are lost in the infinitely small; become bigger till you are lost in the infinitely big. Either way, the infinite prevails. Disconcertingly, the "reality" of the unmeasurable infinite contradicts and overwhelms the common-sense, factual reality of the measurable finite. But if and when, through purification, one is "re-born", then one is no longer found in finitude and lost in infinity, but one is bound in finitude —an appearance to mortal eyes—and finds the Self in the Infinite.

The obvious-to-mortal-eyes existential person is not the whole individual, but is like a signature of his. Mortal eyes see, and the beholder says, "that other man, over there"; and the separatist significance in the mortal beholder's mind, attached to the word "other", is the clear index to his unenlightenment.

Now let the true individual present himself. When he utters "I" or "you", the ordinary sense of "an other" does not cloud his apprehension. His comprehension of full relatedness is so complete, that whilst his physical senses function like any mortal's senses, interpretation by his speech-thought faculty is whole. In his all-embracing consciousness "you" are held, for his comprehension is true to his apprehension. Effortlessly, he is not confined to limited self-consciousness, but is whole-conscious. Being such, he really "knows himself". He knows that he is the undivided from "you". It is this kind of unity which lovers really seek with each other. Can lovers see?

The true individual's whole-consciousness wholly apprehending is omniscience, the sabbaññuta-ñāṇaṁ of the Buddha. The omniscient one realizes the Living God, as manifested through himself—God Immanent reigning in his kingdom—and also as manifested through what is commonly called the not-self, the external universe—Brahman regarded pantheistically, pervading the universe.

But "having established this whole universe with a fragment of myself, I remain."[1] I remain. This is the wholly-other-than, the Transcendent God, Paramātman.

The doctrine of the Person, in His aspects of Immanent God, Transcendent God, and God pervading the universe, runs through the Upanishads, and is also taught in the Gītā. Yājñavalkya

[1] Bhagavad-Gītā, X. 42.

sums up together all three aspects in his answer to Uddālaka Āruṇi's question regarding the Inner Controller, the Immortal, in:

> He who, dwelling in (each element, divinity, material thing, man) yet is other than (each element . . . man), whom (each element . . . man) does not know, whose body (each element . . . man) is, who controls (each element . . . man) from within, He is your Soul (Ātman), the Inner Controller, the Immortal.
>
> Bṛihad-Āraṇyaka Upanishad
> III.7.3–23 (abbreviated.)

Shri Kṛishṇa says in the seventh discourse of the Gītā :

> Earth, water, fire, air, ākāśa, mind, Buddhi and the ego-sense (ahaṁkāra), these form my nature in its eightfold division.
> This is my lower nature. But know that other than this is my higher nature. It is the Life-principle (Jīvabhūtaṁ), O mighty-armed, by which the world is sustained.
> . . . I am the origin and likewise the dissolution of the whole world.
> There is nothing higher than I, O Dhananjaya.
>
> 4–7.
>
> I am the eternal seed of all beings.
>
> 10.
>
> And know that natures that are of the constituents of goodness, passion and dullness are from me. I am not in them but they are in me.
>
> By these natures formed of the three constituents the whole world is bewildered. It verily knows not me, supreme above them and inexhaustible.
>
> 12, 13.
>
> . . . the man of knowledge (jñāni) . . . is established in me, the highest way.[1]
> At the end of many births the jñāni resorts to me, saying, " Vāsudeva is all."
>
> 18, 19.
>
> Those without Buddhi think of me, the unmanifest, as having manifestation, not knowing my higher nature, the changeless, the supreme.
> . . . This bewildered world knows me not, the unborn . . .
> I know the beings of the past and the present, O Arjuna, and those of the future ; but no one knows me.[2]
>
> 24–26.

[1] "I am the way, the truth and the life."—John, XIV. 6.
[2] Cf. Matthew, XI. 27, and John, I. 18.

In the eighth discourse he says:

> But beyond this unmanifested there is yet another state of being unmanifested, eternal, which perishes not when all (other) existences perish.
> This unmanifested is called the Imperishable. It is spoken of as the supreme state. They who win it return not. That is my supreme abode.
> This the Supreme Person, O Pārtha, in whom all existences abide, and by whom all this is pervaded, can indeed be gained by unswerving devotion.
>
> 20–22.

And in the fifteenth discourse he says:

> I enter the earth and support beings with my energy; I nourish all plants, becoming Soma rich in juice.
> Becoming the fire of digestion I resort to the bodies of living beings; united with the out-breath and the in-breath I digest food of the four kinds.
> And I abide in the heart of everyone; from me are memory, knowledge, and their absence. I am that which is to be known by all the Vedas; the maker of the Vedānta and the knower of the Vedas am I.
> These two Persons are in the world, the destructible and the indestructible. The destructible is all beings; standing unshakable is the indestructible called.
> But the Highest Person is another, declared to be the Supreme Self, who enters the threefold world and supports it, the changeless Lord.
> Since I am beyond the destructible, and most high above the indestructible, hence am I in the world and the Veda proclaimed the Highest Person.
> He who even thus unbewildered knows me as the Highest Person, he knowing all worships me with his whole being, O Bhārata.
>
> 13–19

* * * * *

Bṛihad-Āraṇyaka Upanishad (III.9):

> Then Vidaghda Śākalya questioned him: 'How many gods are there Yājñavalkya?'
> He answered in accord with the following *Nivid* (invocatory formula): 'As many as are mentioned in the *Nivid* of the hymn

to All the Gods, namely, three hundred and three, and three thousand and three (=3306).'
'Yes,' said he, 'but just how many gods are there Yājñavalkya ?'
'Thirty-three.'

and so, step by step, Yājñavalkya ascends to two, one and a half, and finally to one god. Then Śākalya asks :

'Which are those three hundred and three, and those three thousand and three ?'
He (i.e. Yājñavalkya) said : 'Those are only their powers. There are just thirty-three gods.'
'Which are those thirty-three ?'
'Eight Vasus, eleven Rudras, twelve Ādityas. Those are thirty-one. Indra and Prajāpati make thirty-three.'

Śākalya enquires which are the Vasus, Rudras, Ādityas, Indra and Prajāpati. Yājñavalkya states they are the elements of the external world, man, time, thunder (Indra) and sacrifice (Prajāpati). Śākalya then asks which are the six gods, the three, the two, the one and a half, and finally :

'Which is the one god ?'
'Prāṇa (Life, or Breath),' said he (Yājñavalkya).
'They call him Brahman, the Yon (tya).'

Śākalaya proceeds to elicit other God-conceptions :

'Verily, he who knows that Person whose abode is the earth, whose world is fire, whose light is mind who is the last source of every soul— he verily would be a knower of every soul—he verily would be a knower, O Yājñavalkya.'
(Yājñavalkya said) : 'Verily, I know that Person, the last source of every soul, of whom you speak.
This very person who is in the body is He.
Tell me, Śākalya, who is his god ?'
'The Immortal,' said he.

The dialogue proceeds in the same strain, and the question, "Who is his god ?" is answered as Women (the feminine element in creation), Truth, the Quarters of Heaven, Death, Life, Varuṇa and Prajāpati. The next phase of the discussion reveals that each of the divinities is based on "the heart", which is within man himself. In the final stage of the discussion:

" On what are you and your Soul based ? "

The answer is Breath, in all its divisions of in-, out-, diffused-, up-, and equalizing-breath. And Yājñavalkya sums up with:

> 'That Soul is not this, it is not that. It is unseizable, for it is not seized. It is indestructible, for it is not destroyed. It is unattached, for it does not attach itself. It is unbound. It does not tremble. It is not injured.
>
> These are the eight abodes, the eight worlds, the eight gods, the eight persons (mentioned in previous sections). He who plucks apart and puts together these persons and passes beyond them —that is the Person taught in the Upanishads about whom I ask you.'

Śākalya does not know the answer. So Yājñavalkya himself gives the final answer:

> 'Brahman is knowledge, is bliss,
> The final goal of the giver of offerings,
> Of him, too, who stands still and knows IT.[1]
>
> 1–16, abbreviated.

God made man in His own image—such is the teaching. God as Godhead, God in His Transcendence, is unknown, and cannot be known as such by the mortality-bound. But the ordinary man can, and does grow in knowledge of himself as the existential human. His sense of God, and his steadily clarifying spiritual vision through living the good life, make him more and more intimately aware of God in himself, the Immanent God who is the image of God Transcendent (image somewhat in the sense in which one says of a baby that he is the image of his parents), who is God slumbering in him. God the Universal Transcendent one worships. But God the Immanent one has to cultivate within one's living being. Any particular human, whether aided or hindered by circumstance, can allow or disallow this Immanent God to grow to His full stature and take possession of the world as its Lord, the world being the bodily man himself. Herein, the human has freedom which he may realize and bring to fruition, and thus become a liberated one, an anointed one, or which he may deny to himself and remain a bond-slave to Māra, caught in the saṁsāric round of births and deaths.

[1] Cf. Psalm XLVI. 10.

The crux of the matter is the human's voluntary effort. God Transcendent compels no person. Granted the voluntary effort, the response of God Transcendent is the equivalent of a good of universal dimensions enveloping, uplifting, purifying and exalting the puny effort of mortal man, till at last it takes him to the pinnacle of immortality. The response of God Transcendent is as inevitable and automatic as the operation of gravity on a body.

This response awakens, and makes grow, God Immanent in each existential human, who thereby grows in knowledge not only of himself as a creature (animal-human) but also as the true individual, as man made in the image of God. The narrow, false "I am" conceit,[1] and selfishness and egoism are steadily done away with as God Immanent comes into His own, and the human achieves full Self-realization, or in other words, true individuality. Herein, he knows God as Person, embodied in himself the God-become: that is, "God as Person" is the verbal expression of his inner realization. For him, God the Universal Transcendent is Supreme Being in a non-personal sense.

For him who has not yet achieved Self-realization, God the Universal Transcendent is Supreme Being in a personal sense, for he cannot but read his own nature into God the Universal Transcendent. Because he himself is a conscious being—loving wise, pure, and in short, the finite embodiment of the moral and intellectual perfections and of the "absolute" spiritual values —the Supreme Being is conceived as being the same, but in infinite measure.

If God-knowing has practical significance it is this: that man, an ethical being, shall live the blameless life, whereby the spiritual Values, which are verily the names of God, shall be made manifest. Thus are the Sons of God—Zarathustra, the Buddha, Shri Kṛishṇa, Jesus and all others who had become Brahman—distinguished from all the millions, the not-yet-become-Brahman.

[1] This is the mistaken conception that rūpa or vedanā or saññā or saṁkhāra or viññāṇa is the Self, the Atta (see above, p. 193 et seq.). The false "I am" conceit must be distinguished from the true "I am", or Self-realization (see above, p. 323).

Ordinary man describes the gods, or God, or himself, according to the way in which he is conscious of the gods, or God, or himself, namely, as a god, or God, or an " I " separate from the gods or God, or other " selves ". As he grows in insight, and love, his " I "-consciousness becomes more and more inclusive. For instance, he who truly loves becomes increasingly conscious of " we ", as if the " you " or " I ", interchangeably, is just " we ", and decreasingly conscious of himself and the beloved as distinctly separate entities. This is, perhaps, most deeply so of a parent's consciousness of self and mate and children. And yet at the same time he becomes more keenly aware of others as being unique, integrated wholes. His own " I "-consciousness, in fact, grows in wholeness. Correspondingly, the not-self, the external world, the gods, become more and more included in a single whole. And so, three thousand three hundred and six gods become One God.

At any stage of development, however, the highest conception of which the man is capable is, for him, true. It is his truth. Three thousand three hundred and six gods are all true gods! As many stages, so many conceptions, so many revelations of truth. Within one particular framework, one particular revelation is valid. As insight deepens, this revelation transforms itself into a profounder one.

Now whereas God as Self-realized by man is the Truth, that very God as orthodoxly taught, believed and described, is less, indeed much less than the Truth. Speech-thought, a line-drawing, cannot convey the bodily content. A mere creed has not the substantial reality of experience. Hence the teaching that man must not take the name of God in vain. Because this teaching, as well as other teaching, is not observed, man commits the most devilish sins in the very name of God, and even invokes the help and blessing of God before perpetrating fiendish actions. God-conception befouled with God-misconception brings tragic consequences for centuries.

And yet, on the other hand, speech-thought is an indispensable means for sharing one's own realization. Indeed, it is a duty to share: " The brāhman whose nature is unsinful, not harsh, unstained, self-restrained, who has mastered knowledge and fully traversed the Brahma-path, he rightly, being brāhman,[1] should announce the Brahma-word." Hence the presentations of the God-conceptions of the great religions. They are an indispensable stimulus and inspiration, and a comfort and guide to us common mortals, the teeming millions who are the ordinary folk. God-faith is a veritable rock of ages. It is a source of peace and healing when one is alone with the aloneness of the bruised self, of betrayed trust and shattered ideals, of the "death of one's soul."

The Indian subcontinent is uniquely rich in God-conceptions; more so now than during the early millennia.

Zarathustra's teaching of Ahura-Mazda is remarkable for being one of the earliest presentations of a wholly spiritual and ethical God, a God of transcendent righteousness and truth. Even as the other Ādityas are to Varuṇa, so the Ameshā Spentās are to Ahura-Mazda, namely His divine powers or attributes. Ahura-Mazda, Lord of Life and Wisdom, is Lord of the divine Good Mind and the father of Truth and Righteousness; He is omnipotent Sovereign; His daughter is Āramaiti, Bountiful Love and Devotion to the Most High; and He is Perfection (or Wholeness or Health) and Immortality. Ahura-Mazda, to be grasped "in purest essence and vision" (Yasna,XXXIII.7.)[2] is one and only Creator, Eternal and Unchanging, source of all Existence and of all existents, Most Radiant Spirit, the unbegotten Supreme Being, All-pervading and Omnipresent, whose own abode is Garo-Demana, the "House of Songs," the Highest Heaven. He is Master and Guide, Father, Friend and Brother to man. He is Just Accountant. He is Ruler, Protector, Watcher, Nourisher and Healer.[3]

A Zarathustrian prayer for well-being begins with the invocation: "In the name of the merciful, compassionate and forgiving Lord."

Muhammad's conception of God perhaps stands unsurpassed for its stark grandeur. God is God. No Trinity. Father of

[1] brāhman = Brahman-become; see above, pp. 355, 356. The passage quoted is one of the utterances by the Buddha on the night of the enlightenment.

[2] See *Songs of Zarathustra* by Dastur Framroze Ardeshir Bode and Piloo Nanavutty, published by George Allen and Unwin Ltd., pp. 21 & 64.

[3] Ahura-Mazda Yast.

men who are brothers in Islam. Alone, Majestic God, Beneficent, Compassionate and Merciful according to His Will; Punisher, too, according to His Will. He is Omnipotent, Omniscient and Omnipresent; Perfect, Eternal, Grateful and Wise.

Says Muhammad:

> God! There is no God but He; the Living; the Eternal; nor slumber seizeth Him nor sleep; His, whatsoever is in the Heavens, and whatsoever is in the Earth! . . . He knoweth what hath been before them and what shall be after them; yet naught of His knowledge will they grasp save what He willeth. His throne reacheth over the Heavens and the Earth, and the upholding of both burdeneth Him not; and He is the High, the Great![1]

And again:

> This is God your Lord. There is no God but He, the Creator of all things: therefore worship Him alone—and He watcheth over all things.
> No vision taketh in Him, but He taketh in (or attaineth to) all vision: and He is the Subtile, the All-informed.[2]

The Judaic tradition presents God, in Genesis, as the Most High, Creator of Heaven and Earth, Almighty, Eternal, the "God of thy fathers". With the leadership of Moses came the concept of Jehovah as a "jealous God", terrible in wrath, yet merciful and gracious. He is Lord of history, First Cause in all events (Amos, III.6), Lord of Nature (Psalm L.10; Job, XXXVIII and XXXIX), Lawgiver, Almighty, Righteous, the Living God, Holy. This Jewish God-conception leads to the Christian: God is the Supreme Being, eternal and infinite Spirit, Creator and Sovereign of the Universe, a Trinity consisting of Father, Son and Holy Ghost, Perfect, Omnipotent, Omniscient and Omnipresent, Righteous, Just and Merciful. He is Truth, Love and Grace. The heart of the Christian conception is that God is Love, a Love so absolute that God Himself, manifest on earth in Jesus Christ, the innocent and sinless one, voluntarily accepts the extremity of suffering in

[1] The Quran, Sura II, verse 256. See Rodwell's translation, The Koran, No: 380 Everyman's Library, p. 366.
[2] The Quran, Sura VI, verses 102 & 103; Rodwell, p. 326.

order to redeem mankind and wash away the sins of the world. The teaching of the boundless Grace of God finds one of its deepest expressions in Christianity.

This idea of Grace occurs as early as in the Ṛig Veda, and more definitely in the Muṇḍaka, Kaṭha and Śvetāśvatara Upanishads, and in the Gītā. The earliest Vaishnavism and Śaivism is pre-Christian. In the later developments of these Hindu monotheisms, the Grace of God is extolled with eloquent fervour.

Viṣṇu is the Supreme Spirit, Creator, Sustainer, Destroyer, the Cause of Salvation, Eternal, Omnipotent, Omniscient and Omnipresent, a God of Love constantly helping all who seek perfection, Lord of Karma, Divine Person, Perfect, joining us in our experiences, sharing our ends and working for the world. Viṣṇu Himself incarnates to save mankind whenever the necessity arises.

Śiva the Self-Existent is Eternal, Omnipresent, Omnipotent Creator through Śakti. Destroyer and Regenerator of the Universe, Liberator of Souls, Saviour and Teacher out of His great Love for mankind. He is Wisdom, Purity, infinite Grace and Bliss. Śiva does not incarnate, like Viṣṇu, but appears to His devotees to test them or to initiate them into truth. He is the only Reality of the Universe. He is infinite consciousness and unrestricted independence.

Guru Nānak taught simply: " There is but one Lord . . . in all is that One supreme." The worship of God is perfectly expressed by Kabir, loveable poet-mystic in whom Hinduism and Islam were most happily wedded: " By performing devotion He is obtained. By sincere love devotees are united with King Raghu."

The most significant, and culminating point in the search for God, is the seeker's union with God. The true brāhman, in the profoundest sense of the word, is the Brahman-become; Perfection, one of the divine attributes of Ahura-Mazda, is the goal of the Zarathustrian; and Jesus teaches, " Be ye therefore perfect even as your Father which is in heaven is perfect." And the Perfected One gives the assurance that " I and my Father in heaven are one"; the Mukta that " I am

God"—asserted in greatest variety and detail in the Gītā; in Upanishadic terms, he who has realized God affirms, "I am Brahman."

In the third chapter of the Tejobindu Upanishad, Śiva Himself, answering Kārttikeya the Kumāra's request to explain the nature of Cinmātra, the partless, non-dual essence, gives a detailed answer, in which there is this statement:

> I am the I that has given up "I",

and also this:

> I am of the nature of Parabrahman.

All descriptive terms in ordinary usage are the terms used by man, the ordinary man who has not given up "I", separate selfhood. To describe God, man uses these terms in superlative measure, thus: man has some knowledge; man is present in a particular place. God is, according to man's description, omniscient and omnipresent. These words can be truly meaningful only to the God-become, for he, being indeed of the nature of Para-brahman, fully understands. They are pathetically misunderstood by the man in the street, who interprets them encyclopædically and spatially.

The God-become uses the word "I" in the sense of the I which has wholly freed itself from the limitations of separate selfhood. The God-become's body is visible to us as any ordinary man's strictly delimited body. But his consciousness, not delimited, is unobstructive to free interplay with the-All; it is harmonious, or, rightly responsive to every influence that plays upon it; it is whole. This wholeness is its "cosmic" or "universal" quality. The God-become is "in tune with the Infinite." Omniscience, omnipotence and omnipresence hold profound meanings for him, as little comprehended by the not-yet-God-become as differential calculus by the primary schoolgoer. But whereas the advanced mathematician has a terminology which the primary schoolgoer can learn easily enough in due time, the God-become's best terminology is silence, and his second best, the one he does use, lends itself more successfully to misinterpretation than to clear understanding.

The God-become, by virtue of his attunement with the Infinite, is fully aware of the wholeness or unity of the universe in every sense, in a manner and to a degree which is well-nigh indescribable. That is his awakened sensitivity to the manifested universe. In the inner, spiritual world of the profounder levels of consciousness, he enters the eighth deliverance in samādhi wherein the limits of human consciousness are transcended and he realizes Brahman. The realized Brahman is Paramātman, and Parameśvar, reached when the yogi is " one with the Father " in prayer. This latter is God Transcendent, Brahman in the aspect of Divine Creator or Creating Spirit, while Brahman in the aspect of Prakṛiti is the root of the manifested universe, the Nature and Universe which are contingent upon the Divine Will of God Transcendent.

All the God-become are the Self-realized and Self-cognizant; and they, together with those philosophers, devotees and others who are nearly God-become, describe God in those terms which are more easily and more nearly applicable to the man-become-God. But God is not a reflection, in the measure of infinity or eternity, of any of the Sons of God, but an integration of the God-become, of a nature so much more profound and holy (more whole), as to put to shame all our superlative human terms of description, leaving only a slender element of truth in them.

So God, certainly God Transcendent, is not Supreme Being, not Person, not a He, nor a She (as with those who worshipped a Mother-Goddess and not a Father-God), not conscious and knowing and merciful and loving as we understand these words. Any described God, that is, any God-conception presented by any man, whether an ordinary person or the very image of God, is but God in the image of man, and merely indicates the limits of man's faculty of speech-thought.

God, the eternal that-which-is, can be experienced by man. God-realization is indescribable; it is the Truth, whole and unanalyzable. God-conception is describable; it reveals man the describer truly enough, but it veils God. And yet, even as the sight of the footprint of the beloved means that the beloved may be found where the footprint leads, even so the veil of God can inspire, work wonders and lead man to the blessed felicity of deathless realization.

Because we can enter profounder levels only by continuously dying to the less perfect, we cannot help defining God at first, and then, with further enlightenment re-defining God, until at last we awake to the fact that we have reached the limits of our minds, and that henceforth, particular, clearly shaped, verbally expressible knowledge must yield place completely to the whole, dimensionless, ineffable, silent and immaculate experience of God—and *that* is the realization of Brahman-Ātman, the Godhead, symbolized by AUM, the non-descriptive sound, the Word.

One can understand why, in relation to Brahman-Ātman, within which is contained, as a part of whole realization, God as taught in all the great religions of the world, those Brahman-become seers, who, like Vāmadeva, " ascended aloft and became immortal ", ended their expositions with " neti, neti."

The depths of Yājñavalkya, Uddālaka, Gotama the Buddha and all the company of the Brahmaputras ever remain un-plumbed by the mere scholar and critic. The peaks of Brahman, Ātman and Nirvāṇa stand inviolate.

He who knows not, reverences with awe a Personal God ; and the simple devotee worships with love the Divine Being. God as Person, in the simple terms of orthodox devotion, is the highest to which the millions can aspire, and is the final and full satisfaction of the deepest human needs. He who sees, in whom God Immanent is awakening from slumber, that is, the man-in-the-image-of-God is stirring into active life, looks to God Transcendent, the Supreme Being of the great monotheisms, the Person of the Upanishads, as the end of his most penetrating spiritual vision. The more he sees, the more he strips God of the personalistic element ; the naïve belief in a personal entity, *a* God who loves me, teaches me, sees me and looks after me, lives in heaven and will make me happy there, changes into God *is* Love, Wisdom, Grace, Knowledge, Existence and Bliss ; *a* God who runs the universe, works in the world, in and upon man, changes into God *is* Action—a creating, sustaining, transforming, transmuting and perfecting activity ; God *is* the universally operative integrative principle, in both the material and spiritual sense. Lastly, for him who realizes, for the Perfected Man who truly knows, God man and the universe are all subsumed in Brahman-Ātman as the ultimate reality. When he affirms, " I am Brahman ", that I is the I which has transcended the " I ", the imprisoned self-consciousness of separate selfhood. This liberated I is Self-conscious. The realization of the Godhead, Brahman, is a transmutation of the individual's consciousness.

In brief, for him who knows not, the highest is Personal God. For him who sees, the Transcendent God. For him who realizes, Brahman.

Man the living existent must realize Brahman. Till then, there are only ephemeral beliefs in a Personal God, theoretical God-conceptions and speculative philosophies of God. When what ought to be done has been done, and sin and mortality have been transcended, the supreme fulfilment of " man made in the image of God " is summed up in Tat tvam asi—That art thou.

* * * * *

In Luke, III.23–38, a line of ascent is traced from Jesus to God. In the centuries earlier Bṛihad-Āraṇyaka Upanishad, II.6 ; IV.6 ; VI.5, a line of ascent is traced from Pautimāshya to Brahman the Self-Existent. This is a line of Master and Disciple (Son). The word used in Luke is " Son ". In each case, the end point of the line is God.

According to the Old Testament, Adam is the first man, and he and Eve are the first parents of mankind. In Zarathustrian traditions, Yima and his sister-spouse Yimak, become the parents of the first mortals. In Vedic teachings Yama and Yamī correspond to Yima and Yimak.

God speaks with Adam, but only in terms of command or question, as a sovereign to a subject. Yima Kshaeta (The Good Shepherd), the third ruler over men and beasts, was one to whom the Kingly Glory of Ahura-Mazda clung. Yama chose death, abandoned his body and passed on to the other world, and became Lord of the highest of the three heavens.

God causes a deep sleep to fall upon Adam, and whilst he is asleep Eve is made by God as a helpmeet for Adam. Long before the days of Adam and Eve, men and women had realized they were helpmeets, each to the other, physically and psychically. Adam, however, on emerging out of his " sleep " (contemplation, or perhaps a trance), attains clear awareness of Eve as his spiritual helpmeet too. In the deeper levels of consciousness, in the spiritual realm itself the masculine and feminine elements of the whole psyche complement each other.[1] Adam (or man) now realizes that he, as masculine man, is completed by his alter ego, the feminine in himself, embodied in flesh and blood in Eve. The alter ego of Eve, as feminine woman, is the masculine in herself, embodied physically and externally in Adam.

In the advanced stages of meditation, the masculine and feminine elements within the contemplative attain an equilibrium (the Ātman is not male, not female.) The " first " man spoken of in the religious traditions refers to the first man who realized God within himself, in meditation. Whoever does so is a Son of God, a Brahmaputra. In St. Luke's Gospel the " genealogy " of Jesus is taken up to " Adam which was the Son of God." It is not impossible that historically the man referred to as Adam did live somewhere round 4,000 B.C. which is the old conventional date assigned to him. But he was the " first man " somewhat in the sense that the king of a country is called the " first gentleman " of that country. Adam represents, not the first human being that ever was on the earth, but the first person out of our own race of true men, which has flourished, it is thought, some twenty thousand years or more on this planet, who, in deep meditation, realized unitary Selfhood, that is realized God, and spoke about his experience to the small circle of initiates, of those who were mystics like himself. Long before Adam's day there were many gods, and innumerable god-conceptions. With Adam's realization, the many gods merge for the first time into God—the One, or That, as in the Vedas. The first profound awakening to the Unity of the Universe takes place. The tradition of this

[1] See below, p. 485 et seq.

awakening is recorded, of course, in symbolical form.

Similarly, in the Irānian tradition, Yima represents the first man who became a Son of God.

The tree of life and also the tree of the knowledge of good and evil of Genesis correspond to the Aśvattha tree of Indian teachings. Adam and Eve both eat of the forbidden fruit and fall from grace. In the very early stages of spiritual development after the first distinct awareness of God, man does not quite know the qualifications necessary for the maintenance of that God-consciousness in everyday life. He slides back into the dualistic consciousness of ordinary sense-mind life. The Serpent, or the Life-force (Prāṇa) in all its contrasting manifestations, " tempts " him. He falls back into associating his self with the fleeting things of everyday life, discriminating as good or evil whatever is pleasant or unpleasant in sense-mind terms. Having succumbed to eating the fruit of the tree of the knowledge of good and evil, he is not allowed to eat of the fruit of the tree of life and become immortal. In other words, by succumbing to the sense-mind life, he cannot establish himself in the full God-consciousness of samādhi, and maintain that God-become state in ordinary life.

Enoch, unlike Adam, transcended the domination of sense-mind life. So " God took him " ; or, he realized immortality here-now. The body, Enoch, of course died a natural death in course of time, just as any and every other body inevitably dies.

Yima Kshaeta,[1] " deceived by the fiend ", becomes " eager for supreme sovereignty instead of the service of Ahura-Mazda " —the usual sovereignty temptation, or egoism—and " The Glory was seen to flee away from him in the shape of a bird." His creatures and mankind perish, but eventually his pardon " originates from the Creator." The failure of Yima is redeemed by Zarathustra, even as that of Adam, successively, by Enoch, by Elijah, whose ascent into heaven in a chariot of fire represents his realization of immortality here-now, and by Jesus.

[1] See the Zamyād Yast of the *Khordeh Avestā*, the *Dadistan-i-Dinik* chapter 29, paragraphs 16-18, and Yasna 32, 8. See also *Songs of Zarathustra* by Bode and Nanavutty, p. 59, note 1.

Now Yama, in the Vedic tradition, chooses death—that is, deliberately puts aside the saṁsāric life—abandons his body and passes to the other world—enters samādhi—and becomes Lord of the highest of the three heavens. The " first man " of the Vedic tradition successfully maintains his God-realization.

The time comes when the seers are not only capable of God-communion through meditation, which is Yoga, but are also Perfected Men in the true and full sense of the word. These Ṛishis, seeking the eternal that-which-is, reached the end point in samādhi. With the stopping at will of the flow of discursive thought and the transcending of sense-mind disturbance, they attain the ultimate realization in super-consciousness. The ultimate is termed Ātman, the within-the-self-Infinite. But in this super-consciousness, within and without have no distinction, and the within-the-self-Infinite is identical with the universal-Infinite, termed Brahman.

No " external " God speaks to man, or controls or guides him. Man, achieving a transcendent consciousness, or, super-consciousness, realizes an indescribable Real, which he terms Ātman or God, Bṛahman or Godhead. The whole of religion is internal to man. With Ātman, man as he is at present constituted, reaches his Absolute, in terms of himself, through religion. But in the course of the millennia to come, through development brought about, this time, by himself in interaction with Nature, a new kind of living being will arise, for whom the transcendent consciousness of our men-become-God will be a common possession, and will not represent his Absolute.

It fell to the lot of individual members of the present, latest type of man on this planet to successfully activate those deeper levels of consciousness, leading to what is termed God-realization. For this reason, the present race of man is the Chosen People. All men in the world to-day are the Chosen People, the beloved of God.

* * * *

The scientist systematically investigates the phenomenal world. He gives a " compendious description of fact ", as one aspect of his work; he states scientific laws or principles as another aspect; he suggests a working hypothesis or presents a theory in relation to origins and fundamentals as still another aspect. He describes phenomena and the things he observes in terms of pointer readings, and of sense impressions. When he explains phenomena, or presents the significance of his objective descriptions of them, he talks of laws or principles, which are not objective entities but are his subjective creations, the product of his mental, or speech-thought activity. But the roots and mechanism of speech-thought activity are sense-functioning, are, indeed, electro-chemical processes in the neurones of the brain. All discursive thought activity is connected with neuronic activity in the brain, though mere neuronic activity may not be the whole of thinking as we understand the word. Perhaps, thinking is the deliberate patterning of this neuronic activity, and a word, or symbol, or sign, or "message" (as when conveyed by the look on a person's face) corresponds to each pattern. Indian philosophy has for nearly three millennia put discursive thought in the category of "material", that is, in the realm of the mortal.

The scientist investigates man in various ways, like physiology, psychology, and so on. The man of religion is primarily interested in the life of the spirit, in mysticism, in God. But, without excluding the material universe from his purview, he probes into what is anterior to, or more fundamental than man's subjective natural laws and universal principles, and man's thinking. His ultimate is called God—unlike scientific terms like energy or matter or primal stuff—immaterial Spirit, eternal and not spatio-temporal. Distinguishing between inner, spiritual world and external, material world, he propounds God Transcendent and Immanent, and as Person. If he recognizes that the Wholeness (the Holy of Holies) is the integration, and not merely the additive inclusion, of the material-energetic and the immaterial-creative (creating out of no-thing), he propounds Godhead, Brahman.

Man investigates the world, and we have science. Man realizes God, and this marks the culminating point of the practical fulfilment of religion. Some men confine, or try to confine themselves to science, others to religion. But it is likely that most men approach the total experience of their total existence through religion *and* science, and also through the other channels of man's everyday life. Science and religion have their specific terminologies, each of which represents the world in a different way from the other. The attempted meeting point of the two, that is, of factual investigation and spiritual realization, is in terms of knowing and of knowledge. There is so deep a meaning to the word, and to the creature, man: a thinker; an apprehender and comprehender; a cognizer and re-cognizer; a right relator, or unifier, or a bringer together of "material" and "spiritual"—and this last is one of the meanings of "Blessed are the peacemakers", for the ultimate and fundamental peace is the peace between body and spirit in each person. This joining together of spirit and matter takes place in the very beginning, in the womb itself, an unconscious joining whose final fruition, if achieved, is the conscious Brahman-realization in adult maturity.

The joined spirit and matter, the manner and point at which the buddhic knowing of God-realization and the manasic knowing of factual investigation attempt to link with each other, is precisely the realm of mystery. This is where a cloud of unknowing, in various senses, "shuts out the light." This realm of mystery has its counterparts in the creation of a work of art by the artist, the intuitive insight of the philosopher, the flash of inspiration of the mathematician and the scientist as he solves a problem, and in other ways. What makes a creation, in contrast to a mere putting together, is the mystery.

By virtue of what he is, man makes one approach to Reality through science, or the knowledge of things. He makes another approach through God-realization in samādhi, or prayer. But the meaning of Reality in the context of the scientific approach shows certain differences from that of the religious. The two meanings cannot be stated in a single form. This is where man is constantly defeated by virtue of what he is at present, constitutionally. He has not that "dimension of consciousness", that faculty whereby he can see or discover how energy is, or becomes matter, how Brahman is, or becomes this-All.

So science of necessity stops short at the world of discursive thought, and of verbal description.

And from samādhi, returning to corporeality, the link between the formless (arūpa) and the formed (rūpa), between silence and speech, between being and becoming, the still and the moving, is suspended.

Like the mountaineer deprived of the will to climb beyond a certain height, is science. Like a mountain-dweller perishing in the plains, is the God-become. No wonder the Buddha said:

> Hard is the infinite to see ; truth is no easy thing to see ;
> Craving is pierced by him who knows ; for him who seeth, naught remains.
>
> Udāna, VIII.2.

Because of the unsolved, and at present insoluble problem, of *how* Brahman becomes this-All, some thinkers muddled up the true individual (the undivided from the Whole) with the fleeting elements of the existential. It was this error the Buddha sought to remove in his anattā teaching. The reality of Brahman he embodied in his " Him I call a brāhman, who . . . "

When a yogi or an arahant " knows " Brahman, when a Christ is in communion with the Father, " praying in secret ", what is the connecting thread between that and his existential sense-mind which does not overleap speech-thought ? Vāyu, the Antaryāmin or Inner Controller, as Yājñavalkya said to Uddālaka Āruṇi ; and ākāśa as the material medium which Vāyu uses, as Yājñavalkya said to Gārgī. It *is* awkward, to always translate Vāyu as wind, and ākāśa as space !

The scientist's investigation of the nature of matter leads him to a dematerialized ultimate stuff, to a concept of energy, as the source of the substantial universe.

The tendency of many religious philosophers is to present God as a concrete real.

What early India thought on these matters may be represented diagrammatically as on the opposite page.

* * * *

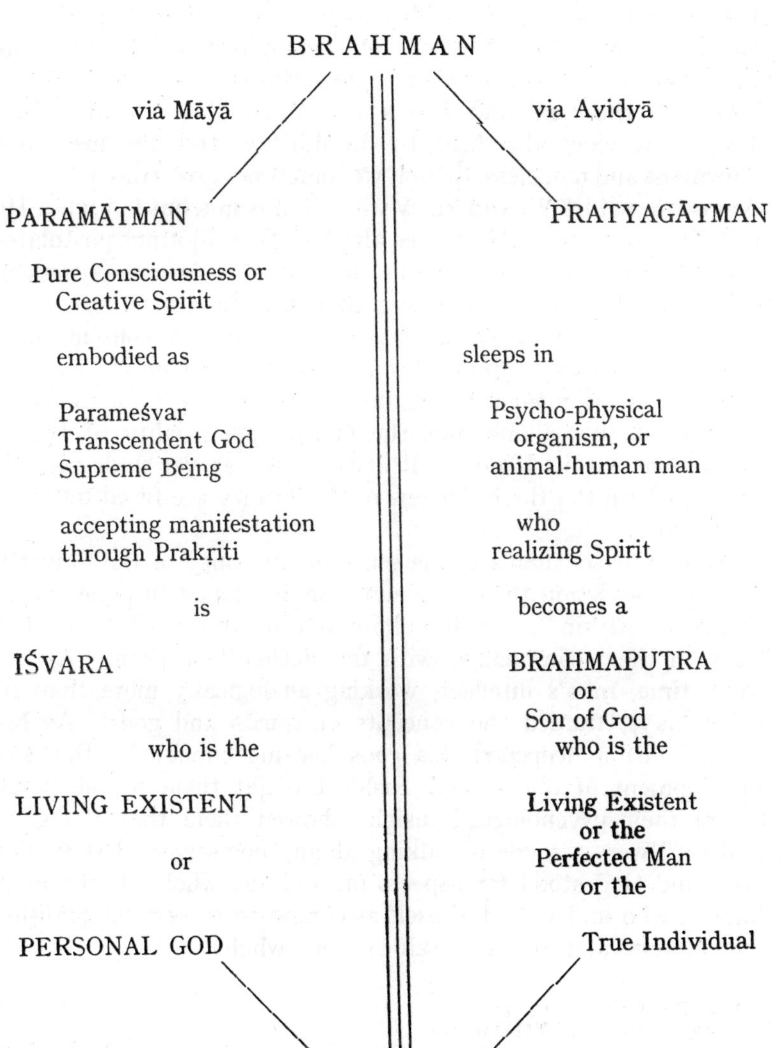
PARABRAHMAN ≡ MŪLAPRAKṚITI
OR
BRAHMAN
via Māyā
via Avidyā
PARAMĀTMAN
PRATYAGĀTMAN
Pure Consciousness or Creative Spirit
embodied as
sleeps in
Parameśvar
Transcendent God
Supreme Being
Psycho-physical organism, or animal-human man
accepting manifestation through Prakṛiti
who realizing Spirit
is
becomes a
ĪŚVARA
BRAHMAPUTRA or Son of God
who is the
who is the
LIVING EXISTENT
or
PERSONAL GOD
Living Existent or the Perfected Man or the True Individual
ĀTMAN

Brahman, the undifferentiated unity, has its correspondences in Greek and Western thought: in Plato's the Good, or the One, relegated beyond Reality, beyond Essence (The Republic, VI.19); before Plato, Eucleides of Megara was the first to identify the Good and the One; Clement of Alexandria, though objecting to "God is beyond Reality", nevertheless says that He is "beyond the One and above the Monad" (Clement, Paed. I.8.71; a view also held by Iamblichus and Proclus), and "formless and nameless, though we sometimes give Him names";[1] Augustine said, "We can know what God is not, but not what He is" (De Trinitate, VIII. 2; see also VII.5);[2] Plotinus postulates the One, which is superconscious and not unconscious, possessing a higher form of consciousness than the discursive reason, or even than the intuitive perception of spirit, a consciousness which is immediate apprehension;[3] Plotinus's One is ineffable, and we can say what it is not, but not what it is;[2] for Eckhart, Godhead is not Being, but the eternal potentiality of Being, containing within Himself all distinctions, as yet undeveloped, and in whom the three Persons of the Trinity are fused into one Godhead.

As very early man's vague sense of the unity of the universe grew in conviction through feeling, he developed the practice of "looking within", which culminated in the samādhi of the yogi, in the "communion with the Father" of Jesus. At the same time, man's intellect, working analogically more than in other ways, framed the concepts of spirits and gods. As his inward vision deepened, his gods became ennobled. But the development of the ancient Ṛishis brought them to the point where their psychological insight showed them that the gods and God were a mode of talking about themselves, that is, the gods and God stood for aspects of, and the whole of, the man himself who understood himself as composed of various qualities and powers, and also as a self-existent whole.

[1] Cf. Ṛig Veda, I. 164. 46.

[2] "Neti, neti", said Yājñavalkya.

[3] Cf. "Brahman is that which is free from all vehicles, which is Absolute Consciousness, devoid of particularities."—Sarvasāra Upanishad; also, the Buddha's eighth deliverance, and the yogi's samādhi; and also, the Bhagavad-Gītā, VIII. 18-21.

The Ṛishi, through dhāraṇā and dhyāna realized consciously that despite the obvious-to-the-senses separateness of his bodily being from " other objects ", to his inner awareness all objects were literally of one primordial stuff, and " his own " consciousness was in reality a whole consciousness, Caitanya, in Hindū terminology, to which the English " Pure, or Absolute Consciousness " is perhaps the nearest equivalent, but which is far removed from consciousness in the sense-mind context.

But just as the man-become-God, the Ṛishi, is Living God, so too, the Ṛishi saw, is the universe ; so too, are " other " men in some degree or other. The difference is that in the Ṛishi, man the microcosm has full awareness of Godhood, which the not-yet-become-God has in dim degree and has still to achieve in fullness. God, to the whole-conscious, is an integrated unity. The Ṛishi sees simultaneously separate men and one Man-kind ; God there, above, beyond the separate objects and individuals of manifestation, and also, God-Allness. The consciousness of the man in the street does not function in that way. To him, the above is a string of words : jargon, if he feels confused or repelled by it ; " strange ideas " if, through a mixed superiority-inferiority feeling, he is fascinated or drawn to it. The earnest seeker amongst ordinary men will partly mis-grasp whatever the Ṛishi says ; for however great a scholar or brilliant an intellect the seeker may be, he will still look *at* God, for he cannot yet know God by being one with God.

Thus the God-is-ness of the Ṛishi who has realized God through conscious, whole experience, is always translated by the non-realizing-through-experience but seeing-from-a-distance sense-mind observer, as God as an entity, a Being, a Person, and so on. He cannot rid himself of the deeply ingrained feeling of I *and* you, of I *and* things, the world, in short, of objective separateness. He cannot realize himself as non-prismatic, as a non-splitter of one light into many colours. So for him, it is always I and God, two separate entities.

Thus God Transcendent, Maker, Creator and so on, a partly or wholly-other-than, a pantheistic or non-pantheistic God, a Trinity or Triune Unity or Single God, are all abstractions made by man's speech-thought faculty. They are extracted out of the living context of the Ṛishi's whole realization by a non-Ṛishi, and then planted before man's gaze as a separate entity to be worshipped. And usually, these abstractions, purporting to describe, or stammeringly confess the eternal That-which-is —for indubitably God IS—plant God outside, over and beyond the universe, or partly in and partly out, and so on.

The difficulty is that one can no more place and time the eternal than one can attempt to measure the specific gravity of a symphony.

Brahman as the subject or object of sense-discursive thought enquiry and statement is unreal, a distorted picture.

Brahman as realization in samādhi is the All-Truth, the whole-reality.

Out of the spoken Brahman, the Śabda Brahman, emerge philosophies—speech-thought activity.

In the silent realization of Brahman is the perfect worship of God.

The philosophies urge and stimulate and make men move about (and moving about may or may not include moving forward) in search of God. They are necessary.

The silent worship, here-now, immortal, makes men live God and manifest God in their every thought and feeling, word and deed. Their lives speak God—they are the figures like Zarathustra and the Buddha and Jesus, if they are in touch with the folk; they are the Pacceka Buddhas if they do not publicly teach.[1] But the Ones who publicly teach, out of compassionate understanding for the limitations of mortals, simply say Father, or Allāh, or Ahura-Mazda, or Rāma, or Mahādeva, using such names as a focal point for strenuous, unremitting endeavour to live the holy life, for that perfect ethical fulfilment which is indispensable to inward, conscious realization.

* * * *

There are those who say that man's innermost longing and need is for a God who is a warm, living Person, and not a bloodless abstraction.[2] They detest "losing oneself altogether in

[1] Nevertheless, "They also serve who stand and wait."

[2] Said the carnivorous tiger to the vegetarian elephant; "How *can* you find sustenance in such bloodless stuff!" The tiger, however, showed no interest in finding out how the elephant did obtain full nourishment from such stuff.

Brahman." So, too, in relation to Nirvāṇa as taught by the Buddha, they recoil from a "bloodless Nirvāṇa." They dub the profundities of Indian thought as nihilistic, meaningless, vacuous.

The truth of God is not to be found as long as a man is conditioned by craving for the satisfaction of his emotional, intellectual and spiritual wants. "Losing oneself altogether in Brahman" is a misinterpretation of union with Brahman. Again, with regard to what is one's state after the death of the body, the Buddha and the Upanishads clearly taught that there is neither survival of separate entity nor annihilation. "What *is* it then?" asks mortal man. "Practise the discipline. Realize the Immortal. And then you will not ask such questions, nor make such statements," is the answer.

All the various conceptions of God have their uses and their significances. They are emotionally and spiritually satisfying and intellectually acceptable to different men according to their stage of development. Each and all of these conceptions—the gods of sky, wind, wisdom, love; or the Father who is maker of heaven and earth and all therein; or the Supreme who is in man and in everything, and is also above and beyond and controlling all men and all things, and so on and so else—can help us to realize that all that is made by God is holy, is sacred. Reverencing all, we can more truly evaluate all, a little more easily work to fulfil "God's Will" for all, and a little more clearly realize the best life in the divine sense. The concept of God as Father, Saviour, Redeemer and so on, is, on the one hand, the supremely exalted reflection of the good in our human selves, and on the other, a consolation and help to us in our helplessness or misery. Best of all, it is an inspiration to us to cultivate those very aspects of fatherhood, justice, kindness and all those virtues which in perfection are the glorious fruition of our humanity. So it is well to accept, and to let be, the conceptions men hold dear according to their own understanding and need. Understanding this, Shri Kṛishṇa taught: "Let not him whose knowledge is complete, unsettle (or mislead) the dull, of imperfect knowledge" (Bhagavad-Gītā, III.28). By the time a man has profited from the inspiration of one concept he is ready for something deeper ; and in fact, if his growth as a whole person continues unhindered, lesser concepts keep transforming into deeper concepts, culminating in profound realization.

Fixed beliefs, fixed intellectual moulds (strings of words), are man's real enemy. All the great faiths present God in much the same terms. All the omni-s are there, and the human virtues and values in supreme degree : an inspiring picture of perfection, even as it should be. But any one picture has a different content of meaning for each single person, for the content depends upon his own development and capacity. Consider, for instance, the changes in the meaning of " father " during one's lifetime : to the baby, he is so strong, so sustaining, so safe ; to the child, he is still these things, and also he is authority which must be obeyed, and to him may be taken all troubles ; in adolescence, one feels that father is at least somewhat like, if not quite like most men, distinguished by good points as well as not quite such good points ; to the adult, father is something different again, and to the mature middle-aged or old man he is something yet more different. And every one of these meanings is in reality only a partial truth about father ; sometimes it is quite an illusion, at times even tragic. How much less chance there is to conceive aright the Fatherhood of God whom we ordinarily know not and see not, if there is such a faulty understanding of father whom we constantly experience !

It is necessary, therefore, to develop psychological and spiritual insight of a high order, to penetrate and grasp the rich content of meaning of religious teachings. For God can work through man only so far as man comes close to God—the human camel must make himself strong enough to carry the last straw of God's overwhelmingly generous gifts. God is sufferingly bound to the extent of man's limitations—look at Him on the Cross to understand this. But man is free to endeavour heroically, with excited joy (and this is the one and only legitimate pleasure in life which man may chase as hard as he likes for all his days), to dissolve away these limitations. In this task he is sweetly compelled by God's Will, so that the Godly purposes may be fulfilled. This impulsion is no compulsion. It is a drive inherent in each man ; but it needs to be harnessed and utilized. Any person, wilfully and self-consciously but Self-unconsciously, can resist this drive. Truly enough, man's freedom is of a peculiar nature. Man is free to resist God either through his ignorance or his wilful choice. But he is doomed to failure if he does resist. He is free to work with God through self-understanding and self-restraint, till through utter self-purification he finds Self-realization wherein is contained his absolute freedom. The fact is that the common or garden meaning of freedom, namely, to do or obtain or think just what one likes, even if brought to heel within the constraints of social living, is false, and all too often leads to evil. It is God's Will alone which ultimately fulfils itself, through evolution, emergence and integration as far as the universal process is concerned, and through the fruition of the religious life where man made in the image of God is concerned. God's Will has its human counterpart in man's disciplined, creative imagination. God's Will is of eternity ; man's creativeness is of time. But time is on God's side, whereas for man as a conscious creature, the speed at which time rolls on is of his own determining. For " Time is too slow for those who wait, too swift for those who fear, too long for those who grieve, too short for those who rejoice ; but for those who Love, time is Eternity." God is Love, and God Loves. And in that Love-Eternity time has no option but to be on God's side. Again, not a compulsion but true freedom. Time, like a sleeping cat looking like a lump of unobtrusive self-existence, lies on the hearthrug of God's Eternity.

On man rests the responsibility of converting time—his time as he experiences it ; interminable, wearying, exciting, swift as lightning—into the Eternity in which God IS from everlasting to everlasting. The man-become-Brahman, who has won the deathless Immortal, is one who has fulfilled this responsibility. So his life on earth is regarded as a thing apart, and his personality is sacred. Hence the masses, with a natural instinct and a justifiable judgment worship the man-become-God as God's vicegerent, or as God himself. And this is the only context in which " He " is a correct and real appellation of God.

One can see now, the need and significance of God as a Person. It is the recognition by man that he himself is a person, not person in the sense of a mask (persona) which hides, but of a real, living appearance which represents the true individual, the undivided from the whole. The word God, the All-Good, sums up as conscious aspiration the unfolding universal process as manifest in man. God Transcendent represents the reservoir of infinite potentiality, universal both materially and spiritually, which is reflected or embodied microcosmically in individual man. God Transcendent answers only one prayer—the prayer to be united with Him.[1] But his divine (= giving) agents, " the gods ", freely bestow what man prays for—a case of the natural functioning of spiritual and psychological law. But let man beware what he prays for, because neither God (obedient Master of His Laws, and hence no miracle-monger of the conjuring trick type, leaving the multitude of devotees, and some others, gaping spiritually), nor the gods can withhold the full consequence of all the not-consciously-desired and not-bargained-for implications involved in the prayer. This is one of the innumerable psychologically wise teachings in which Hinduism is so rich. In any prayer, its godly element evokes God's response, and its devilish element (as in some prayers for success, happiness, victory and all else that is tainted with man's lust and egoism, hatred and delusion) is Satan's opportunity. God's response is invariably purificatory; the devil's, fattening, in preparation for the holocaust to follow.

God the Person—Īśvara, Viṣṇu, Kṛishṇa, Bhagavān, Lord, *my* God—represents the actual culmination which man's personality has to attain. It is the pattern of the perfect fruition of individuality, of self-existent wholeness. Until a man is well on the way to realization, the Personal God concept should not be displaced, and cannot be displaced without peril. The Īśvara conception itself has still to reach its fruition, because man himself has not yet fully understood, through achievement, true individuality.

The devout Buddhist seeing and worshipping the Buddha as God, the Christian seeing and worshipping the highest revelation

[1] See above, p 276.

of God in Jesus Christ, the Hindu in Rāma, or Kṛishṇa, is a necessary step towards the flowering of true individuality, in which the ego is wholly transcended. A man needs a Personal God because he is not strong enough in himself and has to lean on a support, or because he is a devotee by nature and must have a worthy Object of adoration. A man dispenses with a Personal God, naturally and rightly, because he has realized Brahman, or violently and wrongly, because he is ignorant, or arrogant, or a conceited fool.

Now man to-day still mistakes ego-ridden separate selfhood for true individuality. God the Person is also cognized, therefore, as a separate entity instead of as the Self-existent whole. This is the root of egoism and selfishness. The conception of a Personal God who is a separate entity, painted over with all the virtues that a particular man or sect or society approve of (and the virtues are merely ephemeral concepts tenuously held by man in his temporal aspect), is the very root of separateness, division and disunity, of that absurd conceit still afflicting some men, that " I " am God's chosen one appointed to conquer and rule and civilize " you ", and of that lust for spiritual and moral merit which smugly pursues its own selfish ends, provided the pursuit can be hung on the peg of " carrying out the Lord's behests." God, misconceived as a separate entity, is indeed a root of evil! Hence the old saying, " Demon est deus inversus."

Moreover, no proper understanding of the problem of good and evil is possible as long as the fountainhead of existence is a separate entity, a Personal God conceived by man in the image of man's virtues and capabilities.

It is man's task to free himself from his misconceptions regarding his own self. Then only will he become capable of a true Personal God conception, necessary for the flowering of true individuality.

But this involves the understanding of God as impersonal Creative Spirit, for no conception of personality can be whole without the understanding of impersonality.[1] The understanding of the Transcendent " I remain " of Shri Kṛishṇa after

[1] In the modern world, the discipline of science and the scientific method is the most powerful, single aid to man for developing the capacity for impersonal, objective approach and understanding.

" having established this whole universe with a fragment of myself ", of Śiva the " only reality of the universe, He who is infinite consciousness and unrestricted independence ", of Paramātman, enables one to understand God as non-human, non-particularized, and non-limited or infinite Creative Power, the source of all manifestation, without which understanding man can only conceive of the Personal God as a separate, limited, humanized entity. Personality is but limited manifestation, contained within Whole Existence.

But a true understanding of this, in its turn, demands one final stage: the profound, the silent, the full, the void; as Eckhart says, the desert, the darkness. This is other than expressible in speech-thought. Nevertheless, certain considerations may be of some interest. Man presses his enquiry into the innermost nature of things with an objective, extraverted, impersonal, philosophic and scientific approach, or with a subjective, introverted, personal, inspirational, mystic and religious approach. The approaches are only broad classifications; each has elements of the other in it. Along the one path, man ends his quest with Param-Brahma; along the other, with Mūlaprakṛiti. Seeing that either way one touches infinity, "within" along the one path, "without" along the other, and seeing that within and without are in truth but one Whole, it can be seen that Param-Brahma and Mūlaprakṛiti are identical.

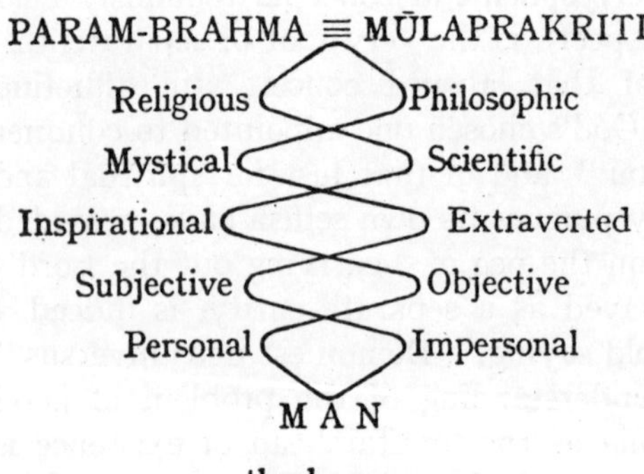

Investigate the way of religion, and man designates the ultimate by the word God; the way of science, and the word is Energy. The word God has remained constant for millennia; whereas with science, the word is inconstant, for the name of Energy only day-before-yesterday was ultimate particles or atoms. But the point to be respected is that it is erroneous to treat science and materialism (" materialism " and " material " in the old sense of the words) as synonymous terms. It would be equally erroneous to hazard the statement that science is proving God. Science and religion each reveal that man has the capacity to investigate the truth, and come to know it, in different ways. What he comes to know, one way or the other, is not *the* truth. His knowledge is only a representation of the eternal that-which-is-through his sense-mind activity.

He represents the what-is in several ways, such as Art, Science, Philosophy, Religion and Mysticism, his particular way being mainly determined by the nature of his own psycho-physical constitution. Each of these ways is the vehicle of a valid revelation of the what-is. The expressed revelation is a representation of his whole-experience, or the measure of his conscious comprehension of what he continuously apprehends. Science neither contradicts nor confirms Art or Religion. But the discipline of science can, for instance, enable a man to know at least some of the senses in which not to translate the word " made " in the statement " God made . . . "

Now science, far from being an enemy of religion and the good life, far, far from dethroning God, is the most potent means for clearing out of our minds our misconceptions of God. These misconceptions are the product of personalistic statements which are correct in the human context, but are false when applied to God. *I* want, feel, command, work and so on. Not for a moment is it true that God " wants ", " feels ", " commands ", " works " and so on. The disciplined few understand the sense in which these personalistic statements are made. The millions either believe them literally in a human sense, or unknowingly misuse words.

The study of science can so discipline our minds—discipline, and not merely substitute the conditioning and limitation of a different set of words—that one can be more wary of the pitfalls while exploring the what-is along the paths of religion and mysticism.

One other point should be noted. Man's simplest physical experiences, the objects of the material world, and his growing understanding of these, are the root-sources of his most abstract concepts, for it is impossible for the technique and faculty of speech-thought ever to come into being in the absence of "matter". Param-Brahma and Mūlaprakṛiti are one.

Science will go on and on, acquiring understanding of the what-is through its investigation of matter and phenomena. The difficulty confronting the world to-day is not due to its becoming materialistic, but to its being insufficiently materialistic. Drive this "becoming materialistic" to its bitter end, and you will suddenly be faced with the God-finder peeping over the other side of the mountain top! Either path, religion or science, is a hard path, driving man to the extremity of endurance. But "on whatsoever path a man approaches me, on that path do I meet him." In that meeting man finds Himself, ennobled and purified, the God-become and no longer the God-seeking.

In the process of seeking, man translates, denominates the God-in-darkness as Personal God, as God Transcendent and Immanent, a subject for talk; and although talk externalizes, it can also inspire. When seeking has ended in realization, Brahman is the Word, the Light of Lights.

What man experiences continuously is spirit-matter. What he tells of is himself. What he realizes is truth, himself-God or Brahman.

In the world of speech-thought exchanges between man and man, each mode of presentation of God is necessary to the other modes. Without Brahman, Personal God and Transcendent God are less meaningful, less true. Without Personal God, Brahman remains less true, even incomprehensible, a mere abstract concept, unrealizable. When God-conception culminates in God-realization, then Personal God and Transcendent God are integrated into the undifferenced unity, Brahman.

This Brahman is realized by the deliberate withdrawal from the disturbance of all uprising and passing away, of all that appertains to and constitutes manifestation and mortality, space and time. This Brahman is realized by the deliberate entry, superconsciously, into the stillness, into the "Peace that passes understanding" which cannot be desecrated by the universal hubbub of thrones, dominations, princedoms, virtues and powers warring against demons and devils, Mammon and

Beelzebub, nor by the hue and cry of wordly activity and process. Here-now, immortally, infinitely, really, is Godhead, Brahman, the Light of Lights, in which is integrated all. No " one " can follow " another " into this Brahman, for all the criteria of the manifested universe and of existential being are not annihilated but resolved into the indescribable Eternal. The one goes directly to the ONE. He who is lighted up as the Light of Lights is the one who truly knows Transcendent and Immanent God, and the Living God, God as Person. God-realization is the perfection of God-conception. Without Brahman-realization, all God-conception is the Real distorted by false conception. But in that supreme Brahman-realization is the Ultimate Reality, is the absolute fulfilment of man.

Section E

KARMA : JUSTICE : REDEMPTION

It is convenient for most practical purposes to regard the world process as a succession of separate acts, or discontinuous events. And again, it is convenient to think of a man as the actor performing acts in a particular situation, the actor, the act and the situation being regarded as distinct and separate from each other. In fact, however, the dynamic world process in its wholeness is one continuous action. The egocentric view puts the viewer out of the context of the whole process and makes him say, " There is the situation, and that is what I did ", instead of recognizing that " This is the process going on here-now." And yet, looking on at another person performing action, this same viewer is quite capable of perceiving objectively, " That is the process going on there-now ", that actor, his action and his environment all being seen as a whole, dynamic process.

This process, which includes nature, man, and the workings of the Divine in and through nature and man, is the karmic process. It is said to take place in accordance with the law(s) of karma, a term which of necessity is very general. It is often equated with the term, the law of causation. This may be accepted, provided cause is regarded not exclusively as something distinct from an effect, but also as that which is taken up into, or becomes transformed into the effect. For instance, when rain falls, we see that a tree gets wet. We also know that the tree absorbs the moisture and continues to grow. Man the observer can arbitrarily separate a cause from its effect, but the actual event is a continuous interaction, or a continuous transforming.

As far as sense-mind observations and experimental verifications go, it is only phenomena with which man can deal. As far as understanding, and the mental processes of framing hypotheses and abstracting generalizations go, it is the sense perception of phenomena which are the "material" for the abstract mental processes. Gravitation, for example, cannot be seen or heard. But a knowledge of the law of gravitation allows us to construct almanacs, or to guide rockets, and so on; and the concept of gravitation enables us to explain certain phenomena in a manner which satisfies our reason. So, too, with the law of karma, knowledge of the law is a guide to action, and the concept of karma enables us to understand various aspects of life in a manner which satisfies our reason. Whether this concept of a universally operative principle will satisfy us or not, depends upon the extent to which our perception and our reasoning faculty are developed.

Partly in the sense in which one speaks of a law of nature, one may speak of the law of karma.

Each society has its system of man-made laws, written and unwritten, in which rewards and punishments play their part. As that society changes with the passage of time, so do some of these laws change, and also the rewards and punishments to be meted out. Just as the reward-punishment ideology plays its part in the life of a society, so, too, is it associated with the operation of the law of karma in the minds of many people.

Further, there are what are called the laws and demands of our being, biological, psychological and spiritual. The laws of our spiritual being, that is, the laws of God Immanent in us, are intimately bound up with the laws of God Transcendent. The laws or demands of our biological and psychological being are in part general, in so far as any and every man is affected by them, such as the urge for preservation and the urge for self-assertion, and in part specific, such as the unique form in which a particular person strives to fulfil these urges. The laws and demands of our biological and psychological being are determined by our individual psycho-physical constitution, which is a product of the karmic process. As we change, those laws and demands also change. For instance, we may live lustily, in response to the demands of the psycho-physical organism, at the age of twenty; whereas at fifty, we could, and may, live sacrificially, partly because of constitutional changes psycho-physically, and partly because God has played, and continues to play a part. God Immanent in us is one determiner of our ethic—and ethic is the main root of the art of living—in the light of which we purify and improve mind and heart and daily behaviour; and God Transcendent is the source of the universal, omnipotent drive to perfection and immortality. The opportunity available to each for utilizing the power of the Will of God, and the extent to which God Immanent in each one of us can creatively utilize this power, transform our natural being, and transmute our unawakened into the awakened consciousness, is the fruit of our karma. Our karma puts no hindrance on the path to perfection. Even an obstacle is in reality a challenging stimulus, indispensable for activating, educating, maturing and perfecting the qualities and potentialities within ourselves. Whether a man sides with God Immanent in him and uses the stimulus for fulfilling the Divine Will, or whether he remains blind to God Immanent in him and is affected by the stimulus to his own confusion and undoing, is largely his own free choice. Largely, but not entirely. For the weight of suffering, the explosion of passion, or the overwhelming consequences of some mistake—each of which is his karma—may prove too much for him. Too much, only temporarily, even if it lasts that lifetime. The man, and his karma (indeed, in a profound sense, the man is his karma) emerge ultimately into Brahman and that Divine Action whose shadow-play is the activity of the manifested universe.

Karma is existential; it is of the realm of mortality. The Maitri Upanishad says:

> For by tranquillity of thought,
> Karman, good and evil, one destroys.
>
> VI.34.

In this context, "destroys" should be understood also as "transcends". What is destroyed is man's bondage to process (the being tied to the wheel of saṁsāra) through the stoppage of self-association with the objects of sense, and the destruction of the āsavas (the taints or cankers). What is transcended is that sullied consciousness (the sundered consciousness which raises up "this" world in disharmony with "that" world) which is the source of all that action (karma) which spells dukkha. Although, even for an enlightened one, consequence in the world of phenomena is unquestionably present while he continues to live bodily, all karma as a force for further self-becoming and the perpetuation of dukkha is destroyed and transcended.

Under karma, then, may be included natural law, human law and divine law. Human experiences, as whole events, involve simultaneously the natural world, the human world and the divine world; these three are one world in reality, but it is convenient to consider the subject under this threefold classification.

The main obstacle to a right understanding of karma is man's tendency to use his personal ideas of fairness, rightness and justice, all of which are significant and applicable only within the limited sphere of human relations, as criteria for judging universal process. Sinner and saint alike are reduced to pulp after an accidental 2,000-foot drop; and the atom bomb exercises no selective action with respect to its victims. Such questions as "Is it fair that the saint should suffer horribly like the sinner?", and "How can we believe in God and justice when innocent[1] women and children by the thousand are so helplessly murdered and mutilated and made to suffer untold agony?", are questions which do not apply to the context of the events concerned. Given all the forces at play under certain conditions, precisely those events must take place. The moral virtues or the unique value of a person to his fellows, or the reverse, have no influence one way or the other upon natural law. The forces which demonstrate natural law, like gravity or atomic energy, are non-moral, un-feeling, un-seeing. According as they are used are the consequences of such use.

The reward-punishment ideology is also a great obstacle to the right understanding of karma. Many believe that since every thought or feeling, word or deed must produce a result, what is pleasant or unpleasant now for an individual is the exact reward or punishment for past good or evil done by the same

[1] Nocuousness, by implication, being a characteristic of the adult male?

individual: an eye for an eye, a tooth for a tooth. Human conventions for exchange and barter, for adjusting or regulating human relations through a social code or a system of law, do form part of the karmic process. But no individual is a wholly separate person, for he is intimately inter-related with others around him. Cause, responsibility and consequence are not generated and borne by, and meted out to each person exclusively. We receive the legacy of others, are interlocked in action and its consequences with others, and bequeath our own legacy to yet others in our turn. It is a fact that many good people go through a life of suffering, many knaves are successful and seem happy, many evil-doers lord it in the world, and that many idealists are frustrated and saints are mishandled, all of which is inexplicable in terms of a shallow reward-punishment theory, or of naïve conceptions of fairness and justice here and now.

Karmic law is not a code prefabricated by a divine or devilish authority at the beginning of time, functioning mechanically as a senseless, merciless, unconstructive, retributive process. If it were, growth, development, evolution, redemption would become inconceivable. The Bṛihad-Āraṇyaka Upanishad says:

> According as one acts, according as one conducts himself, so does he become. The doer of good becomes good. The doer of evil becomes evil. One becomes virtuous by virtuous action, bad by bad action.
>
> IV.4, 5.

> 'Yājñavalkya,' said he (Jāratkārava Ārtabhāga), 'when a man dies, what does not leave him?'
>
> 'The name. Endless, verily, is the name. Endless are the All-gods. An endless world he wins thereby.'
>
> 'Yājñavalkya,' said he, 'when the voice of a dead man goes into fire, his breath into wind, his eye into the sun, his mind into the moon, his hearing into the quarters of heaven, his body into the earth, his soul (ātman) into ākāśa, the hairs of his head into plants, the hairs of his body into trees, and his blood and semen are placed in water, what then becomes of this person (puruṣa)?'
>
> Ārtabhāga, my dear, take my hand. We two only will know of this. This is not for us two (to speak of) publicly.'
>
> The two went away and deliberated. What they spoke of was karma (action). What they praised was karma. Verily, one becomes good by good action, bad by bad action.

Thereupon Jāratkārava Ārtabhāga held his peace.

III.2.12, 13.

" One becomes good by good action, bad by bad action." Precisely! Apart from the immediate pleasure or pain, and the more lasting joy or grief associated with the performance of action, the significant consequence of action is the growth in the skills and qualities characteristic of that action, and not a specific reward or punishment as laid down by a predetermined code. The nature of the total event, or the nature of what happens to us, is intimately related to what we are ourselves. We ourselves are responsible, in some measure or other, in some manner or other, for any and every situation in which we find ourselves. If we act rightly, to the best of our ability, in any situation, moral growth and mental development are the karma vipāka (action and its fruit) of good action, irrespective of the sensational pleasure or pain, and emotional joy or grief experienced in the performance of that action. Since such moral and mental growth is a force for greater good, the trend is towards fulfilment. In the supreme fulfilment is Nirvāṇa, that blissful peace which is the transcendence of both joy and grief. This is made possible through the operation of karma.

Is karma an ethical law or process? Human ethic, and the functioning of human conscience, is each associated with human choice where two or more ways of action are open, such action involving man's relationship and duties towards his fellows and his environment, to himself, and above all, to God. Human ethic cannot intrude into the field of non-moral physical nature. Nor does it intrude upon, but nevertheless leads into the supra-ethical world of God, for it finds its consummation in the transcendental ethic of the man-become-Brahman, in which are subsumed non-moral natural law and moral human ethic. Human ethic or morality, together with human fairness, rightness and justice, by comparison with natural law and transcendental ethic, is the most changeable factor of the three, although certain reciprocal obligations and decencies forming part of human ethic remain stable and rigid through aeons.

Karma, then, is non-ethical with regard to physical nature, sometimes ethical and sometimes unethical with regard to man, and apparently non-ethical but in reality supra-ethical with respect to God. For God, karma is a word descriptive of the way in which the universe is run. Brahman scatters galaxies away from each other, like bubbles blown towards the ends of the universe. Brahman, wearing our Milky Way as a divine halo, evokes our wonder, reverence and delight, and also our apprehension (fear) of the Mystery. Brahman makes the suns, planets and moons run their courses with meticulous accuracy —the Law which deviates not a hair's breadth. Brahman withholds the rain and warmth and light, as believed by ancient peoples, or hurls the storm and tempest at us with devastating fury—dread instruments of the Law of a jealous, angry God! Brahman makes and lets and suffers man to play out his act on the world stage—inexhaustible source of bewilderment, fear, confusion, faith, greatness, nobility and vileness, and also the supreme fulfilment of God-realization—in order that man may learn the whole nature of the Law, the karmic process, the ways of man and God. And in finality, Brahman shows the transcending of the Law regarded as the compulsive, equilibrating and adjusting power in the universe, and the fulfilling of the Law regarded as the beneficent Will of the Supreme who is infinite Love, in the shape of the Dhamma-become, the man-become-God. This is unity with the Will of God, the actualization of "Thy Will, not mine", the ultimate freedom from "karma, good and evil", the remaining unbound by universal process though existing as an integral part of it. God has no problem whether karma is ethical or not. It is the divine Will which runs the universe. In the eyes of man awakened, divine law is supra-ethical.

Man, an integral part of the world process, experiences the resultant effect of natural law, human law and divine law. He cannot make sense of much of his experience and make it fit into his personal conceptions of justness and fairness. He never will, for his conceptions are little cages in which universal process cannot be caught.

The question arises: Does the successful knave, the happy evil-doer, the triumphant oppressor, get away with it?

No.

The Law wholly fulfils itself.[1] It is entirely true, as said in Galatians, VI.7, that "God is not mocked." Each man's action in terms of thought, word and deed, works out and bears fruit through and upon that man, together with his whole environment. In the grand, impersonal sense, perfect justice is done. But it is indeed difficult, perhaps almost impossible for a sufferer, or enjoyer, or mere believer, or, in short, anyone who looks with mortality-blinded eyes, that is, whilst he is still bound in the circle of avijjā, to see the perfect justice of karma.

We look at cause and consequence too separatively: here, in time and space, is a cause; there, in a different time and space, is its consequence. But the Buddha showed, "there being this, that comes to be." At one instant, this prevails. By the very next instant it has become transformed into that. Such change goes on continuously. In the case of any one person, every single thought and feeling, word and action affects him, producing a change which is the resultant of all the forces playing upon him. Since the person is a part of his environment, the environment, which may include other persons, is also affected and changed. Observing the situation impersonally and scientifically, it is not difficult to imagine how karma works out accurately in detail.

Reciprocity is a universally accepted regulating concept where relations between man and man are concerned. To betray trust, to hurt others, to serve one's own interests at the expense of others, all incur universal condemnation; and man demands, in the name of justice, that the wrong should be righted. This means that something should be done to restore that balanced environment in which reciprocity can again actively prevail. Society usually punishes the wrongdoer, hopes to deter potential wrongdoers, attempts to compensate the one who is wronged, and trusts that social equilibrium will be restored. But on all these points, society's conceptions and practices change with accumulating experience. Because of the very fact that a man is in a particular society with its particular conceptions

[1] Jesus said: Till heaven and earth pass, one jot or one tittle shall in no wise pass from the law, till all be fulfilled.—Matthew, V. 18.

and practices, he is involved in the action-process of that society's everyday life. That action-process is karma, of which his karma is an integral element. If he, a wrongdoer, is clever enough not to be found out, or if the procedures of society are such that a formal charge of wrongdoing cannot be brought against him, then it is his karma to escape punishment in one particular form, namely, that inflicted by the law in the name of justice, and it is society's karma to have to endure a particular evil because of its incompetence to deal with it, until such time as society does develop the ability and means to deal with it.

But many a knave cannot be free of the hell of conscience, of restrictions placed on him by other partners in crime, of anxiety and fear (and the physical diseases arising out of fear and anxiety which may plague him till his death), of the horror of being driven helplessly to do wrong after wrong in order to hide the original crime, or to counter or to undo unforeseen developments. Does not this unhappy creature's plight arouse karuṇā, that is, love which is compassion, which is personal grief because of the sufferings, the stern justice of karma, of brother knave ?

In a situation of evil, the knave is always complemented by the fool, the cruel by the weak. It is the personal duty of the knave or the cruel to purify his character and cease to exploit or to oppress others. It is equally the task of the fool and the weakling to rid himself of folly and weakness. For the fool, by being a fertile field for exploitation, or the weakling a good subject for oppression, is a source of temptation for the knave or the cruel strong to do his vile deed.

One cannot legislate or compel another into goodness, and in fact he should never attempt to do so,[1] especially considering that by goodness one means precisely one's own brand of goodness ! (Jesus said : Why callest thou me good ? There is none good but one, that is, God.—Matthew, XIX.17). But one can certainly strive to change oneself, and get rid of foolishness or weakness, knavery or cruelty.

It is instructive to consider how power and resources and abilities have been, and are, well used as well as misused by

[1] Oliver Cromwell is one out of many instructive examples.

all people, according to the prevailing situation—by king and aristocracy, by merchant princes, by privileged classes, by democratic working masses. Such consideration makes it necessary to pause and think very carefully before demanding justice for oneself.

There is a natural outcry by the honest, hardworking poor man against a rich and comfortable man, who is sometimes harmless but useless, and sometimes a heartless parasite on society. The poor man usually has to endure the worst in peace or war, in prosperity or depression. Such a situation is rightly regarded as a social injustice, and calls for reform. But it should be borne in mind that the effectiveness of all reform would be multiplied many times if it is clearly understood that rich and poor alike suffer from similar vices and are graced by similar virtues. In the broad, the poor man become rich behaves like the man born rich, and the rich man become poor like the man born poor. Again, many a man born poor is a heartless parasite, a cruel mammon-worshipper; and many a man born rich is deeply considerate and a power for the alleviation of suffering, ignorance and misery, as evidenced by endowments for hospitals, colleges, research institutes, religious activities and innumerable charities. If only each and every person cleansed his own mind and heart, it would become impossible to prevent social justice from being the natural condition prevailing in the land.

Looking at the plight of rich and poor alike—for each has his suffering in his own well of loneliness—one can only experience karuṇā. And this tempers the passionate enquiry, where is justice? It may also serve to cool the blindfold ardour to be prosperous. At the same time, seeing social injustices as they actually exist, and at the vast misery biting so deeply into the life of mankind, one cannot help but cry out, where is the justice of it?

Now as said in the Paiṅgala Upanishad, " Bondage is through non-enquiry; liberation (moksha) is through enquiry." The enquiry, however, should be correctly framed. It should be formulated, not as " Where is the justice of it? " but as " How did this ill-state come about? " If the enquiry is improperly formulated, one social group will always be at war with some other social group; correctly formulated, at least one important step will have been taken towards ceasing to perpetuate the ill-state.

The inequalities of resources and opportunities between individuals composing a society are the effects produced mainly through the operation of certain qualities, such as greed, egoism, stupidity, ignorance, apathy and inability, which characterize all human beings. Men themselves have brought these inequalities into being. It is unpractical to blame God, nature, parents or heredity, environment, karma or some mythical ill-fate, or, above all, other people. The fact is that each and every person is involved as a cause or as a perpetuator of the ill-state, through sins of omission as well as of commission; and the prevailing extreme inequalities are the inevitable consequence of those sins, in accord with karmic process. There are those who violently resent their own bodily defects, their own lack of intellectual and æsthetic endowment, the misery of ugly environment or distasteful conditions or the cruel deprivations to which they may be subjected particularly on the ground that they, as individuals, were not responsible for such and such an evil. It is true that a man born lame, or with a defective thyroid, cannot be charged with a clearly provable responsibility for having deserved it or brought it about.[1] But is it not equally true, then, that he cannot claim to have deserved or brought about the graces or abilities or favourable opportunities with which he is blessed from birth? Yet he accepts these quite meekly, and with becoming fortitude!

Such situations are clearly a case, as said a little earlier, of cause, responsibility and consequence not being generated and borne by, or meted out to each person exclusively; of receiving the legacy of others, of being interlocked in action and its consequence with others, and of bequeathing our own legacy to yet others in our turn. The element of "deserving" has but little place here.

Whilst self-purification by each and every person is by far

[1] Popular Indian belief would affirm that it is indeed that very man's karma, the consequence of causes generated in a past life.

the most powerful factor for the establishment of social justice, such individual effort must be complemented by collective action, by measures taken by the state. It should be noted, in this connection, that social justice does not mean that the conditional reciprocities which are part of the foundations of social living should be made so narrow and rigid, that a dead equality could be achieved. Equality has a true meaning only in pure mathematics, in mere imagination. Aiming at strictly equal opportunities, equal rights, equal treatment, equal everything, leads to a dangerous forcing into the mould of a stultifying mediocrity. A dynamic equilibrium within a richly varied range of differences, uniquenesses in reality, misconceived as unjust inequalities, offers the best conditions for men's fulfilment in social living.

* * * *

" The ripening of the deed " is a significant Indian teaching, as also the counsel derived from it, " Meet your liabilities immediately, but never demand the settlement of credits."

The way of the untamed is the way of self, a brutish self. The way of the civilized, taught to dwell as wordly citizens, is the way of human reciprocity, a conditional goodness. The way of those who have attained, of the fulfilled, is the way of self transcended, the way of divine sacrifice, in which one feeds the whole flock with one's own handful, a self-replenishing inexhaustible handful.

What is this " ripening of the deed ? " The psycho-physical organism, or body-mind creature, is a physico-chemical system. With every thought or feeling, physical and chemical activity takes place, bringing about changes in responsivity. This is karma vipāka, or action and its consequence, immediately operative. Repetition of a thought or feeling makes it easier and easier to think or feel in that way. What physiologists call facilitation is taking place. A habit of thinking, constructive or destructive, and a type of feeling, pure or impure, lead to a capacity for action, good or evil. Every evil thought or feeling harms me myself, degrades me, makes me ill, obsesses me till I am " possessed of a devil ", and strengthens the impulse to evil action. This holds good irrespective of the fact that another person may have provoked me to feel anger, jealousy, hate or envy, to think ill, to plan revenge or to want to get even with him. Let it be repeated that any evil thought or feeling whatsoever immediately harms me myself. This is my evil karma, internal to me, and growing as a force for precipitating external evil through evil action, which inevitably involves the things and persons constituting my environment.

The precipitation into evil action is one aspect of the ripening of the deed; and in the Indian view, thought or feeling, word, and deed, are mental action, verbal action and physical action. One evil deed actually performed facilitates the perpetration of further evil deeds. Thus this body of Ill, the dukkhakkhandha, grows like a cancer, and becomes increasingly complicated and destructive, spreading sorrow and suffering. Thus, individual life can be frustrated, national disasters can take place, and a world can be plunged into war and ruin.

This is karma as symbolized in the persons crushed under the wheels of the car of Jagannātha. This is hell, and only a part of it, for me the living, existential person, here and now. After "my" death there is no hell for "me", for there is no self-conscious "me" which is any sort of counterpart of the existential "me" living here and now. Nor is there annihilation. Every force for evil set going by me, internal as thought and feeling, external as word and deed, has stamped itself on the whole situation, which includes persons, things, and me. Within the whole situation (after "my death") the transforming process goes on continuously. "One day" in the future stands a man, who, simultaneously is and also is not me of "to-day".[1] For "that" man, the legacy of "my" unresolved discords (the demons of hell), "my" evil, is the hell which "that" man has to tackle. But, everlastingly, "that" man, or any and every "other" fellow of yesterday, to-day and to-morrow through all the infinitude of time, is only another version of "me myself".

Similarly, there is the ripening of the deed in terms of the

[1] This difficult concept might be easier to grasp if we regard a person as an integral part of a total, continuously active and transforming situation, and not in the separative terms of a living person over and against a dead environment. See also, above, pp. 203–205, and 226–228.

good. Every good thought or feeling benefits me, and strengthens the impulse to good action, which, through repeated performance, develops the capacity and the ability to do good. Thus, individual life can be fulfilled, national welfare can be fostered, and world progress can be envisaged through the ripening of the good deed.

This is karma as symbolized in the statue of Śiva Nātarāja with the demon (representing evil) under his foot, whilst his cosmic dance brings the world process to its ultimate fruition, man's fulfilment in Brahman-realization. This is " my " heaven here and now. For " that " man in the future, the legacy of " my " developed faculties, " my " truth-realizations, " my " creative enterprises, " my " wisdom-love fulfilments (the angels of heaven), is the heaven which " that " man has to make more glorious, till in the final consummation the Glory of God fills all heaven and earth, and hell was but a fleeting though necessary disturbance on the path to the supreme beatitude, where karma stands still.

Outside of the consciousness of each living man there is no heaven, hell or purgatory experienced by the living, existential person.

Man begins in the darkness of ignorance, the unawakened consciousness, and slowly grows into the light of God-realization. Because of this ignorance, and its chain of consequence, there is this apparently over-whelming weight of ill, of world woe, whereas true welfare or well-being[1] by comparison, is like one little candle-light in a country on a pitch black night. Hence Indian religion lays so much stress on the fact of the prevalence of evil in the world, and so often exhorts man to transform ill into good. When he achieves this, " his " karma is wiped out, in the sense that " he " has " escaped " from the wheel of saṁsāra, the round of births and deaths, whilst karma, in the sense of the continuous action which is universal process, goes on. Since " he " is not merely a separate, atomistic " him ", but is also interwoven with all mankind, not only does he redeem himself but also all mankind. The karmic process is the mechanism by means of which man fulfils himself.

[1] See also, above, p. 309.

Deeds do not ripen in a simple series-of-parallel-lines fashion. If they did, there might be no end to hell as the product of evil, and to heaven, of good. A mere futility! The human organism, a psycho-physical whole, is a highly complex self-adjusting system. Well adjusted, it is healthy; maladjusted, it is diseased. There are various adjusting forces within man, and also without, interlocked in their workings. Racial legacy, spiritual and cultural heritage, environment, the prevailing way of life, heredity, upbringing and education are powerful factors conditioning a man's moral sense and conscience, his outlook and his behaviour, and his way of setting about his tasks. In all societies, the observation that disobedience to law, or evil action, leads to punishment and pain, and that obedience to law, or good action, leads to reward and happiness, naturally makes for the acceptance of a reward-punishment ideology and practice. The right acceptance of punishment is a necessary expiation of the crime. After expiation, a soul-purging, man is clean again, a true fellow amongst all other good fellows.

Man demands expiation from his fellow man for wrong done. He demands it also from within himself for sin, whether visible or invisible to his fellows, although another aspect of his nature tries hard to escape it, because of the natural revulsion of the organism from the pain of punishment. But it is indeed providential that there is a stern, exacting Justiciar within us, a sort of angry, thundering God who asserts that "vengeance is mine". For human expiation is a link or stage in between the non-moral, conscienceless, "exactly equal and opposite reaction to action" which is the justice of natural law, and the supra-moral, God-conscious, redemptive healing through personal, voluntary sacrifice of the human part of oneself, which is the justice of divine law. Also, expiation is a means for self-purification, for proving repentance, for acquiring the strength and wisdom for the next step forward, and for readjusting disturbed relationships.

Suffering is indispensable for fulfilment. The karmic process, in so far as it involves the operation of natural law and human law, is also indispensable.

Suppose A, deeply united in love and trust with B, through

some trivial but unfortunate circumstances turns faithless, and, wrapped up in the opportunist pursuit of selfish happiness, deceives him with regard to her future intentions ; and taking advantage of physical separation through living in a distant town, she takes refuge in complete silence, offers no explanation, and refuses to set right the broken relationship.

Legal redress, if available, can deal only with physical externals, and can do nothing for souls. B's suffering is due to the fact that he depends for his peace and happiness upon the requital of love from A, and that his trust in her is shattered ; that his ideals and values have been desecrated ; that his personality and self-respect have been sorely wounded ; and that quite part from personalities, a wrong deed, horrible and evil in itself has been perpetrated. Only those who have experienced such suffering know how near it brings one to suicide, to madness, to shipwreck of the soul, to an incapacitation of mind and heart. It seems too terrible and unjust a karma for B to endure. And yet, if B is so sensitive a nature, so dependent upon receiving back love and trust, so attached to the object of his love, so much self-regarding that he insists that A ought to do or not to do so and so, then what else can be the consequence of A's evil-doing to him but that which he does undergo ?

What has happened to B in terms of a soul-catastrophe is similar to what happened to the saint in terms of a physical catastrophe when he unwittingly stepped over the edge of the 2,000-foot precipice. The karma in this case is of the type associated with senseless natural law. Popular Indian belief would affirm that karmic justice does operate here in the full sense.

B's task is so to transform his love by utterly stripping it of attachment, limitation, conditions and self, that it becomes transcendental love. Anything less than transcendental love leaves the lover open to suffering on a sordid account—oneself. Another task is "to turn the other cheek" to A. This does not mean giving a second opportunity to A for evil-doing, for then, through imprudence or sentimentality, B is a partner in evil-doing with A. To turn the other cheek means that B first purifies his own love ; he observes whether A, too, has gone through the necessary purification ; without craving, or attachment, he contrives to produce a situation (unless, happily, it arises by itself) which gives A, now a purified woman, the opportunity to right the wrong done.

When one cheek is slapped, it is folly, sometimes criminal folly, to turn the other cheek also to evil. The other cheek must be turned, rightly and appropriately—and this is a responsibility shared by the wronged with the wrongdoer—to be kissed; kissed with the kiss of Love, not of Judas.

And A? The effects of each and every act live on in her and bear fruit. All pledges, all that is due to B, continue to influence A. The picture of B cannot be effaced from A's mind, whatever she may do to rub it out. (No one should ever attempt to forget. Everything should be faced, and worked out fully.) Those flaws in A's character which made her wrong B so grievously are still there, continuously operative. To-morrow they may harm C or D. But A herself is in constant danger of being trapped and brought to book by those very flaws. Further, A as conscious A cannot deal with subconscious A (except through the purificatory disciplines taught in yoga, by the Buddha, and by other Teachers.) Conscience is a terrible power. For what is more indelicate than such infidelity? More cruel than an unexplained silence? More mean than a cowardly refusal to right the evil done?

The "wrath of God" is an awful reality in the psychical life. For in order to bring about expiation, this very God in his aspect of the stern Justiciar demanding vengeance, will drive A to further temptation and evil. ("And lead us not into temptation" is the Christian prayer, "but deliver us from evil.") In some unguarded moment, despite all cleverness, all subterfuge, all stifling of conscience, A will make some mistake or other and stumble into the abyss.

It is tragic, that man so seldom understands the nature, the significance and the cause of that which happens to him. So it has been taught that

> The fear of the Lord is the beginning of knowledge.
> Proverbs, I.7.
>
> The fear of the Lord is the beginning of wisdom.
> Psalms, CXI.10.

Blessed is the man that feareth the Lord.

Psalms, CXII.1.

Through fear of him, Vāyu doth blow.
Through fear of Him, Sūrya doth rise,
Through fear of Him, Agni and Indra and
Mṛtyu as fifth do speed along.

Taittirīya Upanishad II.8.
and similarly, Kaṭha Upanishad, VI.3.

Fear is not fright in these contexts. It is the courageous man's feeling of concern consequent upon sensing or anticipating danger, which startles him into a state of alertness, of tense apprehension. He is, in truth, on the alert for God, even though he may not know it. God indeed is the danger, which suddenly bursts through his fog of ignorance, flicks away his mask of personality, rips off his armour of ego-conceit, and, through grace, confers upon him the divine vision, as Kṛishṇa did to Arjuna.

Because of egoism, delusion and passion (taṇhā), A does not fear the Lord in time. So she must needs suffer a self-decreed hell. The more she tries to stifle conscience, to wriggle out of expiation, to avoid repentance, to put off the hour of reckoning, the more terrible is the ripening of the deed. Wisely did India teach: meet your liabilities as soon as possible. Worst of all is it to reach the end of one's span without having righted wrongs. There is a profound truth hidden in the teaching that he who dies unrepentent, unconfessed and unabsolved, is consigned to everlasting hell. There is no hell outside the mind of the living person. " Dies ", in this context, means that the person shelves the problem altogether, leaving it unsolved. Hence, within the soul, there is a lifelong, active force for suffering and destruction, namely, the unresolved conflict. In A's case, the demons of " I can't forgive myself for it " and " How *could* I have done such a thing ", of self-hate and a tormenting memory of the past and vain imaginings of might-have-beens or ought-to-have-beens, " roast her in hellfire."

But B, too, should bear in mind that if he fails to do the needful, he, too, will suffer hell for egoistically treasuring an undying grievance, or through despicable self-pity, or through the devilish passion to see A " get what she deserves ". Strange are the ways of karma, even as the ways of Providence.

The stern Justiciar within oneself sees to it that there is a "balancing of accounts", that karma is "paid in full". But if this were all, there would be no redemption and fulfilment.

A's task is to rid herself of the flaws in her character, to eradicate the pursuit of self-gratification, to purify her love, to seek unremittingly, but prudently and skilfully, to right the wrong done to B, to prove her worthiness to "kiss the other cheek" of the person she has hurt. Above all, she must be prepared to make sacrifices, to go through, in full, with willing acceptance, her expiation of her evildoing. Then indeed her repentance is true, for repentance is actually a *faculty* for turning away[1] from evil, and not only an isolated act of turning away from one particular evil deed. And B, too, must repent—from hedging his love with conditions, from the almost universal weakness embodied in the statement, "But I am only a human being."

Afterwards, A can pray for B's forgiveness—continuously, within, in secret, anyone should always pray to God for forgiveness—and B also should seek A's forgiveness. Forgiveness is not a "letting off of payment". Expiation is inescapable by man as long as he is still not an arahant, one who is worthy. When he is Brahman-become, there is no expiation to be done, except in the transcendental sense as in the case of Jesus, or of any sinless martyr. Forgiveness is, in the one part, a foregoing of one's own lust, egoism, hatred and delusion in relation to the other. Only when this is mutual between A and B, wrongdoer and wronged, can there be that other part of forgiveness, namely a forbearing with each other—that unspeakable sweetness of love which demonstrates the love-union wherein, though twain, they are one—instead of a sour putting up with each other, consumed inwardly with mutual contempt and hate.

Such is redemption, the karma vipāka (action and its fruit) which is the justice of God, because of which a new, re-created relationship between A and B, embodied in a right form, can be established. By enduring the complete cycle of experience bravely and wisely, and successfully fulfilling Right, which is Love, both A and B will have gained the skilled ability—" Yoga

[1] **Nibbindati, as the Buddha taught.**

is skill in action" said Shri Kṛishṇa—which will keep them truly secure from making similar mistakes in the future. For if any one experience is fully accepted and understood, and all its consequences are rightly worked out, the complete lesson of that experience is learned, and it frees the individual for ever from that type of karma.

But the vast majority of men and women do not accept experience in its fullness. Usually, A and B will want to go their own separate ways. Falling apart from each other, each seeks security, happiness, love and fulfilment with no truer understanding than before of what they mean. Each is burdened with the same deficiencies of character which ruined the first union between them, and with a somewhat more resentful, suspicious and cunningly cautious attitude than before. Each looks for a new substitute for the old partner. A second union is sought, in the wild hope that the sorrows of the first will be drowned, and the hurts of the past will be forgotten. When there is a second disappointment, the resentments and hurts of the previous experience resurrect with redoubled energy. What is merely repressed into one's subconscious is reborn as a more terrible demon than ever before. With each succeeding attempt to slake one's thirst (taṇhā) and with each succeeding disappointment, all the previous sorrows and pain are felt with ever worsening intensity. Man must therefore learn his lesson that life must not be a pursuit of desire, a craving for the pleasant, an attempt to insure against, to run away from, or to repress the unpleasant. Life (experience) must be accepted and lived in full measure in all its aspects.

Suffering, expiation, cannot be written off arbitrarily. In fact, the truly repentant will intelligently accept, even gladly invite, the suffering consequent upon wrongdoing as testimony of sincere repentance. Thus can man rise to the pinnacle of purity and realize self-less-ness, make it right between himself and God, and fulfil the great law underlying his God-becoming, namely, that organism must sacrifice itself in order that Spirit may triumph. Man always has to wash his sin-stained feet in the blood of his heart.

* * * *

Throughout the entire karmic pattern, justice is fulfilled. Man would like to make this pattern fit into his faulty human concept of justice. Because the pattern fits only in very small measure, he is reduced to despair by perplexing problems like the good man tortured or sick, or like the indiscriminate bestowal by fortune of benefit or loss, or of pleasure or pain by natural phenomena, accidents and atom bombs. And so he rages against the "unjust" ways of God or Nature. The trouble, however, is not with God or Nature, but with his own short understanding, and with his weakness and absurdity in wanting the true explanation of the world process to fit into his limited conceptions of justice.

Karma is the dynamic, whole experience from moment to moment, only partly understandable by man, because of its immensity and complexity. The total consequence of the immediate here-now of action can only be dimly foreseen. Therefore, a continuous, constructive adaptation of the concept of justice is called for to meet the even larger demands and challenge of whole experience. Karma understood bears creative significance for him who understands.

Orthodoxies uphold the dogma of heaven and hell as reward and punishment after death. Millions, out of ignorance and egoism, cling to this falsely formulated doctrine. Men are still inhuman enough to want the satisfaction of seeing that the sinner "gets what he deserves"—the sinner is always "that" fellow—still greedy enough to demand and expect the satisfaction of being rewarded for living the good life—"I", always, am the good man. Money changers in the temple of the Lord! Let them beware of the evil good they do! Encrusted in the shell of self-righteousness they are in danger of sinking deeper into the abyss of their own lusts and hatreds and delusions.

Neither God nor Nature is a paymaster. Let a man live the good life for the Glory of God: the Glory, to which the witness is the quickening of inanimate Nature, the flowering of animate Nature, the redemption of wayward man, and the unity in and with God, the Brahman-becoming of redeemed man. And in this process, the justness of karma is manifest through all its grades, natural, human and divine. No question of sordid rewards and payments. Only the fulfilment of the Divine Will through the Law that functions through the universe.

The natural and human aspect of karma is more within the ken of man than the divine, and is one source of his conceptions of right and wrong. In everyday life, justice is a restoration of the balance according to society's prevailing conceptions of right and wrong ; and in practice, punishment for wrongdoing is a major factor in the administration of justice. The element of retribution is seen in one of its worst aspects in the relations between warring nations. The infliction of retributive justice is uncreative because it is unredeemed by love. Merely retributive punishment debases the inflictor, and stores up a destructive reaction-energy in the sufferer. But if a wrongdoer, himself recognizing that he has done wrong, accepts the necessity for, or even demands punishment as the means for expiation and self-purification, he has the right to receive it. And only he who is free from hate, self-righteousness and personal interest may deliver it. Verily, only the hand that loves may lay the stripes ! Will it ?

As one develops, the use of a punitive and deterrent measure for dispensing justice is gradually replaced by an educative and transformative one, its aim being to protect the unoffending, and also to heal the wrong-doer, to salve (save) him from his ill-state, his ill-thinking or ill-feeling or ill-capacity, and restore him to health. This is the highest aspect of human justice. Herein, the debasing use of violence is abjured. If men in the mass understood this well enough to practise it, fighting for rights and privileges by means which harm others, in the name of justice, will be seen for its true worth.

The perfect answer to the problem of justice was given by the suffering Jesus on the Cross : " Father, forgive them, they know not what they do." No ordinary sufferer can effectively pray thus, but only he who has transcended egoism and desire, for he alone offers no resistance to, and is in fact a perfect channel for, the free flow of God's Love which alone effects the forgiveness. The animal and human in man—limited, not possessing the creative power for transmutation—is not, and cannot be, the forgiver. The animal in man is mechanically reactive, the human reciprocative or equilibrative. The human, at best, is a sacrificial agent, or can offer himself as the willing lamb of God. When the animal and human in man are utterly purified, the Divine embodied in man, the Pratyagātman, at last comes into His own, takes charge, and can intercede with the Father in heaven, the Paramātman, the Lord and possessor of the creative power for transmutation. Man, even man-become-God, as an existential being, cannot forgive in the ultimate and supreme sense. Only God, the integrative (making-new) principle, universally operative, can do so—hence Jesus does not say " I forgive you " but calls upon, intercedes with, the Father to do so—in that magical moment when the karmic situation enables the divine outpouring to take place. That situation of Grace is brought into being, and the forgiveness is effected, through the sinless one, out of Love, himself suffering with and because of the suffering consequent upon wrongdoing by another one, the wrongdoer. The sacrifice by the sinless one demonstrates the truth that Divine Justice is a transmuting, spiritual alchemy, and not a see-saw effort at equilibration.

And in the fulfilment of Divine Justice, in the transcending of all egoism and desire, in the still silence of samādhi, in the union of the sinless one with God, is the end of all karma, " good " and " evil ".

Section F

SIN : GOOD AND EVIL

ETHIC AND TRANSCENDENTAL ETHIC

Whereas forgiveness in the supreme sense is effected through the man-become-God, be he a Kṛishṇa or a Buddha or a Christ or whoever has become sinless, forgiveness is also effected at less exalted levels, bringing healing and re-creation to the extent the forgiver is pure, that is, sinless.

When a child is hurt, the animal in him automatically feels a reactive urge to return hurt. If he succeeds, his tendency and capacity to hurt grows. If he fails, his repressed reactive urge is no asset. Whichever happens, he grows in the power to sin. Contrariwise, through different experiences, he grows in purity.

Throughout life, he experiences the conflict between sin and purity. By virtue of his being an ordinary member of a society which upholds the idea of reciprocity, as is done unto him, so will he tend to do unto others. Instead of true forgiveness, there will be an attempt to " forget all about it ", which is but repression, or a pseudo-forgiveness at best.

If, however, as the decades pass, the erstwhile child grows wise through suffering, and through pity and infinite compassion, and he really sees that hurting is evil, then he ceases to hurt, or at least strives not to hurt any person, including himself. Such insight and the behaviour consequent upon it, is an act of forgiveness. It frees him, the actor, from vengefulness and a sense of frustration. It transforms the evil in the stream of karma into good, for his sacrificial vision and action prevents the "sin of the fathers" from going beyond himself, because he has borne the cross for their sins, and his own children inherit, therefore, the happy opportunities offered in a pure kingdom. Also, it benefits mankind, for whatsoever the individual does affects not only himself but also his environment. In fact, whereas the man himself reaps only in part, MAN reaps the full fruit of that man's sowing.

The evil in the stream of man's karma, which is the stream of man's becoming, is due to Sin.

Sin, in its innermost, at its very heart, is the obscuration of the awareness of God. When I am merely self-conscious, when I am self-associated with the object of my craving, with the victim of my hate, or with the cloud of my delusion, when ego has usurped Ātman, when I am not awake to Brahman, when I am not God-aware, then sin is manifest. This is the root, the origin, of all else that is called sin, of all evil, of the ill-state (dukkha). This is the sin against the Holy Ghost, namely, the state of denial of Brahman or God, the fundamental ignorance, avidyā. This is the sin of which the wages is death, for the God-unaware "I" experiences ceaseless birth and death with each and every self-association with desires and the objects of desire, with sense-functioning and with the unbidden flow of speech-thought. This is the sin referred to by the Vedic seer, Vasishṭha, when he says: "What, Varuṇa, hath been my chief transgression, that thou wouldst slay the friend who sings thy praises? Tell me, unconquerable lord, and quickly sinless will I approach thee with mine homage" (Ṛig Veda, VII.86.4).

The unawakened or ignorant condition is the condition of sin, the being in a state of mortal sin, which is the state of disturbed "worldly" consciousness, and not of peaceful God-consciousness. Sin is not essentially in the mere act, "good" or "wicked", but in the Brahman-unaware or Brahman-denying consciousness whilst acting. The "good" deed done in my name, for your sake, for love, for charity, for king and country, for relieving untold suffering, for church or temple, but done in the absence of God-communion, undedicated to the Eternal, is tainted with sin. Only that deed, be it a mental or verbal or physical deed, done by the God-aware, the Brahman-become, for the glory of God, which is itself a pure deed, wherein the real doer is the

Supreme Self through man as the conscious, cooperative, sacrificial agent, that alone is the unstained good, the ariyan deed, the pure action of him who is sinless.

One's inner consciousness, either in union with God (or unsullied), or divorced from God (or sullied), determines whether one is in a state of sin, of dying, of dukkha, of bondage to karma, or in a sinless state, of life eternal, of well-faring and well-being, of freedom. Thus one can appreciate the far-reaching import of the teaching in the Dhammapada :

> If a man speaks or acts with a sullied mind, then suffering follows him even as the wheel of the wagon follows the hoof of the bullock.
>
> I.1.
>
> If a man speaks or acts with an unsullied mind, then happiness (the well-state) follows him ever, just as his shadow.
>
> I.2.

Sinless, one enjoys the felicity of constant companionship with God here-now. God Immanent in man, reigning in His own kingdom, namely in the living individual who has cast aside the separating veil of selfhood, is the instrument through whom God the universal transcendent realizes man-consciously in the manifested universe His own Godhood. It is not the human who resurrects, but God Immanent in man, for it is He who is continuously slain through the taṇhā and the ego-conceit of the animal-human in man. Side by side with Him, the " I " of the animal-human in me, the man, undergoes continuous birth and death, saṁsāra. His the sacrifice, mine the wages of sin. When through effort, discipline, vision and enlightenment, there comes the final attainment which is the God-becoming fulfilled, and the sinless state is realized, then the purified human, in union with God, at last forgives the self. To forgive oneself in the supreme sense is one of the ultimate achievements of the living individual.

On the night of the enlightenment, the Buddha looks through his entire past, in order that he may consciously relinquish and become freed from bondage to all attachment to that past ; that he may forgo all self-association, all taṇhā, moha and rāga in relation to that past ; and thus effect a complete forgiveness of his self which moved through that saṁsāric stream of the past, and realize the permanent unity with the Ātman. By virtue of the real forgiving of himself, and by virtue of bearing in mind his own past experience, he has complete understanding and compassion for all beings in the " backward " stages, with no condemnation of them as persons, and makes a strenuous and unceasing stand for the good in order to uproot all evil. Thus the teaching embodied in the Brahma-vihāras becomes a reality instead of remaining a charming or pious sentiment.

In ordinary life, if " I " have suffered an " unforgivable " wrong, a release of inner tension occurs after I hear that the wrongdoer has suffered something proportionately grievous. As long as this is the case, there is no spiritual progress ; and if and when I suffer again, I shall await the next satisfaction of my vengeance-passion. As long as blood demands blood, I stick fast at an animal level. But when I have truly transcended wanting the other to be punished for doing me wrong, and would only feel karuṇā if and when the other suffers, then I have transformed the passionate, reciprocal love-hate complex into pure love, mettā, whose foundation in myself is upekkhā, that unperturbable, dynamic poise which is the fruit of self-mastery.

A wrong is " unforgivable " because of one's own egoism. And yet, it is the very experience of unforgivable wrong, of " hurt too great to bear ", which provides a sufficiently powerful stimulus to dissolve away the false notion of separate selfhood, with which lust, hate and fear are associated, and to reach that self-transcendence wherein Love provides the conditions for effective forgiveness. Because of such Love, one accepts all the treachery, cruelty, infidelity or pain inflicted on one, and with such acceptance (an indispensable prerequisite) of the infliction and the inflictor, sinless love converts the sinner.

Since man is usually in a state of God-unawareness, he must constantly " pray to God " for forgiveness—the human in man forgoes, God Immanent in man forbears. By praying to God, a more harmonious reorientation of man's psychical being takes place, and deeper levels of consciousness are activated. Inasmuch as God Immanent in man is in constant and perfect alignment with God Transcendent and Universal, prayer makes the relationship between the particular and the universal, the part and the whole, stronger and richer. In other words, it draws man nearer to God, till in finality, man is integrated into God.

Praying for forgiveness is symbolized in confession and absolution by layman and priest. If a priest is one who has become Brahman, then he, like Jesus, can call upon that Transcendent Power whose Love can effect full forgiveness. But the ordinary priest is a man who has not transcended lust and egoism, hate and delusion. How, then, can *he* forgive? In this connection, the procedure of the Buddhist Sangha is instructive. The assembled priests retire two and two together, each pair kneels down face to face and makes confession of all faults, one to another, in whispers. Then they all kneel and make obeisance to the seated senior priest, saying: " Permit me, Lord, to ask for forgiveness of all my faults committed in deed, or word, or thought." He replies: " I accept your acknowledgment. It is good (for you in turn) to grant me forgiveness." All say: " Permit me, Lord, I forgive you.' The procedure is repeated, successively, by the priests who are second, third, fourth . . . in seniority, with all their respective juniors. Finally, everyone present falls upon his knees and says: " Praise be to the Blessed One (the Buddha), the holy one, the author of all truth." Confessor and confessee each begs for forgiveness from the other.

Does man need to forgive God? Yes, certainly. But unhappily we do not act in the right way in this matter. We slay God continually by remaining in a sinful state. So He does all the forbearing despite our not forgoing. Behold the infinite, tender, Mercy and Patience of God! Lovingly awaiting the Day of Blessed Returning, the Day of Be with Us in all Our Glory and Majesty once again! Behold the infinite sorrow[1] of God, Self-compelled through the ordinance of His Divine Will, to witness man's continual dying, his round of births and deaths, the self-delivered wages of sin, until the Day of Redemption,

[1] So, too, the path of a Buddha is a path of unutterable woe, as he sees man's dukkha.

that is, the Day when each individual awakens to Eternal God, realizes the truth, and is saved from within himself. The great religions promise the Second Advent of their Founders. But there will never be any Second Advent of the persons Zarathustra, Jesus, or anyone else. The awakening, and fulfilment and realization by each one of us individually from within, stimulated by the inspiration of Their past example, is the Second Advent of any one or all of them. And in *this* Second Advent, we, having forgone all lust and egoism, forbear with God. When the forbearance has ceased to be a one-way traffic from God to us, and has attained a mutual, dynamic equilibrium between us and God, then we, too, have forgiven God for His temporary, and only temporal, separation from us, for it is His Divine Will in the first instance which creates us as blind children of mortality.

Does man need to absolve Zarathustra, the Buddha, Kṛishṇa, Jesus, Muhammad, or any of the Brahman-become? Yes, certainly. But unhappily we do not act in the right way in this matter. With painful monotony we repeat the criminal folly of first rejecting, even destroying, the Great Teachers, Those who tread the Mystic Way. It is true that the Buddha, and some others, lived a full span and reached a peaceful end. But Zarathustra, Kṛishṇa, Jesus, and several others, met with a violent death. The God-become, who is unique, associateless and alone, meets the Alone, which is the One Only, and realizes that consciousness of the Brahmaloka, the Heaven World, which, in our eyes, sets him apart from us. He is not one of us, the herd. So we, the sinful herd, sensing the danger which the Purified One is to our way of life entangled in craving and ego, the domain of Māra, deny, revile, persecute, crucify or murder the Lord manifest amongst us. We the dual minded (good-and-evil-minded), we of the sullied consciousness, can slay Him, for we wield that devilish power which is the fruit of forswearing love. Whereas He, by virtue of his lordship of Love and Wisdom through forswearing lust and ego and worldly power, cannot and will not hurt us (the true individual in us, however successfully He hurts and vanquishes Māra or Satan in us), but rather suffers unto death for our sakes.

But when a man, fulfilling his divine destiny, becomes one apart from us, it is incumbent on us to absolve him for that separation. There is only one proper way to absolve him, to forbear with him, namely, to persevere with unremitting effort to become sinless like him.

Confession of sin is possible only if there is awareness of sin. Absolution of sin implies the reinstatement of God-awareness. Within each and every one, absolution is simultaneous with confession in the moment of awareness. The dhāraṇā, dhyāna and samādhi of the yogi, the sammā sati of the Buddha, the watch and pray of Jesus, is the technique of the saving from sin and the restoration of God-consciousness. Within ourselves the confession and absolution has to take place. If death—that is, the end of a particular cycle of experience, momentary or prolonged or lifelong—takes place before confession and absolution, one dies with a sullied consciousness, and the next conscious cycle (the re-birth) starts in sin, suffering and hell.

Thus one can understand the Indian teaching that if the last thought (the inner consciousness) before death is of Brahman, to Brahman he goes. Jesus triumphantly proclaims, " It is accomplished ", on the re-establishment of full communion with the Father ; Bhishma prolongs his life, even in agony, until he unites himself with Brahman ; and the Buddha enters the Fourth Jhāna before the final passing away. But the same teaching applies even more trenchantly to each and every state of consciousness within the life-span on earth. Brahman has to penetrate man's entire life, and then

> He, verily, who knows that supreme Brahman, becomes very Brahman . . . He crosses over sorrow, He crosses over sin.
>
> Muṇḍaka Upanishad, III.2.9.

Let no one be tardy, then, in seeking forgiveness, from God, and from his fellow man. If my fellow is wronged by me, and he were to pass beyond my reach before I seek and win forgiveness, then for all my life I may have to bear the consequence of my unredeemed act, and I may not be able to cross over my sin. Or if I die, in my anger, my evil act, my shameful thought, before I have put it right with my fellow, I slink out of the world as a wicked coward, as one with duty unfulfilled. Hence the prayer, in several religions, "From sudden death, good Lord, deliver us."

* * * *

Clearly, the heart of ethical striving and the crown of ethical development is the establishment of undisturbed God-consciousness, characterized by what the Buddha called upekkhā. He who is thus, lives the Good Life: the Good Thought, Good Word, and Good Deed of Zarathustra.

Good, as manifest in everyday life, is a demonstration of god-likeness in oneself, a measure of one's own God-realization. Whatsoever in spatio-temporal manifestation is a demonstration of the knowledge of God, is good. When it is a perfect expression of the undisturbed union with God, it is the Supreme Good. Whatsoever demonstrates a disturbance in that unity with God. is evil.

Understanding this, one can understand the Buddha's Paṭicca-samuppāda, and appreciate its profundity. The root evil is the unawakened state. In that state, any stimulus leads to a pattern of being, a worldly consciousness and a manifestation in form, to contact, sensation, attachment, and so on through the cycle of the nidānas, which obscure or misrepresent Brahman-awareness. The process belongs to the realm of mortality, of the recurring birth and death cycle. Hence it is Ill. It may or may not be ill considered as a detached, objective, space-time phenomenon. Innumerable passing events and actions are definitely good in the context of the distinctive good-and-evil of human ethic, which is always relative and limited. But each and every one of them is always partly ill in so far as its origin and continuous being are not in God-awareness. For then it is at least partly self-ness, or sinfulness, and not wholly self-less-ness, or sinless-ness, which is at the core of the action, "good" or "bad", it matters not which. For God-unawareness means that the unity of the universe, spatio-temporally, and the one-ness of the One; eternally, is not expressed in man's whole consciousness. The Divine Purpose is that this unity should indeed be expressed. The Good beyond Being and Reality of

Plato, the One of Plotinus, the Silence of Eckhart, Om or Brahman of India, should be the origin and the whole subsistence of the " good " of man. When Brahman-awareness, which is the non-originating and un-dying Immortal, is the source in a man of his good actions, then indeed they are good. No evil can affect such a man ; no evil can issue out of him. He is sovereign lord of self, the " king who can do no wrong ".

The world process, intrinsically, is neither good nor evil. Man, and man alone, is the introducer of evil into life. Any event, as event, is neither good nor evil. To strive to remove disease, or a painful experience, merely because it is unwelcome to us, or to arbitrarily dub it as evil in itself, is a mistake—indeed, it may have a lesson for us of such value that it might be our loss to miss the experience—but to strive to remove it because compassionate action is God in action, is good. Whenever man removes the unwelcome on account of personal antipathy or mere non-acceptance, he has done less than the best ; and what element of relative good there is in his action is spoiled by self-ness, not only in terms of ethical value but also of material fact. For invariably self-ness produces bondage, or complication, or pain, or failure, or sorrow.

The Buddha's Paṭicca-samuppāda is concerned essentially with the Ill which is existential man's divorce from the ultimate Good. Old age, disease, and all the worldly ills are incidental to this fundamental Ill. The Noble Eightfold Path showed the path to the fundamental Good and the complete stopping of the fundamental Ill. The incidental, worldly ills come and go, impermanent, exactly like the incidental, ephemeral, worldly goods, strewn on the pathway of life both before and after Arahantship.

Now there is a goal for man in this world. Nature has evolved him out of the less sensitive and responsive, the less complexly organized and less profoundly conscious, controlling, intelligent and creative, towards the more, which he is to-day. Developing along lines which are unique to him in all nature, namely, the capacity to self-observe, to transcend the limitations of the psycho-physical organism, and to control speech-thought, some men, as pioneers or forerunners, have discovered the Mystery, the Truth, the Power at the heart of things, and termed it Brahman, Ātman, God, and so on. It is for each man to realize this, so that mankind will consist of Self-realized Individuals, or, men-become-Brahman. This is man's fulfilment as expressed in spiritual terms, or in the terms of religion. In material terms, or from the standpoint of a scientific outlook, other modes of expression describing man's fulfilment must be used. Whatever the terms may be, no difference is made to the actuality. In this actuality, Eternity contains all spatio-temporal birth-death existence. The realization of Immortality, in Eternity, is the Absolute Good, the Nirvāṇa towards which God draws and Nature impels man.

To this end, the understanding of the Paṭicca-samuppāda is necessary. For, understanding this, understanding what really is the Ill, one understands better how one must live in order to attain the Well, and make the changeless Immortal continuously shine through the changing mortal. This is living the Good Life, in which " Thy Will, not mine " is continuously manifest : Thy Will—the Will and Purpose of Parameśvar, with which the Will of the Self-realized Individual becomes identical ; not mine—not the desires and purposes of the existential animal-human, the sinful and mortality-bound.

How is this to be achieved ?

The moral code for man in the early stages of development is simple and compulsive. The basic prohibitions in the religions are indispensable to society as a social, economic and political organization, quite apart from religious considerations. Early in history, when the machinery for maintaining law and order, protecting life and limb, safeguarding and promoting individual and community interests and well-being was far less developed and efficient, compared with our own times, the sanction of religion was one of society's most powerful conserving, protecting and improving forces. The sanction of religion lay behind not only the prohibitions but also the moral affirmations, such as the virtues to be cultivated, and the duties to be performed to the gods, the fathers, men, and so on.

A simple, compulsive morality is in use even to-day, where the young, the untutored, or the " backward " are concerned.

Generally speaking, there is less severity, narrowness and unintelligence associated with modern morality and its enforcement, as compared with the past. Moreover, helped by modern social organization, it is increasingly recognized that good commonsense and human decency must underlie morality. A religious sanction, indispensable for exalting simple ethic into a spiritual and psychological tool for the expression of God-realization, is not necessary for ordinary morality ; and indeed, unless a religious sanction is truly understood and willingly accepted, it only makes for a repressive morality which inevitably leads to immorality.

This was clearly understood in the past, in some respects more profoundly than to-day. This profounder understanding enabled the Teachers of the past to tread, and to show others, the path to fulfilment.

Psycho-physical man is in some respects peculiarly mechanical. He is truly a physico-chemical system, wonderfully complex in structure and activities, but functioning in accordance with simple principles. Stimuli produce responses ; actions are answered by reactions, and responsivity, or reactivity, is largely predictable. Man is not master, naturally or effortlessly, of himself or his environment. Compulsive morality largely negatives his natural reaction. If he reacts to a particular stimulus with a desire to kill or to steal, he is confronted with a peremptory "Thou shalt not." If he feels like passing by a beggar, telling a lie, or indulging his appetites, his inclination is negatived by the strenuous upholding of liberality, truthfulness or temperance. The overriding authority of religion asserts that it is God's Wish that it should be so. Afterwards, in heaven, God will more than compensate him for what he forgoes or sacrifices now. But if he is wilful, God will cast him into hell where the devil will administer unimaginable punishment.

Unintelligent repression produces sad results for individual and community alike.

Sooner or later, awkward problems arise. To kill is wrong. But a man does kill, or aids and abets killing for food, for getting rid of pests to his crops, or of sources of disease. Also, a kind, good citizen, with his own gentle hands, kills fellow human beings of other lands, in the process of upholding "freedom, justice and honour against the evil aggressor, the brutal invader." But is kindness, goodness or gentleness skin deep, flesh deep, bone deep or marrow deep ? Or is it of the nature of Eternal God ? Is killing wrong, absolutely, or is it right in some contexts and wrong in others ?

Moral teaching, as codified in the religions, is practised only as a relative ethic, bounded within the circle of human capacities and failings. This is unavoidable. But it serves a very valuable purpose in so far as it stimulates a purity seeker to probe into the depths in order to discover a deeper meaning of ethic and the ethical life.

Then he begins to understand the teaching of Indian ethical philosophy, that the aim is not the mere acquisition of virtues, for that is only an expression of possessiveness, of spiritual greed. Such virtue is often more vicious than naïve, honest vice.

He also understands that his actual behaviour in thought, word and deed is the expression of his whole being and nature ; that he as a whole is living continuously from moment to moment ; and that this living is manifest as a continuously transforming behaviour pattern. So, the good life or the bad life is not a mere sum of separate static acts, good or bad, but a continuous acting, mentally, verbally and physically, the behaviour pattern of any one moment, formed by his interaction with the environment, emerging out of that of the previous moment. And he discovers that this behaviour pattern is never exclusively good or exclusively bad but is always good-bad at once. It is, in fact, a true expression of what he himself is, namely, god-devil at once.

Thus he sees that the religious exhortation to eradicate evil, and to foster and express good, really means that both the negative and positive aspects must receive attention simultaneously. There should not be, and there cannot be a moral vacuum at any time in one's being. But to think of the task as one of driving the devil out and inviting God in, is inaccurate. The devil is oneself. God, also, is oneself. Before fulfilment, one is god-devil. The devil has to be transformed into God, for he cannot merely be driven out. That precisely is the responsibility of the human part of one's whole self, which is animal and human and man-made-in-the-image-of-God. No one else can do this work for the human. By doing it himself, the human " brings forth " the true individual, in whom the transformation of devil into God is complete. One's own effort evokes an active response from the larger Whole of which one is an integral part. But without one's own, constant, deliberate effort as a fundamental pre-requisite, no such transformation of oneself is possible.

The true individual is the Virtuous One, or, the one who has not to acquire virtues. Virtue is the human's strength or śakti. It is soul-strength. The actual, daily life of the virtuous is as naturally true, good and beautiful as the sun is light-giving or the mountain stream is cool.

The central burden of ethical teaching, then, is to show man how to become the virtuous one.

Nature makes the instrument, man's bodily being. Man, the looker into himself, is the seer of the vision, and the exhorter of his fellow man to see also. In the very nature of the instrument lies the obstruction to the fulfilment of the vision. The pleasure-pain mechanism, which plays so paramount a part in the growth and preservation of any living organism, is also the most powerful obstructor of self-transcendence where man is concerned. The origins of the relative good-evil of everyday life are to be found in the pleasure-pain mechanism of the living organism, with attraction-repulsion as its counterpart in physical experiences, love-hate as the emotional counterpart, and the acceptable or worth-while and the unacceptable or not worth-while as the intellectual and value counterpart. The dualism of everyday life is a force which acts like a couple, as the scientist would say, and man goes " round and round " through endless " births and deaths " in everyday life.

Man's difficulty is that he is captivated or overcome by a stimulus, and he lets himself be helplessly swept off in mere reaction to it. He has not enough ability to respond by first calmly examining and fully understanding the stimulus, and then proceeding with a considered, controlled action. The pleasant captures his mind which reacts with liking it and with chasing after further pleasant experiences; the unpleasant imprisons his mind which reacts with disliking it, and he wants to get away or be rid of it. But if and when he masters each component of the dualism of life, then he transcends them both through the integration of the two into something altogether more wonderful: joy-sorrow gives place to Nirvāṇa; attraction-repulsion to Love; selection-rejection to Acceptance; concord-discord to Harmony; agreement-disagreement to Understanding; construction-destruction to Creation; indulgence-denial to Freedom.

Man's sense-functioning is the source of his faculty of speech-thought, which pre-eminently distinguishes him from all other creatures. Once the faculty of thinking is developed, he can continue thinking without seeing or hearing or tasting or smelling or touching. He can abstract himself away from sense-experiencing into an "inner" world of thinking. His thinking is the most powerful factor in his life, so far as he as a human, as distinct from the rest of creation, is concerned. His feeling-thinking, his psychical life, is thus of prime importance.

Now we can follow the process of liberation from compulsive morality, from relative, limited ethic.

Jesus said:

> Ye have heard that it was said by them of old time, Thou shalt not kill; and whosoever shall kill shall be in danger of the judgment:
>
> But I say unto you, that whosoever is angry with his brother without a cause shall be in danger of the judgment ....
>
> Ye have heard that it was said by them of old time, Thou shalt not commit adultery:
>
> But I say unto you, That whosoever looketh on a woman to lust after her hath committed adultery with her already in his heart.
>
> Matthew, V.21, 22, 27, 28.

and, significantly, he proceeds thus:

> And if thy right eye offend thee, pluck it out and cast it from thee; for it is profitable for thee that one of thy members should perish and not that thy whole body should be cast into hell.
>
> Matthew, V.29.

Jesus emphasizes, here, the importance of thought and feeling. The remedy he suggests (in verse 29) is put in a slightly terrifying form. Actually, it means precisely the pratyāhāra of the yogi, and the statement of the Third Noble Truth[1] by the Buddha.

The Saṁyutta Nikāya (Citta Saṁyutta, P.T.S. IV.281) says:

> The eye is not a fetter to material forms, nor are material forms a fetter to the eye; but that excited desire which arises there in consequence of both, that is the fetter . . .
> The mind is not a fetter to objects (of thought), nor are objects a fetter to the mind; but that excited desire which arises there in consequecne of both, that is the fetter.

"That excited desire" is the fetter that binds, the force which impels to sin. Not the senses as such, not sense-functioning, not objects as such, not experience as such, but "that excited desire", the lusting involved in desiring, is the source of Ill in factual life, mentally and physically. This was put in dramatic form by the Buddha in his fire sermon[2]: everything is on fire . . . with the fire of lust, hate and delusion . . . (and the solution is given as) becoming free from desire, he is liberated.

As said earlier, psycho-physical man is mainly reactive. His lusting, as well as his egoism, is a natural uprising born of natural forces. If a male meets a female, and certain conditions prevail, there is an inevitable, natural attraction, and a natural urge for copulation. Each inevitably looks at the other with "lust in the heart". The compulsive morality of the social order lays down the conditions and circumstances in which such copulating may or may not be performed. The feeling and thinking and acting of this man and woman follow from the uprising of the natural desire interacting with the environmental conditions. Desire, as well as the way one thinks and feels, is largely a helpless reacting. This is true of all ambitions, and also of most ideals. The youth wants to pass his school examination and get a good job—*his* fulfilment; as a young man he wants the girl of his heart, and all bliss will be his—*his* fulfilment; middle-aged, he wants to be a good citizen, bring up

[1] See above, pp. 189, 200.
[2] Vinaya, I. 14.

worthy children, engage in altruistic activities, serve God and man through the pursuit of noble causes, deeds of mercy, and in other ways—*his* fulfilment ; and so on. In each case, glands and hormones, upbringing, education, the pattern of one's being, character, experience and circumstance, *determine* the content and shape of his feeling-thinking.

Watch a maiden waiting on a railway platform : the changing expressions on her face ; looking at the clock ; pacing up and down ; sitting down for one moment—an astonishingly long moment to her ! the clock again, and a hasty touching up of lips and nose and hair ; glancing at you, with about three or four changes of expression on her face with the lightning reactions in her mind on seeing you ; the clock again ; rising excitement ; the train comes in ; a flush and a flutter, immense excitement, searching for the one face and body that is the object of pent-up longing ; they see each other, and—all the rest of it ! The tension becomes less ; a few ups and downs of emotion like a jack-in-the-box ; and then—the shadow of the next parting is already on them ! Happiness, for them, is never the bliss that will never end ! There is only a stimulus and a reaction, a stimulus and a reaction, an unending round !

Always there is the impassioned movement to make one, the two which keep falling apart. The desire, or lust, to " possess for ever ", to " never know the shadow of break-in-the-unity ", is inextricably tangled with ego-conceit of separate selfhood. The more powerful this ego, the more fervently is the right mate and the perfect union desired as the uttermost ideal of fulfilment. But this self-same separative ego-consciousness produces, as a reaction, the urge to re-establish consciousness of one-ness with the beloved, or with God, or with Nature, as the case may be. The happiness and sense of fulfilment of the union is expressed, and measured, in terms of the give and take of sensation. Bound by egocentricity, the demand is " you must give your whole self to me " ; bound by stupidity, " I will give you as I think and feel like giving you ", the I-think-and-feel being the product of one's misconceptions (so gross and evil, at times) of oneself ; bound by lust and ignorance, " you must give yourself to me in this, that or the other manner (the manner being the type of sensationalism, physical and psychical, for which I lust), or else I cannot believe you really love me."

A material cause of the sense of incompleteness is the fact of separate sexes. This, which is obvious to the senses, enhances the separate-self consciousness, or the separation-emphasizing consciousness. The manifestation of its contrary reaction pushes one to attract, and to be attracted by others. It is in the nature of the spatio-temporal manifested universe to diversify—impossible without dualism. Man grieves because of the passing away of what he likes and enjoys, and seeks continually to stabilize unity through acts of union, love. Imprisoned by separative selfhood, overcome by regarding anything and everything as an isolated permanent, every act of his, mental, verbal or physical, has a death to it. Therefore his unity-awareness is impermanent. It cannot be anything else as long as there is separate-ego identification with the constantly uprising and dying. He may forcibly hold the unity of the universe as a thought in his mind. But such a string of words is no living realization.

Desire and ego feed each other. The experience of worldly success or happiness, as well as the experience of frustration or misery, strengthens the sense of separate ego. The stronger the egoism (to be distinguished from being a strong personality —a weak character could be more intensely egoistic than a strong character), the stronger is the craving for satisfaction, either as indulgence or as compensation.

Lust and ego besmirch even what seems dedicated living. The separate ego is identified with or submerged in " the cause ": for king and country, for science, for God, for the poor and suffering, for the church. But in each such dedication there is the serpent of vested interest, the poison of " wanting it to succeed ". Every vested interest is a cutting off from the Whole ; it is egoistic and not individualistic ; it is a lack of trust in God, and a begrudging of the whole Glory to God alone. It is true that in actual process one must needs prune, reject, destroy, build up, separate and divide, even as a sculptor works when he releases the perfect form out of the block. But the process is besmirched when " my " interest, or desire and ego, displaces in slightest degree the creative Will of God working through me. Lust and ego inevitably prove their evil presence in so-called dedicated living. One example is seen when proselytizing churches think in terms of their survival in "Arcadia" depending upon a "long battle not only against (a political) 'ism' but against the ancient 'arcadian' religions now reinvigorated by passionate nationalism."

One may ask: How does one know whether ego is involved in what one confidently feels is selfless action? Here is a good, simple test: If personal disappointment or grief follows the "failure" of one's action, or if personal pleasure follows "success", that action is ego-tainted.

The illusion of egoistic separate selfhood is altogether dispensable.

The realization of whole individuality is indispensable.

As ego goes, self-consciousness goes. SELF-consciousness, an expression of the "Divine Mind", marks individuality.

Before attaining liberation, then, man's feeling-thinking is largely mere reactivity. The free Spirit in him is imprisoned in necessitous Matter. Thus, in his feeling-thinking, it is impossible for him not to murder, to steal, to do evil and to be impure. The pure and free state is denied him. He, as psycho-physical man, the organic whole, is the battleground of the prohibitions and affirmations of the ethic of good and evil; he is the constantly furrowed field of the struggle between vices and virtues, and between the lesser forms of virtue and the deeper aspects of virtue. Himself, striving to be virtuous, has to be policeman-warder to himself breaking out viciously. Not a peaceful life!

Indian philosophy has never failed to recognize the importance of the mind in man's life. Since feeling-thinking is what it is, since evil has lust and ego for its parents, and since the root-source of Ill is the not-become-Brahman condition, which is "the condition of mortal sin", what shall man do to remove all Ill? This is precisely where Indian ethical teaching has made one of its supreme contributions to man's well-faring. It has shown that God-consciousness, or "knowing" Brahman, is impossible through mere belief (a string of words), or through a compulsive code of life which is mechanically obeyed. Not mere morality, not mere intellectual perception, even of genius, not mere intuitive spiritual insight, not mere devotion and worship, not mere mediation by any Saviour (a teaching so mistaught, and so misunderstood by millions), but self-discipline —especially the sammā-sati of the Noble Eightfold Path— effects that purification of the mind whereby, as it were, the substance of the mind is transmuted, and the way in which the psycho-physical man functions is altered.

These are some of its central points : constant self-observation without praise or censure, which is dispassionate, scientific observation ; a growing knowledge of oneself, not just of abstract man but of one's particular self as one thinks and feels, speaks and acts, throughout the day ; putting aside, in the light of one's own growing perceptions, the unnecessary, the binding, the evil, step by step, and doing, in that same light of one's own perceptions, the necessary, the good. The voluntary putting away of what one sees through one's own vision to be unnecessary for Brahma-faring, is the true meaning of sacrifice, a making sacred ; and it involves no repression, for it is a true purification through intelligent relinquishment.

Dispassionate observation works like the sun dissipating mists. Mere reactivity, and egoistic functioning and lustful behaviour diminish. Putting aside the unnecessary means, among other things, ceasing to use the senses for deliberately observing or enjoying what does not conduce to Brahma-faring. What precisely does conduce to Brahma-faring progressively reveals itself to the practisant. He grows in wisdom and becomes virtuous, instead of trying to acquire wisdom and virtue. There comes the point when he sacrifices all self-pursuits. Through growing in the power to sacrifice, and through the practice of other aspects of the discipline, comes freedom from the lust for sensations, possessions, power, and moral and spiritual growth, and from egoism.

This is poverty. Blessed are such poor for they are truly dedicated to Brahma-faring. Their fulfilment of all the duties of this dedicated life is chastity. They live in obedience to the behests of the Dhamma, or Truth, or God. The further they progress, the greater is the austerity naturally and cheerfully practised. Desirelessness is indispensable for the highest stages. Hence celibacy is observed, because, more than anything else, this abstinence represents the disengagement of oneself from the root-principle of desire, from the fundamental pleasure seeking and personal gratification, from the most powerful expression of separate self. This is the supreme purity or chastity, indispensable if Love is to be truly universal and utterly selfless.

Forswearing love-lust puts into one's hands oppressive power. But sacrificing all lust together with separative ego makes one capable of unconditioned and undefiled Love, which is Divine, Healing Power. Becoming rid of all delusions and hate, one has perfect wisdom and freedom. He who is love and wisdom incarnate, can bless humanity. Himself utterly desire-less, in him alone "Thy Will, O God, not mine" is a reality. The physico-chemical energy which manifested in the human as wayward personal passion and desire, is the instrument, now, of the Divine Will through him who is the true individual, the Virtuous One.

This is the end of sin. The Self-realized and the Self-controlled are the Self-expressed. They are the peaceful and the free, not driven, helplessly, by reactions. Their feeling-thinking is utterly pure, sinless, for the devil-self has been transformed into God-being.

Indian ethical philosophy clearly teaches, that without complete desirelessness, it is quite impossible to understand fully, and to put into practice, the supreme ethic as exemplified in the lives of the Brahman-become, of the Teachers like the Buddha and the Christ. Man starts life with the handicap of being born God-unaware. This condition of sin is fostered and enhanced by his upbringing and education, which, as far as their defects go, nurture his illusion of separate selfhood, and teach him to work for success and happiness in the sense of egoistic self-assertion and the satisfaction of his "natural appetites and desires." This is not to accuse the world of parents, guardians and teachers, but to recognize a misfortune that afflicts the whole human race. Yet without this misfortune we should be the poorer by a necessary challenge to rise to life's most wonderful adventure—Self-discovery and God-realization. Merely being told about God, or being exhorted or even compelled to live an ethical life, does not bring about God-realization, though it helps one to take a step forward. Only the complete extinction of craving, hate and delusion effects absolution and brings God-realization. Until this is done, any personal desire whatsoever, good and idealistic, or otherwise, is tied up in some way or other with the separative ego, the division maker. Hence "my will", and not "Thy Will", prevails. But when one becomes free of all desire, then no obstruction is put in the path of The Supreme. Then indeed, "Thy Will, not mine" is fulfilled through the true individual.

When all personal desire has ceased, one takes no sides, but un-reactively accepts both sinner and saint, wrongdoer and wronged, with that all-understanding, all-forgiving love which is the Divine Love, which inspires the sinner to climb the pinnacle of saintliness, and the ignorant to touch the depth of omniscience. Then, too, one knows what is the right thing to do, and does it. And *that*, is practicality.

Now, one can make true sense of "Love your enemies, bless them that curse you, do good to them that hate you", and show that sublime teaching to be the natural law of the Good Life. For, by becoming the true individual, the condition of being bound to the mere reactivity of one's feelings or thoughts or actions to any stimulus is transcended, and, having gone beyond the conflict of relative good and evil, there is no problem of repressions.

Now, as the Buddha taught, the Arahant has crossed over the troubled waters of sin to the peaceful shore of the sinless state by using the raft of the virtues. Once safe, the raft is no longer needed, and the Virtuous One lives the virtues to perfection, effortlessly. As taught in the Upanishads, good and evil do not touch the Brahman-knower. When the man-made-in-the-image-of-God is sculptured to perfection, and the Beauty hidden in the heart of the universe is unveiled before mortal eyes, when the Brahma-faring has led a man to that peak which is the fulfilment of the purpose of existence, then his way of life is the expression in this world of a transcendental ethic in operation, beyond the good and evil of ordinary men. And all men are ordinary, except the purified, the desireless, the undeluded, who, realizing individuality (which precisely is the fruit of correctly understanding the Buddha's an-attā teaching), are at home in Nirvāṇa, in the kingdom of God. This means that they have won mastery over speech-thought. No longer earth-bound they can consciously enter that peaceful, ever-creative, Brahma-loka, where Godhead "dwells". They know, that That-Yon is here-now.

The transcendental ethic of the liberated yogi is the hidden source of inspiration, and also the final determinant, of the ethic and morality of Everyman. Though openly manifest in the life of a Gotama, a Jesus, a Zarathustra, it is nevertheless partly hidden, not because it is veiled but because there are not very many who have eyes keen enough to see. This ethic is the ethic of absolute values. As an example, the first teaching of "Love one another" as presented in the Atharva Veda (III.30) is perfect love at the human level—organic, social, reciprocal. Transcendent love is taught by Yājñavalkya in his discourse to Maitreyī, by the Buddha, by Jesus; in another form, by Brahmā to Nārada (Upadeśas II and V of the Nārada-parivrājaka Upanishad); by several others; by Gandhi. Its essence is non-reciprocity: whatever the circumstances, whatever comes from others to oneself, from oneself will go forth only love, even as the sun lightens sinner and saint alike. Transcendent love is not an animal-human reaction but a continuous, healing activity characterizing the sinless, Brahman-become. It has no degrees of affection, no conditions attached.

Being beyond good and evil, transcendental ethic is the absolute Good. It is beyond the limiting world of arguments and considerations. Unlike ordinary morality, and ethical teaching, which change as man develops or circumstances demand, transcendental ethic is not subject to historical process and development.

He who lives in accordance with the transcendental ethic which is beyond our relative good and evil, fulfills to perfection the ordinary moralities as laid down for man. But he lives them not with effort, not with struggling for good against evil, but effortlessly, as second nature, like the effortless technique with which the perfect musician plays his instrument. Hence the form in which the Buddha presents what he calls the trifling, minor details of mere morality[1]—to us ordinary folk it is a stupendous achievement, with nothing trifling or minor or mere about it—is profoundly significant. He presents the negative aspect of the ethic as the prohibition, following it immediately with the positive aspect of the corresponding virtues. He himself lives this ethic. We call such a life the blameless life; but he regards it as just the junior school stage. But in his so regarding it, and because of his effortlessly living it, one can see the transcendental import of the simple prohibitions common to the religions: Thou shalt not kill, because the living creature is the temple of the Most High; thou shalt not steal, nor take what is not given freely, because by stealing thou hast made false division of "thine" and "mine", unlovingly faithlessly, untruly, and hast marred the unity; thou shalt not be unchaste, because by unchastity thou hast misused and desecrated creative power, thy direct link with God the Creator. Again, every act of love in expression is a sacrament. The universal process, and human activities are sacramental: the "study of the sacrifice" mentioned in the Upanishads is the study by which one understands this, and participates in the great, perpetual sacrament of the Universe of which Eternal God is the High Priest.

It is thought by some that ethics can mean little or nothing if God is de-personalized or discarded. The Buddha's teachings, the Upanishadic philosophy of Brahman-Ātman and of Tat-tvam-asi, are thought to leave no room for ethic; and that the moral and intellectual discipline which is undergone is for selfish escape. What sense there is in such thinking, and in other similar thought in connection with Indian religious teaching, can be left to the reader to judge.

The understanding of good and evil is a measure of one's own development. The transforming and integrating process of the universe impels man towards fulfilment, which we may call

[1] See above, pp. 217, 218. See also, Brahmajāla Sutta, D. I. 4-12.

the absolute good, whose content and expression are far removed from our imaginings, but which are an open book to him who is fulfilled, namely the self-less one. Selflessness is non-egoistic, dynamic personality ; it is true and unique individuality ; it is the cessation of thraldom to the dualistic world, through living, as master, in the dualistic world.

Let no man delude himself that he can live by the letter of transcendental ethic whilst he is still unperfected and unfulfilled, although he can march forward inspired by its spirit. No man can really follow in the Master's footsteps by trying to copy His acts or speech or ways. The Master's life is the expression of what He himself is, in His own particular environment. Each of the Great Teachers was unique and original in His Self-expression. Time and circumstance do not stand still, and each person is just himself and not the Master. Unquestionably, the Master's acts and speech are an inspiration to us. But to copy the form of His Self-expression is just to play the ape. Inspired by the Exemplar, each person's duty is to give true expression to what he is in himself, an expression which includes self-restraint or abnegation as and when required. The behaviour which truly expresses each person's own character is like the style distinguishing each creative artist.

The right ethic for each person is the ethic which is true to his actual character and abilities, his striving and his aspiration. It is his Dharma, as Hinduism puts it. If he mechanically observes the formula of a higher ethic, for which he is unprepared because of insufficient self-knowledge and self-discipline, then he merely stores up in the deeps of his psyche an immense reactive force which will explode destructively when time, in its ripeness, presents him with the ineluctable evil situation.

So each man must make sure he does not play at being a Christ or a Kṛishṇa or a Buddha, for he will certainly suffer damnation. Let him, as the Buddha said on his deathbed, strive on with diligence. Thus he will cross over sin, and become the Light that lights the world.

Section G

RELIGION AND THE RELIGIONS

WORLD ORDER : NIRVANA : LOVE

THE MEANS for Brahma-faring and God-realization is religion. He who has realized, lives a life exemplifying religion. The very core of it consists in the at-home-ness in God-consciousness, in which sense-mind consciousness is transcended, which means, perfected and intensified through purification and not discarded or neglected. It is the complete contrast and answer to any ivory tower existence. In that transcendent state, the Perfected One " lives " as God " lives " ; and this, is RELIGION, this is the supreme meaning of the religious life.

RELIGION is the way God lives His life.

This life, beyond the good and evil of relative morality, embodying the Absolute Good of transcendental ethic, is over and above all our familiar, dualistic, sense-mind categories.

RELIGION does not admit of examination or criticism in terms like " world and life negating, or affirming ", " pessimistic ", " optimistic ", and so on. The Great Exemplars, whose life is the embodiment of RELIGION, give teachings showing ways by which others may attain. The forms in which these teachings are cast, the various religions of the world, necessarily include verbal statements. Words belong to the sense-mind sphere, wherein optimism-pessimism, reward-punishment, virtue-vice, good-evil, damnation-salvation have meaning. Since this is the sphere of mortality, its categories cannot be used in relation to the Immortal. But just as a man can have knowledge and talk intelligently of pre-natal conditions (whereas no unborn babe can know or talk of adult man), so the man-become-God can tell how mortal man and all his activities appear to His transcendent vision and values.

It is most significant, therefore, that " this " world, and man's activities and values have been presented by the Great Exemplars in terms which, from mortal man's point of view and in the light of worldly values, are regarded as pessimistic, as world and life negating, as escapism, inactivity, negativity and a flight from reality.

The aim of RELIGION is to enable man to cross over sin, and, triumphing over mortality, to realize the Immortal here-now whilst existent in this living body. Man's dualistic categories and values belong to the transient world of birth and death, of corruption and selfishness, the world in which he is a prisoner on account of his unawakened consciousness, his unbaptised state (unbaptised in the real sense of the word, and not in the exclusively Christian or any ceremonial sense). Therefore, he must completely put aside such values when considering RELIGION. To say that religions like Christianity or Buddhism are pessimistic, and world and life negating, or that religions like Zarathustrianism and some of the Hindu forms of religion are optimistic, and world and life affirming, is to say what is inapplicable in the context. As taught by the Great Teachers, RELIGION altogether transcends pessimism and optimism, world and life affirmation and negation, " world " and " life " being understood in the restricted, mortal sense. By enabling man to realize the Immortal, to " see God face to face ", RELIGION takes man as completely out of the sphere

NOTE.—Just as the unborn babe cannot see the wonderful world into which he will be born, even so an ordinary man, however high his merely intellectual qualifications or however sincere his mere beliefs may be, cannot see the radiance of the state of the deathless Immortal. Again, just as the unborn babe will suddenly use certain latent faculties (the organs for which are already there) only after birth, so, too, ordinary man suddenly uses latent faculties once his inner consciousness stirs in response to the Immortal. The Brahman-become can, at will, stop the unbidden flow of discursive thought, unite himself with the Father in prayer, enter the Fourth Jhāna in samādhi, and know the bliss of Nirvāṇa; he has the capacity for " direct knowing ", by " being " the thing perceived, in full consciousness; he understands, as we do not, the reality of omniscience, omnipotence, omnipresence and creation. But none of these faculties usurp, though they may sometimes enlighten, sense and speech-thought activities; nor in any sense can they dispossess the modes of investigation and expression proper to all the sciences and philosophies and arts of ordinary life. This must be carefully borne in mind in view of statements made by people claiming possession of various " supernormal " abilities, on matters which are legitimately the province of experimental science.

of pessimism-optimism, retrogression-progress, as the new-born infant is taken out of its old world inside its mother. RELIGION is the "life" wherein that dynamic poise, that upekkhā of the Buddha, that unperturbed, active bliss of Brahman, the Peace of God, holds sway. Experience the reality, and all carping criticisms vanish.

But this complete transformation of man's consciousness is the culmination of a process. One of its elements consists in seeing "this" world as the Immortals see it. Hence, what the Great Teachers said, as embodied in Veda and Upanishad, Sutta and Dhammapada, Gītā and Bible, makes the erstwhile bright, joyous, worthy things and activities of mortal striving and existence appear dark, sad and unworthy. Warped judgments passed on RELIGION are a hindrance to fulfilment. One must regard RELIGION, and each of the several religions, from the standpoint of the goal, which is God-becoming, the realization of Immortality, the cessation from being a producer of evil and sorrow, here and now whilst living in the world.

* * * *

In a broad and liberal sense, it is true to say that India is as a spiritual mother in whose embrace the world's faiths are held as children. Despite quarrels, the children live together in the familiar atmosphere of the old home. One or other of these children has thought, and still thinks occasionally, in terms of ousting the others and being the one and only, or of ruling the mother and the other members in the home.

All religions have flourished on Indian soil, and become modified through interaction with each other. Buddhism, which was almost extirpated by Ikhtiyar-ud-Din Muhammad in 1193 with the destruction of Odantapuri and its great monastery, is slowly expanding again. Zarathustrianism has just over a hundred thousand followers. But the other great religions number their devotees in millions.

Modern advances in scholarship and knowledge are revolutionizing many religious beliefs, which have to bear the merciless probe of skilled research, and the fierce flame of challenging criticism. All to the good, for stagnant religion is the devil's fortress. One should welcome with open arms the onslaught of sincere criticism and fearless questioning upon his faith. It is the duty of each person himself to question, challenge, experiment, observe, deny, uphold, discover, and finally, to realize. There are various ways of setting about this task, and it is for each one to find out which way is suitable to his temperament and capacities, and profitable to himself. The truth in the great religions is never in need of defence or apology, for truth cannot be destroyed ; and so the heart of faith cannot be stabbed to death, or its ground be budged a cubit. But the shortcomings in the statements about the truth in the religions is a measure of our own defects, which can be overcome through research and criticism, and through that self-discipline which leads to realization.

Blind belief, miscalled faith, must be rejected, for perverted faith has produced untold misery as history proves. The attitude which asserts " My religion or god is the true one, yours is false ; I worship the holy spirit, you are an idolator ; mine is the revelation by the almighty himself, yours is the doctrine of false prophets ", marks the very nadir of bigotry. All claims by or on behalf of the not-yet-God-become to infallibility are themselves the condemnation of him who calls himself, or is called by his supporters, the infallible one. Convictions, naturally, will be held. But an unalterable conviction is an untruthful expression of the truth one has sensed. As man grows and his perception of the truth deepens, he must needs change the form ; his conviction must be converted into a more suitable expression of the truth.

It would be well if certain men renounced the childish, ego-assertive attitude and effort to " win the world over to Christ ". Time and again, leading figures in world affairs have been guilty of expressing such short-sighted views as : " Only a Christian ethic can save the world ", or, " Only on Christian ideals and a Christian world-outlook can a world order be based." Conceit, spiritual arrogance and militant evangelism are inevitable concomitants of successful aggression militarily, politically and economically. Zarathustrianism was guilty of it in a small way at one period of her history. Islam was guilty of it. And the sinful part of Christendom has brazenly triumphed with it, contradicting in its actual history, the winning over to God by self-sacrificing love as embodied in the sinless, crucified Jesus. Were Christendom to become sinless—worthy of God, therefore—suffer crucifixion at the hands of the wicked world, attain full God-consciousness and then utter, as Jesus did, " It is accomplished ", before giving up the ghost with a loud cry, then, in that divine moment the world will be won over to God—not to an " anity ", a church, an organization, or a vested interest, but to Eternal God.

What would the Christian world feel and do if, say, Hindus were to set about to " win the world over to Hinduism ", or to pronounce, " Only a Hindu ethic can save the world ", or, " Only on Hindu ideals and a Hindu world outlook can a world order be based " ?

It is argued, in defence of Christian militant evangelism, that Jesus was the Son of God. The conception of the Son of God is older than the birth of Jesus, and the Sons of God, the Brahmapùtras, were not unknown in India (and elsewhere), before and after Jesus and are not unknown to-day ; and, moreover, they all were, and are, " born of a Virgin."

Christendom points to the crucifixion and resurrection of Jesus as the marks of his uniqueness and supremacy in relation to all other Teachers. The non-Christian world points out that the teachings underlying the terms crucifixion and resurrection are far anterior to the birth of Jesus, and that they refer to experiences of the person who sets out on the Path of Holiness, and attains fulfilment.[1] He who treads the Path far enough experiences " crucifixion ", or, " the death of the soul ". He is bereft in every way by the world. He is bereft of his convictions, of the bases of his beliefs, of all faith and trust in the world's ways and institutions, in man, in those nearest and dearest to him, in his own inner spirit, in God. The death of the soul is not a subject for investigation by the curious—only he who has passed through and beyond it, safely, can fitly investigate it. It is the most solemn experience, or series of experiences, which the seeker of God can go through. If he comes out of it trium-

[1] See also, above, p. 180.

phantly, as the Jina, the Victor, the one who has " overcome the world ", he comes out as one who has become utterly calm, harmless and undeluded, who is beyond any need for personal security, love, happiness or success, who accepts sinner and saint alike, and who is wholly compassionate, loving, forgiving and self-sacrificial. He is the resurrected one, he is the Brahman-become.

With due understanding for the feelings and faith of Christians, non-Christian India points out the unacceptability of the teaching of resurrection as presented by Christendom. This presentation may have served some purpose in the past ; but it is the true meaning which man needs and seeks. Non-Christians would also draw attention to the fact that the meanings underlying crucifixion and resurrection were known to those who were initiated into certain mysteries—in Egypt, Greece, Western Asian lands, India and Central Asia. One of the initiation ceremonies required the neophyte to lie on his back in a small enclosed chamber, completely immobile as if he were dead. (Mastery of Śavāsana, or the Dead Pose, is one of the practices of training in Yoga.) On the third day, he rose from the dead. During that period, the aspirant went deeper and deeper into the silence. If he could not successfully go beyond what the Buddha called the Seventh Deliverance (see above p. 169), or beyond one of the earlier stages, he fell asleep—compare the falling asleep of the disciples, particularly Peter, whilst Jesus "prays" in the garden of Gethsemane. But if he successfully passed the Seventh Deliverance, he won the superconsciousness of the Eighth Deliverance, where " I and my Father are one " is realized, where the full union of Pratyagātman and Paramātman is consummated. If the initiate is a fully trained yogi, he wins also full physical health, and remarkable physical powers, particularly where fatigue and sleep, hunger and thirst are concerned ; and it is only in this sense that there is a bodily resurrection. When the initiate rose from the dead, he rose as the true individual, the God-become, after which he was fit to " make public ", that is, to teach the earnest disciples, the mysteries which should not be publicly taught till he had risen from the dead.

He who, not merely in symbolical ceremony, but in very truth of living experience has gone through this, knows that " crucifixion " and " resurrection " are here and now. Out of the death of the " life " of the here and now, one emerges into the fullness of the Immortal, here-now. The resurrection means the " accession to the throne " by God Immanent. The Immortal, here-now, is a conscious realization by living man, but the " body ", the psycho-physical organism of each and everyone without exception, dies and perishes in accordance with changeless law, and knows no resurrection.

India respects fervent faith. She herself exemplifies it. But she points out that militant evangelism, an intolerant and illiberal activity, is an expression of egoism and spiritual lust only, and as such is distasteful to her. The greater part of India says: by all means discuss your faith with us; share your views and your experience with us; but let not the gracious code underlying such exchanges be violated. India would like to suggest that the true missionary is one who, by both example and precept, helps the other to live his own faith more perfectly and not forsake it for the missionary's faith, except of his own free will and choice. To give such help effectually, the missionary should be one who really knows the religion of the other person, and also his own. There is no evidence yet of the existence of Christian missionaries of that calibre, as far as their knowledge of Hinduism or Buddhism or Zarathustrianism is concerned. But there is evidence which makes non-Christians wonder, if Christians themselves have plumbed the full depth of the teachings of Jesus, through realization, beyond speech-thought, however well they may have churned the ocean of speech-thought. This challenge, Christendom will begin to answer very soon; so far, circumstances have not afforded either the cause or the means to answer it.

It is stated by Christians that in the person of Jesus, once and for all God intervened, in order to save mankind. The non-Christian world would like the Christian world to put aside its conceit that it is the best and the select, to remember that in a world of unique incomparables there is no real meaning to " best and select " in certain contexts, and then, coolly and with right wisdom, to consider its statement that the Creator, the Grand Architect of the Universe, the omniscient, all-wise Governor who can hold a thousand million galaxies in the palm of His hand, who scattered a hundred thousand million glittering stars all round our own single galaxy for our heart's delight, who made blazing suns, and strange planets and moons moving in a rhythmic ring dance with a perfection that staggers our puny imagination, who made a fifth grade sun as lord of life and light over our sweet green mother earth, who with a mere bit of clay and a puff of exhaled breath from His divine lips made man on earth (perhaps much like man on a hundred million other planets), and who watched him get along for a million years or so reasonably well—this Maker and Father suddenly had to intervene on the eastern shores of that small sea the Mediterranean, *just once and for all*, in order to save mankind! To non-Christians, such a statement is preposterous, and an insult to God's intelligence: preposterous, because the statement, made by ordinary people, implies that these people know the mind of God with respect to the whole of the future; and an insult to God's intelligence because the necessity for a special, once for all intervention implies incapacity for proper governance and management, or it implies capriciousness.

The Brahman-become, those who have realized Ātman, those who have God-consciousness which is the superconsciousness beyond speech-thought, know precisely the meaning of the divinity of Jesus, know precisely what he attained. So they reject this artificial doctrine of a once and for all intervention. They know, as also do other clear-seeing people, including many Christians, the falsity of the claim foisted by deluded devotees, of the exclusive paramountcy of one Teacher. (Deluded devotees of non-Christian faiths have also claimed exclusive paramountcy for their own Teachers.) The time is at hand, now, when men must free themselves from this, and other similar delusions, which have been the bases, too often and too long, for the infiltrations of that quartet, the trader, the missionary, the soldier and the wine-seller.

It is thought by knowledgeable people that man possibly has a life-span on this planet of about one or two thousand million years. Time enough, the non-Christian world feels, for new Revelations, and for the slowly increasing gathering of the Brahmaputras on our earth.

The non-Christian world also feels that the Christian world should consider the fact, that as long as Christians think of converting the world to Christianity, as long as they assert that only on Christian foundations must, or can, a world-order be based, such egoism and purblind vision will make and preserve unholy division between themselves, some eight hundred millions in all, and Buddhists, Hindus, Muslims, Zarathustrians and others, some sixteen hundred millions in all. Christians are guilty of the wholly unwarrantable assumption of their rightness, superiority and their God-chosen-ness in relation to the rest of the world. It is unhappily true, historically, that the adherents of all the rigidly monotheistic religions have been, or still are, guilty of this same evil. Attention has been drawn to Christians rather than to the others simply because Christendom rides the saddle to-day in world affairs. Nations calling themselves Christian hold dominant power militarily, politically and economically, and exercise a very much greater control over the world than non-Christian peoples. Should any other monotheism militantly step into Christendom's shoes to-morrow, remarks similar to those made above in relation to Christendom would apply to it.

If Christendom does not clarify its vision and see that the Christian faith, the Christian way, the Christian formulation of the truth is but one of several others with which it must co-operate, if it does not rid itself of illiberalism and of its militancy, and if it does not see, and abide by the seeing, that just as it has gifts and lessons for other faiths, so too have other faiths much to give and teach it, then Christendom will learn the hard way.

Now in India significant things have happened. The first Christian mission in the first century was received with friendliness. The Gods of Hinduism have never been illiberal or rude, but have always recognized and courteously greeted other guises of themselves. Islam had the misfortune at first, of falling upon her Hindu host's neck somewhat clumsily. The host being much older, fell down before the weight of this robust entry. But the incomparable Akbar, whose life and deeds shouted from the housetops Muhammad's own teaching in the Quran, "Let there be no compulsion in religion", redeemed this to a remarkable extent. After the reign of ill-starred Aurangzeb, a Christian power rose to overlordship in India, and Christian ideals and teaching and missions came to stay, doing good service in certain fields to India.

The work of Christian scholars was perhaps the most powerful stimulus to India's religious renaissance. But whilst their scholarship was of a high order, some of their interpretations of the deeper teachings were faulty. Old boats must be burned. To-day, Indians themselves are once again not merely studying but realizing the profundities for themselves. They see the good and the truth and the beauty of the teachings given by all the Great Teachers of India and elsewhere. Many Indians particularly value the fact that each religion is unique and incomparable. God has not blessed the world with only one kind of flower.

To-day in South India, the Christian Churches, with the exception of the Roman Catholic, have united. It may be, that in course of time the Catholic Church will also join the union of the Churches in South India—a desirable consummation, for the Catholic Church holds a rich share of profound teachings and systems of discipline. Christendom in India is distinguished by simple, fervent devotion. If Christendom the world over has an understanding heart, and ability, it can profit by observing Christendom in India.

Meanwhile, it is not unlikely that non-Christians will increasingly prove a source of fresh inspiration to Christendom, and of help with those interpretations and insights without which Christianity may find itself, by degrees, a spent force.

Without Christianity, the hitherto remarkable development of social justice and the value of the individual, team work and the spirit of voluntary co-operation by free individuals and peoples, could not have taken place. The Personal God concept of Christendom, and Christian congregational worship, which is the most highly developed form in the world of congregational as distinct from individual worship, have been two of the most powerful factors in this development. But Christendom has sinned more than any other, in allowing the culture of the individual to degrade into rampant egoism.

Salvation from rampant egoism and the perfecting of true individuality cannot be effected without the interaction of Brahman and Īśvara (the Personal God). It has been already indicated that Īśvara by itself is the root of separate ego, and of confinement to the realm of manifestation. We may think of it in this way: if you are one of those fortunate ones who is truly united with the beloved, do you realize richer individuality in your inner consciousness, in terms of yourself as a separate self-contained you, or in terms of you and your beloved as a united whole? And if the latter, as it should be, is it not true that what is ordinarily the separate you, far from being lost, is indescribably intensified as self-existent personality through the integrated unity with the beloved? We may also express this by saying: I am more SELF by being not restricted to just myself. It must be appreciated that the inner psychical and spiritual life is very different from, and sometimes apparently contradicts, everyday life-experience. But too often, to our confusion, we apply the criteria of the less developed to the more integrated.

Now Brahman-realization leads precisely to the full consciousness of "I am more SELF by being not restricted to just myself." Most monotheists find it peculiarly difficult to de-egoize, and instead, truly individualize. Hence they easily fall into the naïve misinterpretation of Brahman summed up in such terms as impersonality, de-personalized deity, lost in Brahman. They fight tooth and nail to maintain decaying ego in perpetuity, instead of fearlessly, and dutifully to God, realizing immortality, which, of the Eternal, is neither survival nor annihilation. But if they are able to take that one profounder step, the difficulties in their path will be easier to surmount. The way to be rid of rampant egoism, and to realize true individuality will become clearer. Brahman, Godhead, is the reality. God, Īśvara, is man's conception, only a way of talking.

The coming years will see changes in the religious sphere as great and dramatic as those in the scientific have been in the near past. The living religions will undergo reinterpretation and cleansing ; and far from being replaced by science or by some petty " ism ", they will become a more vital influence in man's life. Already, they are becoming a profounder personal concern to individual men and women in larger numbers. As time passes, more people will have a deeper knowledge and a more sympathetic appreciation of faiths other than their own. There will be a slowly growing tendency for the young to study and to be helped to study all religions, and then, at a mature age, to choose membership in the one which appeals most to them (or to be free of formal membership in any of them if they so decide), instead of being made to belong automatically, as heretofore, to the faith of their parents. Religion will become more a matter for serious investigation, a discipline of oneself, and a root inspiration for all aspects of one's life, and less and less a matter of formalized doctrines and mechanical rituals. God will be not only an object of worship but verily the That-which-has-to-be-realized. The power and place and tasks of the professional dignitaries and servants of all religions will also undergo great changes.

Above all, science, as well as far reaching changes in the politico-economic structure of the world, accompanied by much suffering, unrest and upheaval, will be one of the most powerful forces bearing on the religions. And then will be seen the full fruition of the Upanishadic teachings of Brahman-Ātman and of the Buddha's teachings on the one hand, and of Christ's teaching, after its profounder significances are better understood, on the other.

Closer sympathy and right reconciliations between religions will not take place through syncretism or eclecticism, but through growing insight in individual men and women, through self-observation and self-discipline, and through the study of the sciences. It will be understood that a man being what he is, he accordingly interprets what he sees. The world's religions are different from each other not only in minor but also in major matters. For instance, one of the most profound and remarkable religions, Buddhism, has no doctrines of a Personal

God as a separate entity as conceived, defined and named by unknowing mortals, and of soul or survival, all of which are cardinal tenets of other faiths. Different insights and different expressions are all needed.

It is neither possible to dish up a mere conglomerate religion of all the existing religions, nor is it necessary or desirable. Whatever destroys or diminishes uniqueness is undesirable. Each religion can best help, and constructively influence and co-operate with another, only by retaining its full integrity. At the same time, the proper study and practice of other religions, in addition to one's own, lead to that profounder understanding without which true unity and peace between the religions remains an idle dream.

Whilst it is true that all religions show differences from each other, it is also true that they have affinities and bonds between them, and also some identical teachings. The exhortation to live the good life is one of the focal points where all religions meet. All religions aim at man's fulfilment spiritually, at the transcending of ego and the realization of a summum bonum. They are all idealistic. They are also realistic.

Above all, the great religions find their unity in the root, namely in RELIGION which is the way God lives, the Dhamma-become lives, the Brahman-knower lives. As and when RELIGION is increasingly manifest in a man's life, that man sees that the underlying unity of the religions is far profounder than their obvious differences. The senses and reason increasingly penetrate and tabulate differences ; spiritual insight and Buddhi increasingly relate and integrate the diversities into a single whole. The former can spread confusion, and darkness ; the latter, enlighten.

After attaining realization, a man knows that the different religions are but the different garbs of the single, naked, living truth which is RELIGION. When a man has found the stillness, and is God-become, or has realized the Ātman, every category and limited mode of expression of the manifested universe becomes inapplicable. In the Buddha's words (Udāna, VIII.I.), here is no coming or going, birth or death, thing or thought ; here is only the absolute end of Ill, or, as we may state, here-now is the indescribable, unanalysable, ineffable Well. This experienced God-existence, on our return to spatio-temporal consciousness, inspires a way of life, a religious teaching, which is a guide and a pathway for others to walk to the consummation, God-existence. Whereas God-existence, the Unconditioned, is the one and invariable, the man-ways-of-life, the religions, will necessarily be the several and different, on account of the varying, conditioning forces which characterize this world and its people.

He whose life is RELIGION in manifestation claims to be truly invested with Divine Authority. For him, external knowledge and the exernal authorities—apostolic, intellectual, scholarly, commentarial, all of which are as the gods of Valhalla—are thrown out by that individual God-realization which is finality as far as the Truth of the Spirit is concerned. On ceasing to seek finality—the very seeking spells non-finality, and finality in the sense of a straight-line end is only a dead-end—the sense of finality is here-now; for this sense comes from the Immortal Eternal, the fount of Creation out of no-thing, and not the mere round of making and unmaking atoms and universes. The frantic search for sense-mind finality in the here and now (not the here-now) is like oneself being rushed along like a senseless object by a torrential stream of thought and act. But if that swirl is stopped, one becomes undisturbed, actively poised. Only thus, in the state of upekkhā, one can fully absorb all impressions, or sense-mind activity, and at last see clearly with open eyes, as the born and not the unborn child can see. Then, one sees the finality of the Truth of the Spirit.

There are those who rebel, not unnaturally, against "reading into the actual words of the Vedas and the Upanishads more than what the words really mean." But exact verbal equivalence constitutes only a part of the meaning, of which the vital element is its inner significance. Words cannot convey the whole "flesh and blood" of feeling-thinking, and still less can they convey the content of whole experiencing. It is true that the greatness and beauty of language does consist in expressing varying shades of feeling-thinking, so that more and more of the rich content of our psychical life finds expression in speech, or is effectually suggested by it. And yet, though shades of thought can find rich expression in speech, what words can convey the *light* of thought when thought is set ablaze through inner enlightenment ? An ordinary man and a genius equally say " I see " to express the fact that they have grasped the matter—but one must look with a " third " eye, into the minds of the two to see the difference in content labelled by the words " I see."

We in this literalistic age are somewhat prone to exercise our critical faculties in those fields where it would be more profitable to experiment than to judge. To " take a vow of silence ", practise the discipline, become harmonized, and still, and then see for oneself the inner light, otherwise somewhat obscured, in the word of the Veda and Upanishad, the Gītā and Gāthā, the New and the Old Testament—this is what philosopher and sage did in the old days. Do we, the logical positivists and psychologists and scientists and comparative religionists of to-day, we who are the modern, passing fashion of the intellectual world, do we think we were not foreshadowed in the past ? If we think so, let us call back to mind that Indian, one Kṛishṇa, who of geometers is Lobatchewsky, of gravitationists Newton, of relativists Einstein, of warriors Churchill, of presidents Roosevelt, of statesmen Nehru, of power the atomic ; and who is also the hitlering of an Adolf and the goebbling of a Joseph—wherein is hid a perplexing mystery !

* * * *

As social beings set in a politico-economic environment, men are confronted with the problem of making this environment a happy order, stable enough to ensure the continuity of worthy traditions and of a good way of life, and elastic enough to adapt itself to changes.

In the past, many believed that the acquisition of wealth and the extension of power would ensure such an order, and reward them with greater security and happiness. So they made themselves strong, conquered and ruled other countries, acquired wealth and controlled the lives of men in weaker and less fortunate states. But time and again, as history shows, these dominant states ultimately fell, or were destroyed.

In our own day, too, we see the tide and ebb of power and wealth. To-day, many men hold beliefs similar to those held in the past. Those forces within man's own nature which produce widespread misery, strife and world disorder, are as much in evidence to-day as they were in the past. There is, for instance, the egoism, aggressiveness and self-assertiveness associated with power; there is greed and avarice and the lust for self-gratification; there is the pathetic belief that happiness and fulfilment depend mainly on possession, that money can buy anything, which lashes men on to a frantic scramble for wealth, like Alberich driving the Niebelung hordes. Added to this is the sombre and prize depriving characteristic of most men and women to turn a blind eye to their own responsibility for personal action where world order is concerned, and to look anxiously to others, to organizations or governments to produce the millennium for them.

"The balance of power", "the end justifies the means" and "enlightened self-interest" are three of the active principles which have disgraced human history, particularly in recent centuries. So we behold to-day a dangerous situation in which the upholders of opposing "isms", splitting most of the world into two camps, glower at each other, little realizing that fundamentally they are but man and fellow man. Of a nature akin to those two dull-witted giants, Fafner and Fasolt, slaves of power and lust, these opposing camps threaten all mankind. Hence before our very eyes we see prosperity fast flowing away into immense preparations for defence. Yet all these preparations, though partly reassuring, cannot quite remove the terrible anxiety and fear of war and misery.

In this modern age which witnesses breath-taking achievements through man's exploration and knowledge and control of matter, of environment and natural forces, in this age when man like a magician is performing prodigies well nigh miraculous, in which his developed social justice, his respect for the individual, his humane and liberal outlook and behaviour in at least some parts of the world is glad vindication of his struggles and sacrifices, in this very age we behold anxiety and fear, neurosis and frustration, gigantic greeds and hellish hatreds, strikes and wars, insecurity and misery, heartbreak and disillusionment, poverty despite plenty, slavery despite freedom. Evil abounds everywhere, and sorrow eats away the hearts of men and women lonely in the midst of huddled millions.

Under these circumstances fear gnaws at the vitals of him who dreads the destruction of our civilization and values, or the extermination of the human race by means of the atom bomb and other engines of destruction. One can hardly help wondering, what is this much vaunted civilization worth, if man, its maker, appears so incapable of preserving it? What are his values which leave him cravenly impotent to prevent himself acting like a suicidal maniac?

But it is more to the point to ask, what is wrong? What should we do to bring ourselves nearer to order and peace? What guidance does religion offer us?

At the outset it should be clearly recognized that there is no panacea for the world's ills. It is impossible ever to realize any utopia. No plan can cover the immense range of differences in outlooks, ways of life, abilities, aspirations and strivings of all the different human groups living in the world. Even if the making of a plan covering this vast range of differences is just possible, there is no person to-day, nor any body of people, possessed of the requisite knowledge, foresight and world grasp to draw up such a plan. Moreover, it is only too well known through repeated experience, that whilst foresight may discern trends keenly enough, no one can predict precisely how the stream of life will flow. Life cannot be forcibly confined in a rigid mould. To-day, not many are unaware of the incalculable part played by the unforeseen and the unexpected, of the necessity to deal like a skilled improviser with fresh situations as they arise, and of the importance of redefining the good in the light of advances in knowledge and under changing conditions.

Again, no rigid ideology can be laid down, and masses of men, still less all mankind, be compelled to live in slavish, unquestioning obedience to it. In fact, such compulsion always spells doom. At the very core of his being each individual is free, like God, and the realization of his true freedom should be fostered and served by any and every community or state. The individual for his part, should self-responsibly make his own contribution for the nourishment of society. It is to the creativeness of individuals that mankind owes its real advances in all fields. This is not to deny the necessity and utility of controls and sanctions, to ensure coherence and stability. But, just as one criterion of a teacher's success is the speed with which he enables his pupil to dispense with further tuition, so, too, the speed with which a sanction renders itself unnecessary is a measure of its efficacy and value.

Individuals as well as groups have their own convictions. They have no right, however, to impose these forcibly upon others. All are free to experiment in their own way, conditioned by the simple humanity which requires each not to hurt his neighbour thereby. Regimentation or totalitarianism is the forcible degrading of men to the level of animals. But whereas animals are good animals, no man can be thus degraded but that he is turned into a sullen beast of burden if he is in a humble situation, or into a monstrous beast of prey if he is in authority, ripe instrument, each, for destructive violence. Whoso compels another is something of a devil incarnate; and in denying freedom to his fellow he forfeits his own individuality, his very humanity. It should be remembered, that in actual fact, compulsion is exercised not solely by the totalitarian but also, perhaps not so wittingly, by him who professes liberal doctrines. Let there be no illusion: the devil's domicile is not a particular locality but all the world; whoso can see straight will meet the devil not infrequently on the opposite side of a mirror.

No individual, or racial group, has any self-appointed mission, divine or otherwise, to civilize or rule others "for their own benefit." Such arrant hypocrisy meets only the grim caller, nemesis, at the end of the road. Whoso denies freedom and free living to others is an enemy of both God and man. He may triumph temporarily, worshipping demon might, destroying his opponent. After the blitz, green grass grows over all.

It is well to remember that host of fools, the great tyrants who strutted for a while on the world stage. Men, as individual men, are each unique and incomparable, not superior or inferior to each other. In the happy condition of freedom, one may look for the best thriving. The nature and the degree of freedom suitable for each person depends, admittedly, upon his own development, and is different for different people.

There is, however, a compulsion which each and every person inevitably exerts, namely, that exerted by his very existence. To make that compulsion a creative or inspiring influence for human good, and for world order and peace, is precisely the question on which religion has guidance to give to man.

But this guidance confronts each person with the most difficult problems. There is, for example, the tension between the ought-to-be and the what-is-possible. The ought-to-be has the greatest scope in the smallest organization, each person; the what-is-possible is the only sensible procedure in the sphere of the collective. The former means self-discipline and obedience to the inner categorical imperative; the latter, organization of resources and human energy and skills, the ordered growth and progress of civilized life, and the discipline of daily labour and the laws of the land. The former can develop at the greatest speed; the latter can only make slow progress. Therefore, harmonious co-operation between the most advanced individuals and the less developed masses demands understanding, tolerance and self-abnegation of an order which is not sufficiently in evidence in many parts of the world. In this connection, it should be understood that the ideal, if truly ideal, and the practical, if truly practical, are one and the same. It is the practicable which is neither the truly practical nor the truly ideal. The practicable is the ideal-practical gone partly awry, on account, mainly, of man's drawbacks. But granted a condition of active tolerance, individual idealism and inspiration on the one hand and collective action on the other can interact creatively for the good of the whole, and the practicable can be purified till it is transformed into the truly practical, or, the realized ideal.

Consider, again, the problem of patriotism. Undoubtedly

it is right and good to give oneself for one's land and people. But where do I draw my lines ? Round my village and family ? Country and nation ? World and mankind ? The further question arises : Does patriotism remain a virtue and a value when your patriotism and my patriotism demand that you and I destroy each other ? Is not the raison d'être of patriotism the preservation and nurturing of life and welfare and love between man and fellow man ? All enemies are fellow men, exactly as all friends are ! And what about patriotism to the Kingdom of Heaven ? And unswerving fidelity to Heaven's Master, Eternal God ? How wide, now, and daunting, is the gulf which yawns between the ideal-practical and the practicable !

As mentioned earlier, the mass of people look to a governing authority to solve their problems for them. This governing authority may be a freely elected one, or a compulsorily elected one—as in certain states which persist in using the word "democratic" ! In the case of a freely elected one, the authority consists of those who represent the people's interests, which means, among other things, the people's desires, aims, hopes and expectations. One of the specific tasks of the governing body is to serve the people's interests successfully. Whence do these interests stem ? From vision, knowledge and impersonal duty ? Or from greed and self-aggrandisement ? Or perhaps from hopelessly mixed motives ? To the extent, therefore, that the people are God-unaware, caught in a net of Ill, bent on serving self-interests, to that extent the government (composed of men and women who, after all, are much like those who constitute the governed) are defeated from achieving true welfare and well-being, to that extent the government cannot free politics and economics from the corrosion by ego and lust. Such is also the case, and in far worse measure, with a compulsorily elected government, which, moreover, always stoops to the criminality of torturing truth to fit into the ugly crust of authoritarian ideology.

If one understands the springs of action of men and women everywhere, observes the effect of environment upon them, and the manner in which they react to it, and sees the world situation truly for what it is, then one puts aside all hopes and fears, all evasions and prevarications, all false ideals and wasteful activities. One sees, that short of a miracle, the best that might possibly be achieved is a bare preservation through an immediate first-aid measure. The real healing does rest in each and every individual's hands, but the date of rewarding fulfilment, when the lion shall lie down with the lamb through Love's omnipotent moving, is a top secret with God. But by that date, Love will have grown young again for man's divine delight! Meanwhile, man has to fulfil his duty, to God first and foremost; and in the fulfilling, organism must everlastingly sacrifice itself in order that Spirit may triumph.

The religions, as organized human institutions, involved in worldly life and activities, and compromised by worldly values, the inevitable fate of all human institutions, have an important and constructive part to play where masses of men are concerned. But they have little, and in some cases no part to play in relation to individuals. The clear seeing man knows that the world problem is at root the individual problem. If he, the social person, establishes his own harmony, he is the greatest and most effective force he, personally, can be for putting the world right. To enable himself to become such, he turns to RELIGION.

But the guidance of RELIGION will at first put each man at variance with himself, with his neighbour and with the state. Yet if he will faithfully and steadfastly follow the right road to the very end, his will not be the earthly tomb of an unknown warrior, but a crown of light in the blest abode of Eternal God. And—and this is the practical (not the merely practicable) point—he will have been a champion of Truth, and have created Order and Peace.

All are agreed that they desire, and work for the welfare of all. But what is welfare?

As a creature, man is an economic and political animal; in his human aspect he is a social person; as man-made-in-the-image-of-God, his essential Self, he is an ethical and religious being. Worldly values dominate the creaturely man, reacting to stimuli, struggling for self-preservation and self-aggrandisement, and thirsting for self-gratification. The spiritual values are true of the man-in-the-image-of-God; towards their perfect expression, Nature is moving man and God is drawing him. Man the human—the good or skilled or happy thinker and doer—is the self-responsible link between himself the animal and himself the God-becoming. The human has not to be a peace-patcher. His task is not to make and preserve a static balance between animal and God, but to tame the animal, train the person, and through self-mastery and self-surrender to God, become the awakened one, the perfected man who is the true individual. Whether we regard man from a scientific and evolutionary standpoint, or see him through the eyes of a religious philosopher, his development and fulfilment consist in the fruition of individuality, and in living, as a member of society, an ethical life which expresses the spiritual values.

Such fruition of individuality, which is the fulfilment of the purpose of existence, or of God's Will for man, is the meaning of Welfare. It is God-faring. It is Brahmacariya. And so, RELIGION shows that the criterion of human welfare is fundamentally this: that all men shall be helped to move closer and closer to the holy life, the Brahmacariya. All other criteria are only subservient to this, or false. RELIGION can promise no welfare, can offer no hope of a happy world as a normal home, if man were to remain unaligned with evolutionary Nature, un-cooperative with his fellow man and unawakened to God.

As a man of the world, and as an integral part of a social order, each person is influenced by worldly and social values. As one whose fulfilment is the flowering of true individuality, he is governed by the spiritual values. Here arises a difficulty, for worldly values operate in the sphere of self-ness and are effective for welfare and well-being in a self-concerned sense, whereas spiritual values are truly significant only where there is self-less-ness. This difficulty is overcome through perceiving the truth of self and self's relationship with all, and through sacrifice.

Worldly values must of necessity determine man's economic and political life. Power and wealth, progress and well-being, are not, on the whole, misconceived by the generality of men. But they are misused because men, ignorant of the purpose of their existence and the nature and implications of their own true fulfilment, have a distorted vision of the proper place and use of the worldly values. They are unable to relate themselves rightly to them. Treating power and wealth, national greatness and industrial expansion and all the good things of life as desirable objectives, worthy in themselves, men become slaves to worldliness through their lusts and egoism. Inevitably Mammon ousts God; moreover, men are cheated of the fair fruit of their very objectives.

The misuse of power and wealth, the misvaluation of the good things of life, and in short the world malaise, is best approached by each man as an ethical and religious being. RELIGION cannot directly affect world affairs, for it has no direct concern with them. RELIGION deals directly with each person singly, and moreover is only concerned with the fulfilment of his divine destiny. And to make the prospect look less hopeful at first glance, it is true that sorrow and suffering, deprivation and world disorder are more effective stimuli to seek God-realization than comfort and well-being. But each person is indissolubly linked with his neighbour and with his whole environment. Every step towards his true fulfilment makes him cease more and more from being a producer of evil and sorrow. The bond of love with his fellow grows strong and pure, and he becomes, in his own person, a foundation stone of world order.

RELIGION unequivocally repudiates worldly values. Yājña-valkya said, " Of immortality there is no hope through wealth "; Jesus said, " Whosoever shall humble himself . . . is greatest in the kingdom of heaven ", and also, " He that is greatest among you shall be your servant "; the Buddha wholly repudiated all worldly values for they are the values of the unawakened, of sin-bound mortality.

Therefore, the truly religious man pursues no worldly values, and stands free in his soul. Thereupon he finds that he can apply his natural abilities more effectively than ever for the world's good. A true sacrificer, he is happy and content. But men in the mass do not stand free in their souls. They pursue worldly values to gratify self. Power and wealth are intertwined with aggressive egoism and greed. Men may, and often do see themselves as they are, at least partly. But they supinely accept their own weaknesses or make insufficient effort to be rid of them. He cannot call himself a free man who puts only one foot outside a prison and leaves the other foot inside.

Now man and his schemes are indissolubly linked together. No man, no scheme; and the scheme expresses the man. Thus, any and every scheme or organization for promoting prosperity or well-being, or for establishing world order, is vitiated at the source by the flaws in the character of man himself. Therefore, what little is successfully established for human good is only a temporary makeshift, a fleeting, uneasy lull in the misery.

Prosperity is still understood by too many people as acquiring and possessing more and more, each for himself. When the industrial revolution and all that followed in its train completely changed the economic basis of life and economic relations between states, few if any saw that the day of personal possession was gone and the day of utilization and management as a trustee for the welfare of all had dawned. It was hardly realized that mankind, and not a man here and a man there, was the destined heir of the riches of the world. But men and nations scrambled and fought for wealth, to the deep sorrow of the gods and the derisive laughter of Mammon. Mankind, therefore, is left poverty stricken. Strangely enough, the men who fought and won also pay their price! By all means let us make wealth and more wealth. But let us evaluate it and use it rightly. The penalty, if one merely possesses it, is endless woe. If I do not share all I have with my brother man, I excite his envy, I tempt him to steal, and even to descend to war.

The world thinks in terms of producing, distributing and possessing the maximum. "Maximum" and "minimum" are both dead-ends. What living man needs, and should aim for, is the optimum. RELIGION says the optimum is that which best makes for the holy life. This means a life free of the crushing burden and anxiety of useless possessions for oneself. The optimum implies a diminishing burden of exclusive possession and an increasing utilization of all resources, a utilization by each man purely as a trustee, for the welfare of all and not for self-gratification. He who understands prosperity in this light will understand Jesus' saying: "Seek ye first the kingdom of God and his righteousness; and all these things will be added unto you." For indeed, he who seeks God will divest himself of all that comes between him and God. He will fling away his ten thousand useless wants, born of his lust and folly, and reduce himself to the ten essential needs indispensable for his existence and the perfect execution of his daily duties. And these few needs can be easily added unto him. For under such conditions it may not be so difficult, as it has proved hitherto, to meet everyone's needs, and make the stream of prosperity flow freely through all the channels of human good. (This, however, is quite different from trying to force the result by legislation in accordance with any ideology imposed by the few upon the many.)

Sooner or later, the man growing in wisdom clearly sees that whoso lives in a state of decent austerity is the one who most enjoys prosperity, is carefree, and is least obstructed where true fulfilment is concerned.

With regard to power, man is here not to enjoy lordship over other men or states or empires, but only as a servant to wield power, exercise authority and administer affairs for the welfare of his fellows, of all mankind. He who understands RELIGION sees that world peace and world order are impossible without world-mindedness, greatheartedness on a planetary scale and a global vision, qualities distinguishing too few in our world to-day. On the one hand the parochial outlooks, the restrictive nationalisms and the petty interests of the two thousand millions, and on the other hand the vast power lust, and the gigantic web of big-scale vested interests of the few, lay bare the mind and heart and vision of man the world over.

The two world wars of the twentieth century have not only struck a death-blow to isolationist national sovereignties (though not to integral nationhood), but have also killed the idea and utility of war itself as an instrument of constructive policy. To-day war is indeed an outmoded technique of action. And yet, wretchedly, man is still unable to banish it in practice, however strongly he wishes to outlaw it absolutely. In fact he is piling up armaments. He lives in suspicion of the other fellow, in fear of treacherous assault and of destruction on a scale which would make the Flood an episode too insignificant to remember. Because he himself, everywhere, is wittingly or unwittingly the devil's agent, armaments will inevitably be piled up, and used.

Man and fellow man face each other as enemies because each is held in a fast grip by a particular machinery of life, which serves, or purports to serve the interests of the people concerned. The one party is constrained by an ideology ; the other, more free in certain respects, is conditioned by its own way of life, which is the organic growth of centuries. Each side, apart from its material interests, also has its ideals and values. But neither side has any inkling how much its interests, ideals and values are bound within the circle of sinful mortality. For these interests, ideals and values are rooted too largely in the self-conceit " I am ", the division maker and discord bringer, and too little in the true " I am ", the Immortal.

Some pandits will point to economic rivalries and the jealousy and fear associated with them, and to the violent upsurge of local nationalisms, as the proximate causes of world disorder. Other pandits will point to that strange malady, " the historic mission of the Stultian people, the master race, to become lords of the world ", as the cause. All such causes, real enough, have their roots deep down in man's own greed and aggressiveness. (In the extreme case, it is alleged that man fights for survival, driven by instinct. Fully granted, the instinct. But why does anyone, claiming title to representative membership of the species homo *sapiens*, presume he ought to survive ?) There must be at least two parties before there can be rivalry. If I, as the one party, cleanse myself of striving against you in any shape or form, that puts an end to rivalry between you and me. Peace and world order cannot be established and maintained without continuous sacrifice, without the continuous exercise of loving clearsightedness.

Ordinarily, men descend to the merely practicable, driven helplessly by forces both without and within themselves.

Nations are often the victims of the what-is-possible. In terms of nations as they are to-day, or of a short term policy there is no solution to the problem of war and peace of which we can be certain. The gigantic forces making for disorder, generated in the past, are almost too great to be countered swiftly and effectively. The organized churches of different faiths can, and do play their part for the preservation of peace. But alas! if and when they are unsuccessful in staving off war, they themselves lead the nation's prayers to God for victory! And the enemy nations do likewise! Do we ever hear how sadly God laughs at times? And mutters imprecations in His sleep?

RELIGION has nothing to say to nations, except perhaps something which is not altogether unknown: if you will cleave your brother's head with a battleaxe, it is really impossible for him to remain alive, and equally impossible for you to escape the consequences, self-decreed, of blood guilt.

But RELIGION has everything to say to each person singly. What nations are incapable of doing, an individual can. Let us not forget the story of the little mouse who freed the mighty lion. How strange it may seem that a single individual could be so powerful compared with a nation! But not the least strange when it is understood that the group is bound by conditional reciprocities, whereas the individual can be lord of the free world of absolute values, practically (ideally) fulfilled through sacrifice. Not the nations as they are to-day, but each individual man can outlaw war absolutely, provided he can stay the course in God-faring.

RELIGION declares: you must live by the moral law; you must attain self-mastery; you must find union with God. The moral law says, "Thou shalt not kill". The Buddha taught: "Putting away the killing of living things, Gotama the recluse holds aloof from the destruction of life. He has laid the cudgel and the sword aside; he lives scrupulous and full of mercy, friendly and compassionate to all creatures that have life." He also taught: "Putting away the stain of malevolence, he remains with a heart set free from malevolence; he purifies his mind from the stain of malevolence, (and is) compassionate and kind towards all breathing creatures".

The sinless Jesus, allowing himself to be the sacrificial substitute for the sinner, prayed, " Father, forgive them ", himself pleading the cause of his murderers. The dying Gandhi said, " Rāma, Rāma ", raising the hand of salutation in blessing upon his assassin.

This is not to support the view that blindly, or out of fear or crankiness, one should not kill or participate in war. If one is subject to feelings and thoughts of hate and anger and murder, one is a killer in one's soul ; and so, even if one shrinks from physical killing, those evil psychical forces wreak havoc in some form or other. Only when one truly sees that killing is wrong, when one has really ceased to kill in one's own mind and heart because the mind and heart are utterly purified of all malevolence, anger and hate, then naturally and legitimately one abstains from killing, from any participation in war. The ethic of physical action must correspond faithfully to the ethic of one's inner mental life. Thus can a man outlaw war absolutely because he has truly eschewed all violence and has become harmless. Further, he is also friendly and compassionate to all, understanding, loving and accepting all.

RELIGION shows, therefore, that the way of peace is for each man, individually, to become harmless and non-violent, to understand, love and accept any and every fellow man. If the fellow chooses to be violent, to forbear with him and endure his violence to the extreme limit ; to try to the end to win him over by truth, by understanding persuasion ; and in the ultimate, only to pray, " Father, forgive ", a prayer fully effective when he who prays is the sinless one, the Brahman-become, the true individual.

The message of RELIGION is clear and unequivocal. Until people change, so that their interests no longer stem from lust and ego, any system or organization will be somewhat like a steel and concrete structure cast upon quicksands. World order and peace is not the responsibility of delegates and officials alone. It is also an individual responsibility falling squarely and fairly on the shoulders of each and every living human being. Until there is a sufficiently preponderant percentage of human beings in the world who are sufficiently free of lust and ego, there can be no stable, unanxious, unforced world order and peace. The question which each person should ask is not whether there will or will not be another world war, but " What am I doing to cease from being a cause of Ill and destruction? What am I doing to become a source of Good and peace? " Let no one delude himself that he is not a source of Ill and destruction. Each and every one of us has thoughts and feelings, and performs actions, of anger and hate, and has desires and beliefs which are causes of destruction. Always, and too easily, we blame the other fellow; whereas the fact is that in each and every one of us, excepting in the God-become, is the active cause for destroying what we ourselves set up.

Many people are tried by a perplexing problem: reciprocity largely controls human inter-relations, and people not unnaturally adopt the standard, " I can, and shall abide by the good and the right course, provided the other fellow does not descend too far below the mutually agreed standard of right and good behaviour. If he does so descend, I am reluctantly compelled to do what I hate to do." Most people do live in conformity with this attitude. But all great religions teach that conditional goodness is not the law by which man should try to live. For instance, the Dhammapada says:

> Let not a man heed the perversities of others,
> their sins of ommission and commission;
> But let him attend to what he himself has
> done amiss, and what left undone.
>
> IV.7.

If we do want a world order, it must be clearly seen that the sweeping tide of world affairs is the external concrete shape made by what we are ourselves, interacting with environment. Our institutions and procedures are the product of our desires and hopes, our purposes and aspirations, interacting with conditions and resources. All that happens to us bears the stamp of our own virtues and vices, vision and blindness, capacities and ineptitudes. Unquestionably, the most important change to be made is the change in ourselves. The New World needs the New Man.

If we look at history, we see that an end comes to all beings, all institutions and all things. Rarely is that end a perfect consummation, a divine fulfilment, the benediction by Father Time preluding a blissful sanctification through the mercy and grace of God. All too often that end is the work of Death, the Executioner—(" The last enemy that shall be destroyed is death "—I Corinthians, XV.26)—the ineluctable judgment on man's lust, egoism, hatred and delusion. We need not here consider the effects of natural forces, conveniently dubbed acts of God, for we can exercise but little control over them. What we can control and change is ourselves, rid ourselves of false views and baseless hopes, and so win a chance to build on better foundations. Never need it be feared that victory will lie finally with the evil-doer. Remember that there is only you in all the world, or that I am the only one in the world. " I " am only a different version of " you ". " You and I " are in truth the greater " you " and the richer " I ". You and I, if pure, stay the flood of evil, exactly as you and I, impure, poison the stream of life. Remember that the Lord Himself declared :

> O son of Pṛithā, neither here nor in the next world is there destruction for him (who worketh righteousness) ; for no one who does good, O my son, goes an evil way.
>
> Bhagavad-Gītā, VI.40

Without fear of the present or future, let us work with courage and wisdom ; which means, let us be devoted to the Highest Good which we ourselves, as individuals, can see clearly, accepting the toil and tears, and the adventure and delight of it all in our stride. Let us never calculate upon preserving our wealth and our institutions, or upon crystallizing our way of life. For whatever we do, the forms will inevitably pass away. Therefore let us pay heed to what we shall bequeath to those who issue from us and who will embody us on and on through time. All the past lives in us to-day, and all the future is beckoning to us here at this moment. Shall we bequeath a museum of remains ? Or the Spirit of Life ? Look at the civilizations of the past : their immortality is not of the world but of the Spirit, whose divine legacy to us is clothed in the tenuous garment of an idea, an ideal, a Value.

RELIGION clearly shows that the virtuous man is the foundation stone of world order and world peace. All the virtues may be broadly grouped under goodness (or skilled conduct), truth and love, which cover action, thought and feeling, or hand, head and heart. In the harmony of the three is the full blossoming of virtue, or soul-strength, the śakti or true power in man as a thinking-feeling personality.

The practical expression of such virtue in every walk of life spells human fulfilment individually, and is the bedrock of stable world order. Because of insufficient virtue, insufficient order within himself, man dooms himself to malaise and death; and his world, the insecure, grievous world of external affairs, collapses with monotonous regularity.

The Great Teachers, fully understanding this, left the world of affairs alone, and concentrated their efforts upon the redemptive work of enlightening man, upon setting his feet on the road to the sinless state. The God-become has none of the problems besetting the good-and-evil life of mortality-bound man. He is not concerned with the preservation of anything that appertains to mortality. But he is concerned with the right utilization of everything in the spatio-temporal world as the means for realizing the immortal, whereby the purposes of Eternal God are fulfilled. In this fulfilment lies the divine inspiration, hope and opportunity for perfecting the things of this world. Given a sufficient number of virtuous men who have the manliness and wisdom to accept both the pleasant and the unpleasant, who are not parochial but world-minded and are capable of expressing practically their vision of the universal good of all mankind, then indeed a world order which takes proper account of justice, of legitimate needs not lusts, and individual human dignity not ego, can arise.

It is for each and every one of us to make ourselves worthy citizens of the City of God, of the temple of God which is our own bodily being here and now, the Brahmapura. Unavoidably then, we shall also be good citizens of the world, quite at ease in the cosmos. Not for a moment does that mean that there will be no difficulties and disasters. But these incidental ills of mortality will never be able to shiver to pieces the healthy, living structure of a world encircling human order. We shall live and work as men purified, and when we pass on we shall live enshrined in the mind and heart and body of a humanity at peace on earth, joyfully working out the Will of the Most High. Then, truly, we shall have made practical sense of :

Hark ! the herald angels sing,
Glory to the new-born king !
Peace on earth and mercy mild,
God and sinners reconciled.

In their deep wisdom, the Great Teachers knew that in awakening man they did their whole work, and therein fully demonstrated love. It is in this sense that Jesus exhorted his slowly awakening disciples to love one another " as I have loved you " (John, XV.12 et seq.) Again, what greater love can there be than that a man should " lay down his life for his friend ", that is, sacrifice separate selfhood in order that, having achieved the sinless, the continuously Brahman-aware state, both friend and self are re-born in the unity of true individuality, the undivided from each other ?

* * * *

Being by nature unawakened and self-centred, enslaved by the machinery of the physico-chemical system which he regards as himself, many a man unconsciously approaches religion with the predatory attitude, " What can I get out of this ? " In answer, the organized religions of the world try, on the one hand, to cajole him, to bribe him, to threaten him or to force him into accepting them, and on the other, to minister to his various needs to the best of their ability, and to be a channel between him and God.

RELIGION answers his attitude unequivocally : Descend thou into hell. Wade neck-deep, swim full-immersed through all the seething seas of hell, till thou dost reach, purified, the blest isle of holy living. There is no other way. There is no vicarious expiation, no remission of the work which thou thyself must fully perform. There is, indeed, vicarious at-one-ment by each and every one of the Brahman-become, because of which it is easier for thee, also, to become the sinless one. Remember, O blind child of mortality, that God is Sovereign, Almighty. God's Will is the only will. Thy opportunist " what can I get out of this ? " is thine own self-condemnation, and thou shalt eat only sorrow. Thy stolen pleasures shall line thy face, bend thy back, steal the light out of thine eyes and tear the song out of thy heart ; and take thee to death. Remember also, O beloved sinner, that God is the Immortal, thy divine destiny. And this Immortal is Happiness, is Love. Thine is the task. Upon God the Inexhaustible, embodied in thine own organic being, thine own mad, passionate body, thou canst call infinitely, endlessly, never, never to be refused. But it is thy very own will, tamed, and trained, which must call upon God. Thou art free to do what thou wilt. But though free to cause, thou art not free to say nay ! to consequence. Life maintains its freedom only as long as the universe is the dutiful Son of Necessity. Choose here and now : Wilt thou seek what thou canst " get out of this ", and in a fitful, mortal hour perish like a moth in the fire of thy folly ? Or wilt thou, a man, proving his manhood, plunge into the seas of hell and swim to the Happy Bourn ? The Lord shall be thy strength. Thou shalt not fail. For the Lord Himself declared : " Neither here nor in the next world is there destruction for him (who worketh righteousness); for no one who does good, O my son, goes an evil way."

He who seeks the Ātman, which is the end of Ill, looks within himself. He unravels the tangled skein of cause and effect. He " sees the past ", stretching " aeon behind aeon ". As he sees, with perfect wisdom, he sees the moving panorama of his whole becoming-process : uprising and passing away, by way of cause. He sees the maker and maintainer of the house of Ill : " that excited desire " which is the fetter ; taṇhā ; the false conceit " I am ". And as he sees, undisturbed, unreacting, he casts out each devil one by one ; he sees the destruction of the causes of Ill ; he " heals the soul ". He is the perfect psychotherapist who works a spiritual alchemy. For when the soul is thus cleansed, the false " I am " vanishes, and I become the Self, the one who, gone thus (Tathāgata), is now the Brahman-become. This passage through the temporal becoming-process of the soul, is the passage through the seething seas of hell, and its end is the union with Eternal God. This is the fulfilment of the pledge, " for no one who worketh righteousness, O my son, goes an evil way."

Good-fellow says: But I have no time or energy, no ability for even understanding such things, leave alone achieving such perfection! It is all I can do to get on with the practical business of performing my daily duties satisfactorily!

Yet in his last life he swam Hellespont every night to keep faith with Hero, till that jealous fiend, Death, murdered him! But now he is not at home, or he is busy, or has no skill with a simple goodfellow greeting when his Lord calls on him in his own house! Whither wend his feet of clay? Whither goes his wayward heart? To Happiness? To Love?

* * * *

Experience contains both the agreeable and the disagreeable. Man, the captive of his attachment to the pleasant and aversion from the unpleasant, struggles to perpetuate the desirable and to eliminate, or at least to flee from what he dislikes. By this refusal to accept experience in its wholeness he defiles the holiness of life, and he misses the profounder significance of his experience. He fails to see that as long as there is any personal desire, or any egoism, there is the attendant possibility of frustration, or anger. Anxiety and fear, resentment and sorrow are everlastingly the lengthening or shortening shadows of his every action.

Why does not man see that happiness, as a real value, is not the gratification of craving, and that the truly happy man can be happy, though pained, in the very midst of the unpleasant? Why does he not see that his Self-integrity, as a real value, is independent of the succession of temporary experiences of being exalted or degraded by other people or by fickle fortune, and that it has nothing to do with the false ego, gloating over successful self-assertion or miserable and enraged when humiliated?

The reason is not far to seek. If one observes the flowing tide of humanity in the busy streets of a great metropolis, or in the places of eating or of amusement or of cultural edification, or in the counting house or in the councils of state, one might then enquire : At what level is the consciousness of all these people ? To what is all their energy directed ? To what extent are they God-aware ? Truthful, loving, happy and at peace ? Are they whole individuals, or is each one of them a kaleidoscopic succession of ephemeral personalities, blown off by the next wind of desire or fear or anger, squashed into another shape at the very next impact of sensation ? What do they all talk about ? Read, write, feel, think, do ?

But one must observe with a pure scrutiny, without bias and preconception, without praise or censure, without pronouncing judgment. For all that streaming mass of men is no other than a collection of different versions of oneself, and one can see himself truly, only with a heart that is at peace and a mind that is free. A pure scrutiny will show that most men and women live at a creaturely level : a sensational existence, desire-driven, ego-caged, ignorant. Many of them do not know what they really seek, or why they do much of what they do do. They are swept by the tide.

Man's task is to deepen his level of consciousness from the creaturely to that of the man-in-the-image-of-God. Progress, understood as better housing and sanitation, clothes and locomotion, labour saving gadgets and living standards, has only a slight influence here. Moreover, such progress raises fresh problems with every advance. For instance, better health services mean more and more old people as a charge on the state, and, combined with internal security, a new problem of population increase at a speed with which sufficient food production cannot keep pace. Or again, wresting the secrets of nature, like atomic energy, means greater powers of destruction. Through such progress, which nevertheless must go on, each element of the pairs of opposites becomes bigger and bigger. Life becomes more intensified and not more purified : more freedom in this way, more restriction in that way ; more good on the one hand, more evil on the other. Man's life is thus made into a see-saw game of equilibration, steadily piling up a bigger burden on each side. It is impossible for him to avoid this until he sees that there is a way to transcend this dualistic world of manifestation, to achieve an active poise, and to live thereafter—not to be lived, and be hurled about, and be thrown out ultimately by senseless, amoral process—but to live as a free, creative, happy individual. In this, upbringing and education, and, paramountly, the religious life, play their part. Then indeed, instead of being subjugated by his machines and discoveries and progress and new powers, he will be master everywhere because he is master of himself. His level of consciousness will change only through self-mastery, from the creaturely level to the level of the man-in-the-image-of-God.

Precisely here, Indian religious thought has something to say to man, and show him how to desist from his unpractical mode of life and learn what is true practicality. Salvation comes not from outside but from within. The external is man's tool. He himself must use the tool skilfully. It is each man's personal responsibility to see the truth of things, to know himself and discipline himself, and to become enlightened ; to train himself to remain free from the clutches of sense-impressions, of the urge to grasp at pleasures and thrust aside the disagreeable, of the passion to assert the ego, of every single vested interest and of every worldly value. No one else can do this for him.

Security and power and prosperity cannot be established as a permanent and fixed concrete shape. It is inherent in the nature of all things to arise, to grow and to die. It is not static solutions but dynamic fulfilments which must be sought. For Nature, the bride of God, everlastingly dances with new veils, and he is a fool who seeks the temporal veil instead of Everlasting God

It is but folly to seek prosperity and power and security in the way men do. Any and every situation holds security and happiness and promise, as well as danger and difficulty and pain to the degree that it does hold all these. Each man must accept the whole situation, and extract the full essence out of both the security and danger, the happiness and pain, the promise and difficulty. Only through whole acceptance can come full purification. And that way alone, through transformation of the whole and not through pushing evil out into another corner of the field, will a man leave the whole situation altogether better than he found it, and not with both the evil and the good in it more intensified. In this work, any man is bound to meet with some suffering. But he who shrinks from accepting God's gift of suffering is no man, certainly no lover of God or benefactor of man.

Who is capable of so dealing with the whole situation? Surely, he who has self-mastery.

Some men repudiate what they call the unnatural asceticism, the gloomy world view and the fatalistic attitude of RELIGION, and particularly of Indian religious thought. It might prove more profitable for them to point to peace and security and world order, to happiness and wisdom and love and fulfilment as their *fait accompli*, before rejecting Indian religious thought. The heir to the Greek tradition believes in the enjoyment of his faculties, physical and mental, and in getting the best out of life. But at present he wears a haggard and hunted look with the strain of enjoying his faculties and getting the best out of life!

There are some who ask, what has God or RELIGION to offer them? And they say that they can, in fact, get along very well without God and RELIGION, for they trust their common-sense. God, or RELIGION, makes no offer to man, in the sense of an artful shopkeeper enticing his customer with a tempting bargain. It is for proud man, freely, to seek God, or the Truth, and God will never deny him the fruit of his search. God is no common advertiser of cheap wares. His business includes man and his affairs. And He does it so well, that long ago He threw out Lucifer, man's elder brother, at the psychological moment, and made it a charge on man to redeem both himself and his big brother and go back home, with Power and Glory, Prosperous and Happy. Dispensing with God, man merely gets off the narrow bridge of life, poised in boundless existence; and he falls and falls, and becomes unconscious. And unawakened, how slight is his chance to become enlightened! Man can never get on without God, for God is man's own Supreme Self, his Best Self and not a stranger, not a mythical personage tucked away in heaven, that fool's paradise of man's vain imaginings. Happy is the man who enjoys the bliss of a loving wife and a happy home and this world's blessings.

But 10^{10} times happier is he who enjoys the bliss of the Brahma-world (Bṛihad-Āraṇyaka Upanishad, IV.3.33.) How Excellent is man's Best Self!

Who could be more sensible or more practical minded than Indians? They called Gotama the Buddha, as they call any of the Sons of God, Bhagavā, the Fortunate One! Su-gata, he who has gone well! They call the Arahant, Sukhin, the Happy One! (Saṁyutta Nikāya, III.83.) Far from depriving, or seeking to deprive man of happiness, Indian religious thought has shown precisely, and faultlessly, how man can be happy for ever and ever.

Self-consciousness, in the sense of preoccupation with one's own egoistic desiring and thinking, dims, or even blots out the right awareness of the universal process around one. The cloud of self blots out the sunshine of universal being. When, with self become the SELF, there is intense awareness of the world process, there comes present an indescribable serenity, contentment and happiness, non-sensational, non-critical. This is Nirvāṇa: not a mere feeling, not a mere attitude maintained by effort, not a mere thought, not an illusion, but just the objective reality characteristic of man-become-God. In the nirvāṇic awareness of the "pleasant" aspect of the universal process, is seen one meaning of the Brahma-vihāra of muditā—taking joy in others' joy; in the nirvāṇic awareness of the "unpleasant" aspect of the universal process, is seen karuṇā—compassion; in the nirvāṇic awareness of all relations between all the living, mettā—loving-kindness; and in the nirvāṇic awareness which is the complete acceptance of this-All, in full God-consciousness, is seen upekkhā, in which consciousness, the Brahman-become, like Eternal God, actively embodies and expresses Love-Wisdom-Peace.

What the senses convey, what is read or told, what has been experienced in the past, all these present the nucleus or substance, and the stimulus, for the play of fantasy, on the basis of which a man pursues his own chimæra, believing or asserting it to be good or worth while, and whose attainment or possession will spell happiness. The sense-mind life is full of memories and anticipations. But whoso frees himself from the pleasures of the imagination, as Shri Kṛishṇa and the Buddha taught, whoso masters memory and anticipation—his vain hankerings and expectations, his petty regrets and values, his fond hopes—he is the one who becomes free of time's barb, of the tyranny of wishful thinking, of the heartrending agony of all that is unrequited, of the futile love-longing which makes every moment an eternity of unendurable pain.

By clinging to the dear familiar of worldly existence, by wishing for the other instead of accepting the this-is, by not being fully awake in the immediate now, one is " tied up in knots " and mentally clouded, and there is no health. The ways of the world are the ways of confusion and pain. By being free of such clinging, and by being fully aware of the instant, one finds that whatever be the external shape of the passing event, Happiness reigns supreme.

For Happiness, here-now, is the sense of realization or fulfilment enlivening every experience in the here and now. This is Nirvāṇa. Happiness is the ultimate fulfilment of organic being, just as freedom is the prize of true individuality, and peace is the crown of our spiritual being. The level of consciousness of him who is Happy, is the level to which must rise, through complete sacrifice, the pleasure-seeker and the self-asserter, whose level is that of the untamed. The " level of consciousness " is that region where the process called " as a man thinketh in his heart (not head) " goes on. The free and the happy are those who, having made peace in *their* world (" this fathom-long body ") between matter and spirit, are the givers of joy to the sorrowing and of peace to the disturbed.

When craving and ignorance have given place to purity and wisdom, Nirvāṇa supervenes. In the everyday life, the same objects and the same familiar experiences will be there—the simple things of everyday life as they are called—but there is no anxiety or fear or sorrow in connection with them ; there is only Nirvāṇa, the deathless immortal. Nirvāṇa is not a state, a condition, a belief, a self-hypnosis, an illusion. It has no origin, basis, procession or decease. But when this turbulent, poisoned stream of self-becoming is utterly purified through the extinction of all lust, egoism, hate and delusion, then suddenly, this very stream, for the purified one, is lighted with the radiance of Nirvāṇa. The external world-stream is still itself. It is the purified one who is transformed. But because of him, the light of Nirvāṇa suffuses the dim and dark recesses of the world, and purifies the world-stream, even as the sun, from its great distance, purifies the earth. One should not merely believe this, or take it on trust. One should come and see. One should tread the Path, uproot Ill, and then see if it is possible to say " No " to Nirvāṇa.

In him who knows Nirvāṇa, the immediate, uninhibited response from within to the without is devoid of grasping, aversion, resentment, egoism, or any unbalance. Inwardly, there is a permanent, dynamic poise, and an acceptance of the total world process, with full understanding and love. Then indeed it becomes a practical possibility to transform evil into good. " Come, O Bhikkhu! Tread the Brahma-path for making a complete end of Ill " was the Buddha's greeting to him who sought the Immortal. He who is touched with the transcendent light of Nirvāṇa knows that at the inmost heart of all things lies celestial bliss.

All those who suffer much in this world have a greater stimulus for seeking the Immortal than those who stagnate in comfort, or who are bogged in pleasure. But the break with this life, for the sake of that life, must be complete. RELIGION needs complete self-surrender, without specifically demanding it—no love between lovers is true love without glad self-surrender. But the break must not be made in the spirit of " Will I make a better bargain ? " For then there is hell here and now in this life on earth. The happiness of *that* life is no less and no greater than of *this* ; but its nature is quite different, and its intensity compares with this as intra-atomic energy with mechanical.

Because of attachment, man attempts to bind the elements of experience into permanence, an impossible and painful task. Let the stream of continuous becoming flow past. Each man's business is to help it to flow without flooding, without spreading evil. He can do this through non-attachment, and cross over all sin and illusion. Realizing the Eternal's playful manifestation in the spatio-temporal, all experience has the quality of eternity in it, and the man himself is sugata, happy. There are times in almost every man's life when he is touched with nirvāṇic consciousness. But the experience of the undiscorded wholeness of the sublime moments is impermanent because of the unresolved discords in himself, or of the temporarily damped down fires. Hence the necessity for perfection—not the sterile asceticism which is profitless self-torture, but the fruitful austerity which leads to perfection. The self-excusing musician may make a nice sound; but only the supremely disciplined who has realized perfection, makes music.

Again Good-fellow protests: But how can I put aside the sense life, as taught by Jesus ("if thine eye offend thee, pluck it out") and by the Buddha in the Third Noble Truth? All life is a series of sensations, and if they are put aside, it is the end of everything. This transcendental Nirvāṇa is just beyond me. I cannot understand it unless I can be told how to experience it practically.

Bondage or evil do not lie in process or experience which is a stream of sensations, and ever will be so, or in the course of psycho-physical living in which not only must the sense organs be used, but used in perfection. Bondage comes through "that excited desire" which arises when sense organ cognizes object, and when there is egoistic separation of mine and thine. When the lusting (taṇhic), grasping (upādānic) and wilful (sankalpic) pursuit of the sensual life and objects ceases, then the pure delight of the unavoidable use of the senses and mind is constantly experienced in fullness. "Seek ye first the kingdom of God . . . and all these things will be added unto you"—for when a man seeks the kingdom of God, his self-purification allows his senses to be rightly used at last; and then only the true happiness of the sense-mind life is added unto him. Let it be noted again, this delight is non-sensational. You cannot imagine this delight or think out this philosophy, but you can experience it here-now, in the passing here and now. For example:

Stand quietly, and look into a shop-window, or at that man or that woman; hear the traffic; smell the perfume from the flower girl's flowers; touch, or lean against that pillar-box, or just feel the pavement under your feet. Look, hear, smell and touch without liking or disliking, appraising or dispraising, without hankering, regretting, starting up any fantasy, feeling angry or envious or miserable, without wanting to possess or not to possess. Observe wholly, with effortless concentration, yourself just your whole self, breathing easily, body at ease, mind and heart at peace. Bring no bias or prejudice, no judgment on the basis of some pre-conceived standard, to bear upon the observing. If you succeed in doing this, then you will know what it means to be an individual, and you will know Nirvāṇa, and know it as the ineffable, the immortal, which does not begin or end, come to birth or die. It is the eternal is-ness, which is obscured, shines through, is cut off, or is yours for ever, in you, because of your awakened or unawakened condition as the case may be, and not because of itself. Light is there, always. The rotation of the earth makes night ; the movement of clouds brings darkness ; the condition of the here and now lets in or steals away the light. But the light IS. Even so, Nirvāṇa IS.

Let no man lust for God or Nirvāṇa. For lust and ego separate and enslave. The moment Freedom goes out, grinning Death walks in. Let no man attempt to storm the ramparts of Heaven, for an eagle will eat his liver every night and the wound will heal every day. For Heaven, the "yonder world" of the Upanishads, is not out there, or everywhere or anywhere, or more than or less than this world, but is this very world itself transformed because man is transfigured. The perfect sublimation of the aggressiveness in our nature is supremely demonstrated in the Buddha's "I will not rise from this seat till I have found Deliverance."

Freedom from "I wish, I like, I want, I will go and get" makes possible the perception of what ought to be done (the karaṇiya kataṁ) and how to do it, and is the source of the urge to do it. In this lies happiness, lustrous like pure gold, inevitable and inescapable, thrilling at the core of every experience whether it be painful or pleasurable : life's music in the wistful, plaintive minor key is just as wonderful as in the triumphant major mode. The essence of such happiness is the realization of the eternal as the full immediacy of the here-now, an immediacy which distinguishes the momentary now from the eternal now, the evanescent deathful from the real immortal.

This happiness, this Nirvāṇa, never dies. There is no " Oh, what a pity it is over ! " in connection with it. Any and every experience is over in the here and now, but Nirvāṇa's bliss is permanent in the here-now, distinctive of the consciousness of the God-become, and not merely as the memory of a past exaltation. Indeed, at the heart of all things lies celestial Bliss ! Experience should neither be sought nor avoided, except in so far as wisdom directs that one should not do anything that is evil or unnecessary. This would eliminate the vast bulk of man's foolish, fevered activities, perpetuating Ill. The purified one has not only fullness of heart, but also soundness of head and skill of hand. His activities are practicality *par excellence*. For RELIGION shows that true practicality consists solely in the performance of that which fulfils the purpose of man's existence here, namely to realize immortality and glorify God thereby. Being alive and continuing to live means that experience is inevitable. So let thought, ever watchful, discriminate between unnecessary experience and right experience, and be Nirvāṇa's guardian for man. Individual fulfilment is a leit-motif in the symphony of life. It is a dull, perhaps intolerable symphony which does not contain both discords and concords related perfectly to each other in a dynamic poise which means harmony. Right experience includes, then, both unpleasant and pleasant experience. No fulfilment is a worthy fulfilment, unless one has known the depth of despair and the bitterness of frustration to the very limits of one's endurance.

Thus man learns to integrate suffering into the fabric of his whole existence, for without this he will never know love for his fellows or devotion to God, and he will never know Nirvāṇa.

Let no man look outside, or beyond the grave for happiness. There is no insurance cheque or weekly allowance paid in the hereafter to the simpleton hoping to bargain with God. Indian religious thought is fundamentally real, eminently practical, and shows the way to realize Nirvāṇa here-now in the daily life : not here and now in ephemeral uprising and passing away, but here-now in whole event in which Eternal God is embodied, unsullied by the event—Divine Mystery! The here-now is the transmuting and integrating point. All the past is concentrated, essentially, in the here-now. The Brahmaputras, the Arahants, kings and warriors and lowly folk, the good and the bad, all, all live in the here-now. And through the here-now there goes on perpetually that spiritual alchemy by which the Ill is changed into the Well. *Through* each man, that infinite potentiality which is summed up in the name Paramātman, Transcendent God, the Creative Spirit, slowly works the transformation; *by* each man is that transformation helped or hindered—man's personal responsibility. What begins as the work of the Divine Titan finishes as the product of the Divine Craftsman. The Eternal Artist creates Eternal Beauty—" Behold the universe in the glory of God: and all that lives and moves on earth. Leaving the transient find Joy in the Eternal " (Īśā Upanishad).

Only through the complete relinquishment of the shadow—sensual pleasures and sense-mind disturbance—man finds the substance. Through RELIGION, he realizes his spiritual birthright, Nirvāṇa. The discipline of RELIGION leads him to self-less-ness. Thereupon that ugly dwarf, the ego, goes out. In his place there stands the " Lord of the Universe ", and reigns true Sovereign in his own kingdom. The true individual's consciousness functions out-turned freely (no longer self-centred, impeding the free flow of the Divine Life), and in him, the perfected microcosm, the whole universe comes to life—" Behold my sovereign yoga!" Consciousness, as a lens, focuses the whole and part in perfect relationship to each other. The self stilled, the SELF springs into pure action.

Nirvāṇa, like the silent, invisible smile of the Spirit, awaits release in the heart of all beings. Man can release that transcendent Joy. He can make heaven on earth. Whatever be the nature and condition of the earth on which he stands, he, and he alone, can suffuse it with the light of heaven. In the very flood of his tears and the swirl of his sobs, at the core of his heartbreak lies Joy. The redemption is here-now. " Come unto Me and I will give you rest ". " I am the abode of Brahman, the Immortal, the Inexhaustible, and of eternal righteousness and unending bliss." And also it has been said, " No one cometh to the Father except through Me". But that Me to which a man must go, that I which is the abode of Brahman, is no external God or mediator. It is the inmost Spirit in each man himself, the holy of holies, the free and self-less core of his being. And again it has been said, "To Me have been given the keys of Heaven, and dominion over the world". That Me stands for any man who has become the true individual, for he alone knows the true meaning of "I", "Me" and "Self". Only the Self-realized holds the keys of heaven in his hand, and enjoys dominion over the world, which means over "this fathom-long body", this psycho-physical organism and over the stream of saṁsāra, and not over the planet earth with its inhabitants. In that sense, the Buddha also said: "Victorious over all, omniscient am I."

Man can go to that holy of holies only through the ocean of his tears, only by letting the flood of sorrow sweep away all that was "his", only by letting the flaming sword of suffering pierce and transmute all that he formerly knew and treasured as "himself". That spark in him which dimly senses this truth, has to turn warrior and become a hero like Arjuna. "Stand up and fight" has to be his slogan. "Slain", he will obtain heaven. "Victorious", he will establish heaven on earth.

Not all, however, may rise to the occasion. Of those that rise, few succeed. But all must try, and try unto death, to be the champions of the Spirit. For God, Nirvāṇa, is man's destiny. In the dust and heat of the strife, in every single fragment of his total existence, at the very heart of all things is the Ātman, awaiting the release of its imprisoned bliss and peace. Man, ordinary mortal man, can receive the keys of heaven in his hand and disimprison that supernal Joy. Said the Upanishad:

Brahman is Bliss.

Taittirīya, III. 6.

* * * *

And now, one may see another vision of man's destiny, which RELIGION reveals. Turn again to the Word. From the dim dawn of his spiritual birth, child-man slowly and painfully spelled this divine Word with stammering lips. With true instinct he clutched tight this bread of life. And so he grew. And as the morning mists were dispelled by the Sun of Truth, this babe grown to manhood discovered that the Word spelt his own true and hidden Name, the Name that none may take in vain. And he also learned that the Name which was his was also the Name of IT, the eternal that-which-is.

Out of the unconscious aspiration of his heart towards IT, man conceived in his mind, an Other, a Loving Father, all-Good, all-True, omniscient, omnipotent, omnipresent, Creator, and enthroned Him in majesty beyond the eternal stars.

Let man cherish that Personal Being whom he conceived in his mind and heart, for though our green mansion has been occasionally graced by The Presence, He is still to be born wearing a million bodies.

Slowly, in strange and wonderful ways, that Personal Being whom man has conceived, is being released into manifestation. Nature, the bride of God, has put forth a crowning work in the shape of man. And in man's innermost, secret place, Brahman made a little recess, to lie sleeping (Viṣṇu sleeping, dreaming, on the world serpent), till man himself shall awake. And now it is man's task, as a conscious cooperator with his virgin mother, Nature, through his self-purification, through his conscious, purposively directed effort from within, and through his increasing control of matter, to bring to birth, as the climax of an aeonian evolution, that Personal Being whom he nurses in his heart. In the developmental process, man's conception of that Personal Being will become modified, and gradually perfected, as he himself grows. And in the striking of the hour on the Day of Be with Us, men themselves will be the million expressions of that Personal Being. So shall to-day's concept of God the Person become a concrete reality on earth, and in the aeon whose date is the Far To-morrow, Gods, yea Gods, shall walk the earth, to-day's Word made flesh to-morrow, when no longer will the waters under the firmament remain divided from the waters above the firmament, for heaven and earth shall be one. Man himself, transcending self and realizing Self, will be the stepping stone for the incarnation of God the selfless Self, the incarnation as the fulfilled multitude and not the crucified solitary.

This is one meaning of that saying in the Ṛig Veda, "Daksha was born of Aditi, and Aditi was Daksha's child" (X.72.4), a saying which points to man's destiny as a creator: Man is the father of the Personal God. In this will be the ultimate fruition of monotheistic faith. Wonderful are the ways of Brahman's fulfilling, and in the fulfilling the earth shall be filled with the Brahmaputras, and Viṣṇu shall have awakened from his divine dream.

But for such godlike creation, men and women must learn to love divinely.

RELIGION exalts Love as man's supreme value. The Great Teachers exemplified it in their lives. Love is the deepest spring of happiness in human life, and also the source of the profoundest sorrow. Love is whole and indivisible, the active expression of the unity of the universe, of the one-ness of God, manifesting as creation, preservation and regeneration. Love harms no one. "If you hurt neither yourself nor others, nor both yourself and others, you dwell with a self become Brahman", said the Buddha. Love heals all sorrow; love makes all free; love brings peace; love opens the door to the Beauty of all Beauty. But the essential condition for such realization is that love shall not be aflame with all desire, but shall be at peace. Love which brings personal disappointment and sorrow, is but tainted love. Through man's craving for exciting sensations, through his indulging in the licence of passion, through his thirsting to possess the beloved for himself, love is bruised and battered, and the lover is taut with strain, the prey of anxiety, jealousy, hate and misery. Longing for passion, he mistakes the overmastering play of the physico-chemical system for love. In each and every expression of love in the unawakened or the unpurified, there is seen a caricature of love. When one is released from craving and the egoistic mine-thine, and from the passion to fixate particular forms of love-expression, there comes freedom. And then, man's beloved is not just a particular person but the very next person, his neighbour, or the very next thing, a rose, a dog, a ship, or the sky and the stars,

God and the Devil. Then he will cease to practise the art of stage-falling by falling in love with this and that person. Instead, he will steadily and endlessly love. True loving is continuous, undisturbed and whole, as ceaseless as the streaming of the blood in one's body. This is the Love which is fulfilment and bliss.

Man meets his fellow man on terms other than those of whole acceptance. He meets him desiring to obtain something from him, or being on his guard against the other's seeking ; liking certain aspects of him and disliking other aspects, such like and dislike resting upon the impressions he gets and the judgments he forms, necessarily imperfect, of the other person. In fact the meeting of man and fellow man is always in terms of attraction and aversion, approval and criticism, affection and resentment, grasping and giving, in short, of all that comes within the circle of the deathful, of the Ill. But if and when I meet you without grasping or desiring for myself, without praise or censure, without satisfaction or disappointment, if I see you truly as you are and myself remain poised and at peace, I can accept the whole of you without any reservations and without desiring you to be other than you are. And if you can accept me similarly, then you and I are well met, and our friendship is the perfect expression of undefiled love.

At this stage, I have learned the art of loving my Self, and loving you, my neighbour, as myself. Further, if you or I can meet any one person in this way, we can meet any and every person in that very way, for we have transcended selfishness and malevolence, all illusions about human beings, and all separative selfhood. Our relationship with each other and with all the world is one of perpetual harmony, of which the event of our personal meeting is a visible manifestation. Therefore, in love, you will never be an object of my lust ; in business, an instrument for selfish gain ; in politics, a pawn in my game to be ruthlessly sacrificed if required ; in economics, a field for exploitation ; in community, just " the other fellow " of whom I am not the keeper.

However perfect the reciprocity between any two, confined love maintains an unstable balance. There is always the need for a taking back, however refined. When there is complete freedom from expecting or demanding a return, from any form of taking back, when there is no vested interest in love, no external dependence, then love, unfettered, firm-poised, is free and stable. This is celibacy, which means not merely an abstention from sexual intercourse, but complete freedom from a taking back or needing a return. Celibacy means wisely loving in full measure, giving all that the other can contain. The purified ones, whose undefiled love was truly universal, naturally led a sexually continent life. Holy love cannot be specialized. What is for one is for all. And all love which observes distinctions is less than divine love. Like omnipresent light, holy love cannot be seized and imprisoned, made conditional and reciprocal. Celibacy is natural to the God-become from whom radiates transcendent, absolute love.

When no woman complements a man, or no man a woman, a psycho-physical tension arises, and increases in tautness. This tension urges the person to seek release in sexual love, based on passion-energy. Each partner in the sexual union can experience a sensational peak. Then there is a death to it. After a time, there again arises the tension, again relief is sought in sexual union, and again there is a death to it. The full cycle, constantly repeated, is contained within the circle of mortality, consciousness being confined to avijjā. He who practises the discipline of celibacy, provided he is possessed of right understanding, and capability, can change the psycho-physical into a psycho-spiritual tension, passion-energy being transmuted in the process into spiritual-energy, that is, into a drive to a transformed thinking-feeling-acting, free of complexes, neuroses or psychoses. By dealing rightly with the psycho-physical tension of celibacy, the feminine alter ego in the man, or the masculine in the woman, can be fully activated and harmonized with the usual masculine in that same man, or the feminine in that same woman. Thereby, man fully understands the feminine, and woman the masculine, thus realizing psycho-physical wholeness. When this harmony of the polarities (the masculine and the feminine within oneself) is established, the psycho-physical tension becomes a psycho-spiritual one. Here, no " relief " is sought, or can be sought. The urge is towards union with God, which, transcending the circle of mortality, is free of the sensational round of sexual union (birth)-climax (orgasm)-termination of union (death). The psycho-spiritual tension leads only to the absolute realization of God, of eternity and immortality. Hence the Brahman-become knows "unending bliss". His, or hers, is the perfect physical-psychical-spiritual harmony, the harmony of the self-contained, or the continent.

Such celibacy, however, is only for the few. For the rest, there are other things.

Eros is immortal. Kāma is the parent of all the gods, according to Hindu teachings. Śiva, as lord of ascetics, reduced Kāma, to ashes with a fiery glance. But, as lord of reproductive Nature, Śiva is won as husband by Pārvatī.

Sexual intercourse is the most intense ego-assertion, and it can also be one of the most beautiful and tender expressions of self-surrender; it is a most powerful binding influence, and it can also be a saving liberator; it is the most exciting, satisfying and exalting as well as the most disappointing, frustrating and degrading experience. In the sexual urge, Nature implanted an overwhelmingly powerful drive so that the species may continue, and also that man may awaken to the antithesis of self-assertion and self-surrender, experience abject slavery and a divine intoxication, come to know his incompleteness if ego-contained, become sensitive to the other-than-self and gradually dissipate the barriers between himself and the other, learn the meaning of human love and its mystery, and realize, finally, that he is a creator, like God.

Through the ages man has reverenced creativeness. The first name given to God is Creator. In the dim past, man recognized that in his power to create he wielded a power which was magical. Not only magical, but the source of an ecstasy unequalled by any other experience in the world. In phallic worship he reverenced creativeness: as pure and profound a worship as any other, in essence, and not, as some men of later ages make out, a degraded or savage superstition. In their sexual potency, men and women possess a power whose profundity and holiness they have hardly begun to realize as yet.

Very significant is the view of Indian religious thought on sex. Recognizing the worth and significance of both male and female, Hindu thought presented each of the Persons of the Trinity not as a lone God but as complemented by His Divine Consort, who is His śakti or potency, and through whom there is manifestation.

The Bhāgavata says:

> She is manifestation, Thou the final cause thereof;
> She is sense and body, Thou the soul behind;
> She is name and form, Thou the basic thought.
>
> VI.19.13.

He by himself would be a closed system, unevolving, a wearisome godliness with no scope for creation and the emergence of progressive, subtler and more wonderful orders of manifested being. The holiness of sexual reproduction is emphasized in the Bṛihad-Āraṇyaka Upanishad:

> Prajāpati (Lord of creatures) bethought himself: 'Come, let me provide him a firm basis!' So He created woman. When He had created her, He *revered* her below. Therefore one should *revere* woman below.
>
> VI.4.2.

Lust desecrates. Reverence sanctifies.

Men and women have to learn to reverence each other in sexual love. This learning is a personal responsibility. Upbringing and education impart the traditions and practices of one's society. Circumstance has played, and still plays a dominant role in determining the man-woman relationship. But the time is at hand, when men and women as individuals will have to understand their personal problems, and self-responsibly make their own decisions and abide by the consequences. The thunder and clap of orthodox religion and the law is a stand-by, a controlling and stabilizing factor for society; but as far as the profounder aspects of one's sexuality and the man-woman relationship are concerned, the pronouncements of professional priest and respectable pillar of propriety are not always helpful. Often, they are irrelevant, or behind the times. These problems can be understood and correctly treated only by men and women themselves if they seek purity and aspire to the highest.

The sanctity of marriage lies not in the mere institution, dolled up in social or legal or religious rags, but in the objective biological, psychological, æsthetic, moral, idealistic and spiritual facts of the man and wife concerned. If in truth a man and woman are no longer in active, holy wedlock, but continue, or are forced to continue, with the external appearance of marriage out of fear, or for the sake of sordid, worldly motives such as obtaining money or maintaining social position, or out of slavery to custom and usage, then indeed that "marriage" has less sanctity than a harlot's girdle. But if the external form is preserved out of regard for the children, out of true sacrifice, for the sake of self-purification, with the worthy passion and noble hope to make true, in time to come, what is false now, to make beautiful what is at the moment ugly, then indeed the sanctity of that marriage is undisturbed, and the unsung silent heroism of that man and woman will be inscribed in the tablets of heaven. But both man and wife must be willing, and capable. One must not compel the other in any way, direct or indirect ; nor must an impossible task be stupidly undertaken, especially if children are involved in the situation, for their last state will most likely be worse than the state in which they would find themselves if the parents parted. Those who say that it is God's will that marriages once contracted are indissoluble will never be named Socrates. Marriages are man's responsibility.

Sexual compatibility and harmony between man and wife is the fundamental physical bedrock of marriage. Let that be right, *in the profound sense*, and many other disabilities have a chance of being put right. "Civilized" man hardly takes any steps to make certain that the bedrock is right. He who reverences sexual creativeness may have a better chance here. With the millions, love grows out of sexual fulfilment (not indiscriminate expression) in the young years. After maturity, love can express itself in sacramental relations. The overwhelming, sensational intensity of sexual experience either exalts, trains, purifies, and leads upwards, or it shatters a person's inner nature. It is only through the overwhelming intensity of sensation that man first awakens to a vision of that which is beyond sensation, namely Nirvāṇa, the integration of pleasure and pain, of joy and sorrow.

Man as a physico-chemical system is moved by a compelling drive to touch the extremity of sensation. As an emotion-thought complex, conditioned by the traditions handed down and by what goes on around him, he is a romantic. Nature casts her nets wide for him, so that she be not defeated! Each person feels the tremendous power of that urge to seek his own true love, union with whom is fervently believed to be the highest bliss on earth.

So it is.

But now, what is trying to emerge into consciousness and triumphant realization in this mysterious, irrepressible urge for the Immortal Beloved—the Immortal Beloved not merely as a figure of speech, or an ideal conception, or a symbol of some other thing or truth, but as a flesh and blood reality here and now?

Two matters have been mentioned earlier: phallic worship as expressing reverence for creativeness; and the Indian teachings concerning the Gods and their Consorts, and the reverence with which sexual union must be regarded and consummated. These find their culmination in the concept of the Holy Family, which is one of the worthy contributions which Christian religious art has made to the world, but one which will find fruition in the Far To-morrow. Both Hinduism and Christianity have taught that "marriages are made in heaven". This refers in the first instance to the indissoluble union between God Transcendent, Lord of the Universe, and God Immanent, embodied in each individual man. Man was made in two parts, male and female, each incomplete in itself, but incomplete only in the limited context of psycho-physical organic existence. God Immanent is neither male nor female, but plain God Immanent. Therefore any individual male or female, treading "the path of the Gods" and not "of the Fathers", "ascends aloft" and "becomes immortal". But these Sons of God are comparatively few and far between. Male and female, normally, must wed. To correspond to the indissolubility of the (spiritual) marriage of God Transcendent and God Immanent, Hindu and Christian idealism leaned towards indissolubility of the marriage of male and female psycho-physical organisms—neither wise nor practicable in certain circumstances, but certainly the ideal which men and women must seek to fulfil.

The man-wife relationship is an altogether unique one, and of a sacramental nature. It is not only a question of mutual love and esteem, mutual forbearance, helpfulness and support, but also, beyond the accepted values, a question of how one holds the other in his or her inmost consciousness. Each partner of the marriage is, in deepest reality, the embodiment of Eternal God ; and in those rare, all too rare marriages where there is true union in the innermost spiritual depths, there is the real, whole recognition and acceptance of each individual by the other individual. In such unions, the One manifested as the Many, the Unity as the Diversity, finds its supreme human realization as a true harmony. Each partner of such an union is not " the other person ", but is so held in his and her inner consciousness respectively, that the two form a non-dual male-female unit. Such two-in-oneness is one of the significances of the Hindu teachings of the Gods and their Divine Consorts.

Anyone can be a provider, a supporter, a housekeeper, a cook, a nursemaid. Any man can be a woman's lover, any woman a man's mistress. All the ordinary processes of everyday existence can be attended to by men or women other than the husband or wife. But only a husband can be a husband, only a wife can be a wife. Just that innermost, essential, indispensable, supreme something which exalts a man to the position of husband, and a woman to that of wife, characterizes the man who is truly a husband, and the woman who is truly a wife. It is the personal and solemn responsibility of the man to be just that to his wife, and of the woman to be just that to her husband. He, verily, is God. She, verily, like mother Nature, is the bride of God. The man-wife relationship is a veritable sacrament of worship, essentially Divine, substantively human.

Food and sex are main factors determining the continuance

of life. Food is a matter of cooperative organization. Sex is an individual concern; no one else can trespass here. Most problems arise out of food and sex. Let sex be understood, let the man-wife relationship be made true, and a hundred, a thousand problems will cease to exist, and a million sorrows will be replaced by as many joys. Bring up children in homes where the parents are true husband and wife, and they will grow in the sweet atmosphere of a happiness which is rooted in peace and in which they will learn the art of accepting life in its wholeness.

Now Christian Art has pointed a finger of light to a sublime fulfilment: The Holy Family.

What constitutes a Holy Family?

A purified man and a purified woman, free of lust and hate and delusion, free from "passion, fear and anger" in the words of the Gītā, whole individuals therefore, live in perfect communion with each other, united by a Love that is non-reciprocal, non-conditional, and hence absolute. Their sense-mind life is pure, holy. With right judgment of the appropriateness of the circumstance when it arises, they deliberately perform "that action which causes the birth of beings" (Bhagavad-Gītā VIII.3) The child born of such an union is not merely a produced child, not merely a wanted or an unwanted child. It is a created child, the Holy Child. And the mother of that Child always remains a pure Virgin,[1] howsoever many children she may bear. When sexual intercourse is performed with utter reverence, with full awareness of the unity of one's being with God and Nature and with one's marital partner, with complete dedication to the purposes of the Most High, with full ecstacy of creation, and with the perfect artistry of man-woman loving, then that sexual union is the supreme, real sacrament in man's earthly life. The sacrament of any ritual worship is but symbolical. But the sacrament of Love's expression in sexual creativity is man's profoundest, real sacrament. God's holy activity of creation is supremely embodied in man and woman,

[1] There is no need to descend to the absurdity of literal belief in the miracle of the mothers of Zarathustra, Gotama and Jesus conceiving by anyone other than a human father. A male sperm fertilizing a female ovum is sufficient miracle "to confound a sextillion of infidels".

as true individuals, creating the Child. And in this creative activity, the inmost essence of sensation, and sensation's inner meaning and significance is known, and transcended. Transcended, because in such loving, there is no reaction, no sense of dust and ashes afterwards, no depression, no regret, no conflict between self-assertion and self-surrender. There is only peace, full and deep like the quiet of the solitudes between the stars of heaven.

In the Holy Family will be fulfilled not only the purposes of Nature and of Man, but also of God, by enabling the integrative principle in the universe to bring forth on earth a living god.

But let man beware! Let him not play with fire. Let him not be self-deluded into playing a game. For his slavery to lust and ego will consume him with the torturing fires of hell. Let him unremittingly purify himself; let him aspire, humble and dedicated; let him act with reverence, sacramentally. Then assuredly the day will dawn when men and women will create Holy Children, the Sons of God who will sing praise with exultant joy, like the cry of the morning stars as they speed in their cosmic dance.

RELIGION points to such a consummation of man's God-conceiving. To-day, as men and women, seeking purity, work towards such a consummation, they will find freedom from many a trouble darkening their lives. The day is passing when men dominate and women submit, or women rule and men obey. The time is at hand when men and women shall play their part in full, each freely complementing the other.

* * * *

In finality, the Immortal Beloved is Brahman:

Lo, verily, not for love of the husband is the husband dear,
but for love of the Ātman is the husband dear.
Lo, verily, not for love of the wife is the wife dear,
but for love of the Ātman is the wife dear,
Lo, verily, not for love of sons are sons dear,
but for love of the Ātman are sons dear.

Bṛihad-Āraṇyaka Upanishad, II.4.5.

RELIGION shows that strait gate and narrow path leading to the union with the Immortal Beloved, the path trod by all Great Teachers, the path which They exhort men to tread. It is the path of desirelessness, of undefiled love, of super-knowledge, of perfect wisdom, of skilled action. At its end, one reaches the sinless state, knows the Peace of God which passes understanding, transcending all sense-mind disturbance whilst living the everyday life in the here and the now. Here-now, RELIGION enables man to become the true individual, in constant communion with God, the self-less SELF, thus making him the creative source of world order and human fulfilment. The living of RELIGION is the supreme practicality.

Man cannot escape the pressure of the universal process. He must go on and on, developing mentally, and spiritually. RELIGION shows him which way lies his inner development, which emerges, transcendentally, as the crown and fruition of his biological or psycho-physical, and social evolution. In that fruition he knows the bliss of Nirvāṇa, here-now whilst living on earth. He realizes Brahman, the Immortal, the Beloved.

* * * *

And what chance is there that men to-day, earth-bound, seeking temporary solutions for themselves, will seek God, will endeavour strenuously, tread the Brahma-path to make an end of Ill and realize Nirvāṇa ?

Only a little one !

Yet you and I, the eternal companions, need have no anxiety. For a million years have we sojourned on this planet. Only six thousand years ago, civilization began. Reduce our time scale a thousand times. Now see ! We are a thousand years old to-day ! Only six years ago, when we were nine hundred and ninety-four, we became civilized ! Only three years ago the transcendent vision of Brahman-Ātman illumined us ! Only two and a half years ago the Buddha brought Nirvāṇa, the deathless Immortal to us, and only two years ago Jesus swung open the gates of the kingdom !

Only last month we began to wake up to the fact that we should cast away our follies, our lusts and egoisms, for only last month we really began to see that several paths lead up the mountain side to the divine summit of perfection!

What then, friend, is it seemly that you and I should display the taint of impatience? Of doubt? And betray a poor, faltering faith?

Come, you and I have a long span yet! We are only a thousand years young to-day, and we are promised a thousand thousand to come! Time enough to serve the behests of the Eternal, and know the radiance of Nirvāṇa!

But look! The light of Heaven is already gathering on the hilltops! And the New Day is beckoning *now* to the New Man!

O beloved companion! Let us keep watch together, endeavour diligently, do what ought to be done, enter the raptures and realize the Truth.

And we shall be led to the very heart of Eternal God where Love reigns supreme, where Bliss is unending, and Light Perpetual shines.

BIBLIOGRAPHY

The Corridors of Time	Peake and Fleure, 9 Vols.
Mohenjodaro and The Indus Civilization	Sir John Marshall, 3 Vols.
The Indus Civilization	E. Mackay
Prehistoric India	Stuart Piggott
Ancient India	J. W. Mc.Crindle
India—A Short Cultural History ..	H. G. Rawlinson
India	C. H. Philips
Caste in India	J. H. Hutton
Comparative Religion	A. C. Bouquet
The Legacy of Asia	A. W. Watts
A History of Indian Philosophy ..	S. Dasgupta, 5 Vols.
Indian Philosophy	S. Radhakrishnan, 2 Vols.
Sanskrit Literature	A. A. Macdonell
Sacred Books of the East	edited by Max Muller, 50 Vols.
The Ṛig Veda	R. T. H. Griffith, 4 Vols.
The Atharva Veda	R. T. H. Griffith, 2 Vols.
Vedic Mythology	A. A. Macdonell
The Religion of The Ṛig Veda ..	H. D. Griswold
The Thirteen Principal Upanishads ..	R. E. Hume
The Himalayas of the Soul	J. Mascaró
Thirty Minor Upanishads	K. Narayansvami Aiyar
120 Upanishads (Sanskrit Text only)	Satyabhamabai Pandurang, Publisher.
The Philosophy of the Upanishads ..	P. Deussen
Brahma-Sūtras	Swami Vireswarananda
The Song of The Lord	E. J. Thomas
The Bhagavad-Gītā	S. Radhakrishnan
Viṣṇu Purāṇa	H. H. Wilson
Bhāgavata Purāṇa (Sanskrit Text)	
The Mahābhārata	M. N. Dutt
The Rāmāyaṇa (Valmiki)	R. T. H. Griffith
The Rāmāyaṇa (Tulsi Das)	F. S. Growse
The Yoga Sūtras of Patañjali ..	M. N. Dvivedi

Shakti and Shakta .. .. .. J. Woodroffe
The Serpent Power .. .. .. Arthur Avalon (J. Woodroffe)
Hinduism .. .. A. C. Bouquet
The Hindu View of Life .. .. S. Radhakrishnan
The Science of Peace .. .. .. Bhagavan Das

Buddhism .. .. Mrs. C. A. F. Rhys Davids
Buddha, His Life, His Doctrine, His Order .. .. H. Oldenberg
Buddha and The Gospel of Buddhism A. Coomaraswamy
Buddhism .. .. E. Conze
Buddhism .. .. Christmas Humphreys
The Life of Buddha .. .. .. E. J. Thomas
History of Buddhist Thought .. E. J. Thomas
Buddhist India .. .. .. T. W. Rhys Davids
Women under Primitive Buddhism .. I. B. Horner
Gotama the Buddha .. .. .. presented by A. K. Coomaraswamy and I. B. Horner.
Early Buddhist Monachism .. .. S. Dutt
Sacred Books of the Buddhists
Anguttara Nikāya (Pali Text Society) 5 Vols.
Saṁyutta Nikāya (Pali Text Society) 5 Vols.
Dhammapada .. .. N. K. Bhagawat
Dhammapada .. .. S. Radhakrishnan

Songs of Zarathustra .. .. .. Bode and Nanavutty
The Gāthās of Zarathustra .. .. I. J. S. Taraporevala

Mohammedanism .. .. .. H. A. R. Gibb
The Koran .. .. trans. by Rodwell
The Bible
Mysticism .. .. Evelyn Underhill
The Dialogues of Plato
The Greek Thinkers .. .. .. T. Gomperz, 4 Vols.
The Philosophy of Plotinus .. .. W. R. Inge, 2 Vols.
The Meeting of East and West .. F. S. C. Northrop
Eastern Religions and Western Thought .. .. S. Radhakrishnan

GLOSSARY

(S = Sanskrit P = Pāli)

Acyuta (S) Firm ; imperishable ; an epithet of Viṣṇu, and Kṛishṇa.

Aditi (S) The infinite ; boundless ; the goddess who is the mother of the gods, the Ādityas, in the Ṛig Veda.

Āditya (S) A god, member of the Āditya clan, born of Aditi. Varuṇa, Indra, Agni, Soma and others were the Ādityas, twelve in all.

Agni (S) Fire ; the god of fire, one of the Ādityas, a messenger of the gods, a friend to man.

Ahiṁsa (S) Harmlessness ; abstention from injury to living things ; gentleness.

Ahura-Mazda (Avestan) The Supreme Being of the Zarathustrian religion ; lord of life (Ahura) and wisdom (Mazda). His divine powers, the six Ameshā-Spentās, are embodied in Himself, He Himself being placed at the head of them all.

Ājīvo (P) Mode of living ; livelihood.

Ākāśa (S) The subtlest of the five elements—the other four are agni (fire), āpas (water), vāyu (wind), pṛithvī (earth)—of which the universe is made ; " ether " ; clear space ; sky.

Amata (P) The deathless ; the immortal.

Ameshā-Spentā (Avestan) A divine power of Ahura-Mazda. The six Ameshā-Spentās are Vohu Mano, the Good Mind, Asha, the divine law, Xshathra, the Lord's might and majesty, Āramaiti, divine devotion, Haurvatāt, Perfection or wholeness or health, and Ameretatāt, immortality.

Amṛita (S) Immortality ; nectar.

Anattā (P) Without abiding entity ; soulless ; no-self.

Anicca (P) Impermanent.

Apara-vidyā (S) Lower knowledge; the knowledge of things, of manifestation, confined to the realm of the mortal.

Arahant (P) One who has attained perfection, the summum bonum of religious aspiration (Nirvāṇa or Nibbāna), the supreme worthiness.

Āramaiti (Avestan) Divine devotion or love; one of the Ameshā-Spentās.

Āraṇyaka (S) A treatise produced by a forest-dwelling sage.

Ariyan (P) Āryan; noble, distinguished, of high birth; right, good, ideal.

Arjuna (S) The third of the five Pāṇḍava brothers, the sons of Pāṇḍu by Kunti (also called Pṛithā).

Āruṇi (S) Uddālaka Āruṇi was the sage who gave the teaching of tat tvam asi ("That art thou") in the Chāndogya Upanishad.

Āryans (S) The fair skinned people who came from Central Asia into India.

Āryāvarta (S) The land of settlement of the Āryans.

Āsanas (S) The bodily poses, together with prāṇāyāma, which constituted an important part of the physical discipline of yoga.

Āsavas (P) Intoxicants; cankers.

Asura (S) Spirit, Lord God; evil spirit, demon.

Ātman (S) Soul; life; breath; essence; the universal soul; the unitary Self. In the Bṛihad-Āraṇyaka Upanishad, Ātman is declared to be the same as Brahman, the ultimate reality, the absolute. In some Upanishads the Ātman is animistically pictured as being of the shape of a man, the size of a thumb, and situated in the heart.

Attan (P) = Sanskrit Ātman.

Avatāra (S) Manifestation or incarnation of deity on earth.

Avidyā (S) Ignorance. In Indian religious and philosophical teachings, he who is ignorant of, or unawakened to the reality of the Supreme, is in a state of avidyā, from which he is not released by the mere acquisition of any knowledge in terms of speech and thought; but he is released through realization of the

		Supreme through Brahman-becoming, through attaining, superconsciously, the Silence, the Immortal, Nirvāṇa.
Avijjā	(P)	= Sanskrit Avidyā.
Bhārata	(S)	A descendant of Bharata.
Bhāratavarsha	(S)	Bharata's realm ; Hindusthan.
Bhava	(P)	" Becoming " ; (state of) existence ; a " life ".
	(S)	Birth, origin, existence.
Bhikkhu	(P)	An almsman, a mendicant, a Buddhist monk or priest, a bhikkhu.
Bhikkhunī	(P)	An almswoman, a Buddhist nun.
Bodhisat(ta)	(P)	One destined to attain supreme enlightenment.
Brahma	(S)	The power or efficacy of prayer ; Brahman the Absolute.
Brahmā	(P & S)	The creator of the universe ; the First Person of the Hindu Trinity, God the Father.
Brahmacariya	(P & S)	Self-restraint, chastity, continence ; religious studentship of a brāhman youth, passed in celibacy ; Brahma-faring, God-faring ; the path to the Supreme.
Brahman	(S)	The Absolute ; IT.
Brāhman, or brāhmaṇa	(S)	A member of the brāhman caste ; one who had realized Brahman, or become Brahman.
Brāhmaṇas	(S)	The portion of Vedic literature, or theological treatises, dealing with faith and ceremonies.
Brahmavidyā	(S)	The knowledge of Brahman ; sacred knowledge.
Brahma-vihāra	(P)	Sublime or divine state of mind. The four Brahma-vihāras were : mettā, loving-kindness ; karuṇā, compassion ; muditā, sympathetic joy ; upekkhā, imperturbability, serenity.
Buddhi	(S & P)	Intelligence, wisdom ; the reason of him whose mind is wholly purified, or of him who has attained enlightenment.
Cakka	(P)	Wheel, circle ; collection ; succession ; sphere.
Cakkhu	(P)	Eye.
Cakra	(S)	Wheel, circle, discus, sphere.
Cinmātra	(S)	Pure intelligence.

Citta	(S)	Discursively thinking mind.
Concentration		See dhāraṇā, below.
Contemplation		See dhyāna, below.
Dasyu	(S)	Fiend, foe of the gods, unbeliever ; man of non-brāhmanical tribes ; robber.
Dāsa	(S)	Foe, demon, infidel ; slave, servant.
Deva	(S & P)	A celestial being, a divinity ; a king.
Devadāsi	(S)	A female servant of the devas ; a temple girl.
Dhamma	(P)	The truth, doctrine, gospel ; norm.
Dhammā	(P)	Things, phenomena ; mental objects, ideas, states of mind.
Dhananjaya	(S)	Winning wealth ; victorious in battle ; epithet bestowed on Arjuna.
Dhāraṇā	(S)	Mental concentration. In yoga, dhāraṇā is the practice of retaining a single thought or image in one's mind to the complete exclusion of all else. The supreme object of dhāraṇā is Brahman, and this dhāraṇā, at a certain stage of development, can be practised throughout the day.
Dharma	(S)	Custom, rule ; duty, law ; the way of life laid down as a religious duty.
Dhyāna	(S)	Contemplation. Dhyāna is the step which follows dhāraṇā in yoga. Whilst dhāraṇā trains one to concentrate attention upon a subject, dhyāna enables one to grasp the essential nature of that subject. One of the purposes of dhyāna is to enable the thinker to become aware of the object of thought in such a manner as to overleap the gap between thinking subject and thought object. Dhāraṇā and dhyāna culminate in samādhi.
Diṭṭhi	(P)	View, belief, dogma, theory, speculation ; especially groundless or unfounded opinion, or false theory.
Dukkha	(P)	Ill, pain, suffering—but no English word adequately covers dukkha, which is both physical and mental.
Durgā	(S)	Śiva's consort.
Dyaus Pitar	(S)	Father Heaven.
Govinda	(S)	An epithet of Kṛishṇa or Viṣṇu.
Guṇa	(S)	Fundamental quality ; virtue, merit, excellence.

Guru(-deva)	(S)	Teacher.
Hiraṇyagarbha	(S)	A name of the personal Brahman ; womb of gold.
Hṛshīkeśa	(S)	Having his hair erect ; an epithet of Krishṇa or Viṣṇu
Idappaccayatā	(P)	Having its foundation in this ; connected by way of cause.
Indra	(S)	One of the Ādityas, the god Indra
Īśvara	(S)	God as a Personal Being.
Jagannātha	(S)	The protector of the world ; an epithet of Viṣṇu.
Jarāmaraṇa	(P)	Jarā, old age, and maraṇa, death ;
Jātaka	(P)	A story of one of the Buddha's former births.
Jāti	(P & S)	Birth, rebirth ; existence, life ; state ; rank, caste.
Jhāna	(P)	A meditation, one of the four raptures.
Jīva	(S)	Principle of life ; individual soul.
Jñāna	(S)	Knowledge ; wisdom.
Kālī	(S)	Name of Śiva's consort ; the black goddess.
Kāma	(P & S)	Wish, desire, pleasure, lust, love (sexual); Eros.
Kamma	(P)	Action, deed ; law of cause and consequence.
Kammanto	(P)	Doing, acting, working ; profession, occupation, work, business.
Karman	(S)	Action, work, deed ; rite ; effect ; result of act done in the past.
Karuṇā	(P)	Compassion.
Kaunteya	(S)	Son of Kuntī.
Keśava	(S)	Having fine hair ; an epithet of Kṛishṇa.
Khandha	(P)	Mass, aggregate ; the body of, a collection of ; all that is comprised under, forming the substance of.
Kuntī	(S)	Wife of Pāṇḍu, mother of the Pāṇḍava brothers.
Kusala	(P)	Clever, skilful, expert ; good, right, meritorious.
Liṅga	(S)	Mark, token, sign, emblem, phallus.
Madhusūdana	(S)	Slayer of the demon Madhu.
Madhyadeśa	(S)	The middle region, Midland (the country lying between the Himālaya and Vindhya mountains, Vinasana and Prayāga in the east).
Manas	(S)	Mind.
Māyā	(S)	Art, device, trick ; illusion, phantom ; marvellous power, creative magic.

Māyā		Mother of Siddhattha Gotama.
Meditation		A general term covering various stages of a mental discipline whose main elements are the deliberate abstraction from sense impressions, concentration, contemplation, and communion with the Ultimate, superconsciousness or the union with God being fully realized on stopping the flow of discursive thought.
Mettā	(P)	Loving-kindness.
Mṛityu	(S)	Death, the god of Death.
Muditā	(P)	Sympathy, disinterested love.
Mukta	(S)	Set free, released, liberated.
Mūlaprakṛiti	(S)	Primeval or root matter (also called pradhāna in the Sāṁkhya philosophy.)
Muni	(S)	Inspired or ecstatic man ; sage, seer, especially one who has taken the vow of silence. The true Muni is the one who has achieved the Silence, the stopping of the flow of discursive thought, thereby attaining superconsciousness.
Nāma-rūpa	(P)	Name and body (form), individuality, individual being.
Ñāna	(P)	Knowledge, intelligence, insight, conviction.
Naya	(P)	Method, plan, manner.
Nibbāna	(P)	The dying out in the heart of the threefold fire of lust, ill-will and delusion ; the sense of spiritual well-being, emancipation, salvation, bliss.
Nidāna	(P)	Ground, foundation ; origin, cause.
Nikāya	(P)	Collection (" body "), assemblage, class, group.
Nirvāṇa	(S)	Extinction of lust, ill-will, hatred and delusion ; final emancipation, union with the Absolute ; the indescribable serenity of the Perfected Man ; the ineffable bliss of superconsciousness.
Niyama	(S)	Restraint ; fixed rule, self-imposed (religious) observance.
Pāṇḍava	(S)	A descendant of Pāṇḍu.
Paramātman	(S)	The Supreme Spirit, the Holy Creative Spirit.
Parameśvar	(S)	Transcendent God ; the Supreme Lord.

Parantapa (S) Vexing the foe.
Para-vidyā (S) Higher knowledge; the knowledge of Brahman.
Pārtha (S) Son of Pṛithā; an epithet of Arjuna.
Pārvatī (S) The daughter of Himālaya and consort of Śiva.
Paṭicca-samuppāda (P) "arising on the grounds of (a preceding cause)" happening by way of cause, causal chain of causation; the theory of dependent origination.
Phassa (P) Contact.
Prajāpati (S) Lord of creatures; genius presiding over procreation; Creator; name of supreme being above the Vedic gods.
Prakṛiti (S) Original or natural form or condition; nature; in the original state, unchanged.
Prāṇa (S) Breath, vital spirit, life, inhaled air.
Prāṇāyāma (S) Suspension of breath or breath control.
Prasāda (S) Graciousness, kindness, favour; calmness (of mind); perspicuity (of speech or style); clearness (of water).
Pratyagātman (S) The Ātman as embodied in the individual.
Pratyāhāra (S) Withdrawal of attention from sense impressions.
Pṛithā (S) Another name for Kuntī, wife of Pāṇḍu.
Purusha (S) A man, human being; highest personal principle; Supreme Spirit.
Rājanya (S) Royal personage, noble, man of the warrior caste.
Rajas (S) Quality inflaming or obscuring the mind. In the Sāṁkhya philosophy, rajas is one of the three guṇas, the other two being sattva and tamas.
Rāmānuja One of the greatest philosophers and teachers of South India, born in 1027 A.D. He was an upholder of devotional theism, and a bulwark of the Vaiṣnavite faith.
Ṛishi (S) A bard of the sacred hymns; a sage; a seer.
Ṛta (S) Established order, sacred ordinance, rite; divine law; truth, right.
Rūpa (P & S) Appearance, form, shape.
Saḷāyatana (P) The six-fold sense field: six organs of sense, namely eye, ear, nose, tongue, body (touch) and mind, and six objects, namely, forms,

sounds, odours, tastes, tangible things, and ideas.

Samādhi (S) The final stage in meditation in which God-union is attained. There are two aspects to it; one, where there is still consciousness of separate self; the other where self-consciousness is wholly transcended, all discursive thoughts or words completely cease, and in the absolute Silence the Superconsciousness (the become-Brahman state, the ultimate "knowing" Brahman, realizing the Ātman) is attained.

Śaṁkara He was born in 788 A.D. and died in 820 A.D. He was one of the greatest philosophers. His philosophy is known as the Advaita (or non-dual) Vedānta, a philosophy of unqualified monism.

Sāṁkhya (S) One of the six great systems of Indian philosophy. The sage Kapila is said to be its originator.

Sammā (P) Thoroughly, properly; in the right way; best, perfectly.

Saṁkalpa (S) Resolve of the mind; will, purpose, definite intention.

Saṁnyāsa (S) Abandonment, renunciation of the world.

Saṁsāra (S & P) Transmigration, perpetual cycle of births, cycle of existence.

Sangha (P) Assembly; the Buddhist order of Bhikkhus and Bhikkhunīs.

Sankappo (P) Intention, aspiration.

Saññā (P) Sense, perception, discernment.

Śānti (S) Mental tranquillity, peace.

Sati (P) Mindfulness, alertness, self-possession.

Sattva (S) Being, existence, reality; essence, nature; absolute goodness (or rhythm or harmony, the first of the three guṇas of Prakṛiti in the Sāṁkhya philosophy).

Satyam (S) Reality, truth.

Śiva (S) The Third Person of the Hindu Trinity; the auspicious one. Śiva is the Destroyer-Regenerator. He is lord of reproductive nature, and he is also the supreme ascetic.

Soma (S) One of the Ādityas, the Vedic god of inspiration.

Svarga	(S)	Celestial ; going or leading to the light or heaven.
Svayambhū	(S)	Self-existent.
Śvetaketu		Son of Uddālaka Āruṇi.
Tamas	(S)	Inertia, darkness, ignorance, delusion ; one of the three guṇas of Prakṛiti.
Taṇhā	(P)	Thirst, craving, the fever of unsatisfied longing. Taṇhā is the root cause of Ill.
Tathāgata	(P & S)	He who has gone thus ; an epithet of the Buddha.
Tat-tva	(S)	That-ness.
Uddālaka		Personal name of Āruṇi, the Upanishadic sage.
Umā		Wife of Śiva.
Upādāna	(P)	Fuel, supply, provision ; " drawing upon ", grasping.
Upanishad	(S)	Secret or esoteric doctrine ; the essential Vedic teaching.
Upekkhā	(P)	Equanimity ; unperturbedness.
Vācā	(P)	Word, saying, speech.
Varuṇa	(S)	One of the Ādityas, the Encompasser.
Vāyāmo	(P)	Effort, exertion, endeavour.
Vāyu	(S)	Wind, air ; god of wind ; breath, vital air.
Veda	(S)	Knowledge (sacred knowledge).
Vedanā	(S & P)	Feeling, perception, sensation.
Vedānta	(S)	The conclusion or essence of the Veda.
Vidyā	(S)	Knowledge, learning, science.
Vijjā	(P)	Lore, science, higher knowledge, revelation.
Vijñāna	(S)	Discernment, knowledge (profane).
Viññāṇa	(P)	A mental quality as a constituent of individuality ; the bearer of (individual) life ; life-force (as extending also over rebirths); principle of conscious life ; general consciousness (as function of mind and matter.)
Viṣṇu	(S)	The Second Person of the Hindu Trinity, who out of boundless love incarnates from time to time to save mankind.
Viśvakarman	(S)	The Creator of the universe ; the architect and artificer of the gods.
Yājñavalkya		One of the greatest of the Upanishadic sages.
Yama		Son of Vivasvat, the male twin of Yamī, the first man ; the lord of death.

Yoga (S) Yoking; remedy, cure; means; union; mental concentration. Yoga is that discipline, physical, moral, mental and spiritual, by means of which the individual attains the realization of the Ultimate, or God-union, or Superconsciousness.

Yoni (S) Lap, womb; place of production, origin, source.

INDICES

I. TOPICS *and* NAMES

II. SANSKRIT AND PALI WORDS